Teaching and Learning the English Language

Also available from Bloomsbury

Teaching and Learning the English Language

A Problem-Solving Approach

Richard Badger

Online resources to accompany this book are available at:
www.bloomsbury.com/cw/teaching-and-learning-the-english-language/

Please type the URL into your web browser and follow the instructions to access the Companion Website. If you experience any problems, please contact Bloomsbury at: contact@bloomsbury.com

BLOOMSBURY ACADEMIC
LONDON • NEW YORK • OXFORD • NEW DELHI • SYDNEY

BLOOMSBURY ACADEMIC
Bloomsbury Publishing Plc
50 Bedford Square, London, WC1B 3DP, UK

**BLOOMSBURY, BLOOMSBURY ACADEMIC and the Diana logo are trademarks
of Bloomsbury Publishing Plc**

First published in Great Britain 2018

A catalogue record for this book is available from the British Library.

A catalog record for this book is available from the Library of Congress.

ISBN: HB: 978-1-4742-9043-2
         PB: 978-1-4742-9042-5
       ePDF: 978-1-4742-9045-6
       ePub: 978-1-4742-9044-9

Typeset by Newgen KnowledgeWorks Pvt. Ltd., Chennai, India
Printed and bound in Great Britain

To find out more about our authors and books visit www.bloomsbury.com
and sign up for our newsletters.

I dedicate this book to Tze Siang Choo sine qua non.

Contents

Part IV   Language Skills

Part V   Conclusion

Figures

Tables

Preface

Christopher Brumfit defined applied linguistics as

> the theoretical and empirical investigation of real-world problems in which language is a central issue.
> (1997: 93)

The real-world problem addressed in the book is one faced by all teachers of English – that their learners are not able to use the language as well as either learners or teachers want; and the rest of this book addresses that issue, but here it seems appropriate to discuss what is meant by problem-solving.

Problem-solving involves three stages:

1 Identifying a problem
2 Collecting information about ways of addressing the problem
3 Trying out possible solutions

Teachers may have to deal with problems which relate to how to design a programme or produce a method of evaluating what their learners know, but probably the most common situation in which teachers have to solve problems is when they plan a lesson, and here the question they should be asking is 'what do I want my learners to do better?'

The answers to that question may include things like 'being able to book a hotel in English', 'write a business letter', 'understand a poem', 'use the present perfect tense appropriately' or perhaps 'be better behaved in class'. These answers sound like common sense, but they reflect the ideas and theories that the teachers who are planning the lessons have about language and language learning. So, for example, being able to book a hotel in English implies a functional view of language (see Chapter 2), and a focus on the present perfect tense suggests a focus on grammar (Chapter 9).

Teachers' understanding of what happens in their classes is always based on some kind of theory. When I was teaching in the state system, the visits of inspectors from the ministry of education were big events. When the English inspector was due to visit, the principal asked me if I wanted the inspector to come and watch me teach a particular class because the learners in that class were quiet. My principal's theory of learning was that it was a quiet activity or, perhaps, that was what he thought the inspector's idea of learning was. My choice was a noisier class, which, coming from a communicative background, seemed to me to be a more effective class. Fortunately, the inspector also thought that a reasonably talkative class was a good one, but the key point is that what counts as a good class reflects the theory you bring with you when you teach or observe a class.

A theory is a way of thinking about what happens, and if it is a good theory, it should do two things. It should help make sense of what has happened in your class. For example, if your learners are able to do well in a written exercise on the third-person singular 's' in the present tense but then miss out the 's' when they are having a conversation, a good theory will help you understand why that might be. A good theory should also help you predict what will happen when you go into the class. Whenever teachers plan lessons, they are making predictions about how the class will go and how their actions will lead to their learners learning. If a teacher presents grammar rules to their learners, this suggests that the teacher thinks that knowledge of grammar rules will help people to use the language or, in other words, the theory of learning sees rules as contributing to language development.

All teachers have theories about language, learning and teaching, but not all teachers are aware of their own theories. One of the purposes of this book is to make you more aware of your own theories and to allow you to develop your theories in the light of the ideas that other people have developed.

Once you have identified the problem that you want to address, the next step is finding out how other people have tried to address your problem. Books such as this are a one-point source of information about this, as are your colleagues and online materials. One potential resource is academic research. Teachers make less use of research because subscribing to such resources needs to be paid for. Even where teachers do have access, the research is often written for an audience of other researchers. Researchers' desire to understand second-language learning in general can lead to research which does not give enough attention to the subjective nature of language and learning, and this can make it difficult to work out what the research says about improving language learning in particular contexts and for particular learners (Borg 2007).

In the UK, academics are now being asked what impact their research has on the world beyond universities, and this is pushing academics to consider ways of involving teachers in research from the beginning as well as making research papers available without payment and in forms that are more accessible.

Once possible solutions have been identified, they need to be tried out, but again this has both theoretical and empirical aspects. Two of the theories that my teacher education course suggest would lead to more communicative classes are pair work and authenticity. When I was in the classroom, I was nervous about trying out pair work with a group of thirty teenagers, mainly because it might lead to chaos in the classroom. Reading books and articles about how pair work could transform the class persuaded me intellectually, but the reassurance I needed was empirical. So, when I made the leap of faith and tried out a pair work activity based on an information gap in one of my classes, the very positive effect on my learners persuaded me that pair work activities should become part of my teaching repertoire.

The use of authentic texts was a much less threatening idea. I could find authentic texts, write what seemed to me to be reasonable comprehension activities and use them in the classroom without disrupting normal lessons. However, minor problems arose. Some texts worked better than others, and sometimes using authentic texts led to classes where the learners became bored. While I got better at choosing the appropriate authentic text, what went wrong here was my choice of intellectual tools that I used to think about authenticity. It took me several years to finally understand that there was a difference between an authentically produced text and an authentically received text. Just because a text was authentically produced was no guarantee that learners would be able to engage with it authentically. Once I had this insight, I was better equipped to solve the problem of choosing a text that engaged learners.

My aim as a teacher educator is to support teachers as they try to help their learners use English more effectively, and I hope this book will contribute to the problem-solving that goes on in your classrooms. If you look at the website that the publisher has produced to accompany this book, you will find some interesting videos of language classes and associated materials.

Richard Badger
University of Leeds, UK
November 2017

Acknowledgements

This book is the result of my experience both as a teacher and as a teacher educator, and I would like to express my gratitude to those I taught in Malaysia, Algeria and the UK, as well as to the colleagues I worked with in those places. I would also like to express my gratitude to the student teachers who attended courses of which I was a part and the tutors with whom I collaborated. I have drawn on their ideas throughout the book, but I particularly thank Amhemet Farag for the think-aloud protocol in Chapter 12, Amy Lehman for the web quest in Chapter 12 and James Taylor for his inputs to the chapter on vocabulary. I am indebted to the teachers at the Language Centre at Leeds University, UK, who allowed me to videograph their classes and to Oscar Yan and his colleagues for providing videos of their classes. I would also like to thank the reviewers of the book for their supportive and valuable feedback.

Chapter 1

Introduction

Teaching English to speakers of other languages (TESOL) is an amazingly varied activity. This is partly because there are many different kinds and aspects of English that people want to learn. Some people want to speak like Hollywood actors, some want to be able to read scientific articles, some want just enough language to be able to survive in parts of the world where they can use English to communicate and some just want to get through their next exam.

In this chapter I talk about part of my teaching biography and how I think about these stages of my life in order to explain why I have organized this book in the way it is.

1.1 Some teaching history

1.1.1 Malaysia

My first job after completing a postgraduate certificate in English language teaching was to teach in a secondary school in Malaysia, preparing pupils for the *Sijil Rendah Pelajaran* (SRP) or Lower Secondary Certificate, which they take at the end of their third year of secondary or high school. The exam focused largely on reading, writing and grammar, and a lot of my teaching centred on these. However, I had just been taught about communicative language teaching (CLT) and, when I plucked up enough courage, I wanted to try out ideas that were new to me and to my students, including pair work, information gaps, listening to songs and using authentic material. It was a government school, and I had a course book on which most of my lessons were based; and each week I had to complete a record indicating what I had been teaching that week. This may sound quite constraining, but I also had a head teacher who was expanding the English part of the library and an inspector of schools who was very keen that I should spend time helping my pupils to speak better rather than just get them through their examination.

There were about thirty students in each of my four classes, and each period lasted forty minutes. The classes were streamed. The top class included pupils whose English was very good and, two, whose first language was English. In my bottom class, I had pupils who found English very difficult. For some of them, English was their third spoken language and second writing system, but for all of them, doing well on the SRP was very important and would have a major impact on their lives. So a lot of work had to be done on preparing students for the examination. In many classes, I presented examples of a grammatical structure, maybe the difference between the past simple and the present perfect, or countable versus uncountable nouns, followed by related spoken and written exercises. Sometimes we did some kind of communicative activity. One pupil would be a shopkeeper and the other would be a customer, and they would use sentences like 'How much flour do you want?' or 'I want three durians'. Generally, however, the end of the class would be either some kind of writing activity or a reading comprehension exercise and, especially when I started this job, I often got the timing wrong, and so I would have to have some filler exercise, hangman or some anagram activity.

1.1.2 Algeria

My next job was in a language school in Algeria. The students were all paying fees and came because they wanted to learn English. They were almost all Algerians, but some were French and one or two native speakers of other languages who were working in Algeria. The students were over sixteen. Some of the students were preparing for one of the Cambridge examinations, such as First Certificate or Proficiency. These examinations cover speaking and listening as well as reading and writing and require students to produce language where the grammar is accurate and the vocabulary appropriate.

One big change was that all the other teachers taught English. In the Malaysian staff room, we had talked about sports days and the next assembly; here we discussed course books, swapped worksheets and brainstormed how to make our classes livelier. I was getting lots of ideas about things to do in class, and since I had more experience, I had the confidence to try out different ways of organizing the class.

We had a choice of course books with audio and video material and, while all exam preparation classes used the same materials, this was the choice of the teachers rather than the school or the ministry of education. We kept a record of what work we did in case someone fell sick and another teacher had to take over the class; and once a term, the director of studies came and watched a class.

There were between seven and fifteen students in a class. Students took a test when they first came to the school and were placed in an appropriate group; and they generally moved up a class each term. They were eager to speak in English. When I was working in the Malaysian secondary school, I had had to structure speaking activities and make sure the pupils gained the language skills they needed. Here, students would try out things and invent language or ask me for help in mid-utterance. They were very comfortable working in groups. However, they had much less time than my Malaysian pupils had. They came to the school once a week for a two-hour period and had little exposure to English outside of the classroom. In Malaysia, pupils could watch TV and films in English. In Algeria, their only sources of English were a few English language libraries and radio programmes, such as Voice of America. I spent much less time in class on reading comprehension or writing. These were given as homework. The class was for oral communication and maybe a little work on grammar and vocabulary.

1.1.3 The UK

After Algeria, I got a job in a further education college in the UK. In the summer, our work was fairly similar to what I had done in Algeria but with groups of multilingual learners who were often still at school and saw the course as part of their holiday. For the rest of the year, I was working with students, mainly from Africa and Asia, who were preparing to study for degrees in the UK. The students were fee-paying, but some were sponsored by their governments. They were very motivated. They came to the college for a year and then took examinations in their specialist subjects, such as law, business, media studies and an English examination, which we wrote. This focused on reading and writing but included an element of listening.

I worked mainly with students who wanted to study law. They came with fairly high levels of English and were generally very articulate. They and I attended one law lecture a week given by a local university, and we spent the rest of the week working on whatever topic had been covered in the lecture. We did not use a course book but made extensive use of audio recordings of the lecture and the readings the lecturer suggested. These included sources such as legislation and law reports in which judges explained why they had reached a particular decision.

Classes had between fifteen and twenty students. We had four one-hour classes a week, one each on listening and reading and two on writing. Initially, I used some published materials on listening to lectures, but I soon began to focus on recordings of the lectures and, in particular, the PowerPoint slides the lecturer used. After a while, we started doing this session in the computer lab where the students could listen to the lecture and see the PowerPoint slides at the same time, and my role was to monitor how they were getting on and to field questions about what the lecturer had said or what message had been intended.

To a large extent this mirrored what was happening in the reading class. Students would be allocated a reading text with some questions before the class and would discuss what they had read in their groups. This was sometimes structured as a formal debate. Again, my role was to monitor the students to make sure everyone was playing a role and to stop the more outgoing students from dominating discussions. Writing classes were also mainly organized in groups with students working on producing essays on topics such as the ways in which laws are passed in England and Wales, or giving their opinions on whether a particular set of events would amount to a crime or be the basis on which one person could take another person to court.

1.2 A framework for English language teaching

This description of my own teaching history is intended to illustrate the variety of ways of teaching English. This variety is what makes many people want to teach English, but this variety can sometimes result in chaos, especially for those who are relatively new to the profession. The rest of this chapter describes a framework for looking at the different ways in which people teach English to speakers of other languages. This reveals the parallels between different situations and should allow us to learn from our own and other people's experiences so that we become better teachers of English. The three key questions that need to be asked about any English language teaching class or programme are:

1 What is the aim of the class or programme? This is a question about language.

2 How is the language being learnt? This is a question about learners and learning.

3 How is the language being taught? This is a question about teachers and teaching.

These questions are best answered in this order. Before we can think about how teachers can contribute to this process, we need to think about how learners learn; and before we can think about how learners learn, we need to know what the class is hoping to achieve. The three questions explain the title of this book: *Teaching and Learning the English Language*.

This tripartite division also helped me to make sense of my experiences of English language teaching described earlier.

1.2.1 Language

In Malaysia, the language aims were largely to help the pupils develop their reading and writing skills. The passages that the pupils read in class and in the exam fell into two groups. The most common ones were like entries in a junior encyclopaedia, covering topics such as 'The Pampas', 'Palm Oil' and 'The Planets', but students also had to read formal dialogues between children and, occasionally, between adults about everyday topics such as what they had done during the weekend. The language in these dialogues did not reflect colloquial speech but were presumably intended to compensate for the lack of focus on speaking and listening, which were not ignored but were given less importance compared to reading or writing. The kinds of things the pupils had to write included letters to apply for jobs, something which might plausibly be the kind of writing the pupils would do after they finished school, as well as summaries of texts similar to the factual reading passages, which seemed to be more to do with providing a way of assessing the pupils' language than helping them to use language beyond the classroom. Grammar was important and we covered topics such as conditionals, the past tense, the perfect aspect and countable nouns. Some time was spent on vocabulary, but this almost always related to a particular reading passage.

When I was working in Malaysia, I was part of a programme that the Malaysian government had introduced to improve the level of English in the whole country. Schools across Malaysia received teachers, mainly from the UK, so one of the less obvious aspects of the aims of the class was to do with pupils learning to use a traditional kind of British English rather than a Malaysian variety. This was generally reflected in examinations, so often there were items testing the distinctions between 'who' and 'whom', but some lexical items were also used that would be unfamiliar to most people from Britain, such as godown for warehouse and bungalow to mean a detached house. The differences between British and Malaysian English are more striking in spoken language, and here, after a period of adjustment, I learned to accept questions formed by the addition of the tag 'or not' rather than starting with a modal such as 'You got a pen or not?' instead of 'Have you got a pen?'

The aims here might loosely be described as communication but with a heavy emphasis on written rather than spoken language. In terms of language varieties, there was a preference for British English, but there was some flexibility about local and other native speaker varieties such as American or Australian.

In Algeria, spoken language was much more important, and most of my classes focused on helping students to develop their abilities to listen and speak in English. Grammar was less important compared to the Malaysian context, and vocabulary was given a greater role. Writing and reading also received lesser attention. The variety of English again tended to be British English, but some of the teachers spoke North American varieties, and a most of the voices on our listening materials spoke with American accents. There were also some examples in the teaching materials of nonnative speakers of English from countries such as Holland and Sweden.

As with Malaysia, the aim was to be able to communicate in English but with more emphasis on spoken language. There was a less clear preference for British English, with other native speaker varieties of English being treated fairly equally.

With my law course in the UK, the language aims were much more specific. The intention was to help students to be able to use English to study law. A lot of work was done on legal and academic vocabulary, but reading and writing legal texts received the most attention. The students were learning how to read specific kinds of texts, such as law reports, rather than how to read generally in English and how to write the specific kinds of essays, such as the problem answers that law examiners require, rather than some general idea of an academic essay. This meant that there was a change in focus from looking at language at sentence level to looking at texts. The ways in which texts were structured and the purposes they were meant to achieve were central to the programme.

Again, the aim was broadly to do with communication, but as in the secondary school, the emphasis was on written language; but because the level of the learners was much higher, it had moved towards texts or genres rather than sentence-level features. The aims were more communicative than in Malaysia, largely because the fact that the learners were going to be using English to study law in the following year made it much easier to decide what their communicative needs were. The students were studying Common law, a legal system used in several Anglophone countries such as the United States and some British Commonwealth countries such as Nigeria and Singapore, but the students were mainly reading and listening to speakers of British English. However, the variety of language had less to do with the origin of the speakers than the fact that the language was to do with law.

1.2.2 Learning

The way learning takes place is harder to follow than what is being learnt, because learning is partly a psychological process, and we have limited access to what happens in learners' heads.

The pupils in the Malaysian secondary school had varied levels of motivation. All of them wanted to do well on the SRP examination, but for some of the pupils in the lower classes, English was extremely difficult and they coped with my classes by speaking as little as possible and doing enough not to attract attention. In the higher streams, they knew that English was important if they wanted to go on to university, and they worked very hard, reading books in English as well as completing all the homework I gave them.

In one sense, learning is the acquisition of knowledge, and the pupils acquired knowledge in a range of ways. One kind of knowledge they acquired was grammatical. When I used terms like plural and singular or past and present tense, this may have helped them to notice the difference between 'cat' and 'cats' or 'cook' and 'cooked'. Similarly, when I said a pair of words such as 'light' and 'right' or 'ship' and 'sheep', it may have helped them to notice the difference between the phonemes /l/ and /r/ and /ɪ/ and i:/. This may have also been happening with knowledge and skills they already had. So they may have seen a connection between the Malay word 'dua', meaning two, and the English word 'dual', or between the way they look at the last page of a comic to find out how their favourite character got on and the strategy of looking through a passage quickly to find out where a particular piece of information required by a comprehension question can be found.

Learning is also about using knowledge and skills. So the oral drills and rather tedious written exercises that we did in class may have helped them to get their tongues around some English sounds or to be able to produce the right tense when they needed it. Often they were using language with some kind of support. So when they were answering the questions on reading texts, they may have had support in terms of some discussion about the topic or perhaps looking up words in a dictionary, or, if they chose to write something down before saying it, it would have made it easier for them to focus on how the words should be pronounced rather than their choice of vocabulary. This also happened outside the classroom. The homework generally included some kind of support, and some parents or siblings would help the pupils. Supported use outside the classroom also happened less formally. The father of one of the pupils ran a small shop and, even though his English had weaknesses, the pupil could speak fluently in English because he sometimes needed to use English with customers.

The students in the Algerian language school had paid to attend classes and were highly motivated. However, for most of them, the classes were just one part of a busy life, and they found it hard to concentrate if they had to write a long piece or tackle an extended reading passage. They acquired some knowledge about grammar, vocabulary and discourse, such as how to start and end a conversation, and many of the activities they did in class had similarities with supported language use that I talked about for the Malaysian students. The two main differences between Algerian and Malaysian students were that the former were older and better able to think about their learning. However, they also spent less time on English and lacked the institutional and social support provided by a school. Completing homework was difficult for Algerian students partly because of other pressures on their lives but also because they had few opportunities outside of the classroom to engage in meaningful communication.

The students I worked with in the UK were the most focused. Like the Malaysian pupils they were going to take exam, and this was coming at the end of the year rather than some years away. Also, most of them had chosen to study law in English, while the Malaysian pupils were taking English as a compulsory course, though, of course, the parents of most students in the UK were paying for the course and possibly putting pressure on their wards to make sure the investment was not wasted.

They were getting a lot of information about legal and academic vocabulary and discourse, some of which was explicit, but a lot of which was being picked up through their reading and interactions with fellow students. They were also learning how to use the language . In the law courses they attended, the way the lecturers talked about a case or piece of legislation would help them to see how lawyers reasoned, and the sessions on planning and writing law essays or problem-solving questions helped them to develop the abilities to do such things. Perhaps the most important skill they were developing was how to learn a particular variety of English. At the beginning of the course, many of them expected to be told all the vocabulary they would need to make sense out of an article, but by the end, they had a clearer idea of how they could solve the linguistic problems they faced when readings texts on their own.

1.2.3 Teaching

Teaching in the Malaysian secondary school was my first job after a year studying TESOL and my first formal exposure to the ideas in CLT. CLT is a very broad term, and the weak version that the course had encouraged me to adopt was one which saw the three stages of presentation, practice and production

(PPP) as the normal way of organizing a class, and while the aim was to end with a production stage in which there was a communicative activity, the use of drills and controlled pair work was common. At the time, these ideas about how to structure a lesson and particular classroom activities seemed to be the most important thing that the course had taught me about pedagogy, but the teaching practice on the course and the responses of my tutors also made me realize the importance of reflecting on classes and trying to work out how to teach them better.

The three stages became my standard way of organizing classes. My lessons were often planned around a grammatical item or teaching the learners to write a particular kind of text, but there were also lessons where my aim was more to cover a part of the course book rather than what I was hoping my learners would learn. The fairly conservative style of teaching that I adopted was at least partly due to my concern about managing a group of thirty teenagers and a sense that the class would go more smoothly if I kept control of what happened without allowing the learners too much freedom. I used techniques such as giving the learners a writing exercise if I felt they were making too much noise. It took six months and the incentive of a visit by the school inspector for me to try out pair work. I used an information-gap exercise and was surprised at both how smoothly it went and how keen the learners were to complete it.

The other things which I brought to the classes were skills in using language and knowledge about language, acquired from the course I had just completed. In the Malaysian class, this related mainly to vocabulary and grammar, including some terminology like active/passive and the indefinite article. I was also drawing on my knowledge of phonology when I created minimal pairs. There was even an element of discourse knowledge which informed how I taught the pupils to write a letter. I have a fairly good command of English, and the fact that I was using English in class was an important part of the lesson as was the fact that the pupils knew that they would have to use English rather than Malay if they wanted to converse with me. But even though my knowledge of Malay was limited, I did use it on occasions, and sometimes before class, I would discover the Malay equivalent of a word which I thought would be difficult to explain in English.

While working in Algeria, I felt more relaxed about how the classes were organized, though PPP was still the most common pattern of organization. Some classes consisted of simulations or relatively free discussions. This was partly because of my growing self-confidence but also because of the wider range of teaching materials I could draw on. There were two other important factors. First, discussions about teaching and learning were the main topic of conversation in the staff room, and it was quite common for teachers to use each other's lesson plans or make suggestions about which course book dealt best with a particular problem. Second, I was conscious that my students were paying for the classes, and while many of them wanted to improve their English so that they could study aboard or improve their employment prospects, the majority saw learning English as a hobby. I felt the need to vary the activities so that students should not feel bored, and sometimes I probably thought too much about having a good class and not enough about what the students were learning.

Also my knowledge about discourse had increased so I knew about things like turn-taking, fillers and ways of organizing texts, including a problem solution pattern. Some of these terms I used with my students, but they were mainly part of the range of ideas which influenced what I taught or how I analysed where students needed help.

In the UK, PPP became just one way of organizing the class, and much of my teaching involved blocks that covered two or more periods. My aims were less to do with grammar and more to do with what I was learning to call tasks – how could students read a part of this law report, listen to an extract from the weekly lecture and then produce an essay? The language aims emerged from the problems that my students were having rather than from my own ideas about what language they needed.

I also gave more time to helping learners to learn on their own. For example I would get them to compare versions of an essay or look at the way authors showed what they thought of other people's ideas without saying 'I think this is rubbish' so that when they read texts on their own they would notice and learn how the language was being used.

This notion of helping learners to learn related to another thing that I was bringing to the classes, which might seem a negative – my ignorance. When I attended the weekly lectures, the topics were often things about which I had limited knowledge – the role of magistrates in the English legal system, the moral issues related to abortion – and when I came out of lectures, I needed to teach myself enough about these topics so that I could manage the next week's classes effectively. But I soon learnt that I could not become an expert on all these different topics. What I could do was help the students work out how to learn about these topics, and the students were old enough to realize that, while I might be able to give them an explanation about the structure of the third conditional or why the plural of 'criterion' is 'criteria', the most useful thing I could do when they asked for the meaning of phrases like 'sufficient consideration' or 'reasonable doubt' was to point them to a person or a document they could draw help from.

I brought a different kind of ignorance to technology. The college where I worked installed a computer laboratory for language learning the year after I joined. The range of programs we had was fairly limited – multiple choice fills, cloze tests and some simple simulations, but several programmes allowed teachers to produce their own activities. After some experimentation, we discovered that the students' favourite program was a complete cloze called 'Storyboard', and their favourite activity was listening to a song on a tape-recorder and typing in the lyrics.

1.3 Conclusion

Most experienced teachers look on their careers as representing professional development, and I am no exception. I began with a fairly rigid view of how lessons can be organized, where I was implementing a particular kind of teaching method, and gradually developed a more flexible approach. This was partly because I was learning about different ways of teaching and had a deeper understanding of language and learning, but it was also to do with my own confidence.

However, this partial autobiography also illustrates the importance of context in language teaching and the enormous variation that results from this. The language aims, the kinds of learners, the resources available, and the differences between the institutions in which I was teaching all had an impact on the way I taught, and my experience is, inevitably, limited. I have not taught in Australia, New Zealand or North or South America. People who work in these contexts may bring different insights to the teaching process, but I hope the framework of language, learning and teaching that I have used to make sense of my own experience will be useful to teachers who face different challenges in developing their learners' language abilities. The next chapter looks at this first aspect of language teaching – what we mean by language.

Part I

The Fundamentals

Chapter 2

Language

2.1 Introduction

We produce and process language so efficiently that we hardly notice it. However, teaching English depends on an understanding of the nature of language and, because it is not possible to teach all of a language at once, teachers need a way of dividing language up into component parts that can be used as the basis of a course or a lesson. This information about the nature and organization of language applies to all languages. However, English has taken on such an unusual role in the world that we also need to examine some of the implications of this role. The rest of this chapter addresses these issues by attempting to answer three questions:

1 What is language?
2 How are languages organized?
3 What is special about English?

2.2 Part I: What is language?

English teachers need to understand what language is if they are to teach effectively. The discussion of theories of language will help address the following kinds of comments:

Why can't they tell the difference between 'l' and 'r'?

I have pointed it out a hundred times but my learners still write 'she say' and 'he like' instead of 'she says' and 'he likes'.

When we use authentic texts in my reading class, the learners say they are boring.

A common-sense view of language is that it is a physical object. The words on this page seem to be objects in the same way that a pen or a table are physical objects. When we consider spoken language or writing on a computer screen, things get more complicated but, while sound waves and pixels that form the images on screens are not as tangible as pieces of paper, they are physical objects, and this suggests that language is an object that is independent of the observer. As a writer, I would be surprised if readers of this book did not agree that the first words in this paragraph are 'a common-sense view of language'. If I give some students copies of a list of articles and books I want them to read in a hand-out, it feels as if I am giving them information.

However, when we look at this from the viewpoint of language learners, problems arise. This is easier to illustrate with written language, but the same considerations apply to spoken language. At a basic level, recognizing letters in written language is much more complex than it might initially appear. A physical view of language makes sense with letter like 'O'. The way we recognize an 'O' looks rather like the way we identify a physical object. In the same way as a table consists of a flat surface with some legs, the letter 'O' consists of an oval or circular shape. How do readers know that a particular mark is the letter 'O'? They look for the circle. But identifying the letter 'O' requires more than this. Smith (1994) pointed out that the 'O' in 'LION' is often the same as the 'O' in '100' but is not the same symbol. The two instances of 'O' may be physically identical, but they are linguistically different. More strikingly, the letter 'A' can be written in various ways which have very little in common physically: 'a' or 'A'. Readers who are not familiar with the Roman alphabet would be forgiven for thinking that 'a' is a kind of 'O' rather than a kind of 'A'. To recognize an 'A', you need to know the range of things that count as an 'A'.

A English speaker will see '匕' as a way of writing the first letter of 'tea', whereas a Chinese speaker may see it as first part of the word '匕首' (dagger). A speaker of Malay will understand the word 'air' as water rather than what an English speaker will take from the same combination of letters. When learners encounter what seems to be a new language, it is not just that they do not know what the letters or phonemes of that language are. They do not know what parts of what they are seeing or hearing needs their attention.

An example of this is the discovery of pulsars, a kind of star, in 1967 by an astronomer called Bell (Hewish et al. 1968). What was striking about the pulsars was that they emitted bursts of radiation every 1.33 seconds. This regularity made Bell think it might be a message or at least an indication of some kind of intelligence. She even gave pulsars the half-joking nickname 'Little Green Men'. The bursts are not, as far we know, a message, but the fact that this possibility occurred to her illustrates how difficult it is to work out what might be a language. The only people who would know if it was a language would be the little green men or people who had the knowledge the little green men had.

In a similar way, Figure 2.1 is a photograph of what is supposed to be a non-terrestrial language. It looks like a language because it contains a lot of patterns and also what appears to be the figure 2,000.

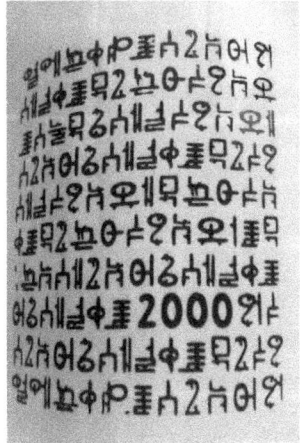

Figure 2.1 An alien language?

However, I have been told that the writing is based on the Old Croationa Glagolithic script. As someone with no knowledge of either the language or the script, this image remains an interesting pattern rather than a sample of language, though the difference is between something which I know to be language but which does not make sense to me and something which is a non-linguistic pattern of shapes or sounds that may not be easily identified.

The letters, the pulsars and the image of the imitation non-terrestrial language are all physical objects, but whether we can call them a language or not does not depend just on what kind of physical objects they are. For something to be language, we need a physical object, but we also need users of that language who can make sense of it. Language is a psychological interaction between users and a physical object.

What is on this page is not letters, words and paragraphs but marks on paper. Readers need to bring information about the writing system of English and their knowledge of how people write about topics such as language to make these marks on paper into language. The letters, words and texts are the result of the interaction between the information in readers' heads and the physical object. A lion is a lion whether or not someone is around, but a word 'lion' is only a word when someone is using it in speech or writing. As Crystal (2010: 81) says, 'texts only exist when they are read'. The remarkable thing is that we are able to communicate at all and this is because expert users of a language have 'a common set of signs' (Harris 1996: 6), but the defining characteristic of learners is that they do not share the set of English signs, so miscommunication is an intrinsic part of the language classroom. If learners were able to understand everything in the language classroom, they would not need a teacher, so learners should not be blamed for misunderstanding something they have heard or read. Unfortunately, many learners have come to feel that not understanding is a failure on their part, so many misunderstandings are kept secret. A key skill for language teachers is identifying what learners do not understand and working out what the learners need to help them overcome this.

The start of this section identified three issues that relate to the nature of language. The first was a teacher complaining about learners not being able to tell the difference between 'l' and 'r'. The fact that learners are not able to distinguish two sounds of English is not surprising. In fact, these learners are using the resources they have from their first language (L1) to provide something which is an approximation of sounds in English. Teachers need to be able to analyse why the learners are doing this and come up with a way of helping them to communicate more effectively.

Similarly, when learners write 'she say' and 'he like', this is probably because when the learners are exposed to a sentence such as 'She likes carrots', the sentence they reconstruct using their limited knowledge of English is 'She like carrots', and so this is what they are likely to write. The learners create their own version of the language to which they are exposed. The extent to which learners' version of the message coincides with the teacher's version depends on the knowledge the learners have. For many beginners, the sound that comes out of their teacher's mouth is not even language; it is just noise. What the teacher says is not always what the learners hear, and effective teachers try to evaluate their learners' understandings and misunderstandings.

The final issue was to do with the use of authentic texts in reading classes. The essential point is that what is authentic for one group of language users is not authentic for a different group. I am trying to learn Chinese and can say some words in Chinese, but I can read almost no characters. If my Chinese teacher gave me an article taken from a Chinese newspaper, it would not be authentic for me because I do not have enough knowledge of Chinese to reconstruct the text in a way that would correspond to what the author wrote. If my teacher asked me to read the text, it would probably be both boring and embarrassing for me.

 Activity 2.1 What is a language?

Which of these samples are language? How do you know?

1 ꭰꭲ Ᏼ Ꮢꮢꭶ
2 Hij gaf me een boek
3 'oH vam Hol
4 他给了我一本书
5 彼は私に本を与えました。

2.3 The organization of language

It is not possible to teach all of a language at once. Teachers need to find a way of breaking it down into component parts that can be used as the basis of a course or a lesson. This part of the chapter describes some ways in which language can be divided up, and two of these then form the organization of most of the rest of this book.

This section looks at three ways of dividing language up into different parts or elements. The first approach is a series of attempts to describe the ability to communicate; the second is based on the stages you need to go through in the process by which you get from the physical trace of language, or expression, to meaning or vice versa. The final approach is a way of dividing up language into the skills of reading, writing, speaking and listening.

2.3.1 Communicative competence

Linguists working within the transformational generative tradition associated with Chomsky make a division between what language users know and what they do.

> We thus make a fundamental distinction between the competence (the speaker-hearer's knowledge of his language) and performance (the actual use of language in concrete situations). (1969: 4)

The most interesting aspects of language users' knowledge for these linguists are the grammar and the phonology/phonetics, because these parts of language seem to have rules and these rules can be used to understand how language is produced. This view led to the idea that linguistic competence

Table 2.1 Hymes (1979) on communicative competence

Ways in which language is used	Criteria for appropriate or inappropriate use	Knowledge underlying use
1. Whether (and to what degree) something is formally possible	Grammatical/ungrammatical	Linguistic
2. Whether (and to what degree) something is feasible in virtue of the means of implementation available	Easy/difficult to use	Psycholinguistic
3. Whether (and to what degree) something is appropriate (adequate, happy, successful) in relation to a context in which it is used and evaluated	Polite/rude	Sociolinguistic
4. Whether (and to what degree) something is in fact done, actually performed and what its doing entails	Common/rare	Frequency

meant knowing the grammar and phonology of the language being studied. This was an influential view, and many language courses have focused on these elements and particularly on grammar.

However, several linguists offer wider views of what learners need to know. The three most important models are those presented by Hymes, Canale and Swain, and Bachman.

Hymes identified four aspects of language knowledge. See Table 2.1. This framework provides a useful way of describing what underlies an act of communication and highlights what learners need to know. The ideas of easy and difficult or common and rare provide useful guides for organizing a course book, and ideas of politeness are important for language learners. However, it is difficult to see how this translates in what might be taught in the classroom beyond a grammatical syllabus.

A second attempt at describing communicative competence was made by Canale and Swain (1980: 29–31 et passim). They identified three elements:

1 *Grammatical competence* – knowledge of lexical items and of rules of morphology, syntax, sentence–grammar semantics and phonology

2 *Sociolinguistic competence* –

   a sociocultural rules of use (what makes language appropriate for a particular context)

   b rules of discourse (how language is organized above the sentence)

3 *Strategic competence* – strategies used to deal with breakdowns in communication

This model has been influential in two main ways. The first is to do with the sociocultural rules of use. This led to the inclusion of functional elements in some language courses (Wilkins 1976). Many course books for elementary learners start with a unit which covers the function of introductions, and this allows course book writers to include different grammatical patterns in the same unit. A strictly grammatical course would treat 'How are you?' as belonging in a different unit from 'Hello' even though they both can be used to carry out the function of greeting people. The functional view of language is still influential, and you may well have functional units or parts of units in the course books you use but, despite Wilkins's efforts, it is hard to use this as the sole basis for an English syllabus. Swan (1985a) has argued that this is because grammar is more useful for learners who want to create new language because functions are less systematic and less generative than grammatical knowledge. Functions are still important in language learning, and there is some further discussion of them in Chapter 11.

The other contribution of Canale and Swain's notion of communicative competence was the idea of communication or compensatory strategies. Many course books now include elements on what learners should do if they do not understand something or what they should do if they do not know the exact word for what they want to say. Approaches involving strategies are relatively common in language learning and teaching, and we will cover some aspects of these in the chapters on skills-based teaching.

Bachman (1990: 87 et seq.) replaces the term communicative competence with the phrase communicative language ability. This is made up of language knowledge and strategic competence (Bachman and Palmer 1996: 67). Language knoweldge in turn is divided into organizational competence and pragmatic competence.

Organizational competence covers what Bachman describes as the formal structures of language and comprises grammatical competence, equivalent to Hymes's linguistic competence and Canale and Swain's grammatical competence, and textual competence, paralleling Canale and Swain's rules of discourse.

Pragmatic competence covers the ways in which language is used to express meaning. The first part of this, illocutionary competence (Bachman 1990: 90) or functional knowledge (Bachman and Palmer 1996: 69), covers how an utterance such as 'it's very hot' may be a description of temperature (ideational meaning), a request to turn on an air-conditioning system (manipulative meaning), an illustration of the

Table 2.2 Bachman's language knowledge

Language competence	Organizational competence	Grammatical competence	Vocabulary Morphology Syntax Phonology Graphology
		Textual competence	Cohesion Rhetorical organization
	Pragmatic competence	Illocutionary competence	Ideational Manipulative Heuristic Imaginative
		Sociolinguistic competence	Dialect Register Naturalness Cultural references

contraction 'it's' (heuristic) or engaging listeners in a story at a journey across a desert (imaginative). The other element in pragmatic competence involves sociolinguistic knowledge, which covers awareness of how languages vary geographically (dialect) or by differences between the discourse domain (e.g. registers of science and law), naturalness and cultural references. See Table 2.2.

These areas of language competence are then used to produce language when language users draw on their strategic competence. This process has three elements – assessment (working out what is needed), planning (working out how to do what is needed) and execution (doing what is needed).

The Hymes, Canale and Swain and the Bachman versions of communicative competence have been important in the way they have made it clear what learners need to know in order to use language effectively. However, the models are difficult to apply directly to the classroom. It would be difficult to teach a series of lessons on frequency or sociolinguistic competence.

The next section examines the notion of language knowledge using the idea of language elements.

2.3.2 Language elements

When babies start using what we might label pre-language, they use a sound like 'ma' or a gesture to mean something, such as mother, and the meaning relates directly to the expression. There is a direct link between meaning and expression, and when adults hear the sound, they go straight from the expression to the meaning. See Figure 2.2.

However, adult languages have three levels (Halliday and Matthiessen 2004: 24), and this enables users of English to combine three phonemes /k/, /æ/ and /t/ to produce 'tack', 'cat' and 'act' and to know that they cannot say */ktæ/ (the asterisk here indicates that something is not possible in a particular language). Instead of going directly from one expression to one meaning, there is an intermediate level. The meaning is expressed in a word and the word is expressed through phonemes. This feature of language is variously called double articulation (Schultz et al. 2011), duality of expression (Hockett 1960: 91–2) or 'stratification of the content plane' (Halliday and Matthiessen 2004: 25). Halliday and Matthiessen see the development of this division as a very important part of human evolution. This division of language 'turned *homo* . . . into *homo sapiens*' (p. 25). Figure 2.3 is an attempt to illustrate this in both everyday and more technical language.

When we understand a spoken message, we take the physical object that is the phonetic expression, and we use our knowledge of the sounds of the language to make it into linguistic substance, phonemes or letters. Phonetic description talks about things like the position of the tongue when you make a sound and is not related to a particular language. Phonemic description is about sounds in a particular language and how they relate to each other. One example of this is tone, which is phonemic in Chinese but not in English. For example, the Putonghua or Chinese word for 'Mother' is written as 'mā' in pinyin

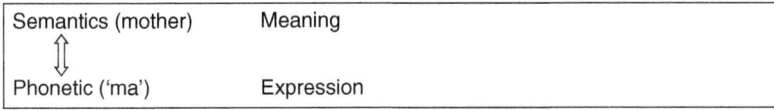

Figure 2.2 Possible levels of pre-language (adapted from Halliday and Hasan 1976: 5)

Word/ing	Semantics	Meaning
	↕	+
	(lexico-grammatical system,	Form
	grammar and vocabulary)	
Sound/letters	↕	+
	(phonological and	Substance
	orthographic systems)	
	↕	+
	Phonetic/graphics	Expression

Figure 2.3 Levels of language (adapted from Halliday and Hasan 1976: 5)

Romanization with 'ā' indicating first tone, and horse is written as 'mǎ', with 'ǎ' indicating third tone. Speakers of Putonghua will hear these as two different words. Most native speakers of English will hear one sound repeated twice because in English, tone is not phonemic. More importantly, they will continue to fail to distinguish between mother and horse in Chinese until they learn, first, that tones are important in distinguishing meaning and, second, to differentiate the tones.

Phonetics and phonology are distinct aspects of the study of language, but for language teaching purposes, they are grouped together and are often treated under the heading of pronunciation. This includes both speaking with an acceptable accent and understanding the way other people speak.

When we understand a written message, we go from the physical substance of marks on paper to letters. This parallels the process with spoken language, so we recognize the range of items such as 'g' and 'G' as being instances of the same letter.

The way we describe the next level, meaning and form, has led to two controversies. The first is signalled by the alternatives of lexis and grammar versus lexico-grammar. Lexis means vocabulary, and grammar is how we order those words. The division between grammar and vocabulary is used widely in language teaching.

The lexico-grammar view, often associated with Halliday, is that there is a continuum from more general meanings, expressed using grammar, to more specific meanings, expressed through vocabulary (Halliday 1961). For example, the difference between 'learner' and 'learners' is a fairly delicate distinction and so it is treated as difference in grammar. The difference between 'learner' and 'teacher' is a greater difference and so it is part of vocabulary or lexis. We can see the continuum view in arguments about whether the difference between 'put on' (e.g. put on your hat) and 'put off' (e.g. put off a meeting) is a lexical or grammatical difference and in the way some language teaching materials focus on topics like collocation and formulaic language. However, at the moment, grammatical descriptions are not able to cover vocabulary, and this book treats grammar and vocabulary in separate chapters. This is also in line with the division in many linguistic theories, for example, Chomsky (2000), and the fact that we have two main kinds of reference books for language, dictionaries and grammars.

Activity 2.2 Grammar and vocabulary or lexico-grammar

Would you treat the difference between these pairs of items as part of grammar, part of vocabulary or something else?

1 Go – went

2 Go – come

3 Throw at someone – throw to someone

4 Take up – take off

5 Happy – happier

6 Happy – unhappy

7 Happy – not happy

8 As happy as Larry – as happy as you

The other controversy at the level of form relates to the units that could be the aim of a lesson. In everyday use, we probably link meaning most closely with words and, for many linguists, the largest meaningful unit of language is the sentence. However, 'it is people who make meanings, not words or structures' (Prodromou 2008: xvi), and people often use units larger than the word or sentence to communicate. Halliday sees the most important unit of meaning as not the word or the sentence but the spoken or written text. When we think about communication, words or grammar contribute to the meaning being expressed, but the important units of communication are texts, for example, a conversation or a letter applying for a job.

A related argument about the importance of texts is the patterns in language that operate over units larger than the sentence. In many languages, conventions exist about how to start conversations; conventions about what you say which restrict the language you can use and these conventions are to do with how groups of sentences are used. For example, speakers of Hausa, a language spoken in West Africa, often start a conversation by asking if the other person is tired, and conversations in Chinese often start with one person asking another if they have eaten. In many varieties of English, a comment about weather is a useful way of starting a conversation. Using Bachman's (Bachman 1990; Bachman and Palmer 1996) terms discussed earlier, the illocutionary force or function of a comment about tiredness, food or weather varies between cultures.

Similarly, written texts are structured. A lot of academic texts have introductions, and course books typically have pages of context and indexes. Using a language effectively requires a knowledge of text structures as well as being able to form grammatical sentences. Language learners need to be able to produce and understand texts, so we need to think of grammar and vocabulary as a means to this end.

Unfortunately, at the moment, most ways of teaching focus on grammar and vocabulary rather than texts, but we are making progress. An important development is genre analysis, a way of describing

Table 2.3 Elements of language and organization of the book

Expression and substance		Form and meaning		
Chapter 7	Chapter 9	Chapter 9	Chapter 10	Chapter 11
Pronunciation	Spelling	Grammar	Vocabulary	Discourse

groups or genres of texts which serve the same function or purpose. Genres are explored in more detail in Chapter 11, and genre in the teaching of writing is discussed in Chapter 14.

Another development is the closely related concept of communicative tasks. The term 'task' is used with a variety of meanings in teaching English to speakers of other languages (TESOL), and most of these meanings are primarily to do with what happens in the classroom.

> A task is taken to be an activity in which meaning is primary, there is some sort of relationship to the real world, task completion has some priority, and the assessment of task performance is in terms of task outcome. (Skehan 1996: 38)

However, the kind of task relevant here is a communicative or target task. Long and Norris say, 'Tasks are the things people will tell you they do if you ask them and they are not applied linguists' (1985: 89). If you want to decide what to teach, you first need to identify learners' needs 'in terms of *target tasks*, the real-world things people *do* [using language] in everyday life' (Long and Norris 2000: 599, italics in original), such as buying a train ticket or applying for a job.

Thinking about language use in terms of tasks is useful as a way of making sure that we remember that language is a means of communication. However, as with genres, our descriptions of language in terms of tasks are limited. Chapter 11 looks at what we know about tasks in more detail. The notion of communicative tasks is also closely linked to the idea of task-based teaching. While this approach to teaching is more influenced by the notion of tasks in the classroom than of communicative tasks, Long's ideas have had an impact. Task-based teaching is discussed in Chapter 4.

This terminology related to language organization about the sentence, texts and communicative tasks can lead to confusion, and this book uses the more general term of discourse to cover both these terms and some associated ideas such as pragmatics. See Table 2.3.

2.3.3 Language skills

We can also divide language up in terms of whether (a) we are working with spoken and written language and (b) we are working with productive or receptive skills. Reading is a receptive skill used with written texts; speaking is an active skill used with spoken texts.

A range of terms are used instead of receptive and productive. Some people use the terms active and passive. The term passive is not a good one, because it suggests that reading and writing do not require the language user to do anything, but the processes of reading and listening are quite demanding. Receptive suggests more activity than passive and perhaps interpretation or re-creation is closer to what happens when someone reads or listens.

Table 2.4 Language skills and organization of the book

Chapter 12	Chapter 13	Chapter 14	Chapter 15
Reading	Writing	Listening	Speaking

While the skills-based approach has the virtue of simplicity, it can lead to teaching where speaking is treated as unconnected with listening. However, the skills-based approach is very useful in language teaching as long as the division between skills is seen as a convenience for teaching rather than a claim that the skills are independent. For these reasons, I use elements and skills to structure much of this book. See Table 2.4.

 Activity 2.3 Organizing a language course book

Choose an English language course book you know well. How does it divide up the language? To what extent does it make use of elements (pronunciation, grammar, vocabulary, tasks) or skills (reading, writing, listening and speaking)?

2.4 Part II: English

The idea that language is created by psychological interaction and the divisions of language by elements and skills applies to all languages. Decisions by teachers of Chinese, Arabic or Spanish about what to teach look fairly similar at this level. For example, all these teachers might well have stretches of teaching where they focus on grammar or reading. However, 'English is different: it appears practically everywhere because it seems assumed to have a global relevance that other languages do not have' (Widdowson 2000: 193). If you are teaching a language to speakers of other languages, you need to decide which varieties of the language you should be teaching, and the fact that English is spoken so widely makes this more complicated than for many other languages.

The reasons for English being so widespread are mainly to do with the fact that the English-speaking UK was succeeded by another dominant power in the world, the Anglophonic United States. This has resulted in there being different native speaker varieties of English associated particularly with what is often called 'the inner circle' of English (Kachru 1983), that is, Australia, Canada, Ireland, New Zealand, South Africa, the United Kingdom and the United States, but for reasons which are not clear, this sometimes excludes other native speakers of English from, say, the West Indies. This multiplicity of native speaker varieties means that many teachers of English have to make a decision about which varieties they wish to focus on or how to deal with the varieties that are included in their teaching material.

However, the number of native speakers is not what makes English different. Indeed, English is not the most common L1 by some distance. Estimates of the number of people who speak English as a

L1 vary between about 330 million (Lewis 2009) and 400 million (Gnutzman 2000: 357), while Mandarin Chinese or Putonghua has about 1.2 billion speakers.

The main reason for the different status of English is to do with the number of L2 speakers, but estimates here vary even more than they do for L1 speakers. Graddol (2006: 62) quotes a figure of 510 million speakers of English as a first or second language, which suggests under 200 million speakers of English as a second or foreign language. Crystal (2010: 370) puts the figure at 1.2 billion, and Graddol (2006) suggests that by 2020 there will be two billion learners (p. 14) which could generate the same number of speakers (p. 96) of English.

> English has become not only an international lingua franca, but the first world language in human history. (Gnutzman 2000: 357)

L2 speakers of English are usually grouped into two categories, those who speak English as a second language (ESL), the outer circle; and those who speak English as foreign language (EFL), the expanding circle (Kachru 1983). People who learn English in a country where English has no official status, such as Japan or China, are said to speak EFL. People who learn English in a country where English has some official status, such as Nigeria or Singapore, are said to speak ESL.

However, this classification is too simplistic for teaching purposes because ESL learners do not form one coherent group. In the United States, migrants learning English have very different needs than, say, someone learning English in India. This has led to a proliferation of acronyms. In the UK people talk about English as an additional language (EAL) for non-native speakers of English at school and ESOL (English to speakers of other languages) at college. In the United States, teachers talk of English language learners (ELLs). Learners who plan to settle in a country where English is a native language may wish to learn the standard language in that country, but they will also need to learn more local varieties. Someone who settles in Leeds will need to be able to cope with Yorkshire English.

In outer-circle countries like Nigeria, there is a standard English which is distinct from native speaker varieties, and in many situations two Nigerians might communicate in English even though they both have other languages in common. These varieties of English are primarily used for communication within a country or region and often have distinctive features of vocabulary and grammar and are a part of the local culture. In West African English, people may say 'two breads' rather than 'two loaves of bread' or read works of literature which include sentences such as 'I was a palm-wine drinkard since I was a boy of ten years of age' (Tutuola 1961: 4). If you are learning English in Nigeria or Ghana, being able to use West African English and the cultures associated with that variety are likely to be more useful than, say, a native speaker variety such as Australian English.

The situation with learners of English as a foreign language is more complex because of the range of reasons for which such learners may need to use English. If they are going to use English primarily with L1 speakers of English, then a variety of English as a native language (ENL) will probably be appropriate. A Mexican who is learning English to do business with people from the United States should probably learn a variety of American English. Similarly, a speaker from Cote D'Ivoire who wants to trade with Ghanaians might wish to learn a Ghanaian or West African kind of English. However, many learners will wish to use English to communicate with others from the expanding circle. A Japanese friend of mine managed a branch of a Japanese company in Germany. I asked him whether he was learning German, and he said he did not need to do this as he only employed people who could speak English. This situation where two non-native speakers of English use English to communicate with each other is very common.

> About 80% of verbal exchanges in which English is used a second or foreign language do not involve native speakers of English. (Gnutzman 2000: 357)

In these circumstances, English is being used as a lingua franca and, for many people, this is the variety of English that they need to learn.

> A lingua franca is a contact language used among people who do not shared a first language, and is commonly understood to mean a second (or subsequent) language of its speakers. (Jenkins 2007: 1)

There is a disagreement of terminology about whether English as a lingua franca (ELF) includes interactions with L1 speakers of English. Prodromou says that ELF is 'the use of English as an international context as a lingua franca between people with a different L1 but excluding L1 speakers of English' (2008: xviii), and he uses the term English as an international language (EIL) to cover interactions between both L1 and L2 speakers of English. In contrast, Jenkins (2007) argues that ELF includes interactions involving L1 speakers of English because so many interactions involve both L1 and L2 speakers of English – 20 per cent according to Gnutzman (2000: 357 supra).

Some people have tried to come up with descriptions of the phonology, lexis and grammar of ELF. For example, Jenkins suggests that the difference between unvoiced and voiced versions of 'th', as in 'three' and 'that' respectively, is not part of the EFL 'core' and there have been suggestions for the omission of certain grammatical features such as third-person simple present 's', as in 'She look happy'. There are also claims that ELF uses fewer idioms than ENL or ESL varieties. However, Jenkins argues that these features should not be used as models for teaching but are simply examples of the ways that ELF interactions happen. (See O'Regan 2014 for the dangers of treating ELF as a variety of English.)

What is important is that ELF should not rely on ENL norms (Jenkins 2007: 25) because

> relying on native speaker norms (or near-native speaker norms) does not necessarily guarantee that the communication will be successful. (Gnutzman, 2000: 358)

Different users will have different varieties of English.

> For instance, if a Chilean, an Indian, and an American attended a business meeting in Hong Kong, each participant might use a variety of English that they were most fluent in – for example, Chilean English, Indian English, and American English respectively. (Matsuda and Friedrich 2011: 333)

A better approach is to focus not on the knowledge of different language levels of those who speak ELF but on the way they use English in an ELF interaction to ensure effective communication.

> What is distinctive about ELF lies in the communicative strategies that its speakers use rather than in the conformity to any changed set of language norms. (Seidlhofer 2005: 38)

Probably the most important strategy is that of accommodation. Users of language need to adjust the way they produce and understand language to ensure that they communicate effectively. Here is an example of three speakers, Jean, Karen and Anna, in an ELF interaction. They are talking about some pictures that Jean's friend has sent to her and which Jean and Karen are looking at (adapted from Cogo and Dewey 2006: 67).

Jean: They have pictures of them you know in Kathmandu, in Tibet, like
Karen: [laughing]
Anna: They sent pictures on the internet.
Jean: It's nice but it's a bit
Anna: . . . too much eh? [speaking at the same time]
Jean: . . . cheesy [speaking at the same time]
Karen: Yeah
Anna: Yeah
Karen: Yeah a bit too much I think (laughing)
Jean: So blue flower, we say fleur bleue [blue flower in French]
Anna: Why? To say that it's cheesy?
Jean: Fleur, yeah, fleur bleue means you know when you have these pictures with little angels of . . .
Karen: Ahh. Yeah
Anna: Yeah
Jean: Fleur bleue
Karen: Kitsch-kitschig [the German for kitschy – a word that English has borrowed from German]
Jean: Kitschig yeah [laughter]

Here, Karen accommodates the way Jean uses the term 'fleur blue' to explain 'cheesy' in a way that is closer to Jean's L1 and, in return, Jean accepts and repeats Karen's use of the German word 'kitshig'. As Prodromou puts it, 'ELF is not a fixed entity: it is a dynamic response to the local interactional needs of the people involved'.

The focus on interactional needs is the key element here. Teachers need to help learners develop the skills they need to communicate, and this will depend not only on the varieties of English that parties to the communication can use but also the relative status of those involved. When a candidate is being interviewed for a job, they will try to use language in a way that is acceptable to the person who is interviewing. Choices of whether to teach one or more kinds of ENL, a second language variety, the set of communication strategies associated with ELF (Seidlhofer and Widdowson 2009: 37–8) or some combination of these will depend on what learners need and – where we are not able to say what they will need – the varieties we think will be most useful to them. These issues are also related to the varieties the teacher speaks. In some contexts, those who own language schools believe that native speakers of English, particularly those from the Britain, America and Australia, make the most acceptable teachers of English. However, the important question to be considered here is who is best able to help learners develop their ability to use English effectively, and this will depend of a variety of factors which may include the varieties of English the teacher uses but also their experience of learning English.

Activity 2.4 Varieties of English

Consider a group of ELLs you have worked with. What were their reasons for learning English? If you speak a L1 other than English, this could relate to your own reasons for learning English.

How would these reasons relate to the variety or varieties of English they or you were taught?

How would their reasons for learning English relate to the identification of who might be an appropriate teacher for these learners?

2.5 Summary

This chapter examined ideas about language in general and argued that language is an interaction between a physical trace and users of that language. The chapter has covered three ways of dividing language up:

a different kinds of competence,

b elements of language (phonology, orthography, lexico-grammar and discourse) and

c skills (reading, writing, speaking and listening).

The chapter also discussed the ways in which English is different from other languages because it is widely used as a lingua franca and argued that this has implications for what kinds of English students of English need to learn.

 2.6 Further reading

My favourite book on language is Crystal (2010), who has written widely and accessibly on most aspects of language. The description of the elements of language is a feature in many current course books, but its rationale is not widely discussed. This chapter was influenced by Halliday's work such as *An Introduction to Functional Grammar* (2004). To know more on ELF, Jenkins's (2007) *English as a Lingua Franca: Attitude and Identity* is useful, as well as Graddol's (2006) *English Next: Why Global English May Mean the End of 'English as a Foreign Language'*, which at the time of writing was available for free download.

Chapter 3

Language Learning

3.1 Introduction

This chapter addresses the second question about TESOL courses: how are languages learnt? This issue has been addressed from two different perspectives. The first is an attempt to identify general principles which account for language learning, and the second perspective focusses on learners. Both these areas have generated extensive literatures, and this chapter aims to provide a foundation for making decisions in the classroom and for examining the literature in more detail by addressing two questions:

1 How do people learn second languages?

2 What is the role of learners in second language learning?

    2.1 What motivates people to learn second languages?

    2.2 How do learners support their own learning?

 Activity 3.1 Learning a language

If you have taken a course in learning a second language, which of these activities featured in it?

a Grammatical rules

b Extensive reading or listening

c Drills and repetition

d Role-play

e Correction

How did these activities help or hinder your learning?

3.2 Theories of learning

The number of theories of learning is extensive and, if you look at the suggested reading at the end of this chapter, you will find several book-length studies of theories of second language learning, but here we focus on three kinds of theory that are the most important. One reason for the number of theories is that different theories concentrate on different parts of the learning process. The first theories covered in this chapter focus on what is special about learning a language. The second kind of theory relates to psychological aspects of learning, and the last theory relates to sociocultural aspects of learning.

3.2.1 Language-oriented theories

This section looks at two language-oriented theories of language learning. The first theory, the monitor model, has been very influential, particularly among teachers, while the second, connectionism, is a more recent development, but both theories are important because they emphasize implicit language learning.

The monitor model

The monitor model was created by Krashen (1981a, 1987, 1989), but his views are an application of the ideas of Chomsky (1969) about first language development to second language learning. One of the issues that Chomsky focussed on was the fact that almost everyone learns to use their first language to a high level of competence. Krashen compared this success with the relative failure of second language learning, and he argues that the best way to help second language learners is to make second language learning as similar as possible to first language development.

The difference between the relatively informal way in which people acquire their first language and the highly structured approach to language learning in many schools led Krashen to identify two kinds of language development.

> 'Acquisition' is a subconscious process identical in all important ways to the process children utilize in acquiring their first language while 'learning' is a conscious process that results in knowing about language. (Krashen 1985: 1)

A distinction between conscious and sub- or unconscious development, or something close to this, appears in several theories of language learning. Krashen, however, goes further and argues that the two processes are separate. If you learn a grammar rule, that rule can never be a part of what you have acquired. You can use what you have learnt to monitor the language you produce as a result of acquisition, but 'two conditions needs to be met in order to use the Monitor: the performer must be consciously concerned about correctness: and he or she must know the rule. Both these conditions are difficult to meet' (Krashen 1985: 2). The lack of connection between what you have learnt and what you have picked up/acquired is a very distinctive part of Krashen's view and has led to his theory being known as the monitor model.

Because the use of the monitor is so limited, acquisition is the most important part of language development, and Krashen makes two claims about how acquisition happens: the need for comprehensible input and the importance of affective factors.

Krashen argues that acquisition requires largely comprehensible input. Unless learners understand what they hear or read, they cannot learn. This idea has been widely, possibly universally, accepted. If you hear something you do not understand, then it is not language for you, and the question of language development does not even arise. This idea is closely related to the idea discussed in Chapter 2 that language is created by interaction. Indeed, the language that is created by interactions with language users is of necessity comprehensible.

Krashen argues that input needs to be largely comprehensible and the largely is important. If learners can understand what they hear or read completely, then their language will stay at that level. If they can roughly understand it, then they may be able to use what they have heard to develop beyond their current level. Krashen says that for language development, learners need to be exposed to $i+1$, where 'i' is comprehensible input and '+1' indicates something that is a little bit above that.

To explain what is meant by input at a level a little bit above what the learners can understand, Krashen borrowed an idea from Chomsky about first language development, the language acquisition device or Universal Grammar. This idea suggests that all humans are genetically endowed with a set of principles and parameters which are triggered when they are exposed to language samples and help them construct the grammar of language to which they are exposed.

For example, languages can be strongly head-initial (like English) so that verbs come before objects/complements (kicked the ball), and position words, prepositions in English, come before nouns (behind John the goal). In strongly head-final languages like Japanese, verbs come after their object (はボールを蹴りました – bōru o kerimashita [the ball kicked]) and post-positions come after the noun (ジョンの後ろ – Jon no ushiro [John behind]) (Saville-Troike 2006: 48). So, if learners hear some sentences with verbs coming before objects, this triggers the assumption that there will be prepositions rather than post-positions in this language. This is a way of explaining how sometimes learners' language develops beyond what might be predicted from their input. In Bahasa Melayu, adjectives come after nouns and so you might expect that mother tongue users of Bahasa Melayu who study English would sometimes write 'meal delicious'. In my experience, this does not happen, and Universal Grammar offers an explanation for this, though the explanation may seem more complicated than the data require.

Universal Grammar explains why second language learners' grammar, and in particular their morphology, develops in similar ways regardless of their first language. 'We acquire the rules of language in a predictable order, some rules tending to come early and other late' (Krashen 1985: 1), and teachers can ensure that input is roughly comprehensible by including grammar points that are just beyond what the learners are currently able to understand. See Figure 3.1.

The second point Krashen makes about acquisition relates to affective factors. If someone is very nervous, then they are not going to learn. Krashen uses the term 'affective filter' to describe this. 'Low motivation, low self-esteem and anxiety . . . can work together to "raise" an affective filter and form a "mental block" that prevents comprehensible input from being used for acquisition' (Bot and Lowie 2005: 36).

This idea would be a rationale for allowing learners who are uncomfortable speaking in order to remain silent. One rather unusual piece of research which supports the notion of the affective filter was carried out by Guiora et al. (1972: 426). They investigated whether drinking alcohol would improve the pronunciation of second language speakers of Thai. They found that 'ingestion of small amounts

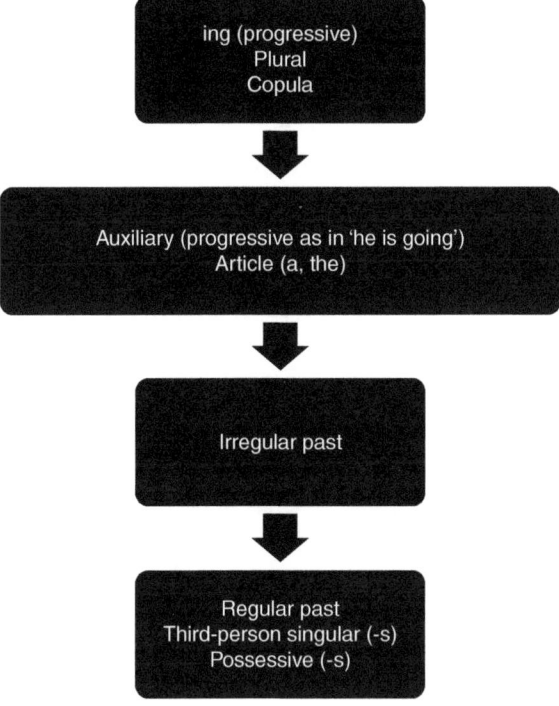

Figure 3.1 The natural order (adapted from Krashen 1987: 13)

Table 3.1 The monitor model

Hypothesis	Gloss
Acquisition/learning	Unconscious language acquisition is separate from conscious language learning
Monitor	What is learned can only be used to monitor language production
Natural order	We acquire the elements of language in a predictable order
Input hypothesis	If learners can roughly understand what they read or hear, this will lead to language development
Affective filer	Learners who are anxious or nervous will not be able to process any input

of alcohol, under certain circumstances, does lead to increased ability to authentically pronounce a second language' but that too much alcohol led to worse pronunciation.

Krashen's ideas focus on learners' subjective experience, and this is problematic for research. It is very difficult to see how to decide whether a text was at i+1 or i+2, and researchers and teachers would find it hard to know when the affective filter is preventing learners from understanding a particular piece of language. As a result, the ideas have not been much explored in the academic world, though many teachers find that the monitor model is a useful way of understanding language development. Table 3.1 is an attempt to summarize Krashen's views.

Connectionism

Connectionism sees language primarily as a matter of patterns in a complex network. The Universal Grammar framework sees sentences resulting from language users applying rule to linguistic units. Within a connectionist model, language users put smaller units such as morphemes and words together to form larger units, such as sentences or texts, based on what the words and morphemes are associated with. So even though sentences might seem to be formed by the creation of grammatical rules, this is just appearance. 'The only relation in connectionist models is strength of association between nodes' (Ellis and Schmidt 1997: 153). The complex apparatus of Universal Grammar is not needed to explain how language users produce apparently rule-governed behaviour.

A similar idea underlies how learning happens. The human brain is a network of neural nodes, and language learning happens as the network in the brain comes to match the network in language use within society. When learners are exposed to examples of language, they identify regularities in what they hear or see, and these regularities will be mimicked in the brain. As learners hear or see the same pattern again, that will strengthen the links between nodes. 'An individual's creative linguistic competence emerges from the combination of two things: the memories of all of the utterances encountered in communicative situations, and the induction of regularities in those utterances based on frequency' (Ellis 2006a: 78).

If an English speaker produces the sound /wʌn/, this could be the first syllable of 'wonderful' or the word 'one'. Most people will, in the absence of other information, understand /wʌn/ as 'one'. Ellis argues that this is because most people have heard more examples of 'one' than of 'wonderful', and that this means 'one' has been primed (Ellis 2006a: 78) and so becomes the most likely interpretation of /wʌn/.

Rather like the monitor model, connectionism suggests that exposure leads to language development. However, again as with the monitor model, it is important to remember that units such as phonemes and letters need to be created by language users and no learning can happen until this processing has happened. If learners do not recognize the sound [w] as the phoneme /w/, they will not be able to identify what other phonemes are associated with it.

Both the monitor model and connectionism provide arguments for lots of exposure to language, and Krashen's notion of comprehensible input is a useful guide to what exposure may lead to learning.

3.2.2 Psychologically oriented or cognitive theories

This group of theories are the most common ways of thinking about language learning. This section focusses on language learning as information processing (Saville-Troike 2006), more or less equivalent to what is sometimes known as skill acquisition (Johnson 1996), and also as the adaptive control of thought (Anderson 2010).

Understanding learning as information processing sees language learning as essentially the same as other kinds of learning. So you will find work in this tradition which has looked at the mathematics (Qin et al. 2004), making cigars (Crossman 1959) and playing chess (Chase 1973). The essential idea here is that learning consists of two elements, acquiring explicit or declarative knowledge (e.g. a grammar rule) and then using that knowledge or, in more technical language, converting declarative knowledge into procedural knowledge (e.g. producing or understanding language using the grammar rule).

This theory differs from the monitor model in two important ways. The first is that this view focusses on explicit learning and sees this explicit learning as leading to unconscious or automatic language use. However, information processing theory does not claim to be an explanation of all language learning, so it does not deny the importance of implicit learning (Dekeyser 2006: 103). Indeed, Doughty and Long (2003: 292) state 'the default processing mode in SLA, as in other types of complex learning is implicit', which suggests the language-oriented views of learning may not be inconsistent with the psychological models.

This focus on explicit learning means that learning a language is seen as different from using a language. While the monitor model would see the communicative, albeit, receptive, use of language as leading to language development, for information processing theory, explicit learning and language use are different processes. Learners have to step outside the act of communication to allow explicit learning. In the model of a vocabulary lesson covered in Chapter 10, comprehensible meaning-focussed input, where the language is being used receptively, is separate from form-focussed learning, where learners are being helped to develop declarative knowledge about vocabulary.

Second, information processing views see practice as leading to language development. Chase, one of the originators of the theory, is reported to have summarized the theory as 'no pain, no gain' (Anderson 2010: 242), but it might also be summarized as saying 'practice makes perfect'.

How do learners acquire declarative knowledge about language

Learners develop knowledge about language by noticing a difference between what they hear or read and their own knowledge of language (Schmidt 1990: 132); for example, if learners see the spelling 'address' and realize they normally spell that word 'adress', that could lead to them acquiring declarative knowledge about the spelling of 'address'. This new knowledge will need to be incorporated into learners' previous knowledge of English spelling and will require that the previous knowledge be restructured.

Noticing is a cognitive process (Schmidt 1990: 130), so teachers cannot tell if their learners have noticed something just by watching, but the importance of noticing fits in well with much that happens in the classroom. Course books are written to draw learners' attention to particular features of English, and teachers go out of their way to identify what learners should be noticing by, for example, using metalinguistic terminology (i.e. the present perfect). Noticing can also result from the negotiation of meaning (Long 1983, 1985) that happens in a communicative activity. Here is an example of two speakers negotiating meaning from Mackey et al. (2000: 486):

A: There are [flurs]?
B: Floors?
A: [fluwərs] uh flowers.

Student A seems to have noticed a difference between her initial pronunciation and the normal pronunciation as produced by student B. The researchers checked this by asking student A to recall what had happened

Recall : I was thinking that my pronounce [sic], pronunciation is very horrible.

Unfortunately, learners do not always notice what teachers might expect them to notice. This is illustrated in another example from Mackey et al.'s research:

C: So one man feed for the birds.
D: So one man's feeding the birds?
C: The birds.

Student D was trying to indicate that the grammar of the verb was wrong and that the preposition 'for' was not needed. Student C's comment on this interaction was, 'When I saw the picture I thought this is a park and I tried to describe' (Mackey et al. 2000: 485), which suggests the student did not interpret the feedback in the way student D intended and did not notice the way the verb or the preposition was used.

Mackey et al.'s research examined the negotiation of meaning as part of a communicative activity, and perhaps some learners find it difficult to switch from using the language in a communicative activity to learning a language, but the fact that they noticed what they were supposed to notice in under 20 per cent of cases where they were given feedback indicates how important it is that teachers do not assume that learners have noticed what the teacher wants them to notice.

How do learners proceduralize their declarative knowledge?

Noticing is not enough because learners need to proceduralize their declarative knowledge before they can use the knowledge to understand or produce language, so it is not surprising that errors that teachers have often corrected are repeated even where the learners have noticed what they had done wrong. The knowledge they have obtained through noticing needs to be turned into action. Unless learners have proceduralized the knowledge from corrections, it will not influence the language they produce.

The first stages of 'proceduralization of knowledge is not particularly arduous or time consuming' (Dekeyser 2006), but it does require that learners have some conscious control over what they are doing. So, they would be able to spell 'address' correctly but would need to think about its spelling to get it right, and this means that, when they are focussing on something else, they can still misspell it. This stage is known as the controlled stage, and the fact that learners need to control their actions means that they have fewer cognitive resources to do other things. So, for example, if they are concentrating on spelling 'address' correctly, they may, as a result, have worse handwriting or make more grammar mistakes.

The notion of learners having limited cognitive resources provides a rationale for repeating activities (Foster and Skehan 1999; Skehan and Foster 1999). For example, if learners are engaged in planning a holiday, the first time around they will need to think about where they are going and how they will get there and their language may be less fluent, accurate or complex than it might be. The second time around, assuming they are still interested in the topic, they should be able to speak more fluently or more accurately.

Gradually learners become more expert at what they are doing and the action becomes more automatic so that it requires less effort to produce or understand language. Once the spelling of 'address'

Table 3.2 Learning language as information processing and related theories

Language learning as a skill (Dekeyser 2006; Johnson 2005)	Information processing (Saville-Troike 2006: 80)	Adaptive control of thought – rational (Anderson 2010: 242–71)
Declarative knowledge	Perception	Cognitive stage
Procedural knowledge: controlled	Controlled processing	Associative stage
Procedural knowledge: automatic	Automatic processing	Autonomous stage

is automatic, learners can use the resources that had been taken up by their need to think about, or control, the spelling of 'address' for other learning or communicative events (Anderson 2010: 243). This explains why learners may be able to produce a new grammatical structure when they are practising it in the classroom but revert back to less sophisticated or inaccurate forms in more communicative activities where the increased time pressure and, possibly, the desire to say something original means they have fewer resources to produce the structure accurately.

Not all practice leads to improvement, and most of us have the experience of our progress in developing expertise in a sport of language stalling. What is effective according to Ericsson et al. (1993) is known as deliberate practice. This has four related features:

1 Learners who want to improve their language not just use it.
2 Learners receive feedback on their performance.
3 Learners monitor how well their performance matches the correct performance on the basis of feedback.
4 Learners focus on eliminating the imperfections in their performance (Anderson 2010; Ericsson 2013: 263).

Table 3.2 is an attempt to summarize the information processing view of language learning and some of the different terminology for related theories that use similar frameworks.

3.3 Sociocultural views: Vygotsky

The main sociocultural theory of language development is associated with Vygotsky (1978), whose interest was in how children learnt in schools. Like information processing approaches, this view sees learning language as the same as learning other things but, perhaps because of the original focus on the classroom, differs from the theories discussed earlier in two important ways. First, learning and language are primarily social and are only internalized later on. 'Any function in the child's cultural development appears on the stage twice, on two planes, first on the social plane and then on the psychological, first among people as an intermental category and then within the child as an intramental category' (Vygotsky 1966: 44).

Second, learning is brought about, or mediated, through people and things around learners. Learners are able to do more if they have support from other people or artefacts around them than they can do on their own, and they gradually internalize the external support. Learners move from other-regulation, where they are guided by more expert users of English to self-regulation or autonomy.

Sociocultural theory sees learning as a process of social interaction. This sounds rather similar to the negotiation for meaning, discussed above. However, whereas in information processing approaches the interactions are important because they change what is in learners' heads though noticing, the sociocultural view sees interaction as 'the development of increasingly effective ways of dealing with the world' (Van Lier 2000: 246–7). The central element is using language (including both production and comprehension) rather than the knowledge that underlies language use.

In information processing theory, the interaction is something that may lead to learning. For people like van Lier who work within sociocultural views, a successful interaction is learning. The teachers need to provide opportunities for interactions and support their learners by providing scaffolding either from other learners or from themselves, or provide artefacts that the learners can use to engage successfully. The two implications that sociocultural theory has for the classroom are, first, what happens in the classroom needs to be as similar as possible to what would normally happen in the learners' target communicative contexts and that, second, learners need to develop control over how they communicate.

Vygotsky says that learners have a zone of proximal development (ZPD), that is, the difference between what they can do independently and what they can do with support or scaffolding, and this is where learning happens. This notion may sound a little like i+1 in the monitor model but, whereas Krashen's idea is primarily to do with how Universal Grammar helps with psychological acquisition, ZPD is about how the interaction between learners and their environment supports or does not support social language development. i+1 is fixed for each learner, while ZPD will vary if the context changes. For Vygotsky, good teachers can increase what their learners can learn. What both the monitor model and Vygotsky agree on is that in a particular classroom, learners have the capacity to learn or acquire some aspects of language and not others.

The support that learners receive can come from other learners or anyone else with higher levels of language ability in their context but will often come from teachers. The fact that sociocultural theory theorizes the role of the teacher distinguishes it from the theories discussed above, but this also means that a key element in learning is teachers identifying what lies within a learner's ZPD and providing the right level of support to the learner at the right stage. Nishidao and Yahima observed a series of low-level classes in Japan. In lesson one, the teacher has to whisper what the learners should be saying (Nishida and Yashima 2010: 484):

Teacher [whispering]	Who are you?
Student 2	Who are you?
Teacher [whispering]	I'm Timon
Student 3	I'm Timon
Teacher [whispering]	I am Nala. Nice to meet you,
Student 2	I am Nala. Nice to meet you,
Teacher [whispering]	Nice to meet you too.
Students 1, 2 and 3	Nice to meet you too

By lesson seven, the teacher just says 'San hai [one, two]' to cue what the learners need to say. Also, S3 is providing support for S2 and this is evidence that S3 has become a more autonomous language user (Nishida and Yashima 2010: 486).

Student 4	E? [Umm? S4 has forgotten what to say]
Student 3	Who are you?
Student 4	A . . . a. Who are you?
Teacher	I'm Nala
Student 1	I'm Nala
Teacher	San hai [one, two]
Students 3 and 4	Nice to meet you Nala

Artefacts can also support language development. This can include any object and, in language classroom, may include the use of digital technologies. However, for Vygotsky the most important artefact is language, and this covers the use of first language as well as second. Saville-Troike collected data from a kindergarten where a four-year-old native speaker of Chinese was often able to communicative successfully with monolingual speakers of English (2006: 118).

Gege	Zhege shi shenme guanzi a? [That is what kind of hose]
Teacher	That's a fire hose.

Gege demonstrates the level of confidence which led to him receiving enough appropriate support to become a fluent speaker of English but, at this stage, he was reliant on the presence of a hose in his immediate context and a supportive interlocutor.

A more self-directed example is given in Table 3.3. A mother tongue speaker of Spanish is producing a piece of writing in English. Normal text indicates what the learner said aloud. Underlined segments indicate text actually written down; italics indicate rereadings and repetitions of that text; translations and descriptions of actions are in square brackets.

Sociocultural theory is not prescriptive about what are or are not effective ways of mediating the development of a second language but, in ways that parallel most models of language learning, the desired result is an autonomous user of English.

Table 3.3 Using the mother tongue

Nowadays nowadays schools must have technological, technological media

Technological. No se si es media. No media es television. [I don't know if it's media. No media is television.]

No *schools must have technological*

Tampoco es technological tecnicos no pues quita eso [it's not technological either technical] [she crosses out 'technological media'] *nowadays schools must must have must have* computers computers for students.

Nowadays schools must have computers for students.

Source: Adapted from Murphy and Roca De Larios (2010: 67)

Activity 3.2 How do we learn?

1 Below are some attempts at producing a question in English by learners of English. Can you identify the sequence in which each group of questions were produced?

2 If you are able to sequence the question attempts, would you see this as to do with some general level of complexity, rather like the idea that some kinds of mathematics are more complicated than other? Alternatively, would you see this as supporting the idea that we all have some kind of universal grammar in our heads?

3 Look at a piece of learner writing that you have marked recently. What strategies have you used to encourage the learner to notice something in the original piece of writing?

Sample question attempts (Lightbown and Spada 2006: 86–7)

Group A	Can you tell me what the date is today? It's better, isn't it?
Group B	Do you have a shores in your picture? Does in this picture there is four astronauts?
Group C	Dog? Four children?
Group D	Is there a fish in the water Where is the sun?
Group E	It's a monster in the right corner? The boys throw the shoes?
Group F	What's the boy doing? How do you say *proche* [a word in the learner's L1]?

3.4 What motivates people to learn second languages? Motivation, identity and investment

Motivation is a concept that most teachers use to explain the success or otherwise of their learners, but the meaning of the term is unclear.

> While intuitively we may know what we mean by the term 'motivation', there seems little consensus on its conceptual range of reference. (Dörnyei and Ushioda 2011: 3)

The term motivation comes originally from the Latin 'movere' – to move – and the metaphor of learners being moved, or not moved, to learn English is a powerful way of talking about why some learners are more successful than others. But the idea of motivation can usefully be supplemented by two other ideas. The first is identity which reinforces the idea that motivation comes from learners (Darvin and Norton 2015; Ushioda 2011). Learners' ideas about themselves, for example, their abilities to learn something new, or ideas about what they want to do in the future, will have an impact on their language learning. As one of Cooke's (2006: 56) adult learners says, 'When I wake up I dream of electricity' which suggests a dynamic attitude to learning.

The other idea is investment (Darvin and Norton 2015; Peirce 1995). The reason for using the term investment is again that learners are not just moved by something outside them but play an active role in their language learning. A second reason is that, just as investors in the stock market build up financial capital, learners who invest in their own language learning build up cultural capital (Bourdieu et al. 1991) which enables them to improve the material conditions of their existence, and this implies some level of consistency in their efforts to learn English. This part of the chapter uses the more common term, motivation, but with an understanding that draws on the ideas of identity and investment.

A particular complexity for language motivation is that successful learners need to have a positive attitude to both the language and the process of learning. This section first examines why people choose to learn English rather than another language and then moves onto the ways in which the learning process may impact on learners' motivation.

3.4.1 Why English?

One of the earliest ideas about why people were motivated to learn a particular second language came out of Canada (Gardner 1985; Gardner and Lambert 1959). Parts of Canada are English-speaking and parts are French-speaking and people in the English-speaking area are taught French and vice versa, but the levels of attainment vary widely. Gardner and Lambert (1972) suggested that this might be because of differences in the way learners relate to the target language community. The more successful learners often had an integrative orientation and wanted to be 'like valued members of the language community' (Gardner and Lambert 1959: 271). This contrasts with an instrumental orientation, where the focus is on the employment or other benefits that might come from speaking the target language, and which in this context leads to lower levels of motivation. The notion of an integrative orientation has been adopted by many researchers but has also been criticized as a way of thinking about why people are motivated to learn English. This is partly because most learners do not live in countries like Canada with large populations of speakers of ENL and partly because English has a different status in the world from many other languages and, even among learners who have achieved high levels of English, few learners aspire to be British or American. See the comments on ELF or EIL in Chapter 2. In addition, instrumental and integrative orientation are not always easy to separate. Indeed, Dörnyei's (2009) research in Hungary led him to see learners as being motivated by having an ideal self which differs in some way from their current ideas of themselves. This is a flexible notion and can cover both a French-speaking Canadian who might aspire to using English like a native speaker of English and a Hungarian who aims to be an expert speaker of ELF. The ideal self applies in other parts of the world too. In Lamb's study of Indonesian learners, one said

> I'm interested in learning English, because people said that maybe a few years in the future, English is going to be used in Indonesia, so I was afraid I wouldn't be able to, so I was really interested. (2004: 13)

Lamb concludes that the ideal self for many Indonesians may 'not be English speakers, therefore, nor even westerners in general, but rather other urban middleclass Indonesians who have already acquired this global identity' (2004: 15). In a Chinese context, Gao et al. (2007: 141) found that being able to speak English was seen as part of being a good citizen of China, combining 'harmonizing the family' and 'putting the country in order'. This situation may be different for those who have moved to an English-speaking community. Cervatiuc (2009: 260) investigated English learners who had moved to Canada and found that some aspired to be multilingual rather than emulating native speakers.

> I am a unique individual with a unique combination of skills and talents. I value the fact that I can speak 3 languages, even if I might never get true native-like ability in all of them.

The notion of the ideal self is a useful way of understanding learner's motivation but is less useful for younger learners who may not have a clear idea of their future. Indeed, Butler (2015: 180) found that young learners were more influenced by their parents.

> Anyway my Mom tells me that I must learn English well; otherwise, I will be like her who knows only a few very simple English words.

Dörnyei conceptualizes this as the 'ought to self', a kind of complement to the ideal self (2011: 82). The boundary between the 'ought to' and ideal selves is not always clear. Some of Gao et al.'s comments about putting the country in order might be seen as more to do with what the learners think they ought to do than what they want to do. However, to the extent that these identities are different, the 'ought self' is probably less effective as a long-term motivator as it is less integrated into learners' views of themselves.

3.4.2 Why learn in this way?

The second source of motivation is a positive attitude to what happens in the classroom. One of the best ways of thinking about this is Deci and Ryan's self-determination theory (1985). They distinguish intrinsic and extrinsic motivation. Where students enjoy an activity in the class, they are said to be intrinsically motivated, but when they are doing it for some reward, such as getting a gold star, this is described as extrinsic motivation. This distinction in attitudes to learning activities has some similarities to integrative and instrumental orientations to English and, like an instrumental orientation, extrinsic motivation is regarded as less effective in the long term. Even worse, 'extrinsic motivation has traditionally been seen as something that can undermine intrinsic motivate' (Dörnyei and Ushioda 2011: 24).

If learners are rewarded for doing well in their English examination by being given sweets, they may interpret this as an implicit message that preparing for the examination is such an unpleasant activity that the only reason why they would want to do the preparation would be to get the sweets. As a result, learners may put less effort into English in the long term. However, whether learners react this way will depend on how they relate the extrinsic reward and the activity. For example, learners who wish to study at an anglophonic university will need to do well on a test such as TOEFL or IELTS, and this could be seen as extrinsic to their English language study but, if the test is seen as closely related to their English ability and their future studies, the extrinsic motivation may not have a negative impact on their intrinsic motivation.

Ryan and Deci argue that intrinsic motivation comes from three basic human needs: competence, autonomy and connectedness (2000: 57), and these concepts can be related to particular classroom practices. Teachers often use praise as a way of helping their class to feel they are competent language learners. So, for example, Alrabai (2015: 174) found that teachers increased their students' motivation by using positive language, such as:

Teacher: Have you finished the exercise?
Student: Yes, I am done.
Teacher: Could you please let me see your paper?
Teacher: Well, you did a great job! However, instead of saying 'I visit my cousin last night', you should say, 'I visited my cousin last night' because this happened in the past. Anyway, don't worry about it. This error is very common and can be made by any student when learning English.

The research on praise emphasizes the importance of learners' interpretation of the praise (Henderlong and Lepper 2002). So, learners may interpret praise for an activity they regard as easy as an indication that the teacher sees them as not very good at language, and this can have a negative impact on the learners' view of their competence.

Teachers also have a range of ways of helping learners to feel more autonomous from fairly simple things like letting them choose where they sit in a class to ideas like allowing them to play a role in deciding what they are taught (cf. the idea of negotiated syllabus proposed by Breen 1987b). Project work can also offer opportunities for learner autonomy.

When the 9th-grade students in our study were invited to individually select books for a final literature project, Davey appeared lost (explaining: 'Ms. V., you know I don't read!') until his teacher realized that she had the answer at her finger tips. Although Davey struggled to connect with novels, rock music sprinkled most of his conversations and seemed to fill his head as he drummed nonstop on desktops. When his teacher allowed him (within strict parameters) to use music lyrics as his self-selected literature, classroom observations found Davey buried under, and engrossed in, stacks of lyrics. (Faircloth and Miller 2011: 265)

Autonomy has also been used to explain why praising learners for their ability (e.g. 'You are good at languages') is less effective, and may even have an negative impact, than praising them for their effort (e.g. 'You have done a lot of work on this') because learners see ability as something they cannot control while they can generally work harder (Henderlong and Lepper 2002).

Connectedness often relates to the relationship between the teacher and learners. 'Develop a good relationship with the learners', is one of Dörnyei and Csizer's (1998) ten commandments of motivation. See Table 3.4. But the connection can be with almost anyone, and the connections can be digital. Prichard found that getting students to writing posts on social media increased motivation (2013: 752).

Table 3.4 Dörnyei and Csizer's (2009) ten commandments of motivation

1. Set a personal example with your own behaviour
2. Create a pleasant, relaxed atmosphere in the classroom
3. Present the tasks properly
4. Develop a good relationship with the learners
5. Increase the learners' linguistic self-confidence
6. Make the language classes interesting
7. Promote learner autonomy
8. Personalize the learning process
9. Increase the learners' goal-orientedness
10. Familiarize learners with the target language culture

3.5 How learners support their own learning: the use of learning strategies

Most teachers have the experience that some learners in the classes seem to be better at learning languages than other. This experience has led to research into good language learners (Naiman 1996) and the idea that good learners are doing something different from other learners. For example, a learner reported in Huang (2016) said:

> We had so many words to memorize . . . I usually worked with my friends in arranging schedules, testing one another, and memorizing difficult words. Working with friends helped reduce my anxiety.

Another learner said that she 'tried to encourage myself and calm myself down before I stood on the stage' (p. 6).

These different actions are described as learning strategies and defined as 'deliberate goal-directed attempts to manage and control efforts to learn the L2' (Oxford 2010: 12). Good language learners seem to make more use of learning strategies. But there is a lack of consensus about whether 'it is the range and frequency of strategy use, the nature of strategies, or the combinations of strategies that is the key to successful language' (Macaro 2006: 321).

Macaro has identified a lack of theoretical rigour in discussion of strategies. Perhaps as a result the terminology is confusing. Learning strategies are different from learning skills in that they are conscious and so more controllable. They are also, at least partially, different from communicative strategies in that learning strategies are aimed at supporting learning while communicative strategies are aimed at enabling communication, but the two notions overlap because in many cases being able to maintain communication will lead to learning. Some commentators use learner strategies as a general term to cover strategies used by learners.

The element of consciousness in strategies means that they are often associated with the information processing model of learning and conceptualized as cognitive, but some sociocultural theorists see them as an element of learner self-regulation within a broadly Vygotskyan framework and tend to conceptualize them as behaviour.

Table 3.5 Learning strategies

Strategies	Purpose
Eight meta-strategies 1. Paying attention 2. Planning 3. Obtaining and using resources 4. Organizing 5. Implementing plans 6. Orchestrating strategy use 7. Monitoring 8. Evaluating	Managing and controlling L2 learning in a general sense, with a focus on understanding one's own needs and using and adjusting the other strategies to meet those needs
Six strategies in the cognitive dimension 1. Using the senses to understand and remember 2. Activating knowledge 3. Reasoning 4. Conceptualizing with details 5. Conceptualizing broadly 6. Going beyond the immediate data	Remembering and processing L2 (constructing, transforming, and applying L2 knowledge)
Two strategies in the sociocultural-interactive dimension 1. Interacting to learn and communicate 2. Overcoming knowledge gaps in communicating	Handling emotions, beliefs, attitudes and motivation in L2 learning
Three strategies in the sociocultural-interactive dimension 1. Interacting to learn and communicate 2. Overcoming knowledge gaps in communicating 3. Dealing with sociocultural contexts and identities	Dealing with issues of contexts, communication and culture in L2 learning

Source: Oxford (2010: 16)

Several attempts have been made to classify strategies, and one recent attempt is given in Table 3.5. However, strategies are problem-solving activities and are a response to particular issues and 'successful students develop their own strategies, of which using their teacher to good effect to promote their own knowledge is only one' (Oxford et al. 2014: 17).

3.6 Summary

This chapter examined a range of theories of second language learning, covering Krashen's monitor model and connectionism but focusing on information processing models and sociocultural theory. The chapter also looked at two contributions that learners make to the learning process – motivation and use of learning strategies.

Activity 3.3 Discussion

1 Consider a group of learners you have worked with recently. To what extent would you see their motivation has to do with their ideas of their ideal or ought selves?

2 Dörnyei and Csizer (2009) identify ten motivational strategies. See Table 3.4.

    a Which of these strategies do you use in your teaching?

    b To what extent can you relate Dörnyei and Csizer's ten commandments with the notions of ideal/ought to self of Deci and Ryan's ideas of autonomy, competence and connectedness?

3.7 Further reading

Several authors have produced books on second language acquisition. Lightbown and Spada's (2013) *How Languages Are Learned* is an accessible introduction. The best known author is Rod Ellis whose *Understanding Second Language Acquisition* (2015) is a good starting point for a more academic account. *Introducing Second Language Acquisition* by Saville-Troike (2006) is clearly written, and Mitchell and Myles's (2004) *Second Language Learning Theories* and Van Patten and Williams's (2007) *Theories in Second Language Acquisition* are worth looking at. Krashen has made much of his earlier work available through his website and, even though you may disagree with some of his arguments, his ideas are worth exploring.

This chapter focussed on two learner variables – motivation and use of learning strategies. A useful introduction to learner variables in general is Dornyei's (2005) *Psychology of the Language Learner Individual Differences in Second Language Acquisition.* Dornyei and Ushioda's (2011) *Teaching and Researching Motivation* is a clear academic introduction to motivation. Norton and Kramsch's (2013) *Identity and Language Learning: Extending the Conversation* is a discussion of how identity and investment can be used to explain why learners do or do not want to learn a language. Cohen and Macaro's (2007) *Language Learner Strategies* and Oxford's (2010) *Teaching and Researching Language Learning Strategies* are useful surveys of the work on learner strategies.

Part II

Teaching Knowledge and Skills

Chapter 4

Teaching Language Learners

4.1 Introduction

This chapter and Chapter 5 address the third question about TESOL courses: How should languages be taught? Chapter 5 covers some of the factors teachers need to take into account when planning a course, and this chapter focuses on some general issues teachers should consider when organizing a lesson. There is more specific advice about teaching the different elements (phonology, spelling, grammar, vocabulary, discourse) and skills (reading, writing, speaking and listening).

Educational institutions vary in how much input teachers have into lesson planning. Sometimes ministries of education, school principals or course book writers choose the language focus and have chosen materials that are based on their ideas of how learners learn. However, at some stage, all teachers have some influence over how their classes are taught. Where teachers have relatively little input into programme and lesson design, these chapters should help them to evaluate the decisions that others have made and, where teachers do have more autonomy, the chapters should support their decision-making. This chapter is structured around four questions:

1 What is a teaching method?
2 How can teachers decide the aim of a lesson?
3 How can teachers choose materials for their lessons?
4 How can teachers sequence lessons?

4.2 What is a teaching method?

The standard way of addressing how language should be taught has been in terms of method. If someone asked a teacher how they teach, the teacher might say they used the communicative method or believe in task-based teaching. However, 'method' has become controversial in recent years. Part of this is terminological, because different writers use a variety of terms such as approach, design and methods to describe closely related concepts. Richards and Rodgers (2014) see an approach as covering how language and learning are conceptualized. While this distinction has merit, in this book I use both method and approach to describe ways of teaching with approach indicating less precision. I would, for example, talk about the audiolingual method but communicative approaches.

Another reason for the controversy about the term method is the proliferation of methods. A look at books on teaching languages – for example, Larsen-Freeman and Anderson (2011), Richards and Rodgers (2014) – or an online search will produce a list of methods such as community language learning, the silent way, suggestopedia, total physical response, the natural method, content and language integrated learning (CLIL) and, more recently, dogme (Meddings and Thornbury 2009) as well as commercial approaches such as the Michel Thomas approach (Block 2003), the Pimsleur method (Pimsleur 1980), and crazy English. One reason why the number of methods is a problem is that it is often quite difficult to tell the methods apart, so task-based teaching (TBT) is sometimes seen as a variant of communicative methods and sometimes entirely as a separate method. Similarly, Brumfit (1991: 135), for example, wondered how 'it was possible for Krashen and Terrell to market "The Natural Method" as some kind of coherent packages without constantly examining the extent to which it overlapped with others traditions in its recommendations. It is also difficult to find differences in classrooms which are supposed to be examples of different methods' (Swaffar et al. 1982).

Methods are also sometimes seen as only working in particular contexts, so teachers have resisted the introduction of new methods because these seem culturally inappropriate. For example, some teachers argue that particular features of communicative language teaching (CLT) are not relevant in contexts where classes are traditionally teacher-centred (Klapper 2003; Lewis and McCook 2002; Takanashi 2004) and changing the way in which languages are taught can be difficult.

More generally, the idea of methods as being implemented by teachers and delivered to learners misunderstands what happens in classrooms. A method is not a fuel-additive which improves the efficiency of any car (Canagarajah 2016: 20). Methods are generalizations about how teaching can happen and differ widely in their implementation. At the level of the teacher, Woods (1996) found tremendous variation in what happened in classes which were using the same materials because teachers were using these materials in different ways.

In addition, learners' experience of the same method and even of the same class varies enormously. It would be difficult to say how similar learners' experience needs to be to make a basis for claiming that two classes are being taught with the same method, let alone one method is better than the other. The lack of evidence that different methods are more or less successful than others is not surprising (Larsen-Freeman 1991: 126 et seq.). Long went further when he said ' "method" is an unverifiable and irrelevant construct when attempting to improve classroom FL [foreign language] instruction. Worse, it may actually, do harm by distracting teachers from genuinely important issues' (p. 40).

Kumaravadivelu (2003a) has argued that we must move beyond method to the notion of post-method where teachers make decisions about what teaching activities are appropriate for the needs of their learners within a particular teaching and learning context. Harmer (2015: 70) argues for a similar approach when he talks about 'principled eclecticism'.

Rather than thinking of teachers selecting what is currently thought to be the 'best' method, methods should be seen as a set of resources that teachers can use to build up their own methods of teaching in ways that fit with their particular teaching contexts. The next section explores the range of ways that teachers

Table 4.1 Teaching methods: a glossary

Method	Explanation
Grammar translation	This method aims to develop the ability to read literature in the target language. Speaking and listening in L2 are not part of its aims. Instruction involves translation between L1 and L2 and the construction of grammatically accurate sentences using metalinguistic rules. Classes are largely conducted in L1.
Audiolingual	This method aims to produce learners who can use language like native speakers, but initially the focus is on listening and speaking. Instruction involves the imitation of sentences and sentence patterns constructed to exemplify grammatical structures. The use of L1 and grammatical explanations is not common. Classes are conducted in L2.
Weak CLT	This method aims to develop learners who can communicate in L2. This often begins with listening and speaking, but all four skills are valued. Instruction involves pronunciation, grammar and functional teaching or the practice of one or more skills. Teaching units are meant to end with a communicative task.
Strong CLT/TBT	This method aims to develop learners who can communicate in L2. A task-based syllabus is based on communicative tasks that learners need to do outside the language classroom. Classes may consist of learners trying to carry out communicative tasks. Where there is instruction, this is based on the problems learners have with the tasks rather than a predesigned grammatical syllabus.
CLIL/content-based teaching	This method aims to develop learners who can study a specific subject in L2 and enhance their general L2 abilities. The teacher would normally be a subject expert who can use L2. Instruction generally relates to problems that arise from the subject instruction, but in many contexts, a language-focused class, often organized on weak CLT basis, runs parallel to the subject class. The use of L1 is not unusual.

might answer questions 3 to 4 raised in the introduction to this chapter. The discussion is structured around five methods which give some indication of the variety of methodologies that teachers currently use:

a Grammar translation

b Audiolingual

c Weak CLT

d Strong CLT/task-based learning

e CLIL/content-based learning

Table 4.1 glosses how each of these methods works.

4.3 What is the aim of the lesson?

Most language teaching methods have the aim of preparing learners to use the language for communication. This is in the title of CLT, but even an approach such as grammar translation does have the long-term objective of enabling learners to read works of literature in English, a narrow but communicative use of language. Similarly, most, but not all, methods recognize that learners need to develop grammatical and lexical abilities and language skills, but the staging of these different aspects of a method varies enormously.

I learned French using the grammar translation approach and spent most of my first-year learning grammar rules and vocabulary lists. I did not get to the communicative objective – in my case, reading a novel called *Candide* – until my third year. In contrast, when I studied Malay in an audiolingual method, I could go into a restaurant and order a simple meal within the first week of my course in a way that I was not able to do until my third year of French. However, my reading skills in Malay remained undeveloped. This was not to do with the audiolingual method but to the shortness of the course. The grammar translation class has different aims at different times, something that applies to several methods. The next chapter will address this change in focus associated with some methods, but this chapter focuses on planning lessons, and the fact that a course of language teaching orients to a particular method or range of methods of language learning does not necessarily mean that the aims of all the classes have to be similar.

4.3.1 Communication versus learning to communicate

A useful way to start planning a lesson is to work out what the learners need and, at the most general level, this is often a decision between communicating and learning to communicate. This distinction has been described in a range of ways but a current, if rather confusingly labelled, approach talks of a focus on forms (learning to communicate) versus focus on form (communication). This distinction started with Long (1991) who described a lesson with a focus on form or learning to communicate as one where the aim 'is the linguistic items themselves (structures, notions, lexical items, etc.); a lesson is designed to teach "the past continuous", "requesting" and so on, nothing else' (p. 44).

In contrast, a lesson focusing on communication or form 'teaches something else – biology, mathematics, workshop practice, automobile repair, the geography of a country where, the foreign language is spoken, the cultures of its speakers and so on – and overtly draw students' attention to linguistic elements as they arise incidentally in lesson whose overriding focus is on meaning, or communication' (Long 1991: 46).

At first sight, a lesson that focused on communication seems to be the most useful. Learners come to the class to learn to communicate in English, and an analysis of what learners need would suggest that the focus should be on communication rather than, say, grammar or vocabulary.

However, learning a language is not the same as using a language. As Gilmore (2004: 371) points out, some non-communicative activities are justified 'in the process of becoming a competent user of another language', in the same way as those who want to become tennis players spend some of their time not on the tennis court but develop skills through, for example, repeatedly serving or watching other people serve.

In addition, one of the distinctive features about learning a second language is that learners bring a considerable amount of knowledge about language to the classroom, and quite often this knowledge can help with the use of the second language (Swan 1985a: 4). Swan's slightly facetious example of this relates to a group of burglars who are learning ESL. The look-out says, 'The policeman is crossing the road'. Even if they have not taken a course in communication, the burglars will be able to use their knowledge of communication in their first language to work out that the sentence is not just a factual statement but is also intended to be a warning. Swan's (1985b: 86) conclusion from this is that a needs analysis should involve four stages:

1 find out what the learner needs to know;

2 find out what he or she knows already;

3 subtract the second from the first;

4 teach the remainder.

Unfortunately, this is not always easy to do, and question 2 is particularly difficult where the teacher does not share a first language with the learners. My experience of teaching academic English taught me that learners with a good knowledge of English often do not know how to write a good essay. The conventions of writing essays vary from language to language (Connor 2002; Connor et al. 2008), and many learners need to be helped to develop the appropriate skills and knowledge to do this. This issue is examined in more detail in Chapter 11. While Swan's point that learners can often do more than teacher expects is important, this does not mean that the only thing learners need to learn is spelling, pronunciation, grammar and vocabulary.

4.3.2 Learning to communicate

Lessons whose aims are to prepare learners to communicate will typically focus on things like pronunciation, spelling, grammar and vocabulary (covered in Chapters 7–10), and we can find this in the grammar translation, audiolingual and weak CLT methods. So, lessons might be structured around a grammar point such as comparative adjectives. In a grammar translation class, the lesson would just cover grammar and possibly some relevant vocabulary, and the learners would only be expected to develop the skills of reading and writing, so pronunciation would not be covered. A distinctive element of the grammar translation approach would be that the learners would be expected to learn to translate from English into L1 and back again.

Within an audiolingual approach, an attempt would be made to embed the grammatical focus, say the use of comparative adjectives, within some kind of communicative context, so Granger and Hicks (1978: 43) use the context of buying a pet to contextualize comparative adjectives. When the shop assistant suggests a tiger, the customer says, 'Haven't you got something a bit quieter?' The lesson would probably also cover the pronunciation of comparatives. While audiolingual approaches typically start with spoken language, reading and writing might be covered later in the class or in a later class. The use of L1 would be discouraged, and learners would be expected to function in English without translating.

Within a weak CLT approach there would also be some attempt at contextualization. So Soars and Soars (2000: 89) introduce comparative adjectives within the more realistic context of buying a shirt. This approach to contextualization is explored in more detail in Chapter 9. A weak CLT approach would also be likely to cover pronunciation and spelling as well. Weak CLT would typically cover all the elements of language (pronunciation, spelling, grammar and vocabulary) and all skills. Translation would not be regarded as an aim, though translation might be used sparingly as a teaching technique.

The alternative approach would be to start with the communicative task of, say, buying a shirt. This would be common in strong CLT and TBT, and the coverage of elements of language and skills would depend on what aspects of the task of buying a shirt that learners struggled to carry out effectively.

Within CLIL, the aims would come from the content of the other subject that is being taught. So a physics and English integrated lesson might focus on Hookes's law, that is, when you hang objects on a metal spring, the amount that the spring stretches is proportional to the mass of the object and again the levels of language and skills covered would depend on what was needed to achieve a lesson on Hookes's law in English (Nikula 2015: 17).

4.4 What materials are being used in the lesson?

Once teachers have decided what to teach, or have been given an aim that they have to follow, they need to think about the materials they will use to achieve this aim. This has two main elements – what kinds of texts or recordings they bring to the class, which is a question mainly about authentic versus constructed texts, and the kind of language that the teachers use. This section focuses mainly on the use of learners' own language versus English.

4.4.1 Authentic and constructed texts

Authentic texts 'have been produced by and/or for expert users of the language for use outside of the classroom' (Roberts and Cooke 2009: 622) or are examples of 'real language from a real speaker/writer for a real audience with a real message' (Gilmore 2007: 97). Authentically produced texts are a feature of all forms of CLT and TBT.

An extract from a newspaper or magazine would be authentically produced, whereas something which a teacher or course book writer produced to help their students develop their language skills would not be authentic. In the later stages of the grammar translation method, learners would be expected to read authentic works of literature in English by authors such as Austen and Steinbeck. This aim here would be to understand English-speaking cultures, but a more recent argument for authentic texts is that

> contrived simplification of language in the preparation of materials will always be faulty, since it is generated without the guide and support of a communicative context. Only by accepting the discipline of using authentic language are we likely to come anywhere near presenting the learner with a sample of language which is typical of real English. (Willis 1990: 127)

This line of argument was a reaction to the teaching materials that were associated with the audiolingual approach. The Granger and Hicks (1978: 43) quotations above came from the following dialogue:

Assistant: I've got some cats
Mr Mole: Oh. Er . . . I don't think my mother would like one of those.
Assistant: Oh doesn't she like tigers?
Mr Mole: Haven't you got something a bit quieter?
Assistant: Yes sir. I've got just the thing for you. A tortoise.

This extract has virtues in that it includes several features of authentic speech, hesitation markers and short forms which might help learners understand more about spoken English. Despite this, it does not seem to be the kind of thing that would be heard in a pet shop. The writers' intention was to produce something entertaining that exemplifies the use of comparative adjectives. However, even with a framework of weak CLT, where there is less of a focus on grammar, and materials writers are trying to construct texts that are similar to authentic texts, what is produced is different from texts produced for non-language learning purposes.

Roberts and Cooke (2009: 626–7) identify important and possibly misleading differences between constructed and authentic versions of what happens when a doctor asks a patient what is wrong. This is the constructed text:

D: Hello. Come and sit down. What seems to be the matter?
M: Well, I haven't felt very well for a few days. I've got a bit of a temperature, and I feel just terrible. I've got stomach ache as well.

This is an authentically produced text:

D: Oh dear what's been happening
K: Ur well I don't know I was urn going away for Easter and um I had a pain in my back (.) in the lung and I had it bad once and um I thought 'uh uh' you know I'll brush it off so I had a very very dry cough last week when I went to work and er I couldn't go in on the Wednesday and then Thursday and Friday I was coughing and coughing but nothing (.) hurt me but last night I never slept at all and I was going to go up to G hospital hospital one minute its hard and one minute its soft and then when I cough (.) it nearly kills me so.

The real patient takes much longer to explain her symptoms and uses colloquial language to present herself as worthy of treatment ('I'll brush it off' and 'it nearly kills me'). The constructed text sounds quite natural, but the two texts show that even natural-sounding constructed texts are likely to present a distorted view of how communication happens, and this may disadvantage learners when they have to communicate outside the classroom.

Roberts and Cooke are working with ESOL students in the UK who may well need to be able to understand language such as 'brush it off', and the lack of authenticity in the constructed text might well be problematic. However, different considerations might apply to those learning ELF in other contexts, where the conventions for doctor-patient interaction might well be different, and so even Roberts and Cooke's authentic text might not be useful for learners who hope to use English in such situations.

This raises the issues of the role of learners in defining authenticity (Badger and MacDonald 2010). Language users create texts from the ink on the paper, the pixels on the screen or the acoustic signal because they have a purpose for which they wish to use it (see Chapter 2), so the authenticity of a text for the learners relates both to whether they have the appropriate skills and knowledge to make sense of the text, and whether the text relates to the communicative tasks with which these users might be expected to engage.

A text which is authentic for the teacher may not be authentic for the learners in the class either because the learners do not have the appropriate knowledge and skills or because this is not the kind of text the learners need to use outside the language classroom. When teachers are choosing texts, they need to choose ones that are authentic for their learners. For example, if a teacher were working with a group of molecular biologists to improve their abilities to produce a systematic review of research into the molecular biology of cancers, the article from which this is taken might well be an appropriate choice of text:

> Improvements in our understanding of molecular alterations at multiple levels (genetic, epigenetic, protein expression) and their functional significance have the potential to impact lung cancer diagnosis, prognostication and treatment. (Cooper et al. 2013: 479)

However, it is unlikely that this kind of text would be authentic for many other groups of learners and, even with a group of molecular biologists whose aim was to improve their listening skills, the text might not be authentic. This is not because the physical text is different but because learners are interacting with the text in different ways. Teachers should use texts that are appropriate for their learners, and this means that they are at the right level for their learners and that they are associated with the kinds of tasks or genres that the learners are likely to be engaged in. See Chapter 11 for more discussion of tasks and genres.

A related notion here is dogme (Meddings and Thornbury 2009), 'a pedagogy of bare essentials'. In this approach, teachers do not make use of any materials specifically related to language teaching and learning but use whatever resources are available in the classroom so that communication emerges from the interests of teachers and learners rather than what is in the course book or the syllabus and so is as authentic as it can be. The dogme approach emphasizes the communicative task of conversation in language development and sees language learning as coming out of conversation rather than learning grammar and vocabulary. This may not be a complete solution to how to teach, but a dogme lesson can help reengage learners who have been put off by course book-oriented lessons.

While authentic texts are generally better materials for language teaching, constructed texts also have their uses. Few teachers would want to prevent the use of learner dictionaries, by definition inauthentic texts. The choice depends not on what is authentically produced but on what best supports language learning.

CLIL materials are usually authentic in the sense that they are 'real language from a real speaker/ writer for a real audience with a real message' (Gilmore 2007: 97), though they have probably been created for teaching purposes. CLIL classes do lead to improvements in learners' reading and writing (Perez-Vidal and Roquet 2015), though it is important to bear in mind that this may not convert to reading abilities outside the classroom without additional support.

 Activity 4.1 Authenticity

Look at the following texts. For what kind of learners, if any, would these texts be authentic, and what would be an authentic way of using the texts in the classroom?

A (Simpson et al. 1999)

S1: alright Sue now it's like uh I dropped like Chem one-twenty-five.
S2: this year? This term?

S1: this_ yes this se- semester right now I [S2: okay] late-dropped because like (xx) I missed a couple of classes my G-S-I instructed me to, [S2: mhm] and secondly it's like uh I told you I was transferring to engineering.

S2: ri- oh but you dropped chem okay.

B (Terry and Wilson 2004)

O: Platinum card service. Rebecca speaking. How may I help you?

C: I've got a few problems with my credit card account.

O: OK. What is your credit card number?

C: Let's see. Huh. It's here somewhere. Ah. Here it is.

O: Can I just take the card number please.

C: Yes it's six double nine two.

O: Six double nine two.

C (Lynch 1996)

Mrs West: I wonder why your country has been involved in almost every war on the continent.

Klaus: The reason for this is its geographic position, I think. Germany is in the middle of Europe and has more bordering states than any other country. Before the last war Germany had ten neighbours. The more neighbours a country has the greater is the danger of war. You British are luckier than we are. You're in the best position. Geographically. You live on an island and you have no neighbours nearer than France, and that is 21 miles away across the Channel at the nearest point.

D (My own data)

I: OK. Uhm uhm, have you been to the movies or to the theatre yet?

I: Yeah. I have been to a movie once.

I: What did you watch?

L: Starbucks

I: Starbucks? Stardust.

L: Stardust. Sorry!

I: Did you like it?

L: Yes, of course. A romantic movie.

I: What was it about?

L: Aah. Just a kind of fantasy. It's about a fantasy.

4.4.2 The students' own language and English

Different methods have taken very different attitudes to the use of the students' own language. In grammar translation, translation from the students' own language into English and back again is an aim of the class, and often the students' own language will be the dominant language in the classroom, at least partly because the aim is to help them develop reading and writing skills in English.

The audiolingual approach was strongly against the use of L1 because it reduced the amount of time when the target language was being used. This can have advantages. When I was learning Malay, the teacher did not provide translations of anything, and we were strongly discouraged from writing things down until we could repeat the day's dialogue from memory. This was quite a difficult thing to do but did mean that when I tried to use Malay outside the classroom, I could do this fairly automatically.

Many teachers working with broadly CLT and task-based approaches to teaching feel they should avoid L1. However, my experience of classes where the learners share a language other than English is that L1 is used regularly, and one of the unfortunate side effects of the exclusion of L1 is that we have relatively little knowledge of when L1 is used and when this use is effective.

Within CLIL and content-based learning approaches, L1 does seem to be used. In immersion classes in Canada, learners often respond in their first language to questions asked in the target language. Some classroom-based research also suggests that L1 can be a resource helping the development of the second language.

> Something I have noticed, and which I consider an advantage, is that when they have mastered their mother tongue and they learn the foreign language the mother tongue is used as a support. They compare the languages and bring different ideas face to face, which leads them to reflect on their own language. (Méndez García and Pavón Vázquez 2012: 588)

The use of the mother tongue in English language teaching has only recently been acknowledged as an important issue for teachers, and I would hope that we will develop a better understanding of when the learners' own language is and is not useful in learning English over the next few years. My own experience is that being forced not to use your own language can be beneficial for a short course, but I am doubtful that this can be maintained for more than a few months. Also, using the learners' first language is problematic in a multilingual class where one learner's own language is meaningless to speakers of other languages. Scrivener suggests that the following may be a useful principle:

> As an ideal, I would like a classroom where learners were free to use their own tongue whenever they wanted, but in fact mostly chose to use English. (2011: 297)

This is a useful guide. The overarching aim is how the use of the learners' own language can help the development of their second language, but this is difficult to evaluate.

 Activity 4.2 Using the mother tongue

1   If you teach learners who share a language other than English, how often do you use that language in your class?

2   Here is an extract from a class taught in an Arabic-speaking country. What do you think about the use of L1? What alternative strategies could have been used to explain the word 'dishes'?

    a   S: What is 'dishes'?

    b   T: Plate

    c   S: How do you say in Arabic?

    d   T: It is something we eat from

e S:سبط [sabat]?

f T: Yes it is سبط.

3 A questionnaire on the use of L1:

Complete this for yourself and get your fellow teachers to respond to the same. To what extent do you agree about the use of L1? What evidence do you have to support your position on the use of L1?

✓✓ means strongly agree, ü× means neither agree nor disagree and ×× means strongly disagree. Complete this questionnaire yourself and ask your colleagues to complete it as well. Can you identify an underlying rationale for you and your colleagues' attitudes to the use of English?

	✓✓	✓	✓×	×	××
1. The teacher should only use English in the classroom					
2. The teacher should use English when providing cultural or background information					
3. The teacher should use English to explain new vocabulary					
4. The teacher should use English to explain grammatical rules					
5. The teacher should translate examples of grammar rules					
6. The teacher should use English when giving feedback on student work					
7. The teacher should use English when students ask questions in L1					
8. The teacher should use English to deal with disciplinary issues					
9. The teacher should use English more with beginners than advanced students					
10. The teacher should use English more with adult learners than young learners					
11. Using L1 leads to a friendlier atmosphere in the classroom					

4.5 What is the sequence in the lesson?

Broadly, the sequence of activities in a lesson depends on whether the teachers aim to teach something and then get the learners to use whatever they have been taught, or if the teachers adopt a problem-solving approach in which the learners try to do something and then are helped to do this better. The first option would result in a lesson sequence that is normally called presentation, practice and production (PPP). This is typically associated with syllabuses where the focus is on grammar and vocabulary. The main alternative is a task-based sequence (Willis 1996; Willis and Willis 2007) which, as the name suggests, is closely associated with syllabuses where the focus is on tasks and which I label as the problem-solving sequence.

4.5.1 Presentation, practice and production

In a PPP lesson, the teacher will start by presenting the new language at the start of the lesson. This might be a grammatical structure, some vocabulary, spelling rules or something to do with pronunciation. It is normally something connected with the elements of language rather than language skills. However, it is possible to use a PPP sequence when the aim is to teach learners how to carry out a communicative task (Nunan 2004). Presentations vary a lot, and there are some examples of presentations in the chapters on language elements. The aim of the presentation is to increase the amount of knowledge that learners have, and so this fits in well the information processing models of learning covered in Chapter 3. The presentation provides learners with declarative knowledge. The teacher might present some language samples and seek to help the learners to develop some implicit awareness of the rules or patterns underlying the language samples. This would be typical of audiolingual or weak communicative approaches.

Even though the term presentation is normally limited to the cognitive or knowledge aspect of language learning, lessons that teachers describe as PPP often involve teachers doing some work on the affective side of learning by trying to engage the learners' interest in what the lesson is about. Harmer (2015: 67) sees this as so important that he suggests the first stage of a typical lesson should be aimed at engaging the learners before the teacher starts the presentation.

Practice, the second stage, involves the learners starting to use their new knowledge and again this fits in well with the proceduralization of knowledge of information processing models of learning. This involves controlled use of the language and often includes activities such as drills and dialogues. Some people regard this stage as focusing on accuracy (Hedge 2000).

The production stage is where learners use the language freely. This might be a role-play or simulation. This stage corresponds to the autonomous stages in information processing or the ACT-R (Anderson 2010: 242) model of learning (Chapter 3).

The PPP sequence has been much criticized (Allwright 2005; Willis and Willis 2007) but is widely used at least partially because of institutional factors. When I worked in Malaysia, I had to record each

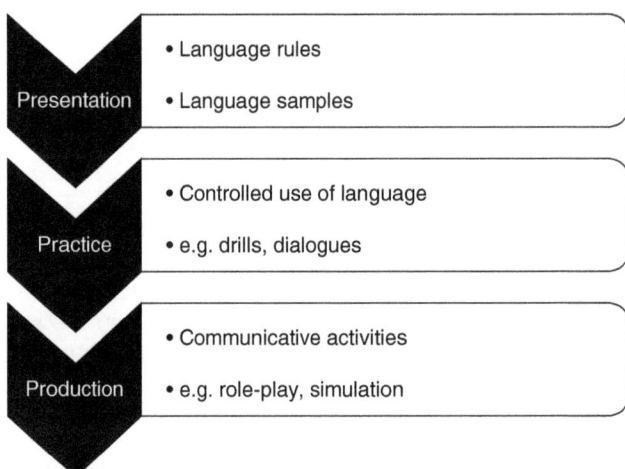

Figure 4.1 Presentation, practice and production (PPP)

week what grammar points identified in the syllabus I had covered in my classes, and this would have made it difficult not to have some PPP lessons. However, teachers can use PPP more flexibly than a simple description of the sequence may suggest. So Byrne (1986) suggested seeing the sequence as a circle. This would have the advantage that the language points that were taught emerged from the production activities attempted previously rather than just from the syllabus.

4.5.2 A problem-solving sequence

A problem-solving sequence has three main stages: pre-task, task cycle and language focus. A more detailed version of this is given in Figure 4.2. The pre-task stage is meant to give the learners some information about the target language item and, in a TBT sequence, this will normally be a communicative task or, in a CLIL or content-based lesson, the topic that is to be covered. This stage should help engage the learners and provide some background information about the task or topic. This may also activate topic-related words and phrases (Willis 1996: 41).

The task stage can simply involve the learners carrying out the task using whatever linguistic resources they have. Normally the task would be carried out in groups within the class. This is intended to be a relatively stress-free environment and so should encourage learners to use the language they already have fluently.

In some classes, some of the groups would then report back to the whole class on the task they have done. This is intended to encourage recycling of language, and the fact that this is more public should encourage students to be more concerned about accuracy.

In the language focus section, the learners work on the elements of language that they need to carry out the task more effectively. This may involve learners comparing how different groups carried out the task or comparing their own performance with that of more expert language users. Where the outcome of the task is some writing, learners might be shown an expert version of the writing. They may also go on to practice elements of language, for example, grammar that come out of an analysis of the differences between how learners carried out the task and how experts would have done it.

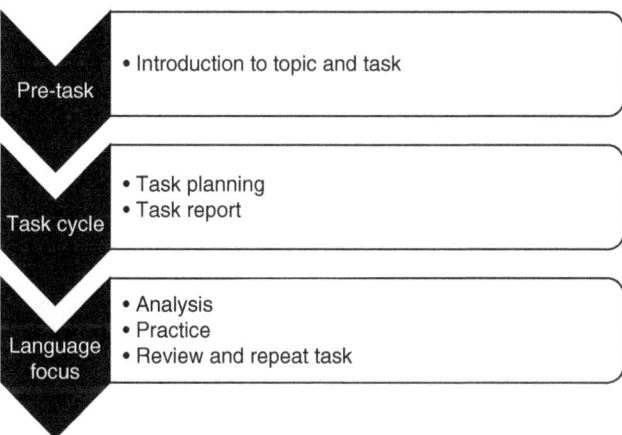

Figure 4.2 Task-based teaching (TBT) (adapted from Willis 1996: 135)

The teacher will need to be able to devise activities very quickly or to have a portfolio of materials that can be given to learners. Some teachers organize their classes so that the language focus happens in a later lesson when they have had time to prepare appropriate activities. In some lessons or lesson sequences, the language focus will be followed by the learners, possibly in new groups, doing the task again.

A problem-solving sequence is also related to information processing views of language learning. At the language focus stage, learners are noticing the gap between what they can do and what experts do. The conditions for noticing are better than they would be in a PPP lesson because the noticing relates to differences between how the task was carried out by the learners and experts.

The problem-solving sequence allows several opportunities for practice. In the task phase, these are mainly to do with repeating the task under different conditions. The argument for this kind of repetition was discussed in Chapter 3, but teachers need to decide when repetition is beneficial for learning and when it may lead to boredom and demotivation.

The version of the problem-solving sequence presented here is highly structured and perhaps reflects the fact that, for many teachers, this is a relatively new approach to teaching, but problem-solving sequences exist in several forms. Many teachers do not have a separate language focus stage and address language issues at various stages throughout the lesson.

4.5.3 Deciding on a sequence

The PPP approach can provide certainty about what is being taught in a class. This is useful in many state systems of education where there is a national syllabus which is specified in grammatical and/or lexical features, and a ministry of education is trying to ensure that there is some consistency about what happens in different schools. For example, a student who has studied at one school would be able to transfer to another school and know that the same parts of the syllabus had been covered. This has advantages for teachers and course book writers because they have a fairly clear idea about what they will need to cover and so plan in advance. In a problem-solving sequence, teachers do not know what language problems the learners will have until they try to carry out the task and so will need to be able to address a wide range of issues. This means that general resources for language learners such as learner dictionaries and grammar reference works and grammar exercise books will need to be available.

The first main argument against a PPP approach is that it is based on an analytical view of language. Learners are regarded as learning a bit of grammar, some vocabulary and they then have to integrate that into a more holistic view of language, such as that represented by the notions of communicative tasks and genres. Sometimes this means that even though learners have been able to use the target linguistic element in the practice stages, they fail to use it when in the production stage because they can achieve the communicative aim without the new language or because they have not fully understood how the target language relates to the communicative task. Knowing the present perfect is not just a matter of being to use the right word endings and understanding the difference between the present perfect and, say, the past simple, but also knowing in what circumstances it is appropriate to use the present perfect, and a task-based approach and a problem-solving sequence seems better able to do this.

The second main argument is that, rather like some views of teaching methods, PPP underplays the roles of learners in the language classroom and misrepresents how learning happens. Presentation is something that teachers do. A focus on learning would centre less on the teacher than on rasing the awareness of learners. This point is highlighted in Thornbury's (2005) recasting of PPP in learner-centred terms as awareness, appropriation and autonomy. In a problem-solving sequence, the language elements that are covered are those that have been problematic to the learners, and this is likely to help with learner motivation.

4.6 Summary

This chapter reviewed the concept of teaching methods and looked at how a grammar translation, weak CLT approach, a strong communicative/TBT approach and CLIL approaches lead to different kinds of lessons. The rest of the chapter was divided into three main sections looking, first, at what would be an appropriate aim for a lesson and, second, what materials are used, focusing on the use of authentic and constructed texts and the learners' L1, and finally on the choice between PPP and a problem-solving lesson sequence.

 Activity 4.3 Discussion

Your English learners are a group of doctors who have been working as doctors in non-Anglophonic contexts. They are now going to practise as doctors in an English-speaking environment. Write a plan for a sequence of lessons preparing them to find out their patients' reason for coming to see them. You should consider your aims, your materials and the sequence of activities.

You may want to use the example of patient–doctor interviews above and two more examples in Tables 4.2 and 4.3.

Table 4.2 Doctor-patient interview (shoulder pain)

D	So what can I do for you today?
P	Well. I have some shoulder pain and and from the top of my arm arm . . . the reason I'm here is because a couple years ago I had frozen shoulder in the other arm, and I had to have surgery and . . . this is starting to get stuck and I want to stop it before it gets stuck.
D	Adhesive capsulitis.
P	Right. I'm losing range of motion in my arm.
D	Well huh can't you tell me the . . .? Wasn't there some trauma, something you swung at?
P	I've had . . .
D	Somebody?
P	No I've had a history of bursitis.
D	There's no recent thing that smashed it. Anything you can tell me that might have . . .?

Table 4.2 (Continued)

P	No.
D	So it's been bothering now since when?
P	About two weeks.
D	Just two weeks.
P	It's getting a little but stiffer and stiffer.
D	Where?
P	Right here in the shoulder joint.

D = doctor; P = patient.

Source: Robinson (2005: 25–6)

Table 4.3 Doctor-patient interview

D	What can I do for you today?
P	Well . . . I feel like there's something wrong down underneath in my rib area.
D	Okay.
P	I don't um . . . I thought I might have cracked a rib um somehow but I have no clue how . . . And I don't even know what cracked ribs feel like. I just know that there's a pain there that shouldn't be. And I'm sitting here it's not bad not as bad but when I'm up and active an moving around and breathing and doing all that you know extra heavy breathing it's really bothering me.
D	Tch. So when you take a deep breath, does that make it worse.
P	Yeah. Yeah.

D = doctor; P = patient.

Source: Heritage and Maynard (2005: 55)

 ## 4.7 Further reading

The two best descriptions of the different methods used in language teacher are Richards and Rodgers's (2014) *Approaches and Methods in Language Teaching*, and Larsen-Freeman and Anderson's (2011) *Techniques and Principles in Language Teaching*. Both these cover the five methods discussed in this chapter. Willis and Willis's (2007) *Doing Task-Based Teaching* is a good book-length description of TBT. Coyle et al.'s (2010) *CLIL: Content and Language Integrated Learning* and Mehisto et al.'s (2008) *Uncovering CLIL* are good introductions to that approach. Kumaravadivelu (2003b) is the classic text on post-method.

Chapter 5

Programme and Lesson Planning

5.1 Introduction

Planning is a central part of all teachers' lives, but the role of planning often changes as teachers become more experienced. When I was studying how to be a teacher and teaching one lesson a day, I stayed up until late at night finding or creating the perfect materials and writing very detailed lesson plans. I very rarely completed my plans and often found myself half-way through the class with only a fraction of my plan completed, but the lesson plans were important in providing me with the confidence I needed in the classroom. This experience was important in teaching me that plans are 'not legally binding . . . We can depart from them or stick to them as we, the students and the circumstances seem to need' (Woodward 2001: 1).

When I was working full-time, I could not devote as much time to preparing my lessons, but I still needed the lesson plan to structure my teaching. I now work in teacher education, and my handouts and PowerPoint slides are my lesson plans but, if I had to walk into a class without any preparation, I could teach a reasonable class, but this would be based on all the planning I have done in the past.

The amount of planning teachers do is also related to the kind of work they do. When I worked in Malaysia, the course book and syllabus were not under my control, and so my planning focused on the lesson and how to use the course book. In Algeria and the UK, I had much more freedom and was also involved in designing programmes and, in the UK, also in the assessment for the programmes. However, even teachers who are given a course book and a fixed number of lessons in which the course book must be covered are still involved in course design and lesson planning. Teachers 'will inevitably have to make decisions about how long to spend on certain activities, which ones to skip or assign for homework if there is not enough time, which ones to modify so that they are relevant to that particular group of students' (Graves 2000: 149). Course books are aimed at generic learners but have to be used to teach specific individuals and, given 'the understandable conservatism of commercial publishers' (Tomlinson 2016: 73), need to be adapted to achieve their purpose. This chapter provides an introduction to the area by addressing the planning of courses and then examining lesson planning.

5.2 Programme design

Woodward identifies six aspects of course design. See Figure 5.1. Conceptualizing content relates to an understanding of language and learning, covered in Chapters 2 and 3, and designing an assessment plan is covered in Chapter 6. The other four aspects are addressed in this chapter.

Figure 5.1 Factors in course design (adapted from Graves 2000: 3)

Planning a course or a lesson should be done systematically but is not an objective process. Lesson and course design are questions of judgment rather than truth. Indeed, perfect plans are not desirable.

> If my course design is so refined, my objectives so detailed, my materials so elaborate that nothing is left to chance then I am creating a teacher-centred environment in which the learners are just pawns to be moved about the game board of curriculum. (Graves 2000: 9)

The discussion of course design focuses on communicative language teaching (CLT), task-based learning (TBL) and content language integrated learning (CLIL). While the grammar translation method and audiolingualism still influence classroom teaching, they have only a peripheral impact on course design, perhaps mainly through the fact that many weak CLT approaches have, at least, a partially grammatical syllabus.

5.2.1 Assessing needs

The aim of this stage of course design is to find out what learners want to mean (Willis and Willis 2007: 179). Taking account of the needs of the learners can be difficult, and many well-known course books, for example, *English File Beginners* (Latham-Koenig and Oxenden 2013), are based on generic description of needs such as the Common European Framework of Reference (Council of Europe 2001). See Table 5.1. While this approach is problematic, indeed this particular framework has been described as 'flawed' because it is not empirically based (Fulcher 2010: 116); general programmes and course books probably have to be designed in this way. However, this reinforces the need, discussed above, for teachers to adapt course books.

Table 5.1 Common European Framework of Reference (CEFR)

C2: Mastery	The capacity to deal with material which is academic or cognitively demanding, and to use language to good effect at a level of performance which may in certain respects be more advanced than that of an average native speaker. Example: *CAN scan texts for relevant information, and grasp main topic of text, reading almost as quickly as a native speaker.*
C1: Effective operational proficiency	The ability to communicate with the emphasis on how well it is done, in terms of appropriacy, sensitivity and the capacity to deal with unfamiliar topics. Example: *CAN deal with hostile questioning confidently. CAN get and hold onto his/her turn to speak.*
B2: Vantage	The capacity to achieve most goals and express oneself on a range of topics. Example: *CAN show visitors around and give a detailed description of a place.*
B1: Threshold	The ability to express oneself in a limited way in familiar situations and to deal in a general way with non-routine information. Example: *CAN ask to open an account at a bank, provided the procedure is straightforward.*
A2: Waystage	An ability to deal with simple, straightforward information and begin to express oneself in familiar contexts. Example: *CAN take part in a routine conversation on simple predictable topics.*
A1: Breakthrough	A basic ability to communicate and exchange information in a simple way. Example: *CAN ask simple questions about a menu and understand simple answers.*

Source: Council of Europe (2001)

For courses in English with a clearer notion of their learners, the needs analysis should provide information about:

a what the learners can do, sometimes known as the present situation analysis,

b the target language use, what the learners need or want to be able to do, and

c a means analysis, what resources are available to enable the learners to move from (a) to (b). (cf. Swan 1985b: 86 supra)

Data related to these may be available, but often teachers and programme designers will need to collect this information. For example, when Woodrow (2006) had to design a pre-sessional programme for learners who were going to study in English at an Australian university; she consulted the students who were already studying similar courses, as well as tutors on the programmes that the learners were going to take. Woodrow took into account the gap between the present situation and target analysis, so the course covered academic writing abilities. However, the means analysis had revealed that the learners could not develop all that was needed during the course, and so learners were helped to develop the skills to research the literacy demands of their academic course to allow them to keep on developing after the course was over. In contrast, Potts and Park (2007) found that university students in Korea who might have been expected to have similar needs to Woodrow's students expressed their main needs as being able to take part in oral interaction, and this became the main focus of the course. With both courses, learners played an important part in negotiating what the aims of the course should be, and in many context this element of learner involvement can lead to more effective course design (Breen 1987a, 1987b). Indeed Woodward (2001: 22) suggests, for any course for adults, that teachers write a letter to the learners to find out what their aims are for the course as part of the planning process. For a CLIL approach, the needs analysis would be based on the content of the other subject.

5.2.2 Formulating goals and objectives

The terms goals and objectives are used with varying meanings but, for present purposes, the goal of a programme is what should be achieved by the end of the programme and the objectives are more specific. This part of course design aims to produce a set of goals and objectives that learners on the course are intended to achieve.

In weak forms of CLT, the goal is communication, but the objectives are generally formulated in terms of language elements and language skills. For example, the contents of *English File Beginners* (Latham-Koenig and Oxenden 2013: 2–3) has three strands – grammar, vocabulary and pronunciation; and *Cutting Edge Elementary* (Moor et al. 2013) has grammar, vocabulary, skills, pronunciation, tasks and world culture. Many courses also have strands which relate to learning strategies such as effective use of electronic dictionaries. Courses which are designed in this way need to ensure that learners are able to combine all the discrete items (Bourke 2006: 281) through something like the task-based activity in *Cutting Edge*.

In task-based teaching, the goal is to engage in real-life communicative tasks, and the objectives would emerge from learners' difficulties, if any, in such engagement rather than being specified in advance. The same task might appear in the final or production stage of a PPP lesson in weak CLT and as the starting point of a task-based lesson.

If some CLIL learners were studying volcanoes as part of a course in geography taught in English, the learners' geography goal might be explaining how earthquakes occur, and their language needs might include being 'able to write the explanation sequence stage of a process explanation to explain how earthquakes occur at different types of plate boundary', and the objectives would include using the following:

1 content-obligatory vocabulary – convection currents of magma, converge, diverge, compressional/tensional/lateral forces, oceanic/continental plates, subduct, friction, plate boundary, energy

2 cause–effect language – verbs (active and passive): create, result in, cause, accumulate, release; causal connectives: therefore, as a result, when, as (Kong 2015: 214).

5.2.3 Organizing the course

Organizing the course means taking the goals and objectives identified in the needs analysis and producing a syllabus by dividing the goals and objectives into teachable units and sequencing the units.

For weak CLT programmes with multiple strand syllabuses, the structure is often based on topics which provide a framework for teaching the different strands. Often the choice of topic also guides the sequence. The topic ' "selects" the new language items, be they structures, language functions, or vocabulary. The topic also suggests relevant listening and speaking tasks, interactive activities (e.g. games, information gap, etc.), reading texts, and a variety of writing tasks keyed to the topic' (Bourke 2006: 282).

Some course books provide a framework through a story which runs through the book, and this has some advantages in terms of learner motivation and can lead to making the text more authentic for the learners (e.g. Coles and Lord 1976).

Where the topic or narrative does not guide the order of the syllabus, course designers often draw on concepts like difficulty and complexity. For grammar, the natural order (Krashen 1987: 13), Figure 3.1 in Chapter 3, provides one view of what sequence a grammatical syllabus should follow, and processability theory offers a similar theory (Pienemann 2006). However, course books seem to have developed their own sequence. See Tables 5.2 and 5.3 for examples from both communicative and audiolingual course books. Perhaps the sequence in these books is based on Bourke's ideas about the topic leading to the grammar accompanied by a recognition that grammatical syllabus are cyclical, with

Table 5.2 *English File Beginners'* grammar syllabus

Unit	Grammar term	Example
1	Present tense of 'be' including negative forms	I'm, you're, he's, she's, it's, we're, they're, I'm not, you aren't etc.
2	Singular and plural nouns, possessive adjectives, possessive ('s) adjectives	A cat, cats, an apple, apples My car, your name, his book, her table, its tail, our course, their drink Christina's book, the cat's tail A red car. The car is red.
3	Present simple including negative forms	I go, you go, she goes, he goes, it goes, we go, they go, I don't go, etc.
4	Adverbs of frequency, word order in questions using 'be' and lexical verbs, can/can't permission and possibility	Always, sometimes, never Are we late? Do they speak French? How old is he? Where does he come from? You can't park here You can get a bus from my house
5	Past simple: be, have, go, get, regular verbs	Was, were, had, went, go Walked, changed, waited
6	There is/are/was/were Revision of object pronouns	Me, her, him, us, them
7	Like + verb+ing Future: going to (plans) Future: be going to (predictions)	I like swimming I am going to buy some milk It is going to rain

Source: Latham-Koenig and Oxenden (2013: 3)

Table 5.3 Practice and progress pre-intermediate

Unit	Grammar term	Example
1	Word order in simple statements	I went to America last week
2	Present continuous and simple	I am having my breakfast I always get up late
3	Simple past	Last summer, I went to Italy
4	Present perfect	I have just received a letter
5	Simple past and present perfect simple	The bird covered the distances in three minutes He has sent a great many requests for spare parts
6	Indefinite and definite articles	He asked me for a meal and a glass of beer He ate the food and drank the beer
7	Past continuous	The detectives were waiting at the airport all morning

Source: Alexander (1993: v)

the same grammar point coming up in different contexts at different stages of the educational process and that a grammatical syllabus is best thought of as a checklist of what learners need rather than a sequence of how they are learnt.

The vocabulary strand in these materials is often topic-related, but where lexical factors are considered the main criterion is frequency. The most frequent 700 words in English account for about 70 per cent of all texts (Willis and Willis 2007: 193) – once learners know 2,500 words, they will know 86 per cent of all texts. Beyond this, vocabulary becomes more specific and should be selected on the basis of what the learners need to do with the language rather than the overall frequency of vocabulary in the language, so what someone who wants to study law needs would be lexically different from those who are more focused on working at travel agents. The vocabulary syllabus should involve recycling but this is harder to do than it is for grammar and, so even though it is desirable, recycling is not often systematic.

Task-based teaching follows a sequence which is not based on linguistic content but task complexity and difficulty. So giving directions from A to B is cognitively easier than giving directions from A to B via C (Robinson 2001). A task-led course book such as *Cutting Edge Elementary* (Latham-Koenig et al. 2013) seems to rely, at least partly, on this criterion, so the first task of finding information is easier than the second task, talking about your five favourite people, and both these are easier than the later task of choosing a holiday activity. However, while cognitive difficulty is a useful criterion, it will not differentiate all tasks, and teachers may need to use the parameters described in Table 11.12 in Chapter 11 to bring tasks to the appropriate level for their learners and, if they are involved in the design of a task-based syllabus, to recognize that the sequencing of tasks is not an exact science.

In many CLIL programmes, learners attend both an English class and a subject-specific content class taught through English (Dalton-Puffer 2007), and here the process of course design for the English class may follow any of the strategies discussed earlier, though it is common for such course to adopt a problem-solving or task-based approach related to the difficulties that arise in the content class, and this may lead to a lack of a clear language focus (Baecher et al. 2014). This is also likely to be an approach where English is not taught as a separate subject and the pressure of teaching to both language and content syllabus may require that extensive opportunities for out-of-class study are needed.

Activity 5.1 Organizing the course

1 How would you sequence the following communicative tasks?

   a Buying a pint of milk

   b Telling a friend about a film you liked

   c Taking part in a conversation with two friends

   d Listening to the news on television

   e Ordering a book through a website

2 If you have worked with advanced learners of English, can you identify a set of grammatical features that present difficulties? Are these difficulties to do with differences with the first language or some other factor? Would the notion of difficulty help you to decide the order of items in a grammatical syllabus for advanced learners?

5.2.4 Developing materials

Material development covers 'all the processes made use of by practitioners who produce and/or use materials for language learning, including materials evaluation, their adaptation, design, production, exploitation and research' (Tomlinson 2012: 143–4).

Materials development can be aimed at developing new skills or knowledge, related – in the information processing model of learning – to declarative knowledge, at improving the ways learners use existing skills and knowledge, or to procedural knowledge, or a combination of both. The first of these will generally involve exposing the learners to spoken or written texts which will:

1 be comprehensible to the learners,

2 contain examples of the linguistic features, and

3 be of interest to the learners. (Tomlinson 2008: 4)

Within weak versions of CLT, this might relate to pronunciation, spelling, grammar, vocabulary, discourse, or one of the four skills. For example, teaching the present continuous might involve part of the transcript from the 2016 televised presidential debates in which the compere, Lester Holt, asked Donald Trump how he would put more money into the pockets of American workers. Trump responded:

> Thank you, Lester. Our jobs *are fleeing* the country. They're *going* to Mexico. They're *going* to many other countries. So we're *losing* our good jobs, so many of them. When you look at what's *happening* in Mexico, a friend of mine who builds plants said it's the eighth wonder of the world. They're *building* some of the biggest plants anywhere in the world, some of the most sophisticated, some of the best plants. With the United States, as he said, not so much.
>
> So Ford *is leaving*. You see that, their small car division leaving. Thousands of jobs leaving Michigan, leaving Ohio. They're *all leaving*. And we can't allow it to happen anymore. (Blake 2016; my emphasis)

Table 5.4 Categories of pedagogic tasks

Task category	Example
Listing	Your favourite foods
Sorting	How to make your favourite food
Classifying	Healthy and unhealthy food
Matching	Matching pictures and recipes
Comparing	Comparing two recipes for the same dish
Problem-solving	Choosing food for a class party
Projects	Producing a video about healthy eating
Story-telling	Talking about a disastrous meal

Source: Willis and Willis (2007: 64–111)

This text contains eight instances of present progressive or continuous (in italics) as well as three elliptical uses of the same tense and might serve as an illustration of the use of this tense in discourse for learners at the appropriate level and with an interest in American economic policy. However, it is surprisingly difficult to find texts in this way and, in many instances, the initial criterion is the theme or topic, and the other language elements and skills emerge from the text.

Where the aims of the materials relate to improving the ways learners use existing skills and knowledge, teachers and materials writers will need to design pedagogic tasks. Willis and Willis (2007) identify six kinds of pedagogic tasks, which are useful in designing classroom activities or supplementing a course book. See Table 5.4.

 Activity 5.2 Discussion

1   You are working with a group of upper-intermediate learners on ways of making requests. How might you use the text taken from an Australian television programme below? It is a conversation between Clarrie, a grandfather, and Helen, a neighbour, about a party that Clarrie's grandson is going to have (McCarthy and Carter 1994: 118–19).

Clarrie: So I said to him, forget your books for one night. Throw a party next weekend.

Helen: A party at number 30! What will Dorothy say about that?

Clarrie: Well, what she doesn't know won't hurt her. Of course, I'll be keeping my eye on things, and that brings me to my next problem. You see these young people. They don't want an old codger like me poking my nose in so I'll make myself scarce. But I still need to be close to hand, you see. So I was wondering, would you be all right if I came over here on the night? What do you reckon?

Helen: Oh Clarrie, I . . .

Clarrie: Oh, I'd be no bother. It'd mean a heck of a lot to those young kids

Helen: All right.

Clarrie: I knew you'd say yes. You're an angel, Helen

Helen: Ha.

2 Here is an example of a task from Breen (1985: 67). What is the task objective? For what age and level of learners would this task be appropriate? Could you adapt the task to make is easier?

The students – working within five or six groups – have been asked to read the teacher's comments on two pieces of handwritten homework multi-copied from the work of a previous year's group. Working in pairs initially, the students had to assess the usefulness and appropriateness of the teacher's feedback on the two original pieces of homework. Now working within their groups, the students are agreeing on their answers to two questions which are written up on the blackboard: 'What comments from the teacher would have been most helpful to the people who wrote the homework?' and 'What kind of homework would you recommend as the most useful and helpful?'

3 Design a listing task related to homework that elementary learners could do in groups.

5.3 Lesson planning

When you observe a good lesson, the process seems effortless. The teacher is relaxed, the learners are motivated, the teaching materials are ready when they are wanted, one activity leads smoothly into another and the whole lesson is coherent. However, such classes only happen as a result of effective preparation and planning (Butt 2008: 2). The four key components for a lesson plan are:

1 *Purpose* – what goals and objectives does the teacher want the learners to achieve by the end of the lesson?

2 *Activities* – what activities will the learners engage in to achieve those goals and objectives?

3 *Resources* – what resources will the teacher need to enable those activities?

4 *Evaluation* – what will be the evidence that the goals and objectives have been achieved?

 Activity 5.3 Lesson planning skills

1 Learning goals and objectives

Which of the following items would you regard as appropriate lesson goals and objectives? Which would you see as too general? Which are not to do with learning?

a Learners will complete the listening comprehension exercise in the course book.

b Learners will be able to communicate effectively in writing.

c Learners will be able to write an informal email.

d Learners will be able to identify new and old information in short spoken sentences.

e Learners will describe a picture using the present continuous tense.

2 How would you sequence these activities within a lesson on houses for upper-intermediate learners (adapted from Rifkin 2003: 176)?

   a Learners read an article from a blog about differences in house design between different regions of the United States.

   b Learners write an essay entitled 'My perfect home'.

   c Learners are given a house plan from a sale brochure. In pairs, they each describe their plan to their partner, sight unseen, who then draws the plan.

   d Learners watch a five-minute extract from a sales video for a house.

3 Giving instructions

   How would you organize the seating for the 'describe and draw' activity in 2c in this activity? Write out instructions in English for the activity that would be appropriate for upper-intermediate learners.

4 Lesson planning

   If you use a course book in your teaching, identify the learning goals and objectives of a sample unit and then evaluate the activities in terms of how they contribute to these aims? How might you edit/supplement or reorganize the unit so that it would be more effective?

Table 5.5 is a lesson form for a four-activity lesson, and an editable version of this is available online. The bottom of the lesson plan has space for comments, where the teacher can write comments on the lesson after it has been taught. Writing comments is an important part of teacher development, and I would encourage all teachers, no matter how experienced, to do this as a way of reflecting on their more and less successful lessons.

Table 5.5 A lesson pro-forma

Teacher			
Class			
Level			
Date			
Time			
Goals and objectives			
Materials			
Activity	Int	S/E	Time
1			
2			
3			
4			
Comments			

Int = pattern of interaction – plenary: teacher to whole class (W); group (G); pairs (P). S/E = language skill or element.

5.3.1 How do teachers identify the purpose of a lesson?

The purpose or goal of the lesson, or for a group of lessons, may come from the course book, the syllabus, a needs analysis or may relate to a language issue that has arisen in a previous lesson. For example, in task-based teaching, teachers may use their diagnosis of how the learners carried out the task in one lesson to provide the language objective of the next lesson, though the goal of the sequence of lessons would remain being able to engage in the real-life communicative task. The purpose is often language-related but, because of the need to enable learning beyond the language classroom, may also be to do with, for example, learning strategies and motivational factors.

Goals and objectives need to be reasonably specific. For a reading lesson, the aim of reading in English is too broad. This would need to be related to the text type and skill involved that learners need in order to be able to read more efficiently. Being able to scan an encyclopaedia entry for a specific piece of information would be more appropriate than being able to read for information. However, teachers should not feel they are bound to have measurable outcomes for all their lessons. Sometimes, their objectives relate to issues like motivation or confidence, where it is more important that teachers and learners can sense some development rather than the teacher being able to put a tick against a particular language point.

The aims of the lesson should not just record what the learners are expected to do in the class. So, taking part in a pair work activity or practicing a reading skill would not be an appropriate objective or goal. The objective would relate to what the learners learn from the activity, such as being able to use a grammatical structure more fluently.

Many lessons have multiple objectives. These may be coordinated in some way, so a reading lesson may incorporate objectives related to particular sub-skills, vocabulary knowledge and information about a particular culture. It is also possible to have 'threads' (Woodward 2001: 55), that is, a sequence that is not closely related to the rest of the lesson but forms a coherent strand over a set of lessons or course. This could be related to language element such as pronunciation and vocabulary or to something more general, such as a discussion of what videos learners have watched. Threads can be useful as a way of incorporating learners' need even where teachers have restricted freedom. In Malaysia in a course book-centred approach, I was able to incorporate threads on extensive reading in response to what the learners wanted.

Learners are not robots and so even in the best planned lesson, they may not achieve all that the teacher hoped they would, so Anderson (2015) suggests that teachers should talk about learning opportunities or affordances rather than aims, goals and objectives. The view that lessons should not be judged on whether the goals and objectives are achieved has merit. Indeed, teachers who deviate from their lesson plan when the planned aims are proving problematic are demonstrating important teaching skills and should be commended. However, specifying aims and the related component of evaluation are an important part of how teachers can improve their understanding of what is and is not possible with one group of learners. This means it is important that aims are expressed in a form that makes it easy for teachers to decide if the aim has been achieved. For example, an aim might be expressed in the form 'by the end of the lesson, learners will be able to hear the difference between the phonemes /p/ and /b/' or 'by the end of the lesson, learners will be able to produce an accurate list of references for an assignment'.

5.3.2 How do teachers choose and sequence activities?

Once teachers have decided the aims of the lesson, they need to select appropriate activities. This will relate to the different lesson sequences discussed in Chapter 4 and the elements or skills discussed later in the book. However, a choice of a problem-solving approach, or PPP, will not provide a complete answer as to how the lesson should be sequenced. Two key stages in lesson planning are the start and the end of the class. Most teachers develop a routine about the start of the class, which might include writing what is going to be covered in the class on the board, a review of what happened in the previous lesson or something less structured such as a discussion of what the learners have been doing since the previous class. Teachers also often have routine endings, a summary of what the teachers hope the learners have learnt in the lesson or setting homework for the next lesson, and some teachers like to end with a game, perhaps chosen by the learners. A game that can be extended or dropped is useful in case other activities in the lesson have not taken the time the teacher expected in the lesson plan. A game might be a thread activity, and teachers often have thread activities which they do at the start or end of lessons.

The other activities in the lesson also need to be sequenced. Ur (2012: 22) suggests that more difficult activities should be done earlier on when learners have most energy, and this is also an argument within task-based teaching for doing the task near the start of the lesson rather than, as in PPP, towards the end. The energy level in the class is an important issue in lesson planning. Teachers in primary schools often talk of stirring activities, which encourage higher energy levels, and their counterpart, calming activities; and this distinction can be applied more widely. For example, teachers may follow a stirring activity where learners are expected to talk a lot, such as a discussion, with a calming activity such as a written exercise. Teachers will often change the order of activities in a lesson if they feel it is getting too noisy or that the learners are getting bored. The ways in which teachers and learners interact is also important. Group and pair work may lead to higher energy levels than where teachers address the whole class.

Task-based teaching makes considerable demand on teachers in terms of activities because a problem-solving sequence means that, until the learners have tried to carry out the communicative task, the teacher does not know what the language elements or skills need to be addressed. This means that in task-based lessons, teachers need to identify possible problem areas and have appropriate activities and their associated materials available. In some task-based courses, the language aims of a second lesson emerge from a task that has been done in an earlier lesson so that the teacher can plan appropriate activities. This might increase the planning time but would essentially be the same as the kind of lessons discussed above, though if learners have different problems, the teacher would need to arrange the class so that different learners or groups of learners can work separately. Whether the language focus happens in the same lesson as the task or later, teachers need to have a bank of resources available, which might be published materials or activities the teacher has designed.

Lesson plans will normally include how long particular activities are expected to last. This can be difficult to judge, and most teachers sometimes struggle with this. The point of these estimates is not to determine in advance what happens in a class. Decisions about timing need to be based on the needs of the learners in the class, not what is in the lesson plan. However, after the class, teachers should note how accurate the estimate was so that future estimates will be closer.

5.3.3 What resources are needed to carry out the activities?

Once teachers have identified what activities learners and teachers are going to do, they need to consider what resources they need. This may include photocopies of materials or activities in the course book. However, the resources may also include the use of particular skills such as drawing on the board, giving instructions for a pair work activity or using a particular app or piece of technology in the classroom. Some teachers make a point of using resources, such as bringing a guest into the class or recording what learners say as a way of extending their repertoire of activities.

5.3.4 How do teachers know if they have achieved their aims?

Woodward (2001: 2) says a good lesson is 'one where there's plenty of language learning going on', so teachers need to know what their learners know at the start of the class and monitor what learning happens during the class in a kind of ongoing and specific needs analysis. Task-based teaching incorporates this into its overall structure with the initial attempt at the communicative task providing information about what learners already know and, if the learners carry out the task again after some language instruction, this will tell the teacher what the learners have learnt. Many activities provide evidence of what learners know after teaching and most teachers probably have a reasonable idea of what their learners know at the start of the lesson. This can be built into activity design. If a course book provides a list of vocabulary items for a reading passage, the teacher can start by finding out what learners know before explaining any of them and, similarly, might try to get learners to produce a particular grammatical structure before presenting it.

5.4 Summary

This chapter has built on the discussion of teaching methods in Chapter 4 by looking at programme and lesson design. Programme design covers needs analysis, formulation of goals/objectives, organizing the course and developing materials. Lesson planning includes identifying lesson aims, choosing and sequencing activities, ensuring the appropriate resources are available and evaluating whether the lesson aims have been achieved.

 Activity 5.4 Discussion

Chapter 4 asked you to devise a lesson for a group of doctors who have been working in non-Anglophone contexts and now going to practice in an English-speaking environment. How would you carry out a target language use analysis to identify what their language needs are and a present situation analysis to identify what they are currently able to do?

5.5 Further reading

The most useful book on designing English language courses and lessons is Woodward's (2001) *Planning Lessons and Course* but, if you are just planning a course, Graves's (2000) *Designing Language Courses* is very good. Both these books contain useful information about material adaptation and design. Harwood's (2010) *English Language Teaching Materials: Theory and Practice* and Tomlinson's (2013) *Developing Materials for Language Teaching* provide more detailed information about materials. I find Willis and Willis's (2007) *Doing Task-Based Teaching* and Ur and Wright's (1992) *Five Minute Activities* a useful source of ideas for activities, but most teachers have their favourite authors in this area. Wright (2005) is good on classroom management generally.

Chapter 6

Evaluation and Assessment of Language Learning

6.1 Introduction

The assessment and evaluation of language learning and the tests that are used to inform the assessment process are important in most educational systems. They attract a wide range of views. Some teachers feel 'fear and loathing' towards tests (Haladyna et al. 1991: 4), struggling to reconcile their commitment to helping their learners become better users of language with the need for qualifications, and learners find many tests stressful so it is important that teachers and others involved in the education process understand how assessment practices work.

Misconceptions about assessment are common, and three of the most egregious are discussed here (Bachman and Palmer 2010: 6–11). The first of these is overconfidence in the information which tests provide. Tests provide a partial indication of what learners can do, and everyone involved in the assessment process needs to evaluate the strengths and weaknesses of the tests they use. The second misconception is that test construction should be left to the experts. In fact, understanding how tests and assessments are constructed enables teachers and other educational practitioners to evaluate the tests they use, prepare their learners for tests and construct their own tests to support their own teaching and their learners' language development. The third misconception is to overvalue certain features of tests or assessments such as reliability, often backed up by statistics. Features such as reliability are important, but the central issue is whether a test or assessment leads to appropriate decisions.

A score from an evaluation procedure 'is the basis for a claim, nothing more, about the candidate's standing in relation to a domain of knowledge or skill or capacity to carry out particular sets of communicative tasks and hence his or her readiness for entry into particular communicative contexts. This point is sometimes obscured by the fact that the claim is expressed in the form of a number or a labelled category on a scale, which seems to give it a spurious kind of scientific objectivity' (McNamara 2007).

This chapter addresses four main issues:

1 The purposes of testing – what decisions will the test data inform?
2 The quality of the test – what are the characteristics of a good test?
3 Creating tests – how can teachers produce their own methods of assessment?
4 Preparing learners for tests – how can teachers prepare learners for language assessment?

6.2 The purposes of assessment

Assessment has traditionally been said to achieve five purposes (Fulcher 2010: 21):

1 Achievement – what aspects of language have the learners learnt

2 Aptitude – what are learners' natural abilities

3 Diagnosis – what are the gaps in learners' language abilities

4 Placement – what language class should the learner be in

5 Proficiency – what level are the learners' language abilities

This list is an oversimplification and the categories overlap, but provides a framework for the necessary first stage of test evaluation. Unless the purpose of evaluation is clear, its success or otherwise cannot be judged.

Achievement tests are often constructed by teachers as a way of evaluating the success of their teaching. Informal achievement testing is a part of most lessons as teachers seek evidence that learners have understood what they have been taught or what is in the syllabus that guides their programme. Achievement tests can also be used to evaluate the effectiveness of educational programmes or teachers. The results of achievement tests are normally specific to the context and are not meant to be generalizable. Achievement tests may have a pass mark based on how much of what has been covered in a programme has been learnt, but this is not a necessary feature.

Aptitude tests (Pimsleur et al. 2004; Rogers et al. 2016) are intended to identify whether an individual has a general ability to learn languages. These are less common than they were, partly because people attribute success in language learning to other factors such as motivation (Green 2014: 11) and partly because the spread of compulsory English language education makes the question of whether learners have the potential to be good or bad at English redundant.

Diagnostic tests are often related to achievement tests in that they are intended to find out the gaps in what learners know or can do and so by implication what they do know or can do. They are part of a larger category of formative tests, that is, tests which provide information to support language teaching, as opposed to summative uses of tests where the information provides a retrospective view of what has been learnt. Two important developments in formative assessment – assessment for learning (Black and Wiliam 1998) and dynamic assessment (Poehner and Lantolf 2005) – are explored in more detail in the section on writing your own tests.

Placement tests are given to learners when they start a new programme or a new stage of an existing programme to place learners in the appropriate class for their language ability. Placement tests are available commercially but are often produced by language schools based on the content of the syllabuses they use for different levels. Generally, if a learner is put in the wrong class, this can be remedied fairly easily so these are low-stake tests.

Proficiency tests provide information about whether the people being assessed have the necessary language ability for their needs. They are typically created by large organizations such as ministries of education and commercial testing enterprises and are based on some kind of specification or construct of the language ability that is being assessed. Proficiency tests can have life-changing impacts as they relate to issues such as study through English (e.g. IELTS, TOEFL iBT) and citizenship (Hill and McNamara 2015) and are contentious. See, for example, Uysal (2010) on IELTS, Hill and McNamara (2015) on the US citizenship test, and Shohamy on the No Child Left Behind programme in the United States (Lazaraton 2010). However, such tests can serve as a relatively fair way of allocating limited resources. One of the earliest proficiency tests set up in China in the sixth century AD 'was established in order to reduce the power of the aristocracy in civil administration and open it up to talented individuals from whatever background they came' (Fulcher 2010: 8). Because proficiency tests are used for selection, they can be norm-referenced. If, for example, government translators need to take an exam before they are employed, it may be that fifty translators are needed in one year and hundred in the next. To reflect this, the pass mark may change. This would make this norm-referenced as opposed to a criterion-referenced approach where everyone who meets the relevant standards would pass the test.

The importance of these kinds of tests and the claims that their results can be generalized make it paramount that educational professionals can evaluate the data produced by such tests and the decisions based on those data, the topic of the next section.

6.3 The qualities of the test: practicality, validity, reliability, consequences

The four most important qualities of a test are that it is practical, valid, reliable and has beneficial consequence or backwash (Green 2014: 58). No test fully satisfies all four qualities. This is not grounds for rejecting tests, but teachers and other stakeholders need to consider the quality of the test when they use the resulting information.

This section discusses the first three issues and relates them to two hypothetical tests designed to reveal whether the candidates can (a) arrange an appointment at a doctor's surgery by telephone and (b) understand an academic lecture. The issue of consequences will be discussed in the section on preparing candidates for examinations.

6.3.1 Practicality

Constructing and/or using some test or other evaluation procedure takes resources. Teachers who want to measure what their learners have achieved must balance the time taken to design and administer an achievement procedure against the activities their learners could be doing if the procedure did not happen. At a larger scale, this decision becomes more complex with security issues, and modes of delivery (e.g. paper and pencil versus computer-based testing) become important. The Chinese college entrance examination, the *Gaokao*, illustrates some of the practical measures taken to ensure that everyone takes the test under the same circumstances. 'During the two days of testing, building sites are closed, aircraft flight paths are changed to avoid low-flying aircraft disturbing students, and test centres are provided with their own police guard to reduce traffic noise and maintain security over test papers' (Fulcher 2010: 7).

The practicalities of a test related to booking an appointment are less dramatic. For example, it would ideally be carried out with the candidate speaking into a telephone with a medical receptionist at the other end. If this were done on a large scale, both would be difficult to arrange, and even for a small group of candidates, the receptionist would likely be replaced by someone simulating the behaviour of the receptionist. The test also involves candidates speaking aloud and so would require that individual candidates are not able to hear each other. This might be difficult to arrange and it might mean that the candidates were instead asked to write down their side of the dialogue, possibly in response to a written version of what the receptionist might say. Some of these practical issues might be overcome by online testing.

Academic lectures typically last a little under an hour. Replicating this length is potentially problematic, and most approaches to the evaluation of lecture comprehension use extracts. TOEFL iBt requires candidates to listen to four to six extracts from lectures each lasting about three to five minutes (Educational Testing Services 2012). Lectures are typically supported by presentational software such as PowerPoint. This aspect of lectures is typically not addressed in tests, though TOEFL iBT does provide a photograph to accompany each lecture extract, providing information about the number of speakers.

6.3.2 Validity

Test developers must be able to justify the intended uses of the test (Bachman and Palmer 2010: 11 et passim). If candidates successfully pass a test on arranging a medical appointment, the test writers need to be able to show that the candidates can book an appointment outside the testing context, that is, the test is valid. Validity is sometimes described as a collection of separate kinds of validity, for example, face validity (Does the test look as if it tests what it is meant to test?) or content validity (Does the content of an achievement test match what has been taught?). It is better to think of these as all parts of the argument about whether the test is leading to appropriate decisions so that the different aspects can be balanced against each other. What is not contested is that 'a language test without validation research is like a police force without a court system: unfair and dangerous' (McNamara 2007: 280).

The amount of validation research will depend on the importance of the decision being made and should be extensive for high-stakes proficiency assessment procedures, but for all tests, the main way of carrying out validation research is demonstrating a link between the assessment and the communicative activities about which it is intended to provide information.

The relationship has been conceptualized in terms of directness or authenticity. For example, if assessors want to test whether candidates have the language abilities to understand an academic lecture, a direct test would include a recording of a lecture. The argument for the validity of the procedure would be that it provides good information about whether candidates can understand a lecture because this is what they are doing in the assessment procedure. If the assessment task matches the target language use, this gives face validity , which can influence how candidates respond to the test. If candidates feel the test lacks face validity, they are less likely to take it seriously. However, directness may not be a good criterion. First, listening to a lecture in an examination hall is different from listening to the same lecture in a lecture theatre and, second, the assessment is intended to indicate whether candidates can understand not just one lecture but lectures in general. Indeed, the notion of a direct test is a misnomer (Messick 1996: 244). Test construction, in all but the simplest contexts, involves some kind of description of the target language use, in testing terms, creating a construct that is the focus of the test. Arguments about construct validity are central to the justification of tests, and these often relate to construct under-representation, where the test does not include the key facets of the construct and construct irrelevance, where the test includes facets which are not part of the construct (Messick 1996).

For teacher-designed assessment, the creation of a construct can be relatively straightforward. If a teacher is writing an achievement test to cover what has been taught over a term, then the syllabus or possibly the contents of the course book would be the default construct, and the assessment should cover as much of the syllabus as possible to avoid construct under-representation, and not cover things that had not been covered to avoid construct irrelevance.

For a more specific test, the construct is often based on intuition. In the assessment about making a medical appointment, assessors might rely on their own knowledge of a typical interaction, perhaps starting with the receptionist asking what might be done to aid the caller and the caller asking for an appointment, eventually ending with the making of an appointment. However, an empirical basis for the construct would provide a more robust foundation because, as Roberts and Cooke (2009) have shown, actual interactions may be rather different from how we imagine them. A second issue is who would be the interlocutor speaking to the candidate. The candidate's teacher would be familiar with the candidate's accent, something which would not be true of the target language use where the receptionist would not have met the candidate before and so this would reduce the validity of the test. However, if the teacher were the interlocutor, this might reduce the candidate's anxiety and, as anxiety is not a part of the construct for the test, reduce construct-irrelevant factors. The validity of the test is a matter of argument rather than objective truth.

If the test has more significance, more empirical data would be needed. The lecture comprehension test could draw on a corpus of lectures such as MICASE (Briggs et al. 2002) or BASE (Nesi 2007), but the data from the corpora would need to be analysed in some way. For example, the analysis might centre on the language elements in lectures and identify typical lecture vocabulary and grammar, and this could be used to create a listening text that represented lectures in some way. The construct might include the use of reporting verbs in:

His equation says/claims/argues that there's a linear relationship between the reaction time and the log of the number of stimulus response alternatives.

The construct should cover what would count as comprehension of a lecture. This could be a summary of the content or the ability to answer specific questions. The fact that TOEFL iBT has four lecture extracts suggests that what is typical of lectures cannot be captured in an extract from a single lecture and the fact that they chose to use authentically produced extracts rather than create their own examples shows that the test writers saw the features of continuous speech as an important part of the lecture construct. (See Chapter 7 for the features of continuous speech.) Using both specific questions and a task involving a piece of writing which is based on what the candidates have heard (and what they have read) suggests two different conceptions of what counts as successful lecture comprehension.

An alternative approach to construct design would include a processing or skill-based view of lectures. In the UK, the construct for mother tongue reading in primary schools separates out decoding and comprehension. (See Chapter 12 for more discussion of these terms.) One part of the reading test tries to evaluate the candidates' abilities to decode without comprehension by asking them to read aloud non-sense words such as *zam, blat, splot, plock, dring, crig* and *tweb* (Clark 2016). This would lack face validity, and any claim for construct validity would need evidence.

The discussion of construct validity often focuses on the relationship between the description of the target language use in the construct and the test. However, Messick (1989) has argued that this should be broadened to explore the extent to which the test is providing the information to reach appropriate decisions and so to evaluate the construct the test is based on. A narrow evaluation of the construct of the non-sense word reading test above would explore if the test provides information about whether candidates can decode. A broader evaluation would ask if the test reveals the reading abilities of the candidates.

The argument for the validity of a test can be supported in a range of other ways than a relationship between the construct and the test. For example, if a related test already exists and has led to good decisions, a statistical correlation between the marks of the two assessments would be an argument for saying that the new assessment is valid (Zahedi and Shamsaee 2012). Cloze tests or gap-filling activities have been used as a test of both reading and listening comprehension on the ground that the results they produce are similar to those of tests more obviously linked to those skills (Oller 1973). Sometimes the results of tests undermine their validity. A test of general language ability which consistently produced results that suggested that those under thirty outscored those over forty would need to be questioned unless the age of candidates was part of the construct.

 Activity 6.1 Validity

The academic module of IELTS is often used to decide whether candidates should be admitted to degree-level courses in an Anglophone university. The writing paper comprises two tasks. For task 1, candidates write a report of around 150 words based on a table or diagram, and for task 2, they write a short essay or general report of around 250 words in response to an argument or a problem.

1 Produce your own construct of the writing ability needed for an undergraduate degree in English. You may like to look at research in writing in universities (Gardner and Nesi 2013; Nesi and Gardner 2012), but you can rely on your own knowledge of undergraduate writing. In other words, what information about writing abilities in English would be needed to decide if a candidate should be admitted to a degree programme taught in English?

2 Would the construct differ for a degree in English literature and engineering?

3 Should information about the difference between more and less successful writing be a part of the construct? If so, what would it be?

4 To what extent are the IELTS writing tasks an effective way of evaluating whether candidates have the appropriate writing ability?

5 If you work with a different kind of test on a regular basis, what information would you need to decide if it is valid?

6.3.3 Reliability

Reliability is to do with consistency of measurement. Lado (1961: 31) expressed it as a question:

Does the test yield the same scores one day and the next if there has been no instruction intervening?

Although reliability is often seen as separate from validity, it is a part of the argument for the decisions based on the test. An assessment cannot be valid if it is not reliable, but it can be reliable without being valid because the assessment is measuring something else. Tests which are reliable indicators of whether students can study in English are not necessarily valid measures for citizenship just as a set of bathroom scales could provide data about weight but not about someone's height. This means that some aspects of reliability are to do with statistical aspects of the internal integrity of assessments. These are not covered in this chapter but are explained in the books listed under suggested reading.

Green (2014: 73–4) identifies seven strategies for building reliability into assessment. See Table 6.1.

If the medical appointment assessment were conducted as an oral examination and success meant arranging an appointment, the result would be fairly reliable. However, the interlocutor is a human and is likely to use different words and phrases with each candidate; this would introduce some variability and would mean the conditions were not the same for all candidates, so there would have to be guidelines about what the interlocutor said and the level of support they provided to the candidate.

For the lecture comprehension assessment, the first issue would be the equivalence of what the candidates heard. A large-scale test with candidates at different iterations of the test would require that everyone heard the same recordings under the same conditions. Diverting the flight path of passing planes might be part of this as would making sure that candidates near the recording device were not advantaged over those at a greater distance. The same issue would arise with the questions used to evaluate the candidates' comprehension. If a lecture related to nuclear physics, this would advantage

Table 6.1 Strategies to improve reliability

Clear tasks	If instructions are clear to everyone, the information will be more likely to reflect the intended language abilities
More tasks	If you ask one question, someone might get it right by chance. The more questions you ask, the smaller the role of guesses
Limit the scope	A test of grammar will be more reliable than a test of grammar, vocabulary, reading and writing
Standardize conditions	Everyone should take the test under the same conditions. This is why flights are changed for the *Gaokao*
Control scoring	Giving training to scorers and/or providing them with marking criteria and answer keys improves reliability
More scorers	A mark that is agreed to by two markers will be more reliable than a mark from one marker
Wide range of ability	Distinctions between high-level and low-level learners are more reliable that those between two intermediate learners

candidates with this kind of knowledge over, say, historians. Similarly, if candidates were asked to produce a summary or a piece of writing based on the lecture, clear criteria about what counts as a successful answer would be needed with guidelines to deal with candidates who had understood the lectures but whose writing or grammatical skills meant they produced a weaker response thanmight be expected. See below on writing your own tests.

 Activity 6.2 Reliability

1 If you wanted your learners to demonstrate their writing abilities as part of an achievement test, how would you ensure the reliability of the marks that this task produced? Which of Green's strategies would be relevant to this task?

2 If you have an internally produced test that you use on a regular basis, how do you ensure that the results are reliable?

6.4 Writing your own tests and assessment tools

Teachers are involved in 'a continuous process of appraising their learners' (Rea-Dickins 2006) as a part of their teaching, but sometimes the assessment needs to be planned and implemented. This has three stages – identifying the aims, designing the assessment instruments and evaluating what the learners have done.

6.4.1 The aims of assessment

Teacher assessment is generally conceptualized as a way of finding out what the learners have achieved, that is, as a kind of summative assessment. However, increasingly, evidence about student achievement is used to improve future instruction (Black and Wiliam 1998), that is, formative assessment, also known as assessment for learning. Fulcher (2010: 73) identifies three strategies that have come out of this strand of research:

1 Feedback should describe what the learners have achieved

2 Feedback should identify aspects of the learners' performance that can be improved

3 Time should be provided to allow learners to reflect on the feedback

This focus has been reinforced by the notion of dynamic assessment, which comes out of the Vygotskyan theories of learning discussed in Chapter 3. Dynamic assessment attempts to collect information about the learning trajectory of the candidates. Two learners with same levels of support who were able to use the past tense might not be equally ready to start working on the present perfect. In Vygostkyan terms, the present perfect might be within the zone of proximal development of one learner but not that of another (Poehner and Lantolf 2005: 234). Both assessment for learning and dynamic assessment have implications for assessment techniques, and these are discussed below.

Teachers need to decide what aspects of language are assessed. This might relate to a particular course, for example, the contents of the first four units of a course book, or to a particular skill or sub-skill, for example, writing a film review. The more specific the aims, the easier the assessment design will be. An aim such as being able to make an appointment at a doctor's surgery is easier to assess than understanding lectures because the construct for the latter is more complicated, and so it is harder to evaluate whether all construct-relevant facets have been included. Where a selection needs to be made from the construct, for example, if the course book has covered too much for it all to be tested, teachers will need a systematic way of making a selection such as what is most important or what can be seen as representative of the whole construct and should cover anything that has not been tested in future versions of the test. TOEFL iBT decided to use extracts from four different lectures rather than a longer extract from one lecture because the four extracts are more representative of the overall construct of lecture comprehension than one would be.

6.4.2 Assessment instruments

To evaluate if a learner can make a medical appointment by telephone, the most plausible assessment instrument is a role-play. The candidate would need to be given a card indicating what has to be done, for example, 'You have a fever and have been vomiting. You call Dr Watson's surgery to make an appointment with Dr Watson as soon as possible. You should write down the day and time of your interview'. The language on the card would need to be as simple as possible to ensure that the learners' performance is not affected by the construct-irrelevant facet of reading comprehension level. The learners would need to know the criteria on which they are being assessed, for example, whether they must simply write down the correct date and time of their interview or if they are being evaluated in terms of their pronunciation or aspects of their grammar.

To standardize the conditions of the assessment, learners would need to be evaluated separately, and the face validity would be enhanced if they spoke on a telephone. If this is not possible, it would be possible for the teacher/evaluator and learner to sit with their backs to each other, but issues related to how easy it is to understand someone with their back to you would need to be addressed. If the learner and teacher/evaluator are able to see each other, the learner will be able to use non-verbal communication, and this would involve a construct-irrelevant factor and so weaken the validity of the assessment procedure.

TOEFL iBT illustrates how a large-scale proficiency test evaluates lecture comprehension, and most of the factors discussed above would also relate to tests produced by teachers. Teachers might, however, have more flexibility about how the test was implemented. MacDonald et al. (2000) have found that learners engaged more with lectures given by their teacher than with recordings of lectures and preferred topics related to familiar subjects rather than those related to what they were planning to study. A live lecture would also make it easier to integrate a lecture with reading texts and would mean that the teacher could prepare PowerPoint slides to accompany the lecture.

The next stage is to create the test item. For comprehension activities, this will probably be a short answer question or a summary. If the test is used with large numbers of candidates or used on multiple occasions, it may be worth investing the time in creating multiple choice questions. These can be done online through authoring software such as Hot Potatoes (Arneil et al. 2017: 124; Chapelle and Voss 2016) or apps such as Socrative. Multiple choice questions need to be carefully constructed so that they have clear and specific aims and avoid construct irrelevance. If, for example, we wanted to test whether the learners had understood the significance of the reporting verb in:

Hick's equation says that there's a linear relationship between the reaction time and the log of the number of stimulus response alternatives.

we might simply give four alternatives to 'says':

Hick's equation a. suggests b. suggested c. said d. says that there's a linear relationship between the reaction time and the log of the number of stimulus response alternatives.

This item would be open to much criticism. First, the choices or distractors cover tense (suggests versus suggested, said versus says), something which is not relevant to our construct as well the lexical choice, which is relevant. Instead, we might go for

Hick's equation a. suggests b. claims c. says d. states that there's a linear relationship between the reaction time and the log of the number of stimulus response alternatives.

The meaning of 'states' is more or less the same as 'says' and so would make it difficult to know if candidates who chose 'c' had a better understanding of the lecture that those who chose 'd'. Multiple choice questions need to have only one answer, or in testing terminology only one key.

More generally, the candidates can arrive at option 'd' solely by decoding what has been said and, if the aim of the item is to test comprehension as well as decoding, the item would also fail for construct under-representation. It might be better to go for an option such as

The lecturer believes that Hick's equation is a. untrue b. partially untrue c. partially true d true

This illustrates the complexity of writing effective multiple choice items. Table 6.2 provides some advice on wring such items.

Asking candidates to write a summary is a more direct way of testing whether they have understood the lecture. For example, to decide whether some candidates had understood this extract from a lecture on sports science related to the speed at which people react to others' actions, we would need to specify what information should be included in the summary.

Now I've got the ball. I'm walking up towards the penalty spot. I haven't put it down yet. You have no information about my body language cues. But what can you get? Am I left footed am I right footed? If you've seen me play, ok. Am I going to kick with my left foot or am I likely to kick with my right foot? Ok. Have you seen me take a penalty before? Do I always go in the top right corner? You can get information about contextual cues: strengths, weaknesses, their preferences. This is prior knowledge about someone's experience. Your experience, your prior knowledge about that individual is key. These kinds of contextual clues shape your expectations and control the speed of your actions.

The central point of this extract is that prior knowledge of a person influences how quickly you respond to their actions, but the extract also includes information about whether the other person is right- or left-footed or if they prefer to shoot at the top or bottom of the goal. These two pieces of information

Table 6.2 Guidance on writing multiple choice questions

1. Each multiple choice item should have only one answer
2. Only one feature at a time should be tested
3. Each option should be grammatically correct
4. All multiple choice items should be at a level appropriate to the proficiency level of the testee
5. The stem should contain all the information necessary to select the key, but should not contain unnecessary material
6. The key to any item should not give a clue about the key to another item. This often happens in reading tests where multiple items are based on the same text
7. Ensure that the key cannot be selected without reading the stem, or any other textual material upon which the item is based
8. Avoid negatives such as 'not' and 'except' if at all possible, as such questions increase cognitive processing and make the item more difficult
9. Randomize the location of the key. If you don't, you will find that (on average) option (C) will tend to be the key than other options
10. Avoid options that use 'all of the above' or 'none of the above'
11. Avoid using qualifiers such as 'always' or 'never', which are less likely to be in the key than qualifiers like 'sometimes' or 'probably'

Source: Fulcher (2010: 172–3); Heaton (1988: 29–30)

might be included in a set of notes but seem to have less importance. A candidate who just wrote down something about left- or right-footed players might not be judged to have understood the lecture extract. If this extract were used in a test, the test writer would need to identify what points would need to be included and what weighting would be given to these before administering the test. For example, a point about footedness for the left or right side might earn one point, but a point about prior knowledge of a person influencing the speed of the reaction might earn two points.

 Activity 6.3 Writing test items

Here is an extract from a lecture on Hick's law. Figure 6.1 is the PowerPoint slide that was on the screen as the words below were spoken. Write a single multiple choice item to test whether candidates have understood this part of the lecture.

> **L:** OK. So Hick's law, a recap. Does someone want to tell me what Hick's law is? Just an estimation, without cheating and looking at all your notes. Simple statement. What happens to simple reaction time as what? Anyone, yep,
>
> **S:** The time it takes you to respond to a stimulus depends on the number of possible responses.

Hick's law... compatibility

Hick discovered that CRT increases by a constant amount as the number of S–R alternatives doubles.

Choice RT is linearly related to the log of the number of stimulus-response akternatives.

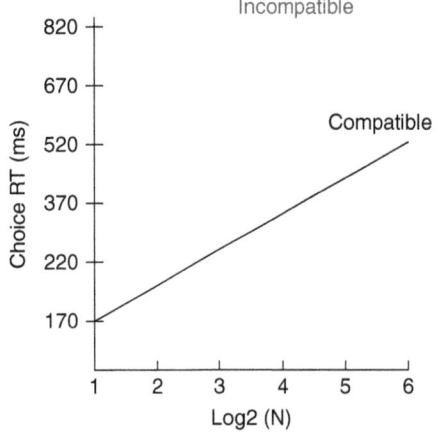

$T=b*\log_2(n+1)$

T= time
b=a constant that
depends on the stimulus
n=the number of choices

Figure 6.1 Slide for Hick's law lecture extract

L: OK. Good. As the stimulus or the number of different stimulus response pairs increases, reaction time increases. The more choices you have the slower your response. OK. Hick also made an equation of this so he worked out an equation so we don't have to. His equation says there's a linear relationship between the reaction time and the log of the number of stimulus response alternatives.

 Activity 6.4 Multiple choice questions

All the items below are problematic in some way. Identify what the problems might be and try to rewrite them. The instructions ask candidates to choose the best answer.

1 You can work out (a) what your opponent is going to do, (b) what is your opponent going to do, (c) what your opponent will do, (d) what will your opponent do.

2 If you want your message to be understood, you (a) can (b) must (c) shall (d) will eschew obfuscation.

3 Sihem did (a)/had (b)/made (c)/took (d) a decision.

4 Very soon the rabbit noticed Alice, as she went hunting about, and called out to her in an angry tone, 'Why, Mary Ann, what ARE you doing out here? Run home this moment, and fetch me a pair of gloves and a fan! Quick, now!' And Alice was so much frightened that she ran off at once in the direction it pointed to, without trying to explain the mistake it had made.

What mistake had the rabbit not made?

a It forgot its fan.

b It thought Mary Anne was Alice.

c It thought Mary Ann was not at home.

d It thought Alice was Mary Ann.

Multiple choice writing software and apps often allow for feedback to be given on answers, and this can be informed by the ideas of dynamic assessment (Poehner et al. 2015). For example, here is an alternative question to the test given in question 4 of Activity 6.4. What mistake had the rabbit made?

a It forgot its fan.

b It thought Mary Anne had its gloves.

c It thought Mary Ann was at home.

d It thought Alice was Mary Ann.

The following feedback would be given:

1 If the first attempt is wrong: This is not the right answer. Read the passage again and have another go.

2 If the second attempt is wrong: Who did the rabbit call out to in the first sentence and what name did he call her by?

3 That is the wrong answer. The right answer is d.

Providing this amount of feedback requires resources, but it would enable a teacher to discriminate between learners who needed more or less support and so could structure follow-up lessons accordingly.

6.5 Backwash and preparing students for language tests

Backwash or washback 'refers to the extent to which the introduction and use of a test influences language teachers and learners to do things that they would not otherwise not do that promote or inhibit language learning' (Messick 1996: 241). While policy-makers may give the impression that changing assessment procedures is an easy way of changing a whole education system, the relationship between testing and teaching is complicated by the number of people involved, particularly teachers and learners, and their variable understanding of what a particular test entails (Alderson and Wall 1993). However, in particular classes and with particular learners preparing for a particular examination, it is possible to see the impact of assessment on teaching and learning.

Many learners come to language classes to prepare for tests, and the results of these tests can have a major impact on the learners, but some teachers have misgivings about such preparation. Haladyna et al. (1991: 4), for example, see designing a curriculum based on a test and the use of commercial materials designed to improve test marks as unethical. Preparing learners for a test might seem to give them an unfair advantage over learners who have not been so well-prepared. In some multiple choice tests, the longest answer is often the correct one, and candidates can be told to use this strategy where they cannot otherwise chose a correct answer, or if wrong answers are not penalized, candidates will be advised to guess the answers to questions they do not know. Similarly, some candidates are thought to commit to memory possible essays which they produce if the title they predicted comes up. These strategies do, in Haladyna et al.'s term, 'pollute' the data the test produces.

However, the issue here is to do with poor test design rather than unethical teaching. A well-designed multiple choice test will not have the longest answer as the key and deducting marks for wrong answers should discourage guessing. Essay writing tasks should not be that predictable, and this may have implications for how often candidates can take and retake tests. More generally, if a syllabus claims to teach the four skills and the test only examines reading and writing, teachers should not be blamed for focusing on reading and writing (Wall and Alderson 1995). The blame belongs to the test designers for construct under-representation. If a test is perfectly designed, the most effective teaching would be to prepare learners for the target language use as specified in the test construct.

Unfortunately, tests are not perfectly designed, and many activities that candidates are required to do in tests – for example, multiple choice questions, fill in the gaps – do not directly reflect the target language use about which the tests should be providing information. This difference between test activities and test construct leads Fulcher (2010: 288) to identify two strands to effective test preparation. The first of these is familiarization with the test format, 'to ensure that the learners do not spend time and effort having to work out what they should be doing during the test'. If a test includes multiple choice items, the teacher should make candidates aware of this format and the scoring system. Where candidates' performances are measured against criteria, they should be aware of what these are, and well-designed tests should make this information available. For example, the Cambridge First Certificate English (2016) test provides information about the four scales for the writing test: content, communicative achievement, organization and language. This familiarity is an important part of test preparation and explains why it is useful to let candidates work through past papers, but, once they are familiar with the test, repeating the process has limited or no benefit.

The other aspect of effective test preparation is helping the learners develop the necessary skills and knowledge they need to carry out the target language use. The test construct provides a target for teachers and learners but does not explain how that construct should be acquired (Fulcher 2010: 282). A test should help teachers decide what they are teaching but will not normally influence how they teach. How they teach should depend partly on the ideas related to assessment for learning and dynamic assessment discussed above but largely on the general pedagogic principles covered in Parts III and IV of this book.

6.6 Summary

This chapter presented testing and assessment as ways of making decisions about learners. The chapter looked at some of the different purposes these decisions relate to and examined how test designers can produce tests which are practical, valid and reliable and so lead to appropriate decisions. The last two sections of the chapter provided advice on how teachers can create their own tests and how they can most effectively prepare their learners for high-stakes tests.

 ## Activity 6.5 Discussion

What would you suggest that the teacher in this context does to design a test to identify which learners have the right skills?

I work in a language school in Vancouver. Many of our learners have part-time jobs in local restaurants but not all of the learners have the necessary language skills to do this well. As we provide the learners with references in support of our learners' job applications, we would like to be sure that the learners will cope with the work in the restaurants. We would like to design a test related to the spoken English that restaurant workers need, but we do not want a test that will take up more than ten minutes per learner.

 ## 6.7 Further reading

The two books I have found most useful on testing are Fulcher (2010) and Green (2014), and these provide some information about statistics. Bachman, on his own and with Palmer, has written three books which provide a solid theoretical basis to assessment policy (Bachman 1990; Bachman and Palmer 1996, 2010), and the third of these is well worth reading. McNamara (McNamara 2000; McNamara and Roever 2006) provides an important reminder that assessment policies can have major social impacts. The videos that accompany this book on the website include several examples of classes teaching EAP, and these may provide you with some insight into how to prepare candidates for examinations such as IELTS and TOEFL iBT.

Part III

The Language Elements

Chapter 7

Pronunciation

7.1 Introduction

The way people speak is the most obvious feature of their speech, and differences in pronunciation can lead to both positive and negative evaluations of a speaker that go beyond their language abilities. At the same time, for many teachers, pronunciation is associated with specialist and opaque terminology which is only distantly connected with actual communication, and so pronunciation, if addressed at all, is dealt with unsystematically. This chapter attempts to address both learners' needs to improve their pronunciation and teachers' desire for 'person-centred learning' (Underhill 2005: vi) by exploring the following questions:

1 What is pronunciation?
2 How do people learn pronunciation?
3 How can teachers best teach pronunciation?

The first question is an attempt to help you think about what aims teachers might adopt for a pronunciation class or a section of a class on pronunciation. The second question addresses how people learn new pronunciations and get better at using the pronunciation they already know. The third question looks at approaches and techniques for teaching pronunciation.

7.2 Understanding pronunciation: what is pronunciation?

The pronunciation of English is an extensive topic. This chapter is an introduction to the field with some suggested reading at the end of the chapter for those who want to develop their knowledge of pronunciation. So this section provides:

1 an introduction to how teachers can identify what models of pronunciation they might chose as a target for their learners; and
2 a description of the most important aspects of English pronunciation.

The chapter does not look at the links between pronunciation and spelling as these are dealt with in Chapter 8.

7.2.1 What varieties should I teach?

When teachers are planning to teach pronunciation, they need to think about what varieties of pronunciation or accents they should be teaching. This can be a difficult decision to make, but the overall aim for learners is to be 'comfortably intelligible' (Kenworthy 1987: 3) when speaking and listening to spoken English, that is, they need to produce speech that is intelligible to the people they are talking to and understand what people say to them. Two main factors need to be considered when identifying the variety or varieties most appropriate for your learners: the reasons for which the learners need English, which will determine who they will speak to, and the resources that are available.

Traditionally, second language learners have been taught native speaker accents of English such as General American (GA) or, what Roach (2010) calls, BBC English (Thomson and Derwing 2015). These are two prestigeous accents in the United States and the UK, respectively. GA is 'the accent of Middle America in both a social and geographical sense' (Pennington 2013: 14) – the accent used by middle-class Americans who come from the geographical centre of the United States. BBC English is more restricted. Hannah and Trudgill, who use the label Received Pronunciation (R.P.), describe it as the only 'genuinely regionless accent within England' (Trudgill and Hannah 2002: 15) but note that it is only used natively by 3–5 per cent of the population of England and that the vowels of BBC English make it 'more difficult for many foreigners to acquire than, say, a Scottish accent' (Trudgill and Hannah 2002: 16). It remains, however, common in much teaching material.

While being able to speak with and understand these accents can be useful for some learners, many learners need to speak other varieties. Sometimes, they need to use the accent that is common in a particular area. Learners going to work in India or Singapore need to learn an accent that is understandable to speakers of English in India or Singapore. Often learners need to communicate with other learners of English, and descriptions of the pronunciation of ELF (Jenkins 2000) now exist. See Chapter 2. The other aspect of what accent learners want to develop relates to how learners intend to present themselves. Learners may wish the people they are communicating with to realize they are not native speakers of English or that they speak ELF rather than another variety.

The second issue in deciding what varieties of pronunciation teachers should teach is the resources available. The primary resource is the teacher and the variety or varieties that the teacher uses. It is very difficult to teach a variety the teacher is not comfortable with, but in some contexts teachers are encouraged to use a particular variety even though it is not one they typically use. So, in a context where a GA accent is considered desirable, teachers who speak other varieties may be encouraged to adopt an American accent. This is not desirable in terms of either teacher motivation or teaching effectiveness.

Teachers may also have access to recordings of different accents. Many published materials focus on GA or BBC English. Online software such as Google Translate and electronic or online dictionaries often use one of these accents, but it is relatively easy to find examples of other native speaker varieties of English or different kinds of EIL online (e.g. Beuckens 2016). If it is difficult to identify the purposes for which a particular group of learners will need English, it makes sense to expose them to a range of accents and let them decide what accent they would like to adopt.

7.2.2 Describing sounds in English

Pronunciation is not at the same level of language as grammar and vocabulary because the relationship between pronunciation and meaning is different from that between grammar or vocabulary and meaning. Morphemes, words and grammatical structures have meaning in a direct way. Individual sounds do not have meanings. For example, neither /e/ nor /t/ means anything on its own. Also pronunciation, unlike other aspects of language, requires fine motor control of muscles in the vocal tract and, for most second language learners, this control is a completely automatic process for the first language.

Another special feature of pronunciation is that it draws on two different areas of linguistics: phonetics (describing how people produce sounds) and phonology (describing how people perceive sounds). Phonetics (a kind of expression in Figure 2.3) is at different level from phonology (a substance), and this is reflected in how the two areas are investigated. Phonetics is a natural science. To find out whether people use their lips when they speak, in technical language whether they can produce bilabial sounds, we would simply observe people when they speak. If you look at yourself in a mirror when you say the name of the capital of Spain, you will see that you use your lips. In phonetic terms, the sound is bilabial. All humans have the same phonetic resources – a tongue, teeth, etc., but these are used differently in different languages, and this is why it is often difficult to learn to speak a new language in the way that expert speakers of the language do.

The phonetic representation of a sound is written in square brackets. So [pin] is a way of representing the word 'pin'. Often this will appear with other marks or diacritics to represent particular features of the pronunciation, so we might represent as [pʰɪn] to show that 'p' in 'pin' is pronounced with aspiration, that is, air is emitted out of the mouth, whereas in 'spin' [spɪn] 'p' is not aspirated and less air is emitted. For most teachers, being able to write phonetic transcripts is not of great importance.

Phonology is to do with the perception of sounds and is more concerned with what people think or understand than what they do. Instead of looking at what people do, phonologists might ask a speaker

Table 7.1 Phonemes of BBC English

Consonants				Vowels (monophthongs)		Vowels (diphthongs)	
p	Pie	ʃ	Shy	ɪ	Sit	ai	Sigh
b	Buy	ʒ	Mea**s**ure	i:	Seat	ei	Say
t	Tie	tʃ	Choke	e	Set	ɔɪ	Soy
d	Die	dʒ	Joke	æ	Sat	iə	Sheer
k	S**k**y	m	My	ɑ:	Start	eə	Share
g	Guy	n	Nose	ʊ	Soot	ʊə	Sure
f	Fly	ŋ	Si**ng**	u:	Suit	aʊ	Shout
v	Vie	w	Why	ɒ	Pot	əʊ	Show
θ	Thigh	r	Rose	ɔ:	Port		
ð	That	l	Lie	ʌ	But		
s	Sigh	j	Your	ə	Wait**er**		
z	Zoo			ɜ:	Bird		
h	How						

of English whether they can hear a difference between 'hit' and 'heat'. Most speakers of English would hear a difference, but this would not be apparent to speakers of many other languages. Similarly, for Spanish speakers the 'r' sound in 'pero' ('but' in English) is different from the 'r' sound in 'perro' ('dog'), but for speakers of many other languages, the two sounds and, so the two words, are the same.

Phonology is particular to a language. A phonological or phonemic transcription of a word appears between back slashes, for example, /bɪn/ is a representation of phonemes of 'bin'. This kind of transcription is more widely used by teachers, and you will find these transcriptions in many dictionaries for learners of English.

Most of the symbols for the phonemes of English are also used in the Roman alphabet. Some other symbols are borrowed from other alphabets, and the pronunciation of the names of these symbols is as follows: θ (theta); ð (eth); ʃ (esh); ʒ (zhe); ŋ (eng); j (yod); æ (ash); ʌ (upside-down v) and ə (shwa).

 Activity 7.1 Describing the sounds of English

The items in this activity should encourage you to think about the individual sounds of English. By the end of this section, you should be able to answer all the questions in this activity, but it will help you to make sense of the rest of the section if you try to answer the questions before you have read the rest of the section.

1 Here is a phonological transcription of the BBC English pronunciation of the start of *Alice in Wonderland* (Carroll and Blum 2008). What would this be in normal English? The back slashes indicate a pause if you read the text aloud. The text starts 'Alice was beginning to get very tired'.

/ˈælɪs wəz bɪˈɡɪnɪŋ tə get ˈveri ˈtaɪəd əv ˈsɪtɪŋ baɪ hə ˈsɪstər ɒn ðə bæŋk/

/ənd əv ˈhævɪŋ ˈnʌθɪŋ tə du/

/wʌns ɔː twaɪs ʃi həd piːpt ˈɪntə ðə bʊk hə ˈsɪstə wəz ˈriːdɪŋ/

/bət ɪt həd nəʊ ˈpɪkʧəz ɔː ˌkɒnvəˈseɪʃənz ɪn ɪt/

/ənd wɒts ðə juːz əv ə bʊk, θɔːt ˈælɪs wɪˈðaʊt ˈpɪkʧəz ɔː ˌkɒnvəˈseɪʃən/

2 Put these sounds in a sequence depending on where you make the sound in your mouth. Start with the sound made furthest back in the mouth and end with the sound made with the lips: b (bee), d (do), g (go), h (hi), ð (that), j (you).

3 Put your finger on your Adam's apple and say the pairs of words below. For each pair, one sound is made with more vibration. Phoneticians describe the sounds made with more vibration as voiced and the other sounds as unvoiced. Write the words in the appropriate column.

(a) sink – zink	(b) fast – vast	(c) din – tin
(d) beat – Pete	(e) choke – joke	(f) core – gore

Unvoiced	Voiced

4 Look at yourself in a mirror while you say the following pairs of words and decide if (i) you say the word with your lips more rounded or spread or (ii) you make them with your tongue near the front or the back of your mouth:

(a)   show   (b)   foot   (c)   feet   (d)   ship.

	Lips spread	Lips rounded
Tongue at the front of the mouth		
Tongue and the back of the mouth		

Not all boxes will have words in them. What does this suggest about the link between tongue and lip position in English? Are other combinations of tongue and lip positions possible in other languages you speak?

7.2.3 Segmental phonology: individual sounds

The production and perception of consonants and vowels are described as segmental phonology/phonetics. This section describes how the consonants and vowels of English are produced in the variety sometimes known as BBC English or R.P. This is a variety of English which, as noted above, is not very widely spoken, but it has been very well described so it is better to see this as an illustration of how you might describe the phonetics/phonology of a language variety rather than an explanation of how to pronounce English. However, the consonants of English are reasonably consistent between different accents. Even if you are more familiar with other accents of English, the description of consonants should be fairly accurate for those accents. Jenkins (2007) sees all the consonants of BBC English as necessary for easy comprehensibility except for the two dental sounds, usually represented in writing by 'th', and Celce-Murcia et al. (2010: 109) note that the two dental sounds have a low functional load, that is, they do not serve to distinguish many words so they may not be very important in non-ELF contexts.

Consonants

To describe the consonants of English, three dimensions are needed:

1 whether the vocal chord vibrates or not (voicing);

2 where in the mouth the sounds are made (place of articulation); and

3 how the sounds are made (manner of articulation).

If you put your fingers on your Adam's apple when you make the sound [z] and then the sound [s], you should feel a vibration for [z] but not [s]. This vibration is voicing, and the sounds [s] and [z] only differ by this. English has several pairs of consonants which are differentiated by voicing. Table 7.2 gives these pairings, and this also contains the answers to the third part of Activity 7.1

The second dimension needed to describe consonants is place of articulation. Phoneticians need greater degree of precision in the terms they use than are common in everyday, and so they use specialist terminology. These terms may seem abstruse, but they are needed for an accurate description of the geography of the mouth. The best way to become familiar with where the sounds are made is to try making different sounds and feel how the different parts of the mouth are being used to create sounds. Those who are able to speak languages other than English will be able to investigate the differences in the consonants in English and in other languages.

The second part of Activity 7.1 asked you to put the following six sounds in order depending on where they were made in the mouth: (bee), d (do), g (go), h (hi), th (that), y (you). The sequence should be: [b], [ð], [d], [j], [h].

The third dimension needed to describe consonants is the manner of articulation. There are three main ways of producing consonants. A plosive (sometimes known as a stop) is produced by blocking

Table 7.2 Voiced and unvoiced consonants

Voiced	b	d	g	dʒ	v	ð	z	ʒ
Unvoiced	p	t	k	tʃ	f	θ	s	ʃ

Table 7.3 Place of articulation of consonants of BBC English

Bilabial	With the lips	p, b, m, w
Labiodental	Lips and teeth	f, v
Dental	Tongue touching the teeth	θ, ð
Alveolar	Tongue on the ridge behind the teeth	t, d, s, z, n, l
Post-alveolar	Tongue on the hard part of the roof of the mouth behind the alveolar ridge	tʃ, dʒ, ʃ, ʒ, r
Post-palatal	Tongue on the boundary between the hard and soft part of the roof of the mouth	j
Velar	Tongue on the soft part of the roof of the mouth	k, g, ŋ
Glottal	In the throat	h

the air passage and then releasing it in a small explosion. When [p] or [b] is produced, the lips are closed and pressure is built up and then released. The sounds [t] and [d] are produced in a similar way, but the blockage is created by the tongue pressing against the alveolar ridge. Nasal sounds are made by pushing the air through the nose rather than the mouth. When [m] is produced, the air moves through the nasal passage and, unlike [p], the lips do not open. The third main manner of articulation is fricative. This is where there is no complete blockage and, as a result, the fricative sounds such as [s] or [z] can be extended in a way the plosives such as [t] or [d] cannot.

It is possible to combine the explosion of a plosive or stop with the continuity of the fricatives in two sounds [tʃ] and [dʒ], and this is reflected in the fact that both these sounds are written as combinations of stops [t] [d] and fricatives [ʃ] [ʒ].

The final grouping of consonants in terms of manner of articulation is approximants: [w], [l], [r] and [j]. These are sounds produced by bringing two parts of the mouth together but not interfering with air flow. These sounds are produced in a more fluid way than other consonants. This fluidity can be illustrated with /l/. In the word 'lull', the first and second 'l' are pronounced very differently but still count as the same phoneme. This fluidity is reflected in the fact that some phoneticians describe approximants as semi-consonants and semi-vowels (Pennington 2013: 47).

Table 7.4 summarizes the description of the consonants of English.

Vowels

BBC English has eleven simple vowels or monophthongs and eight glides or diphthongs, where creating the sounds involves moving from the place where one simple vowel is made to the place where a second simple phoneme is produced.

The simple vowels can be described in terms of where in the mouth they are made. Vertically, vowels can be made at the top of the mouth, for example, [iː] in 'sheep'; the middle, for example, [e] in 'bet'; and the bottom, for example, [æ] in 'cat'.

Horizontally, sounds are made at the front of the mouth, for example, [e] in 'bet'; centre, for example, [ɜː] in 'bird'; or back, for example, [ɔː] in 'port'. See Figure 7.1 for an indication of where in the mouth the tongue is typically placed. When these sounds are produced, the lips are also affected, the front vowels typically made with the lips spread and the back vowels with the lips rounded.

Table 7.4 Consonants of BBC English

Place → Manner↓	Bilabial	Labiodental	Dental	Alveolar	Post-alveolar	Post-palatal	Velar	Glottal
Plosive/stop	p/b			t/d			k/g	
Nasal	m			n			ŋ	
Affricative					tʃ /dʒ			
Fricative		f/v	θ/ð	s/z	ʃ/ʒ			h
Approximant	w			l	r	j		

Source: Adapted from Roach (2010: passim)

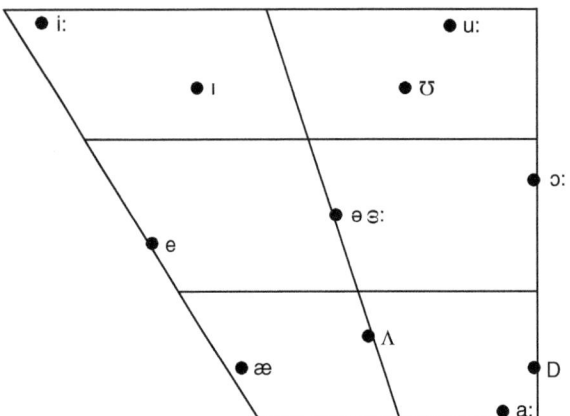

Figure 7.1 The simple vowels of BBC English (Roach 2004: 242)

Most descriptions of the vowels of BBC English use the length of vowels symbolized by a colon (:) as an indication of length. So we have the following pairs:

Top and front	[ɪ] ship	[i:] sheet
Bottom and front/back	[æ] cat	[ɑ:] cart
Middle and centre	[ə] alone	[ɜ:] word
Top and back	[ʊ]look	[u:] Luke
Middle/bottom and back	[ɒ] cot	[ɔ:] caught

The pairing of long and short vowels is not as neat as the voiced/unvoiced pairs for consonants, and it is important to note that the difference between these pairs is not just a difference in length. Indeed, Wang and Munro (2004) found that the quality of vowels was more salient than its length. So [ɒ] as in cot is produced at the bottom of the mouth unlike [ɔ:] which is produced half-way up the mouth. It would be possible to produce a description of the vowels without introducing length. Jenkins (2002) found that vowel length was important for comprehensibility in ELF.

The eight diphthongs of BBC English fall into three groups depending on whether the second half of the glide is /ə/, /i/ and /ʊ/. The diphthongs ending in shwa /ə/ are less important than the others because in many varieties of English they are pronounced with /r/ rather than /ə/, for example, dear which is pronounced /diə/ in BBC English is pronounced /dɪr/ in GA (Trudgill and Hannah 2002).

7.2.4 Suprasegmental speech

Suprasegmental speech covers stretches of language longer than individual phonemes such as syllable structure, changes to speech that happen when it is continuous, word stress, sentence stress and intonation.

Syllable structure

Individual sounds combine to form syllables. Languages have different rules about how to form a syllable. The simplest syllable in English consists of one vowel, for example, 'are' /a:/. English also has a small number of syllables without vowels where there is a syllabic consonant like the final 'l' in 'little' /litl/ or the 'n' in 'didn't' /didnt/. These are written phonetically with a line under the consonant, for example, [lit̩].

Aside from these syllabic consonants, syllables in English must contain a vowel. English limits what can appear in different parts of the syllable. For example, a syllable cannot start with /ŋ/ or end with /h/. This is an area where English is changing. Until recently, syllables did not start with /ʒ/, but borrowed words like 'genre' and 'Jaques' now start with this sound. Also the rules vary between accents. One of the most striking features of BBC English is that /r/ cannot appear at the end of a syllable. In BBC English, 'bar' is pronounced /ba:/. This feature had led to BBC English being described as non-rhotic, that is, without 'r'. Many varieties of English are rhotic, and Jenkins (2000) suggests that pronouncing the /r/ in words like 'bar' leads to more comprehensible speech in ELF.

English allows for a syllable which has up to three consonants at the start of the syllable (e.g. 'splints'/splints/), a vowel and then up to four consonants at the end (Pennington 1996), for example, 'twelfths' /twelfθs/ but, in practice, English allows no more than six consonants in a syllable, but this is much more than in other languages.

Word stress

Where a word has more than one syllable, one syllable will be stressed more than the other(s). This is often indicated by /'/ in dictionaries. So 'student' would be represented as /'stju:dənt/ to indicate that the first syllable is stressed and 'decide' as /dɪs'aid/ to indicate the second syllable is stressed. Stress here is a phonological term relating to how words are perceived. Phonetically, stress may mean that one syllable is louder, longer or lower-pitched than its neighbouring syllable or any combination of these three features (Underhill 2005: 52). Generally, unstressed syllables have a shwa /ə/, short /ɪ/, short /ʊ/ or a syllabic consonant.

Even where a word has three syllables, there is usually only one stressed syllable. 'Decision' would have the stress on its second syllable, and the two other syllables would be unstressed. However, it is possible to have three levels of stress in a word, so 'pronunciation' is written phonologically as /prə,nʌnsɪ'eiʃən/, indicating that the main or primary stress is on '-a(tion)' and the secondary stress is on '-nunc' and the other syllables are not stressed.

Word stress is not easily predictable. Celce-Murcia et al. (2010) identify two general rules. First, words of Germanic origin such as father, elbow and hammer are stressed on their first syllable. Second, words with affixes are stressed on the first syllable of the root words. So the prefix 'de-' means that 'decide' and 'decision' are stressed on their second syllable, and the prefix 'bene-' means 'beneficiary' is stressed on its third syllable. 'Threaten' and 'friendship' are stressed on their first syllable rather than on the suffixes '-en' and '-ship'. These are not universal rules, and one important exception to the affix rule is that suffixes borrowed from French are often stressed, for example, questionnaire, volunteer, balloon and cassette. A second complication is that some suffixes change the stress pattern of the root word, so we have groups of words such as

Photograph	/'fəʊtəgrɑːf/
Photography	/fə'təgrəfɪ/
Photographic	/fəʊtə'græfɪk/

The importance of word stress in ensuring comprehensibility is the subject of debate. Native and non-native speakers of English find that two-syllable words which are normally stressed on the first syllable are difficult to understand when they are stressed on the second syllable, for example, /'stjuːdənt/ being pronounced as /stjʊ'dent/ (Field 2005) but not when the change was in the other direction, for example, when 'decide' is pronounced as /'diːɪsid/ rather than /dɪs'aid/. More generally, Jenkins (2002) does not see word stress as part of the ELF common core, so the importance of word stress is probably best decided by what happens with a particular group of learners.

Continuous speech: changing phonemes and rhythm

Producing a word in continuous speech often leads to modification of the pronunciation. For example, saying a word with a complicated syllable structure like 'twelfths' requires considerable effort and often it will be pronounced as /twelfs/ without /θ/. The elision of a consonant is common in all but the most deliberate speech. 'Next' is often pronounced /neks/ rather than /nekst/. Elision is more usual in consonant clusters at the end of the syllable. It would be very unusual for 'splints' to be pronounced as /spɪnts/ or /slɪnts/ but /splɪns/ is common. O'Neal (2015) found that consonant deletion reduced comprehensibility.

Sounds may also be changed through assimilation. This can be illustrated historically. For example, the prefix 'in' in 'insufficient' has become 'im' in 'impossible' because the influence of the bilabial /p/ has led to /n/ being transformed to /m/. Similarly, the 'n' in 'bank' is pronounced as the velar /ŋ/ because of the following /k/. These two examples have become part of the standard pronunciation, but this phenomenon is widespread in continuous speech. An expression such as 'tin pot' will usually be pronounced as 'tim pot'. When speakers are pronouncing the /n/ in 'tin', their vocal tract is preparing to produce the bilabial sound /p/ and this results in a bilabial nasal sound or /m/.

Vowels can also be elided. The elision of 'o' in 'not' is recognized in the spelling of 'didn't', but also words like 'suppose' can be pronounced /spəʊz/. More often vowels are reduced to either /ɪ/ or /ə/. This is particularly true of function words. So 'she' /ʃiː/ and 'of' /ɒv/ are usually pronounced /ʃɪ/ and /əv/. Some words have a range of pronunciations so 'you' may be /juː/, /jʊ/ or /jə/ depending on how important they are in a particular utterance.

Some of these variations also occur in other languages so in Spanish the /n/ in 'Un beso' (a kiss) is often labialized into an /m/ because of the following /b/. Unfortunately, other languages have different kinds of variations. In German so the /n/ in 'geben' (give) is sometimes pronounced /m/ because it assimilates to the preceding sound of /b/.

Elision helps the regularity of English rhythm (Celce-Murcia et al. 2010: 164). In a sentence such as 'Who is to give the prizes?' there would be sentence stresses on 'who', 'give' and 'prizes', and the other words would be reduced or unstressed /hʊz tə gɪv ðə ˈpraɪzəz/. The pattern in this sentence is very regular with a strong syllable followed by a weak syllable.

The rhythm is not always as regular. In 'the prizes are on the table', 'prizes' and 'table' are stressed, but 'are', 'on' and 'the' would be unstressed and this is reflected in the use of weak vowels on these words /ðə ˈpraɪzəz ər ən ðə ˈteɪbəl/.

This flexibility is sometimes described by saying that English is a stress-timed language unlike languages which have more regular rhythms such as French and Chinese. Such languages are said to be syllable-timed. The claim is that in a syllable-timed language each syllable takes about the same amount of time to be pronounced, whereas in stress-timed languages there is more variation with gaps between stressed syllables being more equal. However, Roach (1982) found no difference in syllable length between languages classified as syllable- or stress-timed. Differences in rhythm between English and other languages are best explained in terms of the features discussed above, for example, syllable structure, word stress and the use of short vowels (Cauldwell 1996).

Sentence or tonic stress and intonation

Stress also operates at sentence level. A sentence like 'We went to Madrid last summer' will be stressed differently depending on which element in the answer is new information to the listener.

1   Where did you go last summer? We went to MADRID last summer.

2   When did you go to Madrid? We went to Madrid last SUMMER.

3   Are you going to Madrid this summer? We went to Madrid LAST summer.

However, the unit here is often less than a sentence and in the intonation literature (Beaken 2009; Brazil 1997; Thompson 2003) the unit is often described a tone unit. So a sentence such as 'one day a big black crow found a large lump of meat' might be spoken as three tone units, each with its own stressed or prominent syllable: one DAY; a big black CROW; found a large lump of MEAT (Beaken 2009: 351). The stressed or prominent syllable will be said with a particular intonation depending on whether the speakers sees the information as something the listeners will know or not. So DAY and CROW might be said with a rising intonation to indicate that they are part of shared information and MEAT would be said with falling intonation because this is something new.

7.3 Learning pronunciation

Two main factors impact on how learners improve their pronunciation. The first of these is our general understanding of how learning happens (Chapter 3) and the second is what learners bring to the classroom in terms of linguistic knowledge and attitudes to English.

7.3.1 Theories of learning and pronunciation

All the theories of learning covered in Chapter 3 can be applied to learning pronunciation. However, the most useful one is the cognitive group of theories. In particular the idea that learning involves learners developing declarative knowledge and then proceduralizing that knowledge implies that learning pronunciation needs to start with learners listening to spoken English so that they can notice the features of their target variety before they try to pronounce those features. Most learners find it easier to notice differences in meaning rather than linguistic features like whether a sound is produced by contact between the teeth and lips (i.e. labiodental sounds such as [f] and [v]) or the tongue and lips (dentals sounds such as [θ] and [ð]). Pronunciation needs to be embedded in a meaningful context such as the difference between /fin/ and /θin/ so that learners can understand what distinctions are meaningful in English. Phonology and perception come before phonetics and production.

This is not to say that learners may not find phonetic descriptions of sounds or phonological transcriptions a useful form of what sociocultural approaches would describe as scaffolding at some points in the learning process but that these are not good starting points. A second important notion for pronunciation learning that comes from sociocultural views is the notion of accommodation (Matsumoto 2011) where the pronunciation of two people engaged in conversation will tend to become more similar. Trofimovich investigated the impact of accommodation on learning about word stress in communicative activities which involved the use of three- and four-syllable English academic words with the stress on the second syllable (e.g. *consider, intelligent*). This is an extract from one activity (Trofimovich 2016: 415):

A: Depression is often deTECted among teens with stable families, many friends, and appreciate ('appropriate') social behaviours. These teenagers hold their depression until sym . . . symptoms became extremely sever ('severe').
B: Many people have the asSUMption that extra weight caused by stripping . . . err . . . skipping breakfast.
A: True?
B: Yes, true.

Speaker B here produced the correct stress pattern on 'assumption' after hearing this pattern in the way A said 'detected'. Students produced correct stress patterns in three and four syllable words more than twice as often when they had been exposed to another student producing the correct stress pattern.

7.3.2 What learners bring to the pronunciation class

Second language learners bring their knowledge of their first language as well as a sense of how they might relate to English and this will have a major impact on how they learn to pronounce English.

Learners will start by hearing English through what Trubetzkoy (1969) described as the 'phonological sieve' of their first language so a knowledge of the phonology of the first language is necessary to support learners as they develop their English pronunciation. The pronunciation of the learners' first language can be described using the same framework that we used for English. In terms of segmental features, they will be able to recognize and produce the phonemes of their first language so speakers of the languages have a nasal bilabial phoneme /m/ will need little instruction to learn to pronounce an English /m/. However, speakers of languages do not have, say, the dental sounds /θ/ and /ð/ will find this pairing difficult to acquire. There are also problems where language may have the same phonemes but with phonetic differences. So French makes a distinction between /p/ and /b/ which is similar to the distinction in English but, whereas in English an initial /p/ as in 'Paris' is aspirated, that is, produced with a puff of air, in French it is not and this can lead to the French /p/ being heard as a /b/ in English ears. A native speaker of French who says 'pear' may be heard as saying 'bear'.

Suprasegmental issues also arise. In many languages, word stress is much more predictable than it is in English and the weakening of vowels is very rare. So many French learners of English will expect 'student' to be stressed on its second syllable because stress on the final syllable is common in French and the same feature of French may also lead to students having difficulty in identifying word boundaries.

Languages also have different rules about syllable structure. So, while English allows the initial consonant cluster /sk/, Spanish and Malay do not and so the cognates of 'school' in those languages 'escuela' and 'sekolah' respectively, add an extra syllable so that the /s/ and /k/ are separated. Speakers of these languages may produce non-standard pronunciations of words such as 'sky'. Similarly, Japanese syllables tend to end in a vowel and this will lead to learners inserting sounds in English words in ways that may make their speech less comprehensible.

Rhythm and intonation also differ. In Mandarin, tone is phonological and a change in tone can change the word for mother into the word for horse. Speakers of Mandarin who are learning English will need to learn that in English tone operates at a suprasegmentally level and in particular will need help using intonational patterns over units longer than the word. Teachers who regularly teach speakers of particular languages will benefit from an understanding of the ways those languages are pronounced.

Learners do not just bring their knowledge to the classroom and various learner variables have been seen as related to effective learning. Age is a particular focus. The critical period hypothesis (Flege 1987; Singleton 2005) suggests that there is biological window for language learning. Learners who start learning a second language after puberty often struggle to attain native-like pronunciation (Moyer 2013). This claim is problematic for at least two reasons. First, the evidence is mixed and a small number of learners who start learning English after puberty seem to be able to achieve a native-like pronunciation which suggests that this is not a purely biological phenomenon. Learning to pronounce a new language is influenced by a very wide range of factors and so drawing any firm conclusion from the research is extremely difficult. Second, learners of English may aspire to use any number of native or non-native accents of English and this means judgments about the success of the learning process are complex (Moyer 2015).

A better approach to understanding the learning of pronunciation comes from the concepts of motivation and identity. An individual's pronunciation of English is an important marker of who they are and many learners use 'their L1 accent as a means of expressing their own identity in English rather than identifying it with its L1 English users' (Jenkins 2002: 125). Equally, learners in an Anglophone context may be motivated by the desire not to be different from their English speaking friends and so seek out the opportunities to develop native accents of English. 'If you aren't really proficient with the language or you have a strong accent it's probably true that it's harder to make contacts' (Moyer 2015: 6).

A final factor to bear in mind about pronunciation is learner anxiety. For some learners speaking in a foreign language can be very stressful and it is important that learners do not develop a fear of speaking in English.

7.4 Teaching pronunciation

Pronunciation is a very personal matter so it is important that teachers take account of learners' views. Moyer (2015: 12) suggests that, where possible, learners should be involved in identifying how they will use language and use that as a way of deciding specific pronunciation goals as well as citing the types of pronunciation activities they most enjoy

Teachers rarely devote whole lessons to pronunciation and many teachers lack training in teaching pronunciation (Henderson et al. 2012) so pronunciation is often taught in a problem-solving way, where the teacher responds to a particular problem that comes up in a communicative activity in a way that parallels task based learning (Chapter 3) or focus on form. This approach has much to commend it because it embeds pronunciation in a communicative context but Henderson's work suggests that it may lead to a focus on the more obvious segmental issues and so may need to be supplemented with a teacher initiated programme which would be based on some analysis of the learners' languages, using something like the framework for describing pronunciation in the section 'What is pronunciation'. It is also possible to embed particular pronunciation points within more communicative activities as Trofimovich (2016), discussed above, did with word stress and Saito and Lyster (2012) incorporated work on /r/ and /l/ within a teaching on argumentative skills by including words with these phonemes in the language they used to set up the argument task.

Reactive pronunciation episodes are often limited to the learners repeating something that the teacher wrote or a demonstration of the articulation of a problematic phoneme. However, a greater degree of structure is also possible. Pennington (2013: 225) makes a suggestion which parallels the PPP or AAA approach to lesson design. See Chapter 8. This starts with an activity designed to make the learners aware of a feature of English pronunciation, a period of practice with varying degrees of freedom and a final 'discussion of the students' real life issues or concerns'. These activities might be distributed over a series of lessons.

7.4.1 Awareness of pronunciation

The language that is used to describe the pronunciation of a language is quite technical and is probably not directly usable in the classroom except with very metacognitively aware learners but should inform much pronunciation teaching. A more practical approach is to focus on awareness.

Table 7.5 A set of minimal pairs

/t/	/θ/
Mats	Maths
Part	Path
Tank	Thank
Tin	Thin
Taught	Thought

Table 7.6 A minimal pair sequence

Word 1	Word 2	Number of fingers that learners hold up
Mats	Maths	2
Part	Part	1
Thank	Thank	1
Tin	Thin	2
Thought	Thought	1

A common approach to awareness raising is based on the concept of the minimal pair. If learners' difficulty understanding or producing the difference between 'mats' and 'maths' is causing communication problems, teachers would need to develop a set of four or five minimal pairs for /t/ and /θ/. A minimal pair is a pair of words which only differ by one phoneme, for example, /mæts and /mæθs/ or /pɑːt/ and /pɑːθ/.

The teacher would then say a word and either say the word again (e.g. mats and mats) or its minimal pair (e.g. mats and maths). The learners would then indicate whether they had heard one word said two times by holding up one finger or two different words by holding up two fingers. The teacher would continue with the other minimal pairs either saying the same word twice or two different words. So you might get a sequence as in Table 7.6.

This can be followed up by the teacher saying one word and the students holding up a finger to show whether it contains the sound /t/ or the sound /θ/. It is also possible to get learners to say the words either to the whole class or to a single partner. Minimal pairs can also be used in games such as Bingo.

Minimal pairs can be used for other aspects of pronunciation such as word stress. So it possible to create a set of minimal pairs of words who differ in terms of stress (e.g. 'refuse and re'fuse) and versions of this kind of activity can be done where students have to decide if a word they hear is stressed on the first ('student) or second (de'cide) syllable.

Activities combining awareness raising and production can be constructed for aspiration. (Celce-Murcia et al. 2010: 86) describes an activity which relates to the fact that word-initial unvoiced consonants are aspirated and their voiced pairs are not. Teachers would hold a lighted match or piece of paper in front of their mouth when saying the following pairs of words

	/p/ /b/	/t/ /d/	/k/ /g/
Aspiration	Pat	Tan	Cave
No aspiration	Bat	Dan	Gave

The word with an unvoiced initial vowel, for example, pat is produced with a puff of air and this should make the flame or paper flutter. The words with voiced initial consonants are not aspirated and so there should be not be a puff of air. The students can try this with just their hands in front of their mouths and see if they can feel the difference.

Activity 7.2 Minimal pairs

1 Find five minimal pairs for i. /r/ and /l/; ii. /e/ and /æ/; iii. /ɒ/ and /ɔː/.

2 Along the lines of the aspiration activity above (Celce-Murcia et al. 2010), what difference would be visible if someone silently mouthed the words 'mum' and 'numb'? Can you identify any other minimal pairs where their difference can be identified when the words are silently mouthed?

Speech recognition technology has great potential for helping learners to become aware of the similarities and differences between their own and their target pronunciation but, at the time of writing, it is difficult to evaluate different technologies. Brett (2004) used a free publically available program called PRAAT (www.praat.org) to give feedback to his learners on their vowel production. He chose this software because it is freely available and can be modified by the user. He found the program useful but that the feedback needed to be faster to help learn development. Wang and Young (2015) found that automatic speech recognition software designed by the National Tsing Hua University helped both adult and young learners to improve their pronunciation over an eight week course. Whipple et al. (2015) used Adobe Flash and software jointly created by the Dublin Institute of Technology to create a representation of sentence stress in a library of recorded utterances as in Figure 7.2.

Many teachers find that phonemic symbols such as the BBC English version in Table 7.1 can be used to make learners more aware of the different sounds of their target variety. This also provides learners with a useful tool when they are using their dictionaries. Underhill and Casey (2011) have produced an app which can be used by learners and teacher to become more familiar with phonemic symbols and Underhill (2005) provides many examples of how to use phonemic script in the classroom.

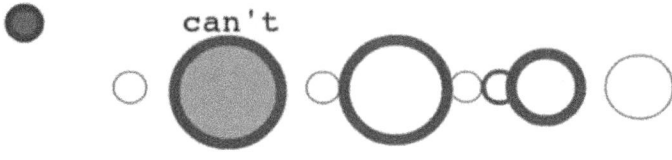

Figure 7.2 Syllable circles (Whipple et al., 2015)

7.4.2 Practising pronunciation

Practising pronunciation can be an embarrassing for learners. Their mistakes are very public so it is important that teachers handle pronunciation practice sensitively. Choral work, where all the learners are speaking together, group work, where they have a smaller audience, or one-to-one interaction with the teacher minimize the learners' possible loss of face. Many learners now have access to ways of recording their own voices and find this a useful way of practising pronunciation (Ducate and Lomicka 2009) whether their teachers get to hear the recordings or not. In Chinese universities, it is common to see English learners reading aloud in public but to no audience as a way of practicing their pronunciation.

The most common method of pronunciation practice is probably learners repeating what teachers say (Murphy 2011). This can be a useful activity if used sensitively and not overused. Other repetition activities can be beneficial. Getting students to repeat minimal pairs after the teacher can help them get used to making particular phonemes and can be embedded in sentences (That's the wrong path/part) to make them more realistic. English has many tongue twisters which can be used to practice different aspects of pronunciation. Tongue twisters such as 'She sell sea shells by the sea shore' incorporate many instances of the same sound in a form that many learners enjoy repeating

The following poem for children can be used to practice the /r/ /l/ contrast:

Row, row, row your boat

Swiftly down the stream

Merrily, merrily, merrily, merrily

Life is but a dream.

Pennington (2013: 266) suggests that learners could work on a poem like this in a group of four with each learner being given one line, which they then memorize. The learners then say their line to the group and try to work out what the best order would be for the whole poem.

Many teachers have a set of poems and tongue twisters that they use on a regular basis.

Reading aloud can also be used to help develop pronunciation. Beaken (2009) argues that this is particularly true for intonation. Before reading learners can identify the tone units and identify information that the reader would want to mark as known or unknown.

Controlled communicative activities can also incorporate particular pronunciation elements. Tables 7.7 and 7.8 are sample sheets for /l/ and /r/ but these can be adapted for different aspects of

Table 7.7 Describe and draw worksheet 1

Q: What is Luke's favourite colour?
A: Blue

	Rory	**Luke**	**Harry**	**Billy**	**Your partner**
Colour	Blue		Brown		
Sport	Football		Rugby		
Food	Ice cream		Lollipops		

Table 7.8 Describe and draw worksheet 2

Q: What is Rory's favourite colour?
A: Blue

	Rory	Luke	Harry	Billy	Your partner
Colour		Red		Yellow	
Sport		Rounders		Lacrosse	
Food		Chocolate		Brownies	

pronunciation and level of student. The learners work in pairs and one person in each pair is given sheet 1 and the other is given sheet 2. They then ask their partners questions to enable them to fill in the blanks on their chart. These sheets include the first question each learner should ask and also have a column so that they can ask each other about their own favourite colours, etc. but this kind of activity can be organized differently.

Similar activities can be designed using describe and draw activities based on the pronunciation problems that particular classes face.

Underhill (2005: 202–3) describes an integrative activity called the 'humane dictation'. The students chose or write a text for the dictation. They read the text and identify any mistakes they think they might make with the dictation and estimate how many mistakes they will make. Underhill suggests that learners' names and estimates of numbers of mistakes be written on the board. The text is removed from the learners and read aloud by the teacher, or a student, phrase by phrase, trying to maintain the conventions of connected speech. Teachers will need to adapt their speed to their learners at this stage to ensure that learners are largely successful. The learners then check their version against the text and write the number of mistakes against their original prediction. This should lead to a discussion of why they over or underpredicted. Then learners identify their 'best' mistake and try to explain why they made this mistake.

7.5 Summary

This chapter looked at the teaching of pronunciation and tried to do three main things: provide an introduction to the description of pronunciation, discuss how people learn grammar, and look at some of the strategies a teacher might adapt for the teaching of pronunciation. Following Celce-Murcia et al. (2010: 284–8), the chapter tried to help you to be able to do the following:

1 Know your learners' aims and current abilities
2 Help learners to become aware of specific pronunciation features
3 Practice these features individually and in group with a general movement from controlled to freer activities
4 Provide appropriate and sensitive feedback

This chapter has not looked at real-life communicative activities, but most of the activities included in Chapter 11 can either be used as they are or adapted to address particular aspects of communication (Trofimovich 2016).

Activity 7.3 Discussion

What would you suggest that the teacher in this context does to help the student improve their pronunciation?

I teach in a private institution in northeast India, helping students prepare for undergraduate study in the Australia, Canada, UK and the United States. A small group of students have a good command of English but speak with strong Indian accents. They are concerned that this will cause problems for them when they are in the UK. My own experience as an Indian in the UK leads me to think that the main problems related to this are not to do with lectures and seminars but informal interaction with British and International student and with those outside academic, for example, shopkeepers and waiters. I want to prepare these students to cope with these kinds of communication.

 ## 7.6 Further reading

The two books which I have found most useful for the teaching of pronunciation are Celce-Murcia et al. (2010) and Underhill (2005). Pennington (2013) offers a good description of phonology and phonetics and their application to the classroom. Jenkins (2007) discusses the issues of identifying and pronunciation particular for ELF speakers, something which is also relevant for learners with different aims. For a description of English (primarily British English) for linguistic rather than pedagogic purposes, I would suggest you read Roach (2010).

Chapter 8

Spelling

8.1 Introduction

Spelling does not get very much attention when English is taught to second language speakers. Stirling (2005: 263) says, 'I have heard vocabulary, writing, and pronunciation all described at some time as the Cinderella of language teaching, but my nomination for the most neglected drudge of all Cinderellas goes to spelling.' A piece of writing that is misspelt often leads to very negative judgments about the author, and most learners of English need to learn to spell, so the lack of attention is surprising. Perhaps this reflects an assumption that English spelling is illogical. 'Fish' could equally be spelt 'ghoti' where 'gh' stands for /f/ as in 'enough'; 'o' stands for /ɪ/ as in the first syllable of 'women'; and 'ti' stands for /ʃ/ as in 'nation' (Mayer 1874). The process of learning is also unclear with long-standing debates over whether spelling is taught or caught (Peters 1985), and many people have memories of being taught rules like 'i before e except after c', which combine memorability with uncertain functionality. This chapter seeks to provide a more solid basis for pedagogy by addressing three questions:

1 What is spelling?
2 How do people learn to spell?
3 How can teachers help learners to spell better?

8.2 Understanding English spelling: what is spelling?

Writing systems develop as ways of representing the spoken language, so understanding English spelling is largely to do with the relationship between spoken and written English. English has adopted a phonographic writing system, that is, one where the symbols, the letters of the alphabet, represent sounds (Sampson 2015: 24). Other writing systems, and in particular Chinese, are logographic or morphographic, so the single symbol 人 represents the word or morpheme 'ren' or 'human' in English. Numbers in English use a parallel system, so the symbol '1' stands for the word 'one' or /wun/. English is predominantly phonographic, but it has some logographic elements or, more precisely, some morphographic elements. Both phonographic and logographic elements are discussed below under the headings of consonants, vowels and morphemes.

The Roman alphabet is used by several languages, and the link between spelling and pronunciation differs in these languages. To illustrate this, Figure 8.1 contains equivalent sentences in Spanish

Spanish	L	a		o	r	t	o	g	r	a	ph	i	a		e	s		f	a	c	i	l
	l	a		o	r	t	o	ɣ	r	a	f	i	a		e	z		f	a	θ	i	l

French	L'	o	r	th	o	g	r	a	phe		est		f	a	c	i	le
	l	ɔ	ʁ	t	ɔ	g	ʁ	a	f		e		f	a	s	i	l

English	S	p	e	ll	i	ng		i	s		ea	s	y
	s	p	e	l	ɪ	ŋ		ɪ	z		iː	z	ɪ

Figure 8.1 Phonological transcription of three languages

('La ortografía es facil'), French ('L'orthographe est facile) and English ('spelling is easy'). The transcriptions are written with different conventions because the phonemes of the three languages are different. So /ʁ/ in French is not quite the same as /r/ in English. In Spanish each letter stands for one phoneme, except for the two letter combinations, or digraph 'ph' which represents one sound /f/. French has several digraphs and trigraphs which represent one sound 'th', 'phe', 'est' and 'le' as does English with 'll', 'ng' and 'ea'. The close link between spelling and pronunciation in Spanish means it is described as having a shallow orthography, while both English and French are said to have deep orthographies.

8.2.1 Consonants

The Roman alphabet has twenty-two consonant letters (including 'y'), and BBC English has twenty-four consonant phonemes. This mismatch creates some problems. However, many English consonants typically represent their corresponding phoneme, for example, 'b' generally stands for the phoneme /b/. The letters 'b', 'd', 'h', 'k', 'l', 'm', 'p', 'r', 'v', 'w', 'y', 'z' and, 'f' if 'of', pronounced /ov/, is excluded generally represent the sounds they would be expected to represent. Where these can be doubled (e.g. 'bb' but not *'hh') they represent the same sound. 'J' does not represent the visually equivalent phoneme but is regularly pronounced as /dʒ/. There are also a number of consonant digraphs with regular pronunciations. See Table 8.1.

Some consonant individual letters and digraphs regularly represent more than one phoneme. See Table 8.2.

Table 8.2 overstates the complexity of this aspect of English spelling. The letter 'n' is only pronounced /ŋ/ in front of 'k' and 'c' is pronounced as /k/ when it is followed by 'a', 'o', 'u' or a consonant and as /s/ when it is followed by 'e', 'i' or 'y'. However, it underestimates the flexibility of the digraphs 'ch', 'gh' which sometimes are not pronounced at all, for example, 'yacht' and 'taught'.

The system for spelling consonants is complex but is in many ways a reasonably close approximation of the pronunciation of English and much easier to understand than the vowel system.

Table 8.1 Consonant digraphs

L	P	Example	L	P	Example	L	P	Example
ch	tʃ	Chose	kn	n	Know	qu	kw	Queen
ci	ʃ	Delicious	mb	m	Climb	sc	s	Science
ck	k	Back	ng	ŋ	Sing	sh	ʃ	Show
dg	dʒ	Fudge	ph	f	Graph	ti	ʃ	Deletion
gn	n	Sign	ps	s	Psychology			

L = letter; P = phoneme.

Source: Brooks 2015: 242

Table 8.2 Consonants which regularly represent two or more sounds

L	P	Example	L	P	Example
c	k, s	Cat, place	th	θ, ð	Thigh, that
g	g, dʒ	Go, wage	s	s, z, ʒ, ʃ	Bus, is, measure, sure
gh	f, g	Cough, ghost	w	w, h	Why, who
n	n, ŋ	Ban, bank	x	ks, z	Box, xylophone
t	t, tʃ	Cat, tune			

L = letter; P = phoneme.

Source: Brooks (2015: 267 et seq)

 Activity 8.1 Consonants

1 'G' can be pronounced as /g/ or /dʒ/. Put the following words into groups according to how 'g' is pronounced and identify a rule accounting for this: gap, general, giant, glow, go, great, guess, guy, gypsy, magic.

   Try out your rule on any other words you can think of and try to account for the silent 'u' in 'guess'.

2 'Ci' can represent two sounds as in 'city' and also be a digraph as in 'delicious'. What patterns can you identify in how 'ci' is pronounced? Here are some examples: artificial, city, civil, decide, delicious, precious, social, special.

3 Several consonants represent the same sound whether they appear singly or are doubled. Can you identify a rule for when the single or double form is used when the one-syllable words below are inflected?

   Big/bigger, fit/fitting, group/grouping, head/headed, hid/hidden, mean/meaning, moan/moaned, run/running, seat/seated, stop/stopped.

   What exceptions can you find to this rule?

8.2.2 Vowels

The Roman alphabet has six vowel letters (a, e, i, o, u, and the ambivalent 'y') with which to represent twenty vowel phonemes. BBC English, or Received Pronunciation, also uses 'r' and 'w' as vowel supporters to indicate length but also sometimes with no apparent value. It is possible to identify sounds which are most often associated with vowel letters as in Table 8.3, but the exceptions are numerous.

As with consonants, English uses digraphs to compensate for the lack of vowel letters. These combinations may be contiguous, for example, 'ea' as in 'hear' or split as 'a.e' as in 'plate'. Table 8.4 provides information about vowel digraphs.

Table 8.3 Vowel letters and phonemes

L	P	Example	%	L	P	Example	%
a	æ	Hat	50	o	ɒ	Top	41
e	e	Bell	47	u	ʌ	But	44
i	ɪ	Hit	*	y	ai	Try	*

L = letter; P = phoneme; % = frequency with which the letter represents the phoneme.
*Frequency data are not available for 'i' or 'y'.

Source: Brooks (2015: 346 et seq)

Table 8.4 Vowel digraphs with their most frequently realized phoneme

L	P	Example	%	L	P	Example	%
a.e	ai	Came	68	i.e	ai	Bike	97
ai	ei	Paint	79	ir	ɜː	Fir	100
ar	ɑː	Start	78	o.e	əʊ	Bone	99
au	ɔː	Sauce	80	oi	ɔɪ	Boy	100
aw	ɔː	Saw	100	oo	ʊ	Book	51
ea	iː	Beach	73	or	ɔː	Or	72
ee	iː	Free	100	ou	aʊ	Shout	48
e.e	iː	Scene	99	ow	aʊ	Cow	45
er	ə	Waiter	65	oy	ɔɪ	Boy	100
ew	juː	Few	84	ue	juː	Tuesday	59
ie	iː	Brief	73	u.e	juː	Pure	89
i.e	ai	Bike	97	ur	ɜː	Turn	70
ie	iː	Brief	73	y	ai	Try	*

L = letter; P = phoneme. % = frequency with which the letter represents the phoneme.
*Frequency data are not available for 'y'.

Source: Brooks (2015: 346 et seq)

Activity 8.2 Digraphs and pronunciation

1 Table 8.4 shows that vowel digraphs have an uncertain relationship with phonology, so longer letter combinations may be more useful. The vowel digraph 'a.e' represents /eɪ/ in only 68 per cent of instances because of words like 'garage', 'courage' and 'moustache'. Create a list of ten words with the rhyme 'ake' and calculate the percentage of times this is linked to /eɪ/.

2 When a suffix is added to a word which ends in 'e', the 'e' sometimes stays as in 'noticeable' and sometimes is deleted as in 'arrival'. Using the following words, account for why this happens: advantageous, arousal, baking, changeable, manageable, moving, noticeable, noticing, staging, traceable.

8.2.3 Morphemes

Writing was historically developed as a representation of speech but needs to be easily processed as written text. So some of the patterns in English spelling are to do with making words easier to read, and this means that the link to meaning, normally through morphemes, is more important that the connection with phonology. For example, the 'c' in 'medical' and 'medicine' are not pronounced the same, but using the same letter helps readers see the connection between the morpheme 'medic' in both words orthographically and presumably semantically. If English had a shallower orthography, we would have something like 'medikal' and 'medsin' which would match the phonology more clearly but would obscure the similarity in meaning.

A similar point applies to the regular past tense of verbs. The past tense of 'cook' is pronounced /kʊkt/, the past tense of 'boil' is /bɔɪld/, and the past tense of 'roast' is /rəʊstɪd/ but all three morphemes are spelled '-ed'.

Spelling can also sometimes help to highlight the differences between morphemes. If English were being redesigned, we would probably not use /ðeə/ as a possessive pronoun, an adverb of place and a short form for 'they' plus 'are'. However given that we do have these homophones, the existence of the spellings 'their', 'there' and 'they're' helps readers. Similar arguments would apply to 'to', 'too' and 'two'.

Many functional words such as 'the' (/ðə/ or /ðɪ/), 'of', (/əv/), 'to' (/tə/) and 'and' (/ænd/ /ənd/ /ən/) are spelled in ways that are more helpful for reading than as an indication of how they are pronounced.

 Activity 8.3 Morphemes

1 To make a regular noun plural, English adds an 's'. However, this is pronounced differently. Look at the following data and identify how 's' is pronounced in each case and explain why it is pronounced that way: bags, boxes, buses, cats, cups, dishes, dogs, pears, ships.

2 How would the words 'photograph', 'photography' and 'photographic' be spelt if English had a shallower orthography?

3 English has different spellings for the homophones pronounced /fɔː/ and /ai/ but not for /tɪl/ or /bɑːk/. Would the benefits for readers in having different spellings for the last two outweigh the disadvantages?

8.3 Learning to spell: how do people learn to spell?

Most models of learning to spell come out of an information processing framework. See Chapter 3. Spelling requires two kinds of information – rules about the links between letters and sounds which help writers to assemble words from their sounds, and a lexical store, where writers produce whole words or morphemes as a unit (Brown and Ellis 1994: 6). This parallels the distinction in spellings based on consonant and vowel sounds, on the one hand, and spellings based on morphemes, on the other.

An alternative explanation of how people learn to spell is offered by connectionism (also covered in Chapter 3). This downplays the division between assembling words and recalling them as wholes (Brown and Loosemore 1994; Heuven 2005). This approach to human learning is based on computer models and the essential learning mechanism is the strength of links rather than notions of rules. The computer models produced in this way are able to simulate the ways in which first and second language learners develop the ability to spell. A connectionist model would see the main mechanisms as learners developing an understanding of spelling patterns rather than using rules.

Most spelling research has investigated first language learners, and while this provides some insight, second language learners differ from first language learners and in particular their knowledge of writing in their first language. So Chinese learners who are familiar with a logographic writing system are less likely to use letter–sound links than, say, Korean speakers who use an alphabet (Nam 2017; Wang et al. 2003). Similarly, Arabic speakers who are familiar with a consonantal writing system which does not always represent vowels (Sampson 2015: 73 et seq.) may suffer from 'vowel blindness', that is, they may omit vowels or find it difficult to recall the correct vowel (Saigh and Schmitt 2012) and so make more spelling errors with vowels than those from a writing system which is more similar to English. Korean learners whose writing system is shallower than English may find the fact that the use of some symbols in English as both individual letters ('m' as in 'ham' and 'b' as in 'lab') and as digraphs, for example, 'mb' as in 'lamb' English is confusing (Nam 2017).

Learners who use the Roman alphabet will also be influenced by their first language. So speakers of Dutch which does not have the phonemes /θ/ or /ð/ or the digraph 'th' write 'badroom' for 'bathroom' and 'clodes' for 'clothes' (Berkel 2005: 113).

More generally, second language learners of English can often read in their first language and usually learn to both speak and read English at the same time, and this may mean that they make less use of phonological knowledge. Zhao et al. (2016) found that bilingual users of English were better at spelling real words than monolingual users but were worse at spelling non-sense words. This may mean that bilingual users make less use of the spoken language in their spelling than do monolingual users.

8.4 Teaching spelling: how can teachers help learners to spell better?

This section first discusses what teachers should focus on and then explores some spelling activities. Few teachers devote whole lessons to spelling, but spelling can be treated as a ten or fifteen-minute thread in a lesson programme.

8.4.1 What to teach

Some curricula include a list of words that learners are expected to be able to spell, and teachers then need to decide how to divide up the list. Where teachers are not provided with such a list, they may choose to draw on word lists online, for example, Nation's webpage (2017), the Dolch word lists (function words whose spelling does not indicate their pronunciation) or the many vocabulary course books (e.g. McCarthy et al. 1997.). These are not organized around spelling issues but can be used as a starting point. Gerlach (2016) argues that beginners need to be able to spell the 300 most common words in English, many of which have idiosyncratic spellings and which would overlap with the Dolch word lists.

A more learner-centred approach is to use errors from learners' writing and words about whose spelling they have asked and analyse these to identify what should be the focus on your spelling instruction, bearing in mind that 'the task of spelling instruction is not to correct mistakes the child has already made, but to help the writer not to make that mistake the next time' (Torbe 1978: 39). The focus needs to move from addressing mistakes to understanding learners' overall spelling system. The learner who produced the text in Figure 8.2 needs help with 'o'clock' (though the occurrence of 'o'clock' suggests some awareness of 'ck' as representing the phoneme /k/) but is also struggling with double letters, for example, swimming, tennis, and shopping. 'Friend' and 'Saturday' are both frequent items and probably also need attention. This kind of analysis may reveal problems which are common to a class but is also likely to reveal that learners have different problems and require individual attention. One way of dealing with this is for teachers to build up a store of the kinds of activities described below on paper or online that can be used when a learner has a particular problem.

Once teachers have decided what they need to teach, they need to consider how they will first increase learners' awareness of the relevant aspects of spelling and then practice those spellings.

8.4.2 Spelling activities: awareness

The most common spelling awareness activity is probably teachers' feedback on learners' written work. Teachers have a range of choices when correcting spellings. Activity 8.4 covers some feedback strategies.

On Saterday In the morning I go to sweming at 11 oclok I have lunch at 12:30 pm I read eamel at 4:00. In the evining I watch t.v at 10 oclock. On Sunday I go to park with my frend at 11:00. I play teanes at 11;30 I go to shoping at 3:00. At 8 oclok I go to senema. At the night I go to bed at 10 oclok.

Figure 8.2 A text produced by an Arabic-speaking English language learner. (Geertzen 2013)

Activity 8.3 Respond to spelling mistakes

Here is a sentence from an Arabic-speaking English learner:

On Sunday I go to park with my frend at 11:00 I play teanes at 11.

Below I list some of the ways a teacher might chose to respond. What would you see as the advantages and disadvantages of these strategies?

1 This sentence contains two spelling mistakes. Can you correct them?

2 'Frend' is misspelt. Check your dictionary to find the correct spelling.

3 Fr_ _nd   t_nn_is

4 On Sunday I go to park with my frend at 11:00 I play teanes at 11.

                               friend   tennis

5 On Sunday I go to park with my frend at 11:00 I play teanes at 11. Remember for 'friend', 'I' before 'e' except after 'c'.

Spelling awareness activities focus on identifying an aspect of spelling which seems relatively regular, for example, the pronunciation of 'g' and 'c' discussed earlier. Some teachers use flash cards to introduce new words. The impact of using flash cards on spelling can be enhanced by using cards which highlight the overall shape of the word. If a teacher were working on words with 'ake', the flash cards in Figures 8.3 might prove useful. Using a flash card without any letters can help learners to recognize the overall shape of the word.

Again with split digraphs, it would be possible to ask learners to focus on, say, 'ake' through a word puzzle based on brake, fake, lake, make, shake, snake and take. You can do this manually, or websites will create word squares for you. A useful related activity is a crossword. Where appropriate, learners can be encouraged to identify the regularities in English spelling. See Table 8.5. This can also be used to highlight groups of words where spelling reflects morphological rather than phonological aspects of the word such as medical, medicine, discussed above, or words like sign, signature, resign.

Although patterns do exist in English spelling, many learners still struggle with particular words such as 'friend' in Figure 8.2. Torbe suggested that learners be encouraged to use the sequence of 'look, cover, remember, write check' (Table 8.6) as a way of working on these independently.

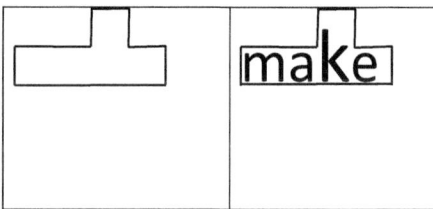

Figure 8.3 Flash cards for 'make'

Table 8.5 Worksheet for single and double letters

Write the correct '-ing' word next to the base verb? What pattern do you notice about when to double the final letter?

Cook

Hit

Keep

Read

Stop

Swim

What is the '-ing' form of these base verbs: eat, heat, run, shop, sleep, sit?

Table 8.6 Worksheet on 'how to help yourself to spell'

Look	• Look at the word; say it to yourself
	• If you have difficulty remembering how to write it, trace it with your finger
	• See if it looks the way it sounds
	• Mark the bit of the word that causes your difficulties
Cover	• Shut your eyes; see the word in your head. Do this for at least 13 seconds
	• If you can't see it in your head, say the word to yourself and see if the sound reminds you of how it looks
Remember	• If that doesn't work, look again at the word and say it in a way that will remind you of how it is spelled. Exaggerate it. Pronounce the bits separately – but remember how it is spelled
Write	• Cover the word: write it from memory. Try and see the word in your head as you write
Check	• If you're not sure about it, look at it again
	• Check back to see if you got it right. If you didn't, do it again
	• Later in the day, write it again from memory. If you're not sure of it, look it up before you try

Source: Torbe (1978: 46)

8.4.3 Spelling activities: production

All writing activities are spelling production activities, and a key question for teachers is the amount of support. One common piece of advice to learners is to use a dictionary, to look up words about whose spelling they are uncertain, or, where they are writing using a word processor, the spellchecker. If the learner who produced the text in Figure 8.1 were able to identify the misspellings in their text, something which would be difficult for a poor speller, they would identify the nine items in Table 8.7. If the learner looked up the misspelt words in the *Macmillan English Dictionary* (Rundell 2002), the help would be variable. Looking for 'oclock' would take them straight to 'o'clock' and looking for 'shoping' would take them straight to 'shopping'. They would find 'Saturday' on the second page if they looked for words starting with 'SAT', and if they looked up 'SWE', they would find 'swimming' on the third

Table 8.7 Using a dictionary and spellchecker to correct misspellings

Misspelling	Dictionary	Word processor suggestions
Saterday	2	1
Sweming	3	1
Oclok/oclock	1	1
Eamel	16	2
Evining	−1	1
Frend	5	1
Teanes	7	Not suggested
Shoping	1	1
Senema	−1047	3

Table 8.8 A mnemonic for mnemonics

Personalized	It might be better if learners made up their own
Amusing	If it is funny, it's more memorable
Meaningful	Meaningless mnemonics take more effort to remember than the spelling
Pictorial	If the mnemonic creates visual picture in the learner's mind, that will help
Easy to remember	Not too complicated
Rude	Yes, sorry but it seems the ruder the better

page. It is unlikely that the dictionary would help them find the correct spelling for 'eamel', 'frend', 'teanes' or 'senema'. The spellchecker in Word is generally more successful with correct suggestions coming up first for most words, but the suggestions for 'teanes' ('teams', 'teases' and 'teens') did not include tennis. This is not an argument for the use of spellcheckers but evidence that dictionaries and spellcheckers cannot solve all spelling problems.

For the dictionary column, 1 means the correct word was on the same page, 2 means on the second page and negative numbers mean the word appeared earlier in the dictionary.

Some learners find mnemonics useful to help them spell difficult words. For example, the spelling of 'rhythm' can be remembered by 'Rhythm Helps Your Two Hips Move' or learners may find 'I have a front and back door at my address' to remember the two 'ds'. Stirling (2011: 148) suggests a mnemonic to remember the good features of mnemonics. See Table 8.8.

8.5 Summary

This chapter covered spelling in English. We first described some generalizations about spelling in English, mainly related to the links between pronunciation and spelling, with consonant having a more regular connection than vowels, and also morphemes. We then examined how spelling is learnt focusing on information processing models and connectionism before exploring how teachers might decide what they should be teaching in the spelling sections of their classes and some of the activities they might use in class.

 Activity 8.4 Discussion

How might a teacher who has received this piece of work from a native speaker of Cantonese respond to help improve the learner's spelling?

My family

My family is a large family, having six people live together in the hous. Each one has different way to help them relax. And also the way they thought is relaxing, having giv me too much angry. For example, my youngest sister is luv chinese music, therefor whenever she at home do her homwork always has the music on. That bother me a lot. Becoz she and I liv in the room making me have to go with the arcument with her.

 8.6 Further reading

Relatively few books go into much detail on spelling. Stirling's (2011) *Teaching Spelling to English Language Learners* and Shemesh and Waller's (2000) *Teaching English Spelling: A Practical Guide* are useful sources. Brooks's (2015) *Dictionary of the British English Spelling System* is a reference guide to the spelling of British English, and Sampson's (2015) *Writing Systems* provides interesting and well-written background information about the range of writing systems that have been used to write languages.

Chapter 9

Grammar

9.1 Introduction

Grammar is regarded as the core of language by many linguists (e.g. Chomsky) but also by many teachers and learners, so most teachers spend a lot of their time teaching grammar. The first stage in teaching grammar is for teachers to decide what their aim might be in a grammar class or in a section of a class on grammar. Teachers working within a task-based, content and language-integrated learning or content-based learning are unlikely to have a whole lesson on a grammar point but may well address grammar issues with the context of the task or content that is the focus of the lesson. Most other approaches to teaching English have syllabuses that include a grammatical strand and lessons whose main aim is teaching grammar. Once teachers have decided on their aim, they need to consider how people learn new grammar and become better at using the grammar they already know, and this should then inform how they teach grammar. This chapter explores the teaching of grammar by addressing three questions related to these points:

1 What is grammar?

2 How do we learn grammar?

3 How can we best teach grammar?

9.2 Understanding grammar: what is grammar?

The grammar of English is a vast topic. It is not possible to cover the whole of English grammar here and, even if that were possible, it would not be particularly useful as what teachers need to know is the grammar their learners need. So this section tries to first

a give you an introduction to some key grammatical concepts,

b provide you with the tools you need to evaluate descriptions of English grammar, and

c develop your skills in identifying what grammatical problems your learners have.

9.3 Some key grammatical concepts

Grammar is to do with meaning. When communicative language teaching was becoming popular in the 1970s, some people thought that a concern with communicating meanings meant that teachers should not teach grammar. I am not sure how widespread this view was, but it is based on a misunderstanding of grammar. Grammar is a way of expressing meaning by choosing between different grammatical structures, and a good description of grammar will explain what different grammatical elements and structures mean as well as how they are formed.

When we talk about learners being good at grammar, this generally means that they are able to use the grammar well rather than being able to describe the grammar of a particular language and one does not imply the other. Many native speakers of English are able to produce grammatically accurate sentences without being able to describe the differences between, say, countable and uncountable nouns. Being able to use grammar is a skill. Some writers use the term 'grammaring' to indicate that this is the aspect of grammar they are talking about (Larsen-Freeman 2003), and our aim is to help learners to produce grammatically accurate language rather than being able to describe grammar.

For many teachers, learners are helped by knowing the rules or patterns of grammar. This is the view of grammar as knowledge, for example, 'A singular subject takes a singular verb, while a plural subject takes a plural verb.' Knowledge of grammar also includes the terminology or metalanguage that we use to describe language. This ranges from parts of speech such as noun, verb, adjective, etc., to terms such as 'aspect' to describe different uses of verbs, as well as – if you are prepared to spend time studying particular models of grammar – to words such as ideational and ergative (Halliday and Matthiessen 2014). The next section introduces some metalanguage which is useful for thinking about teaching grammar.

 Activity 9.1 Grammatical metalanguage

1 Identify which of the following terms are (a) ones that you are familiar with and (b) which you would use with your learners.

   a Phrasal verbs

   b Modal verbs

   c Infinitive

   d Base form

   e -ing form

   f -en form

   g Past participle

   h Present tense

   i Past tense

   j Future tense

2 What grammatical inflections, if any, can you identify for the following words? This first one is done for you

   a Girl. *Girl's Girls Girls'*

   b Arrive.

   c Dark.

d Soon.

e Of.

How does the grammatical morphology of English differ from other languages you know?

3 Identify the parts of speech incidated in bold in the following passage. There are two nouns and two verbs so you should identify the sub-categories for these words.

Alice was beginning to get **very tired** of sitting **by** her sister on the bank, and of having nothing to do: once or twice she had peeped into the book **her** sister **was** reading, **but** it had no pictures or conversations in it, 'and what **is** the use of a book', thought Alice 'without **pictures** or conversation?' (Carroll and Blum 2008: 1)

Alice – *Proper noun*	very	tired
by	her	was
but	is	pictures

4 If you speak a language other than English, try to identify examples of the word classes in Table 9.1 in those languages. How easy is it for a word to change word class in that language?

Grammar is traditionally divided into morphology (how word parts contribute to grammar) and syntax (how words are arranged to make sentences). In English, the difference between singular and plural is signalled mainly by morphology, for example, chair and chairs, child and children, mice and mouse. The distinction between declaratives and interrogatives is mainly signalled by syntax, for example, 'You are a teacher.' 'Are you a teacher?' 'Chen has got a nice house.' 'Has Chen got a nice house?' However, it is more complicated than this as illustrated by pairs such as sheep (singular) and sheep (plural), where there is no morphological signal of the difference between the singular and the plural, and the relationship between 'You cooked your lunch' and 'Did you cook your lunch?' which is to do with both word order and morphology ("cook" and £"cooked").

Grammar is hierarchical. For most grammarians, sentences are the largest unit in grammar, and sentences are made up of one or more clauses; clauses are made up of one or more phrases and so on. See Figure 9.1.

Morphemes

Morphemes are the smallest meaningful units of the language. A morpheme may be a word (e.g. open, cat) or a part of a word, for example, '-ing' in 'opening' or 'cooking', '-s' in 'cats' or 'doors'. The central issue here is meaning so morphology ignores changes in spelling like the loss of an 'e' when '-ed' is added to 'live' or the change of 'f' to 'v' when '-s' is added to 'knife'. Grammatical morphemes are known as inflections. English also uses morphemes, labelled derivational, to make new words. See Chapter 10.

English does not have many inflections compared to other languages but one of the complications of learning English is that we sometimes use the same spelling for two different morphemes. So '-s'

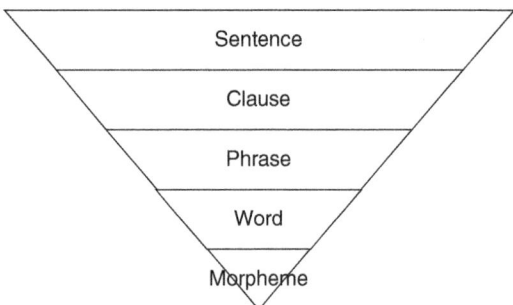

Figure 9.1 The grammar hierarchy (adapted from Jones and Waller 2015: 25)

can represent the plural morpheme in 'books' or the morpheme signalling the singular third person of a present tense verb as in 'cooks' and '-ed' can represent the past tense as in 'He cooked' or the past participle or -en form in 'He has cooked'. English also presents problems for learners because the same morpheme is realized in a range of ways, for example, the plural morpheme as in 'books', 'children', 'mice'.

Word classes

Understand the syntax of English requires an understanding the differences between parts of speech. Table 9.1 identifies the nine main word classes that I would recognize.

The terminology is difficult for two reasons. First, other descriptions of word classes are slightly different. Scrivener (2010: 14) treats pronouns as a separate class; Biber et al. (1999: 56) uses the term 'insert' for what I would call an interjection. These kinds of differences are not very significant, but for teaching purposes consistency will makes things easier for learners. Second, English differs from some other languages in that the same word can be used in more than one word class. Many words can be both a determiner (**This** book is good) and a pronoun (**This** is my book). Biber et al. (1999: 60) show how 'round' can be used as five different word classes

1 I think he deserves a round of applause (noun)

2 I can round up Dave and Peter (verb)

3 Just give me an idea in round figures (adjective)

4 It takes a long time to bring them round (adverb)

5 That's just round the corner (preposition)

Phrases

There are five main kinds of phrases in English. These can be recognized from the 'head' or central word in the phrase. The head of a noun phrase is a noun, the head of an adjective phrase is an adjective and so on. See Table 9.2 where the heads of the phrase are in bold

Table 9.1 Word classes

Part of speech	Sub-category	Short definition	Examples
Noun (N)	Common	Denotes abstract or material objects	Freedom, drink, table, tables
	Pronoun	Replaces a noun	It, his, mine, those, everything, which
	Proper	Denotes a person or place	Obama, Paris, Schipol Airport
Verb	Lexical (V)	Denotes action, process or state	Run, ran, drink, see, own, be
	Auxiliary (AUX)	Supports a main verb and provides information about tense/aspect and clause type	Be, do, have. may
	Modal (MOD)	Supports a main verb and provides information about the certainty and necessity of the main verb	Can, may, should
Adjective	ADJ	Modifies a noun	Red, tall, younger
Adverb	ADV	Modifies a verb, an adjective or clause	Quickly, rather, very, actually
Preposition	PREP	Describes the relationship between two nouns	On, of
Conjunction	CONJ	Links two words, phrases or clauses	And, when
Interjection	INT	Is an exclamation	Wow, damn, gosh
Determiner (DET)	Modifies nouns		
	Article	Specifies whether the noun is definite or indefinite	The, a
	Demonstrative	Specifies if the noun is near or far from the speaker/writer	This, those
	Numeral	Specifies the number of instances of a noun	Five, seven, two hundred
	Possessive	Connection with other nouns	Her, your, its, Shima's
	Quantifier	Specifies the number or amount of the noun	Some, many

Clause elements

When phrases are put into clauses, they serve functions within the sentence. In English, the functions are: subject; predicator (often called verb phrase); complement (subject or object), object (direct, indirect, prepositional) and adverbial. Examples of these are given in Table 9.6. Clause elements can be represented in tree diagrams. There are different conventions about drawing tree diagrams

Table 9.2 Phrases in English

Phrase	Examples
Noun (NP)	**Alice**, **she**, the **rabbit-hole**, my poor little **feet**, **pictures** hung upon pegs, the **people** that walk with their heads downward
Verb (VP)	was going to **happen**, might **catch**, was no longer to be **seen**, would not **open**, was **coming**, must be **growing**
Adjective (AdjP)	very **remarkable**
Adverb (AdvP)	**suddenly**, very **slowly**
Preposition (PP)	**for** it, **in** another moment, **to** her great disappointment, **right** through the earth, **into** the loveliest garden you ever saw

Note: Heads of phrases in bold.

Table 9.3 Elements in a clause

Subject (S)		**Alice** opened the door
		I shall be late
		'Ahem!' said the **mouse** with an important air
		What made you so awfully clever?
Predicator (P)		Alice **opened** the door
		I **shall be** late
Complement	Subject (SC)	I shall be **late**
	Object (OC)	What made you **so awfully clever**?
Object	Direct (DO)	Alice opened **the door**
		She generally gave herself **very good advice**
		I don't care **what happens**
		What made **you** so awfully clever?
	Indirect (IO)	She generally gave **herself** very good advice
	Prepositional (PO)	She got **to the door**
Adverbial (A)		'Ahem!' said the Mouse **with an important air**
		In another moment down went Alice after it
		Alice had not a moment to think about stopping herself **before she found herself falling down a very deep well**

and many writers see a sentence as essentially comprising two elements, the subject and the verb phrase. I prefer a three-way division reflecting subject predicator and object. See Figures 9.2–9.4. Tree diagrams are widely used by linguistics but are not central to most language teachers and you should only make use of them to the extent that they help you to make sense of the syntax of English.

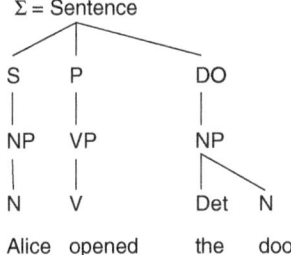

Figure 9.2 A tree diagram of 'Alice opened the door'

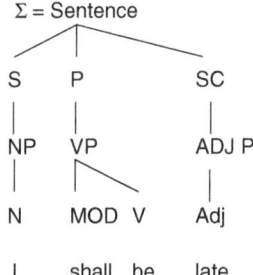

Figure 9.3 A tree diagram of 'I shall be late'

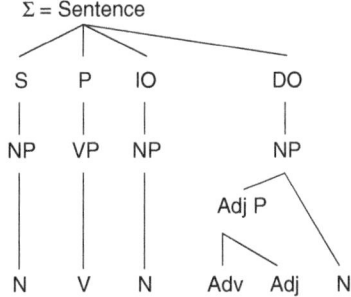

Figure 9.4 A tree diagram of 'She gave herself very good advice'

? Activity 9.2 Tree diagrams

Try to produce tree diagrams for the following sentences.

1 She got to the door.

2 What made you so awfully clever?

3 I must be growing small.

4 Her foot slipped.

5 I don't care what happens.

Table 9.4 Different kinds of sentence

Sentence function	Examples
Declarative	She got to the door
	Alice was not a bit hurt
Interrogative	What made you so awfully clever?
	Who did that?
Imperative	Drink me!
	Tell us a story

Table 9.5 Categories of sentence

Category	Example
Simple	She got to the door
	What made you so awfully clever?
	Drink me!
Compound	She was now only ten inches high, and her face brightened up at the thought
	She tried her best to climb up one of the legs of the table, but it was too slippery
Complex	However, **this bottle was NOT marked 'poison'**, so Alice ventured to taste it
	when she got to the door, **she found she had forgotten the little golden key**

Source: Carroll and Blum (2008)

Sentences

There are three kinds of sentence functions in English – declarative, interrogative and imperative. See Table 9.4. These roughly correspond to statements, questions and orders but English allows some flexibility. A declarative sentence like 'You must do your homework' is in discourse terms an order.

Sentences can consist of more than one clause and so they can also be categorized in terms of complexity. Simple sentences have one main clause. Compound sentences consist of two equal clauses linked by links like 'and', 'or' and 'but'. Complex sentences consist of one main clause and one subordinate clause. See Table 9.5.

9.3.1 Evaluating descriptions of English grammar

The ways in which grammars of language are produced has changed in the last forty years because it has become possible to use computer programs to analyse large samples or 'corpora', of naturally occurring data. This means that most reference grammars are based on examples of what language users do. They are corpus based. This is an important development because it means we can look at rules that have been widely promulgated such as 'Do not split an infinitive' and find out whether this matches how most people use the language. Grammars based on how people actually use the language are often described as descriptive (Thornbury 1999: 10) and seen as better than prescriptive grammar (Willis 2015) which often misrepresents the way language is used. However, teaching grammar is prescriptive because teacher need to tell learners what they can and cannot do in English. What is important is that the grammar that is taught is a proper reflection of the way that the kind of English your learners need is used.

Swan (1994) identifies six criteria for evaluating rules. His criteria are

1 Truth	Rules should be true
2 Demarcation	Rules should identify the limits on the use of the relevant grammar
3 Clarity	Rules should be clear
4 Simplicity	Rules should be simple
5 Conceptual parsimony	Rules should make use of terms and ideas that are familiar to learners
6 Relevant	Rules should address the issue that concerns the learner

These rules provide a useful framework for evaluating rules, though there are many aspects of English grammar where truth is something that we aim for rather than something we achieve. The strength of these criteria is that they are learner-focussed. So when Swan says that rules should be conceptually parsimonious, he is warning against using metalanguage that learners may not know. When teachers have spent time and effort in learning the metalanguage related to a particular grammatical aspect, there is a temptation to assume that the language that has helped them to understand the grammar will help the learners to understand the same thing but this is not necessarily the case. Similarly, clarity, simplicity and relevance will vary depending on which learners the rule is for and this is one reason why the grammatical explanations given to learners may change as their language ability develops.

Swan also indicated the importance of knowing when to use one grammatical structure and when to use another by the criterion of demarcation. This goes back to the idea that grammar is a way of expressing meaning by making choices. Being able to use the definite article involves knowing how to the use the indefinite article and the meaning comes from the fact that language users decide which kind of article to use in a systematic way. Learners will need to know what they can and cannot do.

 Activity 9.3 The present perfect

1 Look at these three descriptions of the present perfect from three well-known grammar books and evaluate how useful they are using Swan's criteria. These are extracts from these books and do not include rules for the formation of the present perfect. You will find longer explanations if you go to the actual books.

   a In general terms, the present perfect is used to refer to a situation that began some time in the past and continues up to the present. For example, the sentence
   But now she's gone on holiday for a whole month. describes a past action (leaving for a holiday) that creates a situation (or result) that extends to the present (Biber et al. 1999: 460).

   b The present perfect (simple and progressive) is used to refer to events taking place in a past time-frame that connects with the present: . . .

So what's been happening since the last time we met? (from that moment till now)

In fact, alligators have killed only eight people in Florida in the last half century (in the fifty years up to the time of writing) (Carter and McCarthy 2006: 613).

c   We use the present perfect to talk about events in the past – but it is a 'present' tense. How is that possible? The key idea with this tense is that it is about the past as it affects the present – that is, there is always some link to now. All present perfect meanings connect the past to now in some way. This is a rather complex concept – and quite hard to convey to students (Scrivener 2010: 163).

I've been to four different countries in Africa (and the experience of visiting these countries is still live and important to me. It doesn't feel like a distant, dead event).
She's bought 20 copies of the book (and she still has them now).
He's eaten camel meat (and he is still a person who knows what that tastes like).

2   The extracts just aim to explain the meaning of the present perfect. They do not explain how the present perfect differs from, say, the past simple, what Swan describes as demarcation. How would you describe the difference between the present perfect and the past simple?

9.3.2 Identifying grammatical problems in learner language

A lot of grammar teaching comes in response to problems that learners have in communicating. This is built into task-based teaching and the problem-based sequence described in Chapter 4 but is a feature of most, if not all, classrooms, when teacher give learners feedback on the grammaticality of their language. There is some information about feedback on written language in Chapter 14, but here I want to look at how you might evaluate sentence-level grammar mistakes.

The first stage is to identify what your learner meant. So, for example, if the learner wrote

   'Dream are not limit to rich peoples.'

I would guess that the learner meant

   'Dream**s** are not limit**ed** to rich **people**.'

Of the three grammar problems here, the first two seem fairly straightforward: the use of a singular noun instead of a plural noun (dreams) and the use of the base form instead of the past participle or -en form to make the passive. The third one may be that the learner does not know the word 'people' is plural or it could be that somehow the 's' from dream was transferred to 'people' and this would of course mean that original analysis of 'dream' was wrong. My judgment would be that this a misplaced 's' because the learner elsewhere used 'people' correctly (see Activity 9.7) but I would emphasize that this is a judgment and you might reach a different conclusion, particularly if you had other information about the learner.

A key part of the information about learners is what languages they speak other than English because learners will quite often apply the rules or patterns in languages they know to English. Teacher who are fortunate enough to know the other languages that their learners know will have a clearer understanding the ways the learner use English. Han (2000: 91) explained that the persistence of structures such as 'The letter has not received' by speakers of Mandarin, not as due to a problem with the passive (i.e. 'has not been received') but due to two aspects of Chinese grammar. First,

Chinese allows a subject pronoun to be omitted when it can be understood from the context, in this case 'I' as the subject of 'received'. Second, Chinese allow the main topic, in this case 'the letter' to appear at the front the sentence even when it is an object. In written English, the sentence the learner intended would have been

I have not received the letter.

This analysis would suggest that the learner needs help with something other than the passive. If you do not know your learners' other languages, you can also look up examples of errors associated in books such as Swan and Smith (1987) and learners can often explain what it is that they meant to convey.

9.4 How do we learn grammar?

The monitor model sees grammar learning happening mainly because of learners' being exposed to intake without any particular focus on grammar. A lot of learners learn a lot of grammar without explicit instruction. However, many teachers and most course book producers give considerable importance to explicit instruction of grammar. Research evidence does suggest that grammar instruction does help (Norris and Ortega 2000) but it is important to note that, despite the amount of research, the evidence is mixed (Ellis 2006b: 86). My own view, perhaps influenced by a desire not to see the many hours I have spent teaching grammar as wasted, is that teaching grammar does help but that many grammar explanations are not understood by many learners. What follows offers a way of understanding how that learning might happen but learning cannot happen if the learners do not understand what they are being taught.

Both cognitive and sociocultural view offer plausible explanations of the development of grammatical ability. The cognitive view sees this as a two-stage process. First, the learner develops declarative knowledge' probably through noticing as a result of something the teacher does or some negotiation for meaning (as in Activity 9.8) and then this is transformed into procedural knowledge. The declarative knowledge is generally understood as a rule but this does necessarily mean that learners can state the rule. Learners seem to be able to learn quite complex grammatical patterns without being able to explain the rule (Dekeyser 1995: 382). Research on grammar pedagogy shows that learners can successfully acquire grammatical knowledge without explicit rules (Denhovska et al. 2016: 161). The declarative knowledge can be quite deeply buried. When the brain has developed an algorithm for processing or producing the grammatical structure, the declarative knowledge is forgotten or become less accessible. The key insight here is that teachers need to decide if they are aiming to help learners acquire knowledge or helping them proceduralize what they already know.

 Activity 9.4 Negotiating for meaning

Look at this extract from a communicative activity and consider how it might lead to learning for student 1. What has student 1 noticed about English grammar? What does student 1 **not** notice about the difference between the language she uses and the language student 2 uses?

S1: This woman is walking on street and sees a nice dress in window of a shop.

S2: The dress is expensive.

S1: Quite expensive and so she stop looking at dress. It is very red.

S2: She stops looking? She walks away from the dress.

S1: No, no, she keep looking at dress. She like the dress so much. She stop looking at the dress for a long time.

S2: I can't understand. She stops looking. She is in a hurry? So she finishes looking and goes on.

S1: No. She stop so she can look.

S2: Ah. She stops to look at the dress.

S1. Exactly. She . . . how you say? She stop to look at dress.

S2: You are right.

S1: OK. She stop to look at dress for a long time. She want to buy the dress.

The sociocultural view sees learning as happening because of the learners either understanding or producing the new grammar with help and that help being gradually withdrawn until the learners can use the grammar independently. A key aspect of this is that learners can only use grammar that is within their zone of proximal development so this means that the teacher need a clear idea of what grammar is appropriate for their learners.

9.5 How can we teach grammar

Borg (1999: 20) notes that a consensus about how best to teach grammar has not been achieved but the target in teaching grammar should always be to get the learners to use the language in a communicative task. This final stage of teaching grammar is covered in Chapter 11 while this chapter covers grammar explanations and grammar practice.

Chapter 4 distinguished between a PPP lesson, where the starting point might be a grammar point, and a problem-solving approach, where the aim would be a task but a grammar point might emerge from this. While the problem-solving pattern of organization is very different from a PPP lesson, if the language focus that emerges from the learners' attempt to carry out the target task is to do with grammar, the teacher will need to demonstrate or explain the grammar in the same way as the PPP teacher who has started with a grammar point.

Once the grammar has been explained or demonstrated, the PPP teacher will move on to the practice stage. A problem-solving teacher may also have a practice stage but this will depend on whether the teacher feels this is necessary. Sometimes an explanation is enough. The approaches are similar after the new grammar point has been introduced and practiced when a PPP lesson moves to the production stage or and the problem-solving teacher would get the students to have another go at the communicative task.

Whichever lesson structure is being used, the key decision, once the teacher has decided that the learners need grammar instruction, is whether to teach the grammar by starting with a rule or starting with examples of the grammar. This choice has been described in a range of ways but the most common is deductive approaches (starting with rules) and inductive approaches (starting with examples or consciousness-raising). Many teachers will use both rules and examples, so the decision here is usually to do with sequencing not what is included.

9.5.1 Deduction: teaching with rules

Generally, Swan's criteria for a good rule discussed above provide guidance for producing or evaluating rules. But it is also important to keep on checking that the explanation is meaningful to your learners.

A grammar rule will need to include information about the form and the meaning. In addition to the kind of information given in Activity 9.5 the rule will need to cover the way that we used 'have' as an auxiliary with the past participle or -en form to form the present perfect. One of the issues about describing the form is how much metalanguage you will use. It is difficult to avoid all metalanguage but the extent to which metalanguage is used will depend on your learners. When you are explaining the meaning of a piece of grammar, demarcation is important. Your learners will need to understand how choosing one grammatical structure rather than another will affect the meaning they are expressing. When you introduce the passive, you need to explain to learners why they might choose the passive rather than the active.

The meaning of a grammatical items can be conveyed in a range of ways. It is common to provide an explanation in English plus some examples. If the learners share a mother tongue this may include using their mother tongue. Thornbury (1999: 38–40) suggests using translation to teach 'used to' to elementary learners who speak Spanish so that the learners understand the difference between English and Spanish grammar. The equivalent verb in Spanish, 'soler' can be used in both the past and the present whereas the English 'used to' is only used in the past. Meanings can also be conveyed diagrammatically or with pictures. After explaining the form and the meaning of the grammar structure, teachers need to decide whether to start with form or meaning. Activity 9.5 explores the range of choices teachers have when providing grammar rules.

 Activity 9.5 Giving a rule

Here is an example of a teacher's explanation of the passive for pre-intermediate learners.

1 What strategies have been used?

   (a) metalanguage (b) use of the mother tongue (c) examples in English (d) demarcation (e) diagrams

2 In what order were the strategies used?

3 Would you have used a different or additional strategies? Would you have ordered the strategies differently?

In English, old information normally comes at the start of a sentence and new information at the end. So in the sentence 'He broke the window', 'he' is the old information and 'broke the window' is the new information. If I asked the question 'What has Tom done now?', then the answer would be 'He broke the window'. But if

I asked the question 'What happened to the window', the answer would be 'It was broken by Tom' because 'it' or the window is the old information and 'Tom' is the new information.

'He broke the window' is an active sentence because 'Tom' or 'he' broke the window.

'It was broken by Tom' is a passive sentence because something happened to 'it' or the window.

In English the passive is made with the verb 'be' plus the past participle. 'Was' plus 'broken'.

4 If possible, record one of your own explanations of a grammar rule or use a rule in a course book that you are familiar with. What strategies have you or they used to explain the rule and how effective do you find them?

9.5.2 Induction: teaching with examples

Inductive approaches start with examples. Because grammar is usually seen as stopping at the sentence, examples are often sentences.

Invented sentences

Many teachers or course book writers will invent the example sentences they use. This is partly because of convenience. It is easier to create a new sentence rather than to find an example from something you have heard or read. But there are also pedagogic reasons for this because it is important that the sentences are comprehensible to the learners. This means that the new grammar element should be the most difficult part of the sentence. The learners should not be distracted by the vocabulary of the sentence when the aim is that they notice the grammar. In Activity 9.5, the teacher's examples were

He broke the window.
It was broken by Tom.

These seem reasonable examples because the use of the passive is the most complicated part of the sentence. If we took another pair

She must have offended the mouse.
It must have been offended by Alice

The grammar point is equally well exemplified but the use of the word 'offend' may not be clear to the learners and, even if they understood 'offend', trying to understand how one might offend a mouse might distract them from the grammar.

It is also important that the meaning is conveyed by the grammar that is the focus of the teaching episode. VanPatten (2002), who was writing about learning Spanish rather than English, argued that learners pay more attention to vocabulary than grammar and that if the vocabulary provides a reasonably sensible meaning, the morphology will be ignored.

Dicen	que	Julieta	está	enferma	y	que	no	viene	a	clase.
They say	that	Julieta	is	ill	and	that	not	come	to	class.

Spanish grammar requires that adjectives should agree in terms of gender with the noun they modify. 'Enferma' is a female form because it agrees with the female 'Julieta'. When learners see or read this sentence, they are not likely to notice that 'enferma' is feminine, because gender is already encoded lexically in 'Julieta'.

A better example would be using the name 'Jo' which could be male or female because then the ending of 'enferma' would be needed to let the readers know if 'Jo' is a woman or a man.

Dicen	*que*	*Jo*	*está*	*enferma*	*y*	*que*	*no*	*viene*	*a*	*clase*
They say	that	Jo	is	ill	and	that	not	come	to	class.

Another way to encourage your learners to notice what you want them to notice is by using demarcation through the technique of minimal pairs. This means two sentences which only differ in terms of one grammar item.

a He <u>has lived</u> in Leeds for two years.

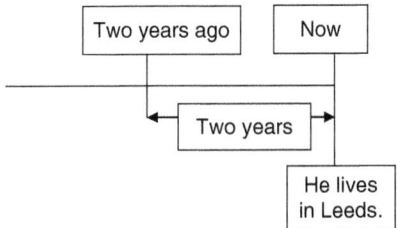

b He <u>lived</u> in Leeds for two years.

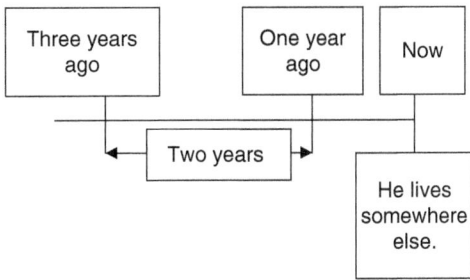

The learners will need to understand the sentences. Sometimes hearing or reading the sentence will be enough but teachers may need to support, the sentences with mime, *realia*, pictures or diagrams to explain the meanings.

We might distinguish between the Leeds sentences above by using a time line.
Alternatively, a grammar point might be illustrated by a picture. See Figure 9.5. A teacher might ask learners to decide which sentence went with which picture.

The examples given in this section are written but teachers will often provide examples orally. This has many advantages related to the development of the learners' ability to process oral English and

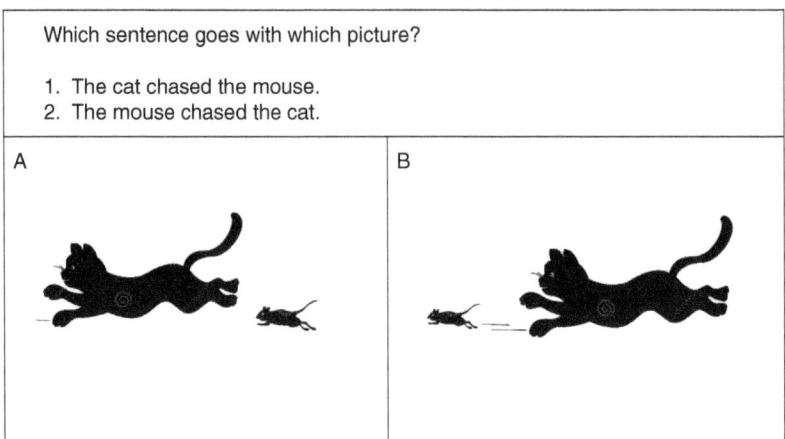

Figure 9.5 Pictures and grammar

helping them with their spoken English. However, it is important to remember that the purpose of the examples is for learners to develop new grammatical knowledge and that written language enables learners to process and review language at their own pace, rather than that of the speaker. This may make noticing new grammar easier.

Concordances

Corpus linguistics has transformed how we describe language and is starting to have an impact on teaching. For grammar teaching, corpus linguistics provides a useful way of producing large numbers of examples of a grammatical point. This is sometimes called data-driven learning (e.g. Lin and Lee 2015). Teachers who want to use data-driven learning need to access a corpus and use a piece of software called a concordancer to do this. Several publicly available websites exist or some teachers create their own corpora and generate example that way. Allan (2009) created a corpus using graded readers because of the difficulties learners have with other corpus data.

One example of a concordance is managed by Brigham Young University and available at http:// corpus.byu.edu/bnc/

 Activity 9.6 What can come after the word 'decide'?

Look at the following sentence and divide them into three groups according to the grammatical structure after 'decide'. What is the difference between the three structures?

a 'Technically you should go back there, but I think you've already decided against that.'

b Anne had now finally decided that she couldn't take it anymore.

c Finally, he decided that The Housemartins were contributing nothing to his life.

d Charles decided to be stubborn more than apologetic.

e Peter Yeo decided to prod gently.

f Robson again decided against summoning a replacement.

g The Bush administration decided against a visible or military role.

h The management one day decided to spread mirrors across the walls of the gym.

i Then, he decided to study to become a librarian.

j Wildski decided that Tokyo was the hat capital of the world.

Most learners are not familiar with concordance data and will often be expecting a continuous text rather than a set of sentences or, with some concordances, parts of sentences. Also concordance software requires that you start with a word or group of words and so you would have to think about how you could use this for the passive.

One of the main advantages of data-driven learning is that it can become something that learners can use independently if teachers can help them to use the range of materials that are currently available (Lin and Lee 2015). Using concordance data for teaching is also covered in Chapter 10.

Texts

Because grammar is meaningful, a text is often required to provide learners with enough information to understand how a structure is used. Many course books provide examples of texts which can be used to illustrate a grammar point.

Authentically produced texts are generally best for this because of the danger that a constructed text will conform to the writer's idea of how language works rather than representing how it actually works but a text must be authentic for the particular learners (Badger and MacDonald 2010) and may need to be adapted so that the learners understand it and are likely to notice the particular grammar point.

Below is a text taken from *Alice in Wonderland* to illustrate mixed conditionals for a class of intermediate second school learners. In particular, I wanted them to think about how the author expresses different levels of certainty in the main clause in conditional sentences. I have adapted the text. The first sentence started off as

This time she found a little bottle on it, ('which certainly was not here before', said Alice,) and round the neck of the bottle was a paper label, with the words 'DRINK ME' beautifully printed on it in large letters.

You will see the changes below. These were partly to do with making the extract comprehensible and coherent but were intended to leave the text as much like the original as possible. I considered removing the word 'poker' which I thought would not be familiar but decided that it added interest.

Alice found a little bottle on the table it, with the words 'DRINK ME' beautifully printed on it in large letters. It was all very well to say 'Drink me', but Alice was not going to do THAT in a hurry. 'No, I'll look first', she said, 'and see whether it's marked "poison" or not'; for she had read several nice little stories about children who had got burnt, and eaten up by wild beasts and other unpleasant things, all because they WOULD not remember the simple rules their friends had taught them: such as, that a red-hot poker will burn you if you hold it too long; and that if you cut your finger VERY deeply with a knife, it usually bleeds; and she had never forgotten that, if you drink much from a bottle marked 'poison', it is almost certain to disagree with you, sooner or later. (Carroll and Blum 2008: 5)

Once the text has been have found and/or adapted, teachers need to check that the learners understand the text and then can explore how particular grammatical structures are used. For this text the key difference are between 'will burn you', 'usually bleeds' and 'almost certain to disagree with you'.

It is quite difficult to find texts to illustrate particular points but many teachers develop a library of texts that they can use in their teaching and some patterns are repeated in many texts. For example, many newspaper articles start with the present perfect and then switch to the past simple.

Generative situations

A more flexible alternative to using an existing test is what Thornbury describes as a 'generative situation' (Thornbury 1999: 61). A generative situation is one that is likely to result in the use of the target grammar activity. The context of buying a pet might be used to generate comparative adjectives.

A learner is given a set of animal pictures and takes on the role of a pet shop owner.

Teacher: I am looking for a pet. What can you suggest?
Learner: I have got a tortoise?
Teacher: Have you got something faster?
Learner: What about a tiger?
Teacher: Have you got something tamer?

A generative situation can be an extremely effective way of introducing a new piece of grammar and can also be used to elicit some grammar that is partially known. Creating generative situations is not easy but course books quite often present grammar points through them and these can be adapted for your own purposes. In some ways, a generative situation is part of the way to a communicative task and so is less predictable than the other ways of using examples discussed in this section but it is also more like communication outside the classroom.

Practice activities

Once learners have got the new grammatical knowledge, they need to proceduralize that information by practising it. Practice activities can be more or less controlled. With more controlled activities, the language which learners produce is predetermined and this should help them learn to use the new grammar more automatically. Table 9.6 includes several examples of practice activities.

9.5.3 Corrective feedback

What do you think of errors?

Errors are conceptualized in different ways in different theories of learning. In behaviourist theory errors are bad habits, probably caused by the first language, and evidence that something has not been learnt and must be corrected immediately (Skinner 1974). This view would mean that a teacher should correct all errors and then get learners to repeat the correct version. In the Monitor Model, errors are an

Table 9.6 Controlled activities

Activity 1: A substitution drill

Student 1	I went to the theatre last night
Teacher	My aunt's house
Student 2	I went to my aunt's house last night
Teacher	Visited
Student 3	I visited my aunt's house last night
Teacher	Yesterday

Activity 2: Gap fill

Fill the gaps in the following text with either the present perfect or past simple form of the verb in brackets.

The International Red Cross has appealed for help for thousands of Mongolian herders who have lost their livestock because of extreme cold. Millions of animals _____ [perish] in the country's hardest winter in years. Those animals who survived are running out of food. Temperatures in Mongolia _____ now [drop] below −40C. Local residents call it a 'dzud' – a severe winter following a very dry summer, which ____ _____ [leave] reserves of fodder low. According to the Red Cross, nearly 10% of Mongolia's livestock ____ _____ [die] since December. The agency _____ [say] it needed money to provide emergency food aid to more than 3,000 families who _____[lose] the bulk of their herds and to help them restore or diversify their livelihoods.

Activity 3: Rewriting

Here is a list of things that John decided to do. Can you rewrite them as in the examples? Sometimes there is more than one possible answer.

a. He (John) would stop smoking *John decided to stop smoking*
b. Smoking was not contributing to his life. *John decided that*
c. Mike was his best friend. *John decided that*
d. He (John) would not buy another packet of cigarettes. *John decided not to*
e. He (John) would buy Mike a big present. *John decided to*
f. He (John) would not buy Mike a bottle of whisky. *John decided against*

Look at the following less controlled activities and decide:

What grammar point each is likely to involve? How controlled is the language? How motivating it would be for your students?

Activity 1: Find someone who

The teacher draws a grid on the blackboard and then elicits three musical instruments, three types of singing and three kinds of dance.

Play	Sing	Dance

Table 9.6 (Continued)

Each student then decides on an instrument, a kind of song and a kind of dance. The students are then told to get up and to find someone who plays the same instrument, sings the same kind of song and dances the same kind of instrument as they do.

Activity 2: Describing the group
Students are put into groups of four or five. They must find the name of a TV programme they have seen, a book they have all read and a kind of food they have all eaten in the last month. Then they have to find for each person in the group, either a TV programme that only that person has seen, a book that only person has read or a kind of food only that person has eaten.

Activity 3: Objects
You can model this activity for the class. Choose some humble, unassuming object you've got with you, e.g. a watch, show it to the class and tell its story in the first person, being as inventive as you like, and including lots of passives. The learners then guess your object.

I was produced in a factory in Korea about five years ago, packed in a big dark container with lots of other telephones and sent on a long journey across the sea. I felt quite seasick at times and I was glad when we reached dry land at last. [. . .] When I was bought I was put in a handbag but I was taken out all the time to take pictures of my owner.

a. Tell the learners to choose an object and give them a couple of minutes to invent some episodes in its life – or, of course, to recall some real events that have happened to it.
b. They tell their stories to each other in pairs or small groups.
c. They circulate and find a new listener or a new group of listeners (or you might need to organize this more strictly and tell them who should talk to whom).

Activity 4: Questions
Write to somebody in your class.

a. Take three pieces of paper and write the name of three different students in your class at the top of each sheet. On each piece of paper write a different question to each person.
b. Give your questions to each of the three students, who should write a reply and return the sheet to you.
c. Tell another person about each of the questions you asked and the replies you received.

Example: 'I asked Carmen what she was doing tonight and she told me that she was washing her hair.'

indication of the stage of learning that learners have reached and disappear as learners receive more comprehensible input (Krashen 1989). This view would suggest that errors should be ignored because over time they will disappear.

Within a cognitive or skill learning approach, an error may be due to either

a a lack of knowledge, in which case the best response would be to help learners develop that knowledge or

b a lack of automatization, in which case learners need a lot of practice (Anderson 2010; Johnson 2002) (or sometimes both of these things).

In a cognitive approach, learners' recognizing or noticing their errors is an important element in learning. This relates to the idea of negotiation for meaning. See Activity 9.4.

Within a sociocultural view, errors are an indication that learners that learners need more scaffolding from people or artefacts (Lantolf 2007; Van Lier 2000). The cognitive and sociocultural views are largely consistent but I find the cognitive model more useful as it indicates what kind of support learners need if the teacher can identify the cause of the error.

How do you respond to errors and mistakes

If a learner makes a mistake, the teacher has a range of options. One possibility is to ignore the mistake.

Learner: I lived in UK since 2006.
Teacher: Really. What about you, Tom?

Teachers may do this because they feel that this mistake will disappear over time, or because they feel that this is not an appropriate point to correct the mistake because, for example, it might interrupt the communication and/or have a negative impact on learners' motivation. Teacher often do respond to learner errors. See Table 9.7 for some strategies for responding to learner errors.

Table 9.7 Strategies for responding to grammar mistakes

Rule	
Learner	I lived in UK since 2006.
Teacher	We use the present perfect with 'since'.
Clue for self-correction 1	
Learner	I lived in UK since 2006.
Teacher	I have lived in . . .
Clue for self-correction 2	
Learner	I lived in UK since 2006.
Teacher	No. there is a mistake there.
Metalinguistic identification of error	
Learner	I lived in UK since 2006.
Teacher	Tense
Clarification request 1	
Learner	I lived in UK since 2006.
Teacher	Do you still live in the UK?
Clarification request 2	
Learner	I lived in UK since 2006.
Teacher	Sorry.
Reformulation 1	
Learner	I lived in UK since 2006.
Teacher	You have lived here since 2006, have you?
Reformulation 2	
Learner	I lived in UK since 2006.
Teacher	I have lived here since 2006 (emphasis on 'have').

9.6 Summary

This chapter looked at the teaching of grammar and tried to do three main things: introduce grammatical descriptions; discuss how people learn grammar and look at some of the strategies a teacher might adapt for the teaching of grammar. This last section covered, first, introducing new grammar using rules or example and, second, practicing grammar.

This chapter has not covered the final P of the PPP lesson production. This is covered in Chapter 11.

 Activity 9.7 Discussion

What would you suggest that the teacher in this context does to help the student improve their grammar?

Last summer I taught on a summer school course for teenagers. Most of the students came from a range of southern European countries, for example, Spain and Italy with some Thai, Chinese and Arabic students. The students were aged between fourteen and sixteen and had an elementary level of English. They had a range of grammatical weakness but one which was common to almost all the students was problems to do with the use of the ways they talked about the future. Most of them overused the 'will' future. So they said things like 'I will go to York at the weekend' or 'I will have a conversation class after lunch'. They rarely used the 'going to' future and often referred to the future in incorrect ways, for example, 'I go back home in July'.

 9.7 Further reading

There are several excellent grammar reference books available. Two comprehensive ones are Biber et al.'s (1999) *Longman Grammar of Spoken and Written English* and Carter and McCarthy's (2006) *The Cambridge Grammar of English: A Comprehensive Guide*. There are also books which are aimed more specifically at teachers such as Parrott's (2010) *Grammar for English Language Teachers* and Scrivener's (2010) *Teaching English Grammar: What to Teach and How to Teach It*. As the name suggests, Scrivener also provides useful information about how to teach grammar. Thornbury's (1999) *How to Teach Grammar* is a useful book for most teachers and contains several sample grammar lessons.

Chapter 10

Vocabulary

10.1 Introduction

This chapter examines the teaching of vocabulary and the ideas which underlie how this happens. The chapter is divided into four main sections looking at:

1 What do we mean by vocabulary?
2 What do learners need to know about vocabulary?
3 How do people learn vocabulary?
4 How can we teach vocabulary?

10.2 What do we mean by vocabulary?

10.2.1 What is the unit in vocabulary?

The obvious unit for vocabulary is the word. We might say that a learner knows a thousand words or twenty thousand words. This sounds like a very precise way of discussing language knowledge compared to the imprecise way we measure learners' abilities in, say, reading or even something that is easier to quantify – grammar. Few teachers say their learners know ten items of grammar or have mastered seventeen of the sub-skills in reading, but many talk about their learners' vocabulary size. However, there is some ambiguity about what exactly a word means.

Types and tokens

The first ambiguity is the difference between the meanings of 'word' in the following sentences:

1 How many words do you know?
2 Write two hundred words on your favourite hobby.

In the first sentence, 'words' means different types of words; in the second it means tokens of words. Consider this sentence:

Reports of the number of words in English range from four hundred thousand words to over two million.

This sentence has sixteen different types of words and eighteen tokens of those words. When we ask learners to write an essay of two hundred words, we are talking about *tokens* of words, and when we are talking about how many words we want to teach them, we are talking about *types* of words.

Functional and content words

The aim of vocabulary teachers is to teach words, but some words seem to be more to do with grammar. So, for example, determiners such as 'a' and 'the' or prepositions such as 'of' and 'to' mainly serve a grammatical purpose. In a sentence such as 'The cost of living has increased', 'the' and 'of' seem more to do with signalling grammatical relationships. These kinds of words are described as function words, whereas 'cost', 'living' and 'increased' in the same sentence are described as content words. Generally, nouns, verbs, adjectives and adverbs are content words, but this is not always true. 'Has', a verb, is a content word in the sentence 'She has a large car', but is a function word in 'she has driven a long way'. More specifically, 'has' is an auxiliary verb. See Chapter 9. Other words which can be both content and function words include 'is' and 'do'.

The point of this division is that some words have very general meanings and are probably easier to learn and teach as part of the grammar of English, and others have more specific meanings and so can be taught as part of the vocabulary of English. This is not always a clear-cut distinction, and it is not very important where the person who teaches grammar is the same as the person who teaches vocabulary. However, in course books vocabulary items tend to be verbs and nouns with some adjectives and adverbs but not prepositions. This may be a problem if items such as prepositions are not covered in either the grammar or the vocabulary class.

 Activity 10.1 When does knowing one word mean you know another word?

Imagine you have a learner who can understand the word or phrase in bold in sentences (a) below. Do you think they would be able to understand the word in bold in (b) and sometimes (c) sentences?

1 a Ioanna replaced the light **bulb** in the hall.

   b Achilleas has planted all the tulip **bulbs** in the back garden.

   c Before you start the engine, pump up the fuel line **bulb** on the outboard tank.

2 a If you need to change some money into Euros, you should go to a **bank**.

   b Hillary and Bill have a lovely house on north **bank** of the river.

3 a Indira was **admitted** to hospital after a bad fall.

   b Sanj.ay **admitted** his mistake.

4 a I **like** watching old movies.

   b Yusuf will do whatever he **likes.**

   c There was not enough turkey for my **liking**.

5 a We'd also be **happy** to discuss future developments for your website.

   b Frank sat on the bench **happily** munching peanuts.

6 **a** We **put him up** in a very comfortable hotel.

   b It is often easier to **put up** with difficult employees than to dismiss them.

   c If you are interested in economics, you shouldn't be **put off** by the maths.

7 **a** Mei **glimpsed** a kingfisher on the edge of the lake.

   b Yuchen **caught a glimpse** of the thief's face as he ran around the corner.

Polysemes and homonyms

Quite a lot of words have more than one meaning. We can talk about a human foot, the foot of stairs and someone being three foot tall. These uses of the words are related. The foot of the stairs is metaphorically linked to a human foot, and the foot as a measure of height or length is linked to average size of a human foot. These kinds of words are polysemes.

There is another category of words such as 'bark'. We can talk about a dog's bark and the bark of a tree. These meanings are not obviously connected, and so these are treated as two words which just happen to share the same spelling and pronunciation. Such pairs of words are called homonyms. This distinction is normally made on historical grounds. So polysemes are historically related, while homonyms are historically different but have somehow come to look and sound the same. This is a useful starting point for vocabulary teachers, but teachers are more concerned with the knowledge of their learners. For learners who can work out the meaning of 'foot' in 'foot of the stairs' from knowing what a human foot is, foot is polysemous. For learners who cannot, this is two items.

Lemmas and word families

With polysemes, many learners will be able to use their knowledge of one way of using a word to understand the same word being used in a different way. However, most learners will also be able to work out the meaning of words that are formed from a word they already know plus an affix, for example, they can work out 'tables' from 'table'. Vocabulary theory offers two frameworks for dealing with the fact that knowing one word can sometimes help learners understand another word: lemmas and word families. See Table 10.1.

Table 10.1 Lemmas and word families

Base form	Lemma	Word family
Arrive (verb)	Arrive, arrives, arriving, arrived	Arrive, arrives, arriving, arrived, arrival
Fool (noun)	Fool, fools	Fool, fools, foolish, foolishly
Happy (adjective)	Happy, happier, happiest	Happy, happier, happiest, happily, happiness
Stimulate (verb)	Stimulate, stimulates, stimulating, stimulated	Stimulate, stimulates, stimulating, stimulated, stimulation, stimulative

The division between grammar and vocabulary also comes up when we look at affixes. When someone knows the word 'decide', they probably know the words 'decides', 'decided' and 'deciding' as well, because of their general knowledge of the grammar of English. For teaching purposes, it is more sensible to teach the word 'decide' and assume that learners will be able to work out the meaning of other words without being taught directly.

In technical language, the lemma 'decide' includes 'decides', 'decided' and 'deciding'. The idea of a lemma is limited to grammatical affixes, sometimes called inflections. For nouns, we are talking about the ways plurals are signalled, and for verbs, it includes the third-person present tense 's', the past tense, the -ing participle and the -en form or past participle. For 'choose' the other forms of the lemma are 'chooses', 'chose', 'choosing' and 'chosen', but for most verbs such as 'decide' the past tense 'decided' and the -en form or past participle are the same.

The lemma does not include affixes which change the grammatical category, sometimes called derivative affixes. So 'decision' is not part of the lemma, because 'decided' is a verb and 'decision' is a noun. More advanced learners with a knowledge of derivative affixes may be able to work out 'decision' from 'decide', so lemma may be too narrow a term for these learners. A broader concept is the term 'word family'.

What are word families?

A word family is the base word plus the derivations. Learners are assumed to be able to work out what 'decision' and 'decidedly' mean if they know 'decide'. The difficulty here is knowing how good learners are at working out derived words. If learners know 'revolve' at what level will this mean that they also know 'revolution'? What about 'revolutionary' or 'anti-revolutionary'?

Bauer and Nation (1993) suggest six levels of knowledge of affixes, with the size of the word family growing in size as the knowledge of affixes increases. For beginners 'develop' and 'develops' would be as different as 'bad' and 'had', whereas advanced learners who know the word 'develop' would not only be able to work out the meaning of 'develops' and 'developing' but also 'redevelopment'. This is a very plausible way of describing vocabulary knowledge and is extremely useful for teachers who are trying to decide which affixes to teach to which learners but it is important to bear in mind that this is a generalization and may not apply to particular learners so teachers need to be careful about checking the extent to which the levels approach applies to their learners. It also creates some difficulty for teachers who are trying to make sense of vocabulary levels in curricular documents or course books, many of which use the word family as the unit of vocabulary teaching and learning.

Multiword expressions

We write English with a gap between words and this encourages us to think that it is quite easy to see where one word ends and another begins. There are some problems. 'All right' and 'alright' are written as one and two words respectively but often treated as realizations of the same word. Generally, the conventions of written language are regular enough for identifying a word. However, for teaching purposes some groups of words seem to function as what are called lexical or vocabulary items. There are quite a lot of terms for this (e.g. idioms, phrases and chunks) but here I will use the term multi-word expressions.

Course books vary in how they deal with multi-word expressions. Where teachers are designing their own materials, the concept of multi-word expressions may be useful in working out what language should be taught in the vocabulary class. This is an area which attracts a lot of attention from corpus linguists because of the large number of multi-word expression that appear in natural language. Pawley and Syder (1983) suggest that expert users of English are able to write and speak so fluently because they use a lot of multi-word units. (see also Howarth 1998; Laufer and Waldman 2011; Nesselhauf 2004).

There are two particular categories of multi-word expression that could be taught as single lexical units. The first is one that is often addressed in course books: phrasal verbs. Phrasal verbs are verbs composed of a verb plus an adverb or preposition such as 'take off' and 'put down'. Some descriptions of phrasal verbs use the term particle instead of adverb and preposition to avoid having to make the distinction between adverbs and prepositions. Learners do have grammatical problems with phrasal verbs such as why the sentences in one are acceptable but the sentence in two is not

1 He took off his hat/He took his hat off/He took it off

2 *He took off it.

However, most issues are to do with the meaning of the phrasal verbs as in these two examples:

1 The fighter plane took off from an air craft carrier.

2 She took off her crown.

Lists of phrasal verbs can be found online or in reference works. Table 10.2 gives the list of phrasal verbs that appear more than ten times in every million words (Biber et al. 1999: 401).

The second kind of multi-word expressions that need special attention are what I call delexical verbs (Carter and Mccarthy 2006: 899; Sinclair 1987: 147) but are given other names such as 'light verbs' (Nesselhauf 2004). The main delexical verbs in English are 'have' (e.g. 'have a good look', 'have dinner', 'make' (e.g. 'make sense', 'make use of'), 'give' (e.g. 'give a thoughtful response/answer') and 'take' ('take a bit of a chance', 'take good care'). English quite often expresses an idea that other languages do through a verb by using a verb with a noun, for example, 'have dinner' would normally be just 'dîner' in French or 'cenar' in Spanish. The verb is described as delexical because the meaning is expressed mainly through the noun. Where learners speak languages which handle the meanings that English can express through delexical verbs in a different way, teachers may need to think about teaching these items.

Table 10.2 Phrasal verbs

Come on	Come along	Take up	Find out
Get up	Sit up	Take on	Give up
Sit down	Go ahead	Get back	Point out
Get out	Get in	Get off	Come off
Come over	Pick up	Look up	Run out
Stand up	Put on	Set up	Turn out
Go off	Make up	Take off	Go on
Shut up	Carry out	Take over	

So far the discussion has covered what can be treated as words or lexical units when deciding what vocabulary to teach but teachers also need to think about how much knowledge learners need of each word, lexical unit or phrase.

10.3 What do learners need to know about a word

Activity 10.2 is intended to illustrate how learners' mistaken knowledge of words can lead to language problems.

 Activity 10.2 How much do learners know about words

What aspect of word knowledge do the learners who produced these sentences lack? I have put my interpretation of what the learners meant in brackets after each sentence.

1 We stayed in a bread and breakfast hotel. [bed]

2 He had a long grin on his face. [broad grin]

3 My mother is the kindness person I have ever seen. [kindest]

4 She prepares our food in the chicken. [kitchen]

5 Social media are a feature of temporary society. [contemporary]

6 He is kind and considerable. [considerate]

7 The city is very grown. [developed]

8 They will travel by leg. [on foot]

9 You need to count his pulse. [take]

When we say that learners know a word, this can mean different things but we can get some idea of what advanced learners might be expected to know from looking at a dictionary entry. Here is the entry for the word 'lazy' from the *Macmillan English Dictionary for Advanced Learners* (Rundell 2002: 806):

Lazy /'leizi/ adj **

1 Not willing to work or do anything that involves effort: *It was hot in the garden, but she was too lazy to move.♦ He's a lazy slob who sits in front of the TV all day.*

2 Spent relaxing and not involving any activity that needs effort: *a lazy afternoon in the sun.* 2a. a lazy movement or smile is slow and relaxed: *a lazy grin –* **lazily** adv, **laziness** noun [U]

The basic information here is what I would call the substance (spelling: lazy and pronunciation: /'leizi/) and the meanings given above. With this level of knowledge, learners would be able to understand most instances of either the spoken or written form of the word, though even at this level teachers need to bear in mind some possible limitations. First, the meanings of most words are fuzzy and, even if learners can recognize what is meant by 'a lazy boy', they may not be able to understand what is meant by a 'lazy river' or a 'lazy stereotype'. Second, learners who know how a word is spelt many not necessarily be able to recognize the same word in speech. Third, for most people, the number of words we understand, our receptive vocabulary, is bigger than the words we use in speech or writing. Learners who can understand receptively a word may not be able to use it productively.

Word knowledge is more than spelling/pronunciation and meaning. There is also quite a lot of grammatical or syntactic knowledge. So the dictionary entry includes the fact that lazy is an adjective and this means that we know it can be used with nouns as in 'lazy slob' or as a complement as in 'she was too lazy to move' but not as a verb as in *'They lazy on the sunbeds'.

The dictionary writers have assumed that learners will know the other forms of the lemma, 'lazier' and 'laziest' but they have included some morphological information with the use of the '-ly' suffix to make the adverb 'lazily' and the '-ness' suffix to make the noun 'laziness' so that we can see learners are not expected to know the word family based on 'lazy'.

The other information which the dictionary gives relates to collocation. In English, we say, 'a lazy grin' rather than *'an idle grin'. Collocation is an area of vocabulary knowledge that is attracting a lot of attention and as learners progress this becomes a very important part of their word knowledge. They need to learn at some stage that we can say 'lazy stereotype' but not *'idle stereotype' but we say 'the machines lay idle' but not *'the machines lay lazy' (Lewis 2000; Nesselhauf 2003; Sinclair 1991).

The other information which the dictionary gives is the ** which indicates that 'lazy' is a frequent word. Frequent words will be used in most contexts. Less frequent words might be limited to one or two contexts. A word like 'judicial' will mainly appear in legal or news contexts. Table 10.3 describes what it means to know a word.

Table 10.3 Word knowledge

Substance	Spoken	R	What does the word sound like?
		P	How is the word pronounced?
	Written	R	What does the word look like?
		P	How is the word written and spelled?
Form	Morphology	R	What parts are recognizable in this word?
		P	What word parts are needed to express this meaning?
	Syntax	R	In what patterns does the word occur?
		P	In what patterns must we use this word?
	Collocation	R	What words or types of words occur with this one?
		P	What words or types of words must we use with this one?
Meaning	Concept/referents	R	What is included in the concept
		P	What items can the concept refer to?
	Associations	R	What other words does this make us think of?
		P	What other words could we use instead of this one?
	Frequency/register	R	Where, when and how often would we expect to meet this word?
		P	Where, when and how often can we use this word?

R = receptive; P = productive.

Source: Adapted from Nation (2001: 27)

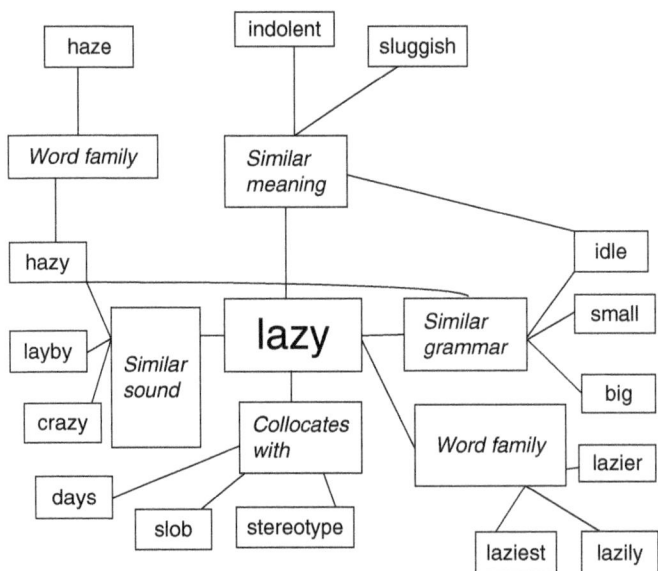

Figure 10.1 Links to 'lazy'

The range of knowledge that learners need for a word is quite daunting but it also indicates that when we are introducing vocabulary to learners we need to think about what kinds of knowledge of the vocabulary we want them to learn and how often they will need to come back to the same words to know enough about it.

It is also useful if trying to understand why learners make mistakes with vocabulary as in Activity 10.2. So, for example, when a learner writes 'bread' rather than 'bed', this suggests that in their mental store or 'lexicon' 'bed' and 'bread' are stored close together, presumably because they sound similar. If learners talk of a 'long grin' instead of a 'broad grin', it suggests that they store words with similar meanings together. This example also implies that for expert users of English there is a link between the collocates 'broad' and 'grin'. 'Count his pulse' instead of 'take his pulse' is also to do with collocations. Expert users of English may either have a link between the delexical verb 'take' and 'pulse' or they may store 'take someone's pulse' as one lexical item. The learners who write 'count his pulse' may also be using the collocation that works in their mother tongue.

Figure 10.1 is an attempt to represent part of a networks related to 'idle' in the mental lexicon but we should bear in mind that 'mental maps are unlike real-life maps in that they have to depend on inspired guesswork, since we cannot easily look into the head and see the connections we hypothesise' (Aitchison 2003:37).

10.3.1 How many words do learners need?

Learners often ask how many words they need to learn. This is a very difficult question to answer partly because it is hard to say what we mean by a word or what knowing a word means but also because the answer depends on the learners' purpose for studying English.

English is estimated to have a million words (Payack 2014). *Chambers English Dictionary* has about 250,000 definitions (Schwarz et al. 1988). These figures suggest that the task of learning vocabulary is one that will never be completed. This is true for all speakers of English. Native speakers of English are estimated to know 20,000 word families (as opposed to words) (Nation and Waring 1997). Twenty thousand word families, though daunting, seems a much more achievable aim. Indeed Milton and Meara (1995) found that able adult learners could learn over 2,500 words in their year abroad.

Nation suggests that, rather than taking this as a target, focussing on the most common words, plus, if relevant, words that relate to the areas that are important to specific learners. There are about two thousand high-frequency word families and this is probably a threshold for being able to use English effectively. Laufer and Shmueli (1997: 90) suggest that learners need to be able to understand 3,000 to 3,500 word families to pass Cambridge First Certificate, an upper intermediate examination.

Several lists of the most common words are available online. One of the earliest, and still in use, is the General Service word list (West 1953) and this has been revised with corpus data (Brezina and Gablasova 2015). Several more specialized lists of words for learners with specific aims have been compiled. The best known of these is probably the academic word list (Coxhead 2000).

10.4 Learning vocabulary

The most useful framework for understanding how learners learn vocabulary explicitly is provided by cognitive models so we really need to think about

1 How learners get knowledge of vocabulary – that is, how learners develop declarative knowledge of vocabulary, largely by noticing something new.

2 How learners learn to use that knowledge – that is, how that knowledge is proceduralized.

As with learning grammar, implicit learning as the result of reading and listening also makes a great contribution to language learning.

10.4.1 Developing declarative knowledge of vocabulary by noticing

Learners first need to notice that there is something new in what they are hearing or reading. If they are encountering a word for the first time, they need to see the connection between a group of sounds or letters and a meaning. If they are learning new things about a word they already know, then this can relate to any of the areas of word knowledge discussed above.

Noticing something requires some motivation from learners. This may be provided by the teacher, for example, by showing an interesting picture, but it is likely to be stronger if the reason for noticing the word comes from something within the learners. If learners come across an unknown word in a text or realize that there is something they want to say but they do not know how to say this in English, they are more likely to notice it than if the teacher or course book tells them that this is an important word. Laufer and Hulstijn (2001) argue that learning new vocabulary happens best when learners need the word to complete some task.

Nation (2001) says that noticing involves decontextualization. This may be the teacher writing the word on the board or the learners thinking 'That is a new word' or 'I did not realize that those two words can go together to mean that'. But learners need to step outside the communication 'to give attention to a language item as part of the language rather than as part of a message' (Nation 2001: 64).

Learners also need to relate the information to the knowledge they already have. If they are learning something new about a word they already know, this will mean that they add another link to the word in their mental lexicon. If the word is completely new they will need to link it to other words that they know which are similar in terms of meaning, pronunciation or other aspects of word knowledge. If the learners only know a few words in English the link may be to a word in their mother tongue or other languages they already know.

10.4.2 Proceduralizing word knowledge

Getting the words into learners' memories is the start of learning a word. If nothing more is done the word will be forgotten quite quickly. Learners need to use the words so that the knowledge is proceduralized. In Chapter 3 proceduralization was divided into controlled and automatic use. Other words are sometimes used by those who study vocabulary development, so Nation talks of retrieval and generative use, terms which share a lot with controlled and automatic. Retrieval means that learners find the word in their own memories, either because they need it to express an idea or because they have come across the word again in something they have heard or read. Each time this happens the links between the word and other areas of knowledge in the mental lexicon are strengthened. Generative use covers the situation where 'previously met words are met or used in ways that differ from previous meetings with the word' (Nation 2001: 68) so this will often involve the creation of new links.

Unfortunately, retrieval and generative use are not enough to guarantee that learners will retain the new vocabulary. The links in the mental lexicon are weak and unless retrieval and/or generative use happen repeatedly words will be forgotten. The research is not clear on how many repetitions are needed to ensure something is remembered, but Thornbury (2002: 24) suggests that 'words stand a good chance of being remembered if they have met at least seven times over spaced intervals'. The spacing of the repetitions is important. Rather than spending ten minutes in a block trying to remember a word, it is better to spend two minutes on the first day, two minutes on the next day, then two minutes of third day, two minutes on seventh day and two minutes a month later. This is biologically plausible (Baddeley et al. 2009) because the delays give the neurochemicals in the brain time to reinforce connections or create new nodes.

Spacing can be influenced by teachers but learning is ultimately a matter for learners and unless the input is taken in by learners it will not bring about any vocabulary development. Laufer and Hulstijn (2001) found that when learners were more involved in the task for which vocabulary was needed, they learnt more.

10.5 Teaching vocabulary

The previous two sections of this chapter were meant to help teachers decide what to teach in the vocabulary lessons and how learners might be helped to learn that vocabulary most efficiently. This section now attempts to put these two things together to come up with suggestions about how best to teach vocabulary.

Vocabulary teaching makes many teachers think of learners going through a list of vocabulary, what I would call explicit vocabulary teaching, but a lot of vocabulary learning happens in classes or beyond them, where the aim is not vocabulary teaching, what I would call incidental vocabulary learning. Teachers need to be able to teach vocabulary explicitly but they also need to be able to support learners to develop their vocabulary incidentally, either by using tools such as dictionaries or by exploiting what happens when their learners read or listen to texts in English.

Nation (2001: 2–3) suggests the following sequence for teaching vocabulary:

1 Comprehensible meaning-focussed input – a communicative activity where the focus is on meaning

2 Language- or form-focussed learning – learners focus on particular words or aspects of word knowledge

3 Meaning-focussed use – learners use the new vocabulary or new aspects of word knowledge in a controlled way

4 Fluency development – learners use the new vocabulary in a communicative task in ways that are close to expert users

This relates closely to his ideas about learning described in the previous section with stage two being to do with noticing and stage three to do with retrieval and the first and final stages being communicative tasks.

This also has some similarities with presentation, practice and production (see Chapter 4) with presentation being divided into a contextualized and decontextualized phase. Nation suggests that each of these strands should get equal amounts of attention and, while the evidence supporting this division is limited, this is a useful rule of thumb. For this chapter, I am assuming that the learners have already engaged in some comprehensible meaning-focussed input or meaning-focussed intake, and have some ideas about some final communicative task that is end of fluency development, and will only cover stages 2 and 3.

10.5.1 Language-focussed learning

The language focus stage involves two elements, noticing and the provision of information. This probably makes it sound more complicated than it is in practice. If a learner asks 'what does "zebra" mean?' that indicates that the learner has noticed a gap in his mental lexicon related to the meaning of 'zebra' and if the teacher says something like 'a kind of wild horse with black and white stripes', the teacher has provided information about the meaning to fill the gap.

The key feature of noticing is that this must be done by the learners so it is generally better if the learners identify what vocabulary they want to learn. Rather than the teacher or course book writer identifying what words in a reading or listening passage need to be pre-taught the learners should read or listen to the text and identify what words they think they need to learn. This is a kind of incidental vocabulary learning but does seem to lead to fairly good retention (Sonbul and Schmitt 2010).

Another way of making sure that learners have noticed the relevant word is a communication breakdown and the resultant negotiations for meaning, a topic covered in Chapter 3. Here is an example from two learners doing a picture description task in which learner one describes a picture to learner two. Learner two does not have the picture and is trying to draw the picture (Gass 1998: 237).

Learner 1	Woman has a [dok]
Learner 2	Duck?
Learner 1	[dok]
Learner 2	[dʌk] Oh I see
Learner 1	A [dok]
Learner 2	What kind of dog?
Learners 1	I'm not sure. The usual one . . . The dog wear some clothe.

Here learner two identifies that she does not understand what learner one has said and, after a couple of goes, learner one realizes that the problem is to do with pronunciation. When learner two says 'What kind of dog?' this seems to be enough for learner one to start pronouncing the word in a more standard way.

Some teachers may want to limit vocabulary teaching to communication breakdowns or learner questions but most teachers are happy to draw their learners' attention to what they think should be learnt, often through questions, but also through techniques such as pretending not to understand what learners mean.

Once the gap in word knowledge has been identified, the question of how to fill that gap is raised. Sometimes there is little choice about how the information is provided. In the 'dog' example above, the gap related to the pronunciation of 'dog'. Learner two could have said 'you need to voice that final consonant' but just saying the word 'dog' seems more likely to connect with learner one's knowledge. Providing models is also a good, if not the only, way to deal with spelling and can be useful for grammar and collocation.

Where there is more choice, the information is best presented in a way that relates to the knowledge the learner already has. For low-level learners, one way of communicating the meaning of a word is translation and some research suggests that translation within a broadly L2 using classroom is more effective than the provision of synonyms in the L2 (Laufer and Shmueli 1997). Translation needs to be treated with care.

Translation has the advantages of being quick, simple, and easily understood. Its major disadvantage is that its use may encourage other use of the first language that seriously reduces the time available for use of the second language. (Nation 2001: 86)

It is also possible to relate new information about meaning to learners' existing knowledge of the world though the use of actions, showing objects, sometimes called *realia*, or using pictures or diagrams.

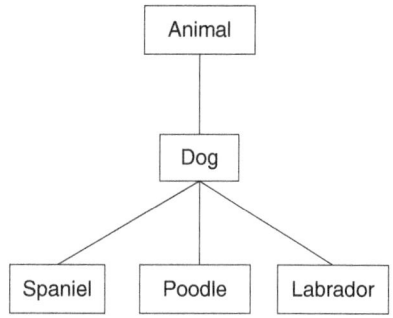

Figure 10.2 Superordinates and hyponyms

When learners have more knowledge of English, this can be used to help them understand meaning, though definitions and lexical relationships such as synonyms, antonyms or opposites, superordinates and hyponyms. See Figure 10.2.

Animal is a superordinate of dog. Dog is a hyponym of animal and a superordinate of spaniel, poodle and labrador. Spaniel is a hyponym of dog.

Definitions are also a useful way of helping learners understand the meaning of words or phrases. These definitions need to be short and simple. Laufer and Shmueli (1997) found that learners do not take in more complicated definitions. It is worth spending time helping learners use paper or electronic dictionaries to find information about words.

Where learners need information about other aspects of meaning such as grammar, collocation and register, examples of how the words are used can be very helpful. Some teachers can provide multiple examples without preparation but dictionaries and corpora are also useful. Here are some sentences taken from the *British National Corpus* for the word 'grin'. These are intended to illustrate what kind of adjectives are used with 'grin'.

1 Amsterdam gave his aunt a lopsided grin.

2 Billy replied, with a mischievous grin.

3 Diana, Barry's wife of 35 years, doesn't mind him meeting all the great screen goddesses. 'I think she feels I'm safe', he says with that famous lopsided grin.

4 'Duty calls', he said with a wry grin.

5 He gave her a wide toothy grin, and immediately realized it was exactly the wrong approach.

6 Her face broke into a mischievous grin that was pure Sally-Anne.

7 She gave a wry little grin, realizing she had no real plan of action.

8 Then his face broke into a sheepish grin.

9 Then his smile became a sheepish grin and his shoulders hunched in a giggle.

10 When he saw me, he grinned a wide toothy grin.

This is an example of what Nation (2001: 94 et seq.) describes as rich instruction and this is only appropriate for words which are particularly important to a specific group of learners.

Activity 10.3 Concordance-informed activities

Here is a set of rich instruction material that I devised about the difference between 'tall' and 'high' for upper-intermediate students. It was quick to produce, but you will need to decide how effective this is for your learners.

What kind of things can be described as 'tall'?

1 The noise brought in the new officer, a **tall** and muscular young lieutenant with a sad, world-weary face.

2 Under the eyes of a serious, **tall** Palestinian with a gun, they were singing.

3 We were sitting on rather low chairs, and he was very **tall.**

4 They planted **tall** trees in the middle of the road.

5 Both are inner-city areas, with **tall** buildings.

6 I don't know what it was, but I felt almost ten feet **tall.**

7 Some girls are **tall** and some girls are short.

8 George and Simon are **tall** and walked with that kind of lithe confidence.

Write a list of things that can be described as tall here.

What kind of things can be described as 'high'?

1 They fired **high** over our heads.

2 **High** prices were paid for prize specimens.

3 In general, Labour seemed to suffer from **high** tax levels.

4 Often buildings are many storeys **high.**

5 A **high** income brings a middle-class self-identification despite having a manual occupation.

6 First, of course, because it only affects **high** earners, that is, those earning more than £75,000 a year.

7 They amazed us by leaping **high** out of the water and somersaulting two or three times before nosing beneath it again without missing a beat.

8 Dealers welcomed the rise in other countries' interest rates as it closes the gap with Sweden's own **high** rates.

Write a list of things that can be described as 'high' here.

Fill in the gaps with either high or tall.

1 And Arsenal were offering an unusually _____ salary for a football manager.

2 For a while this may happen easily, not least in circumstances when interest rates are very _____

    _____.

3 He was able to sell the leaves for _____ prices.

4 Most of the women are _____ so they don't wear _____ heels.

5 The farm workers are _____ and proud in their bearing and though they have a slim build they are surprisingly strong and agile for their size.

Rehearsal

Several games provide useful ways to rehearse vocabulary. Here are some examples but the literature contains many other examples and your fellow teachers will have their favourites.

Lexical sets

This is a way of getting learners to rehearse words which they have already studied. The left-hand column is either written on the board or given as a hand out and, the learners hopefully end up with the right-hand box column, either based on their own knowledge of using a dictionary or other support if that would be useful

Arrange these words into three lexical sets	**Answer**
cat, chair, goldfish, hamster	Cat, goldfish, hamster, rabbit
March, rabbit, settee, sidle	Chair, settee, sofa, stool
Sofa, stool, stroll, walk	March, sidle, stroll, walk

Guessing the word

The class is divided up into two or more groups and each group is either given or comes up with a list of a given number of words that have been studied by the group over the last two weeks. The words are then written in lists on the board. One person from each team comes to the front of the class and faces the other learners. The rest of the learner's team then shouts out clues to the word but they are not allowed to say that actual word on the board. Within a given amount of time, learners guess as many words as possible.

Stories and songs

Primary age learners often like to hear the same story several times and this is a very useful way of getting them to recycle vocabulary. Songs and poems (Coyle and Gracia 2014) are also useful sources of repeated vocabulary. Serialized stories often include quite a lot of repeated vocabulary and this can work well with older learners either as a group or individually.

Vocabulary records

Keeping a vocabulary record (Mccrostie 2007; Schmitt and Schmitt 1995) is extremely helpful for vocabulary learning and rehearsal. These can be physical notebooks, a card index or there are now apps which allow learners to create these on tablets or phones. Card indexes and apps have the advantage of allowing for word cards to be rearranged to help with learning. Notebooks encourage learners to revisit words and to add information to entries as they learn more about words.

Apps for learning vocabulary such as *Memrise* are now available and these can often be a useful supplement to what happens in class.

10.6 Summary

This chapter has looked at what might be the aim of a vocabulary class, how learners might develop their vocabulary and what a teacher can do to help learners do that. The chapter covered

1 What is meant by a word (types, tokens, polysemes and homonyms, lemmas, word families, multiword expressions)?

2 What it means to know a word?

3 How words are learnt (how information gets into learners' heads, helping them learn to use that knowledge)?

4 How can words be taught?

    a How do you help learners notice words?

    b How do you help learners practice words?

 Activity 10.4 Discussion

1 Think of a teaching situation in which vocabulary is being studied, which you know either from the point of view of a learner or a teacher, and try to address the following questions:

    a How good is your learners' vocabulary? In what ways would you want your learners to be able to deal better with vocabulary? What makes you think this?

    b How many words are taught in a typical vocabulary lesson or part of a lesson?

    c How are the words chosen? Did the teacher choose the words? Were they related to a reading or listening text or did the learners choose the words?

    d What kind of knowledge about the words did the teacher cover? Meaning? Spelling? Pronunciation? Grammar? Something else?

    e How did the teacher present the vocabulary?

What did the learners do with the vocabulary?

2 What would you suggest that the teacher in this context do to help the student improve?

I work with ELLs aged nine to eleven. These students have been in the United States for several years and can communicate well in most everyday situations. The local policy for ELLs is push-in. This means that they go to normal primary school classes but they are supported by their ELL teacher, and in this case, that is me. The main teacher is not trained in dealing with ELLs and I find that I spend most of my time answering whispered questions about the vocabulary that the main teacher is using. I have now been given two one hour withdrawal classes, when I work with the ELLs on their own outside their normal classes and I am not sure what I should do with them.

3 Here are some extracts from vocabulary teaching classes (Xie 2013: 438–9). For each extract identify

    a What is being taught?

    b How the learners are being encouraged to increase their declarative knowledge of the new item?

    c How the learners are being encouraged to proceduralize that knowledge?

Extract 1: From a reading class

> **Learner 1:** What does **in fact** mean?
> **Teacher: in fact**. What do you think **in fact** means**, Jean**
> **Learner 2: In fact**. In real.
> **Teacher:** More or less. Really. **In fact** means really.

Extract 2: A picture

> **Teacher:** [holding up a picture of a tulip.] What is this?
> **Learner 1:** A flower
> **Teacher:** A flower. Good. What kind of flower?
> **Learner 1:** A red flower.
> **Teacher:** Yes it is a red flower. But what kind of flower?
> **Learner 2:** From the Netherlands.
> **Learner 2:** Tulips.

Extract 3: Negotiation for meaning

> **Learner:** I have a cat with a stripped tail
> **Teacher:** A stripped tail?
> **Learner:** Yes, a stripped tail. Stripped. White and brown
> **Teacher:** Striped? Like a zebra. A zebra has black and white stripes.
> **Learner:** Ah, stripe. A stripe tail. Like a zebra.
> **Teacher:** A cat with a white and brown striped tail

Extract 4

> **Teacher:** Next one, We're going to have a welcome party in his honour. (Reading from the course book). 'In one's honour' means 'to do something for somebody' ok. To have a party in one's honour' means 'to have a party for somebody'. For instance, our university gave a performance in honour of the freshmen. WO MEN YAO WEI TA BAN YI GE WAN HUI. (Supplying a Chinese sentence for students to translate).
> **Student:** We will have a party in his honour.
> **Teacher:** ZAI TA TUI XIU ZHI QIAN, WO MEN JUE DING GEI TA JU XING YI CI SHENG DA DE JU HUI. (Supplying a Chinese sentence for students to translate.)
> **Student:** Before he retired . . . (Students translating all at the same time.)
> **Teacher:** Before he retired, we decided to hold a big party in his honour. Pay attention, 'honour' has two spellings: honor and honour. (Writing on the blackboard).

10.7 Further reading

There are several useful books on vocabulary learning and teaching. The most authoritative is Nation (2013). Other useful books are McCarthy et al. (2010), Schmitt (2000), Thornbury (2002) and Webb & Nation (2017). If you are interested in the mental lexicon, Aitchison (2003) is a very clearly written introduction to the topic.

Chapter 11

Discourse

11.1 Introduction

The aim of communicative language teaching is to enable learners to engage in real-world communicative tasks, and understanding what this phrase means is vital in producing curricula for communicative language teaching and for identifying the aims of lessons or programmes.

> The real-world tasks may be required for academic purposes, for example, locating a journal in a university library, writing a lab report, or attending a graduate-level economics lecture . . . They may be for occupational purposes . . . for example, while stationed at an embassy, interviewing visa applicants, issuing instructions to security personnel, or delivering an after-dinner speech. (Long 2016: 6)

This list indicates that the number of different kinds of communicative tasks is extensive, if not boundless. A complete set of communicative tasks does not exist and probably could not exist. However, the danger of this kind of list is that it encourages something akin to the directness or authenticity argument used in testing (Chapter 6), that is, what we should be doing in the language classroom is replicating what happens outside the language classroom, and the same rebuttals discussed then apply here. Delivering an after-dinner speech in a language classroom is not the same as delivering a speech after a formal dinner, and also the aim of the class is to help the learners develop the skills for giving after-dinner speeches in general rather than this specific speech.

This is not to say that simulating life beyond the language class is not useful, just that it is not a complete response to how learners can be helped to engage in communicative tasks beyond the language classroom. Language teachers need generalizable accounts of real-life communicative language tasks with an understanding of how these accounts may be used in learning and teaching.

Readers will also have noticed the terminological issue implied by the gap between the focus on communicative tasks at the start of the chapter and the chapter title – discourse. This reflects the fact that research into communicative tasks has largely taken place under the head of discourse analysis and is why this chapter addresses the following questions:

1 What is discourse?

2 How do people learn English discourse?

3 How can teachers help learners develop discourse abilities?

11.2 Understanding English discourse

Discourse analysis and the associated field of pragmatics both provide descriptions of how people use language for communication in context. Pragmatics has focused more on how context impacts our understanding of language, while discourse analysis is more interested in how texts are contextually structured, but there is considerable overlap. Both areas have generated a vast amount of research, and this chapter is necessarily selective, but the selection attempts to represent our understanding of communicative tasks by looking at four related key elements:

1 What is the purpose of communicative tasks (speech act theory)?

2 How do the people involved in communicative tasks interact (politeness theory)?

3 How are communicative tasks structured (patterns in text)?

4 How purpose, interaction and structure can be brought together (genre theory)?

The section on further reading provides suggestions if these areas pique your attention.

Table 11.1 contains a transcript of one kind of a real-life communicative task, a service encounter in a shop, and the rest of this section shows how different approaches to discourse analysis can help us understand the transcript.

11.2.1 Speech act theory

When the customer says, 'Can I have a small postal bag please, [a] jiffy bag?' this is a request, but even though it contains the word 'can', this does not seem to be a question about ability or permission. Indeed, in some languages, for example, Malay, a question formulated in this way would be odd. Expressing a request in English using 'can' has become conventionalized as a request, but the assistant could answer, 'No, you need to go to a stationery shop', which suggests that some interpretation is necessary. Speech act theory is a way of explaining how what is superficially a question about ability is interpreted as a request.

The theory originates from Austin's (1962) insight that when people use language they are not simply describing reality but also doing things, for example, naming a ship, and getting married. When the registrar says, 'It therefore gives me great pleasure to declare that you are now legally married' at the end of a wedding ceremony, this is not just a description of the registrar's emotional state but means the couple

Table 11.1 A service encounter (Ventola 1984: 282)

S	1	You're right. /rising tone/
C	2	Can I have a small postal bag please, [a] jiffy bag? /3 secs – S gets the bag and hands it over/
S	3	Twenty cents. /C hands over the money and S receives it/
S	4	Thank you very much.
C	5	Thank you.

S = shop assistant; C = customer. Comments between back slashes were added by the researcher.

Table 11.2 Felicity conditions for a request

Felicity condition	Example for request
Proposition content	Predicts future act by the hearer
	Speaker believes hearer is able to perform act
Sincerity	Speaker sincerely wants hearer to perform act
Essential	Utterance counts as an attempt to get the hearer to perform act

Source: Holtgraves (2002: 13)

are married (Leeds City Council 2017). However, this is not limited to special uses of language. When the customer above asked about the 'jiffy bag', this was intended to carry out the function of a request. All language use involves doing things, that is, all language is functional and so needs to be evaluated in terms of whether it successfully realizes the speaker or writer's intention, or, in terms of speech act theory, it meets the 'felicity conditions' of the speech act. See Table 11.2 for the felicity conditions for a request. Except for the final condition in that table, that the utterance counts as an attempt to get the hearer to perform act, most learners will be aware of these conditions from their first language.

Austin does not discuss the issue of scale. The jiffy bag request was one sentence long and involved two people, while a wedding ceremony is much longer and – in the UK – minimally requires the presence of the couple getting married, the registrar and two witnesses. Most speech act research has focused on individual utterances, and this meant little attention has been paid to the internal structure of speech acts, though this has been explored in the work on patterns in text and genre, discussed below. More work has been done on the different kinds of speech acts. For example, Searle (1976: 7–11) identifies five categories:

1 Commissives – the speaker is committed to doing something, for example, promise, guarantee and oath.

2 Declaratives – the speaker's words change the world, for example, baptise, declare war, name.

3 Directives – the speaker wants the listener to do/say something, for example, advise, invite, order, permit and request.

4 Expressives – the speaker's words describe a psychological state, for example, apologize, congratulate, greet and thank.

5 Representatives – the speaker represents an aspect of reality, for example, boast, complain, conclude and state.

This is a useful framework, though declaratives are probably a minority interest for most language learners, but is at a high level of generality. Tsui, for example, identifies three different categories where Searle just identifies directive (O'Keeffe et al. 2011: 97):

Elicitives	to elicit an obligatory verbal response or its non-verbal surrogate
Requestives	to solicit non-verbal action with the option to carry out this action
Directives	to solicit non-verbal action with no option of whether or not the addressee will carry out the solicited action

This level of specificity is useful when it comes to identifying language learning aims, but it also highlights that interactions are negotiations and the interpretation intended by the speaker may not be the same as the interpretation of the listener. Grundy (2008: 148) reports how a question in an email 'Can you tell me how to get to the airport from X?', which was intended as a request to be taken from a hotel to the airport, resulted in an extensive set of travel instructions.

The insight that language is functional has had a great impact on language teaching, and most course books and syllabuses make use of at least some functional labels, for example, greeting, making requests. See Chapter 2 but also Swan's critique of functional approaches in Chapter 4.

11.2.2 Politeness

Some of the language used in post office dialogue seems redundant. When the customer wanted a bag, they could more simply and quickly say 'Give me a jiffy bag', and at the end of the interaction, both assistant and customer say 'thank you'. These elements of dialogue could be omitted, and the interaction would have been just as functional, so functionality is not all that involved here. As well as buying and selling a bag, the participants want to be polite to each other.

Linguists see politeness as to do with the way that people maintain their own status, or what is described in politeness research as 'face', or interfere with the status of others. For example, when the customer asked the shop assistant for the bag, this was a minor threat to the shop assistant's face because the shop assistant was being asked to do something. The customer in this dialogue chose to mitigate the threat by formulating the request as a question which gave the shop assistant the opportunity to say 'no'. This kind of mitigation is described as negative politeness because it reduces the demands on the other person and recognizes their independence. The mutual expressions of gratitude at the end of the dialogue would also be treated as negative politeness because they are an acknowledgement that neither participant needed to engage in the interaction.

English has a wide range of mitigation techniques so the customer could have said 'I was wondering, if, by any chance, you might have some jiffy bags'. The use of a statement means that there is no requirement that the assistant has to reply, the use of the past tense suggests that this is not an immediate problem, and the 'by any chance' indicates that the customer will not be overly disappointed if the assistant cannot provide a jiffy bag (Leech 2007).

It would also have been possible for the customer to have used other strategies such as addressing the assistant by name or perhaps engaging in a conversation as a way of indicating that the two are not just linked by the service encounter before making the request. The strategy of building up the other person's face is described as positive politeness. Both positive and negative strategies require more linguistic resources than the bare 'Give me a jiffy bag'.

Speakers may choose to perform face threatening acts more indirectly. This would be difficult in a shop, where a customer is speaking to a shop assistant because the context strongly implies that the customer will ask for something. But, if someone wants to invite a friend to a party, they might start with a pre-sequence (English Web 2013 (enTenTen13)).

Anna: Hi Philip. How's it going?
Philip: Not bad. Listen, are you free on Saturday?

Anna: Sure. Why?

Philip: It's my birthday on Thursday, but most people are working that day, so I want to have a little get-together on Saturday

When Philip asks Anna if she is free on Saturday, this allows Anna to turn down the invitation before it is even made and so without a threat to Philip's face. Even more indirectly, the speaker can go off record as in (Paltridge 2012: 77):

A: I'm dying for a drink (an off-record invitation to go for a drink).

B: Yes it's really hot, isn't it (an off-record rejection of the invitation, signalled by the absence of a reference to going for a drink).

However, the use of these strategies is not simply a matter of personal choice. Brown and Levinson (1987) identify three contextual factors which influence the choice of strategies:

1 the power difference between speakers, where people without power are more polite;

2 the social distance between speakers, where strangers are more polite than friends; and people who know each other well are less polite and

3 the degree of threat, where asking to borrow £1,000 requires more politeness than borrowing £5.

Politeness theory offers a useful way of thinking about how relationships between speakers and listeners impact on language use. What counts as polite may vary from context to context or culture to culture so it is important that language teachers make themselves familiar with the politeness strategies learners bring to the classroom as well that the strategies described above. Politeness theory does not offer an account of the structure of complete communicative task and some kinds of communicative task, for example, conversation may not have an obvious structure. However, for tasks which do have structure, we need to look at research into patterns in text.

 Activity 11.1 Speech acts and politeness

1 Here is a dialogue from a course book for beginners. If A had wanted to be more polite, what language could A have used (Oxenden and Latham-Koenig 2009: 84)?

A: Can I have a memory card, please?

B: Four gig or eight?

A: Four please. How much is that?

B: Four ninety-nine.

A: Can I pay with Mastercard?

B: Sure.

2 Some speakers of Japanese were asked how they would ask a friend to close the window because of the cold. This is what they would say in English to an English friend: Could you close the window for me?/ Hey yo, close the window, would you?

This is what they would say to a Japanese friend in Japanese: Isn't it a little chilly?/ It's cold, don't you think? (Paltridge 2012: 75).

Can you account for the differences?

3   Greeting: English has adapted a question about health as a way of greeting. Here are ten instances of 'How are you?' from the British National Corpus. What is the typical response to the question?

   a   'So how are you,' he said, 'this morning?' 'Fine', she said brightly.

   b   'How are you, Andy? 'OK thanks, Younis', replied an American voice

   c   'And how are you, my boy?' 'Fine, sir'.

   d   'And how are you, my dear?' 'I'm quite well, thank you', she said,

   e   'Maggie! how are you? Are you OK? Where have you been?' 'I'm fine'.

   f   'Oh . . . em, Catherine, how are you?' 'Fine, Duncan'.

   g   'How are you?' 'I'm fine'

   h   'Hi, Kate, how are you?' 'Fine . . .'

   i   'And how are you?' 'Fine'.

   j   'Hello, Mammele, how are you?' 'We're all fine, Dad'.

Is 'how are you?' still a question about health?

   Other languages have also adapted questions as ways of greeting (e.g. have you eaten? where are you going?). In any language that you know can you say to what extent these questions have lost their primary meaning as questions and become simple greetings?

11.2.3 Text patterns

The jiffy bag dialogue has a simple sequence, from the shop assistant's acknowledgement of the customer to the concluding 'thank you'. Spoken monologues and written texts allow for more planning by the speaker or writer and so often have a more complex structure than jointly constructed spoken interaction. The most widely recognized pattern in English language teaching is the problem-solution pattern, most associated with Hoey (1983). This four-part structure is illustrated in Tables 11.3 and 11.4.

Table 11.3 A minimum discourse version of the problem-solution pattern

Situation	I was on sentry duty
Problem	I saw the enemy approaching
Response	I opened fire
Evaluation	I beat off the attack

Source: Hoey (1983: 68)

Table 11.4 An authentically produced problem-solution pattern

Situation	Helicopters are very convenient for dropping freight by parachute
Problem	But this system has its problems. Somehow the landing impact has to be cushioned to give a soft landing. The movement to be absorbed depends on the weight and the speed at which the charge falls. Unfortunately, most normal spring systems bounce the load as it lands, sometimes turning it over
Response	To avoid this, Bertin, developer of the aerotrain, has come up with an air-cushion system
Evaluation	Which assures a safe and soft landing

Source: Hoey (1983: 68)

The longer example of a problem-solution text in Table 11.4 also illustrates the grammar and vocabulary elements which are associated with this pattern. Words like 'but' and 'unfortunately' often signal that something is a problem and 'to avoid this' signals that something is a response or possible solution.

 Activity 11.2 Analysing a problem-solution text

Here is an example of a recursive problem-solution text, that is, it has several problems and several solutions. Identify the different elements in the text and any signalling vocabulary. Some sentences may need to be divided in two.

1 Once upon a time there was a beautiful princess.

2 She was a bit bored and so she decided to get married.

3 First, she went to England and she met a very nice man who took her to eat fish and chips but he wore a bowler hat all the time and she found that very off-putting.

4 Then, she went to Scotland and she met a very nice man who cooked her some very nice haggis, turnips and potatoes but he wore a kilt and, even though he was very nice, she was worried she would get tired of looking at his knees every day.

5 Then, she went to Wales and she met a very nice man who cooked her nice lamb with seaweed but he sang the whole way through the meal and she did not think she could marry someone who was always singing.

6 So she went home and started a restaurant specializing in fish and chips, haggis and lamb and lived happily ever after.

11.2.4 Genre analysis

Genre analysis is an approach to analysing the characteristic of groups of texts. It encompasses elements from all the approaches we have discussed so far. So, like speech act theory, the key element in a genre is the purpose for which it exists. Swales (1990: 58) explains 'A genre comprises a class of communicative events, the members of which share some set of communicative purposes'. For many purposes, the communicative events will be text and for many people genre analysis is a way of categorizing texts. This might not seem quite the same as a communicative task. However, the view of language discussed in Chapter 2 means that texts do not have an independent existence but need to be constructed by those who use them so a text is always in some sense a task (cf. Graddol 1994). If, for example, teachers or materials writers wanted to teach a unit to help learners define words they might analyse the set of texts in Table 11.5.

Genre analysts have different views about how to look at texts but one useful view draws on Halliday's ideas about language (1978) and is associated with Martin and Rose (2008). For Halliday, when we use language we are simultaneously constrained by the people involved in creating and interpreting language (what Halliday calls the 'tenor' and which has some links to politeness theory), what the text is about, what Halliday calls the 'field' and how the text is delivered, which he calls 'mode' and incorporates text patterns.

In this framework, genre analysts are basically asking questions about the overarching issue of purpose and the three meta-functions (to use Halliday's term) of field, tenor and mode. See Table 11.6.

Table 11.5 Texts for a genre analysis

au-then-ti-cate /ɔːˈθen.tɪ.keit/ US /ɑːˈθen.tɪ-/ *verb* [T] to prove that something real, true, or what people say it is. *They used carbon dating tests to authenticate the claim that the skeleton was 2 million year old*	**ge-net-ics** / dʒəˈnet.ɪks/ US /- net-/ *noun* [U] the study of how, in all living things, the characteristics and qualities of parents are given to their children by their genes
leap-frog /ˈliːpfrɒg/ US /-fr ɑːg/ *noun* [U] a children's game in which a number of children bend down and another child jumps over them one at a time.	**pseud** /suːd/ *noun* [C] *UK INFORMAL DISAPPROVING* a person who tries to seem to have detailed knowledge or excellent judgment of a subject, esp. in art, literature, music etc. • *He's such a pseud with his talk of 'lambent harmonies' and 'melting appeggios'.*

Source: Woodford and Jackson (2003)

Table 11.6 A genre analysis of dictionary definitions

Dimension	Question	Response for dictionary texts
Purpose	What is the purpose of the texts?	The texts are intended to help people use words
Field	What are the texts about?	The texts provide, orthographic, phonological, grammatical and semantic information about the words
Tenor	Who are the writers/speakers/readers/listeners related to the texts?	The writers are language experts (and we could find out more precisely what kind of people they are), the readers are, probably mainly language learners (but again we could find out more precisely who they are), and the writers have more authority than the readers
Mode	How are the texts put together?	The texts are presented in written form, with a basic form of the word followed by a phonemic transcription etc.

It is difficult to talk about genre analysis in Martin's model at the level of language without a knowledge of Halliday's functional grammar (e.g. Halliday and Matthiessen 2014, Bloor and Bloor 1995, Downing and Locke 1992), but a genre analysis would also try to identify grammatical and lexical features of the genre. For example, the information in the dictionary entries is not presented in sentences, which means the authors, in terms of what they say (the field), do not have to identify any entities except the words, and, in terms of tenor, can maintain a very distant relationship with their audience. The textual organization is, however, highly structured, with the order in which it appears acting as the main signal to readers as to what kind of information is being presented, for example, we partly know that *noun* [U] is grammatical information because it comes after the phonemic information.

When a group of texts has been collected one of the most striking features is often the text structure, or the mode. In one of the best known examples of genre analysis, Swales (1990) identified a very clear structure in the introduction to research or academic articles. See Table 11.7.

Genre analysis has largely focused on written texts, but Ventola did produce a genre description of service encounters. Her analysis of the jiffy bag text is given in Table 11.8.

Table 11.7 Swales's structure of a research article (1990: 141)

Move 1: Establishing a territory	
Step 1	Claiming centrality **&/or**
Step 2	Making generalizations (s) **&/or**
Step 3	Reviewing items of previous research
Move 2: Establishing a niche	
Step 1A	Counter-claiming **or**
Step 1B	Indicating a gap **or**
Step 1C	Question-raising **or**
Step 1D	Continuing a tradition
Move 3: Occupying the niche	
Step 1A	Outlining purposes **or**
Step 1B	Announcing present research
Step 2	Announcing principal findings
Step 3	Indicating RA structure

Table 11.8 A genre analysis of a service encounter

Service bid	S	1	You 're right/rising tone/
Service	C	2	Can I have a small postal bag please, jiffy bag?
Goods handover			/3 secs – S gets the bag and hands it over/
Pay	S	3	Twenty cents
			/C hands over the money and S receives it/
Closing	S	4	Thank you very much
	C	5	Thank you

Source: Ventola (1984: 282)

The lack of genre work on spoken interaction is a major weakness of this approach and has contributed to the lack of its attention to negotiation, but it is perhaps the most useful approach for communicative tasks built around written texts.

 Activity 11.3 Genre analysis

Look at the following corpus of texts from *Stirling Observer* (2001) and answer the questions which follow.

1. BROWN Keith and Gillian are delighted to announce the birth of their son, Reece, on 3rd April 2001, at Ninewells Hospital. Many thanks to all concerned.	2. ROSS SINCLAIR Willie and Lainey are delighted to announce the arrival of their son 7th April 2001 at Perth Royal Infirmary. Another grandson for Kate & Frank Neil and Mary & Gordon Ross. A huge thanks to all nursing staff concerned.
3. FALLON David and Nicola are proud to announce the safe arrival of their daughter, Rachel Ann, at P.R.I. on Friday 6th April 2001. A sister for Claire and Emily. Many thanks to all involved.	4. RUSH George and Eileen (nee Holden) are delighted to announce the birth of their lovely son Jamie George on Tuesday 4th April 2001 at Stirling Royal Infirmary. A brother for Kirsten and Hollie and grandson for George and Helen and Harry and Christine. Thanks to all maternity staff at Stirling Royal Infirmary.
5. COCHRANE Keith and Fiona are pleased to announce the safe arrival of their son, Gregor Armstrong, art Perth Royal Infirmary on 7th April 2001, a little brother to Jennifer. Thanks to all staff for their care and attention.	6. YOUNG Colin and Fiona (nee Fergus) are delighted to announce the birth of their daughter Katie Margaret on 28th March 2001 at York District Hospital. Granddaughter for Iain and Margaret Fergus and Scott and Isabelle Young.
7. MYLES Steven and Alison (nee McDonald) are delighted to announce the birth of their daughter Jasmine, on Monday 2nd April 2001 at P.R.I. A first grandchild for Bob and June and Sonia and Willie.	8. YOUNG James and Carole are delighted to announce the safe arrival of James and Allan, on 23rd March 2001, little brothers to Robert. Many thanks to The Red Team and Doctors involved. Off P.R.I.

1 Why were the texts written? Why would they be read?

2 What are the texts about? What information is required and what is optional?

3 Who are characteristic readers? Who are typical writers?

4 How are the texts organized? Are there any noticeable aspects of grammar or vocabulary?

Genre analysis has often drawn on techniques from corpus linguistics. For example, my own research into law reports (Badger 2003) showed that 'prosecution' can refer to the act of prosecuting a defendant or the people who prosecute the defendant. Examining the concordance lines from the corpus of law report I had constructed for my research (Table 11.9) enabled me to identify differences in how the two meanings were signalled by the definite article.

Table 11.9 Concordance lines for prosecution

1. The **prosecution** alleged that the men were responsible for the deaths
2. There was insufficient evidence for **prosecution** under the new War Crimes Act
3. The **prosecution** alleges that en route to Scotland, the goods were stolen
4. He was stabbed in broad daylight, the **prosecution** alleges
5. A bargain was struck beforehand between the **prosecution** and defence
6. He would have to throw away the haddock or risk **prosecution**
7. The **prosecution** alleges that the CEGB is in breach of statute
8. A transsexual should not be able to avoid **prosecution** for soliciting
9. But she added that **prosecution** by a criminal court was not appropriate
10. The **prosecution** alleged that witnesses identified the defendant
11. Twenty five people are facing **prosecution** in four countries
12. The Act allows for **prosecution** for offences committed elsewhere

11.3 Learning to use discourse

All the theories of language learning that we examined in Chapter 3 would see the need for learners to be exposed to example of discourse as a necessary part of their language development. The cognitive view would, in addition highlight the importance of learners developing declarative knowledge about discourse structure, along the lines of the descriptions of discourse covered above. Cognitive models and sociocultural views would also highlight the importance of learners participating in discourse as a way of proceduralizing their declarative knowledge or as a way of moving from other- to self-regulation. Exposure to and participation in discourse and, in some cases, awareness raising, are the main processes leading to the development of the ability to engage in discourse and communicative tasks. However, learners bring knowledge and ability related to discourse in their first language to the English language classroom and the rest of this section examines how this might impact on the way they learn English discourse.

Once, in a restaurant in France, the waiter offer me some wine and I said 'merci' (thank you). He walked past me without giving me any wine. Later he came around with a basket of bread rolls and again I said 'merci'. He did not give me any bread. The third time, he came around with a carafe of water and this time I said 's'il vous plait'(please) and he filled my glass. In English, 'thank you' indicates that you want your glass filled, where as in French 'merci' means that you are grateful for the offer but do not want any wine. This kind of miscommunication about the function of a phrase such as 'Thank you' is often harder for teachers and learners to recognize because it does not relate to the grammar or vocabulary.

The different ways in which Japanese speakers reported making requests to English and Japanese friend, reported in Activity 11.1 illustrates how learners' L1 can impact on their English speech acts. This is more likely to be an issue for teachers with groups of learners who share a mother tongue. Björkman (2011) found that among speakers of ELF, overt misunderstandings were relatively rare, perhaps because the participants could use a range of strategies to make sure communication was effective.

Learners will also bring a knowledge of politeness strategies from their first language. For example, Gu (1990) identifies differences in the way inviting takes place in English and Chinese. If a Chinese speaker has invited someone to dinner and been turned down, it would be common for the invitation to be repeated. In many English-speaking cultures, this would be regarded as impolite as it would be a threat to the independence of the person receiving the invitation. In some Chinese cultures it would be impolite not to repeat the invitation as it would indicate that the original invitation was not sincere (Gu 1990: 242). Similarly, Holliday et al. (2004: 199) note that the range of ways people behave in bars in different cultures can lead to misperceptions of rudeness.

> A Spanish man greeting strangers in a bar in England would probably be disappointed in the lack of reciprocity of his greeting. The locals would be suspicious or amused; the Spaniard would feel the locals are perhaps unfriendly. He may be seen as dishonest or evasive if he doesn't offer to pay for the first drink he asked for upon being served that drink.

However it is important to note that many cultures share ways of expressing politeness. For example, Backhaus (2009) reports that in both Japanese- and German-speaking contexts, nurses used complements as positive politeness strategies when giving instructions to patients in ways that replicate behaviour in English-speaking environments after actions that threatened patients' independence.

Research into differences in the ways different cultures organize written texts is described as contrastive rhetoric (Conor 1996) and can be traced back to Kaplan (1966). Kaplan argued that English cultures organized texts linearly, perhaps reflecting the fact that the way a culture organizes texts seems linear to people from that culture. While most teachers of writing will have come across learners who produce texts which are organized in ways that do not conform to expectations and indicate that Kaplan's claims contain an element of truth, the notion of culture here can be very specific. In the UK, many school leavers struggle with the rhetorical organization of the essays they are expected to write at university and this reflects a difference in culture between school and university. Learners on degrees in Physics will for this purpose be from a different culture than those who study History. The problem-solution pattern that was covered above seems widespread, if not universal, but this may well reflect the limits of my own rhetorical experience.

The notion of culture in contrastive rhetoric is built into genre analysis (Martin and Rose 2008) and means teachers need a good understanding of the discourse knowledge that their learners bring to the classroom and the discourse needs that the classroom instruction is intended to meet.

11.4 Teaching discourse

This section presents the teaching of discourse as having three elements, exposure, awareness and practice, though not all teachers will have choices in how these three elements are realized.

11.4.1 Exposure

Many teachers have to follow a set curriculum or course book but where teachers play a role in identifying what is taught, the first stage in teaching discourse is identifying the kinds of discourse or discourse features to which the learners need to be exposed. Ideally, this would mean an empirically based needs

Table 11.10 Written school genres

Purpose for using language	Text type
To tell a story as a means of making sense of events and happenings in the world. It can be both entertaining and informing	Narrative
To reconstruct past experiences by retelling events and incidents in the order in which they have occurred	Recount
To present factual information about a class of things usually by first classifying them and then describing their characteristics	Information report
To present information and opinions about more than one side of an issue: it may end with recommendations based on the evidence presented	Discussion
To explain why things are as they are or how things work	Explanation
To advance of justify an argument or put forward a particular point of view	Exposition
To show how something can be accomplished through a series of steps or actions to be taken	Procedure

Source: Butt et al. (1995: 17)

analysis (Long 2005), something which is explored in more detail in Chapter 5 on programme design. There may be existing information which can be used from the research literature. Table 11.10 identifies the written genres used in schools in New South Wales. A similar set of genres exists for university study assignments (Gardner and Nesi 2013; Nesi and Gardner 2012). Many teachers are sufficiently knowledgeable about their learners needs to be able to identify the relevant communicative tasks.

Once the communicative tasks have been identified, teachers need to obtain exemplars of the target texts. For example, if service encounters were a target task, a teacher might decide to expose the learners to the dialogue in Table 11.9 because this is an authentic text. Authenticity can be a problematic criterion for text selection. Table 11.11 provides another authentically produced service encounter dialogue. This has a much more complex structure with three participants and this might not be appropriate for all learners. Gilmore (2015: 516) suggests that teachers and material writers should base their exemplar texts on authentically produced samples but adapt them so that they are appropriate for their learners, what might be described as their receptive or interpretative authenticity, and that learners need to be exposed to several examples so that they understand that task can be carried out in different ways. You may like to consider the merits of the course book dialogue in Activity 11.1.

The service encounter is a spoken genre so learners would need to be exposed to a spoken version, though good pedagogic reasons may exist for also exposing them to written versions of the text.

11.4.2 Awareness raising

Teachers can make learners aware of a discourse feature by presenting information about that feature. For example, Liu et al. (2014) found that presenting a particular text pattern known as a story grammar (Rumelhart 1975) (with some similarities to the problem-solution pattern) led to an improvement in the quality of stories their learners produced.

Table 11.11 A more complex service encounter (O'Keeffe 2011: 94–5)

Customer 1	How are we doing?
Shop assistant	Hi there how are you? <sound of till> That's one seventy-seven please.
Customer 1	Alright seventy-seven give it to you now
Shop assistant	Not a bad day shur it's not?
Customer 1	Naw it's cold though
Shop assistant	Cold
Customer 1	'Twas nice earlier on the sun was shining
Customer 2	Turning cold out there now, is it?
Customer 1	It is yeah
Customer 2	I'd say we'll get a right cold spell of it
Customer 1	I'll give you twenty-seven there if you don't mind
Shop assistant	Grand no problem
Customer 1	Sound yeah I'd I agree with you I don't mind the cold you know as long as it's not raining
Shop assistant	As long as it not raining is the main thing. Thank you very much
Customer 1	That's right. Thanks. Good luck.

A less teacher-centred approach would be for the learners to take on the role of language researchers. This is illustrated in the section on genre approaches to writing in Chapter 12, particularly Activity 12.1 and Negretti et al. (2011) described there. Murray (2012) suggests that learners translate communicative events from their own language into English and discuss the norms of different speech communities as a way of identifying how this works for different communities.

11.4.3 Practice

The target of the communicative language class is for learners to be able to participates in the target communicative task in a context that as closely as possible matches the actual task. However, most learners will need to practice before they attain this stage. The notion of deliberate practice, discussed in Chapter 3, is a useful guide to structuring this progress. In addition, guides to what factors influence task difficulty exist (Foster and Ohta 2005; Foster and Skehan 1999; Skehan 1998, 2003, 2014; Willis and Willis 2007). See Table 11.12.

11.5 Summary

This chapter provided some insights into the description of real-life communicative tasks from discourse analysis and pragmatics, focusing on speech act theory, politeness theory, research into patterns in text and genre analysis. After a short discussion of how learners develop the ability to participate in real-life communicative tasks, the chapter examined the teaching of discourse under the headings of exposure, awareness raising and practice.

A story created by the control group

(1) This is a beautiful world. (2) Ducks and elephants got ready to fight. Suddenly they heard a sound (sawing sound). (3) This was ever once a beautiful forest. (4) It was A-Pan sawing the trees. (5) A-Pan said sorry to the animals and he won't do it next time.

A story created by the experimental group

(1) This was how a forest looked like. Many animals walked in this forest. (2) When the animals walked in it, there were two people preparing tools to ruin this forest. (3) The two people who wanted to ruin the forest came to a big and old tree. A man, called A-Da, came to stop them. (4) 'You two stop!' said A-Da. 'None of your business. We will make a lot of fortune!' said the two people ruining the forest. 'If you don't stop, I'll call all the animals to save this old tree!' Suddenly, the government officer came and the two people who want to cut the tree left.

Figure 11.1 Impact of story grammars on writing (Liu et al. 2014)

Table 11.12 Task parameters

Parameter	Gloss
Task outcome	Closed outcomes and interim goals make tasks easier
Starting point for the text	Easier starting points make the task easier: visual cues are generally easier than text cues; building on the learners' experience is easier than building on others' experiences
Pre-task preparation	Allowing learners time to plan makes tasks easier

Table 11.12 (Continued)

Parameter	Gloss
Control of agenda	Providing more structure to the task normally makes tasks easier. Time constraints make tasks harder
Interaction patterns and participant roles	Allocating participants roles leads to more equal language use. Working in pairs, three or large groups influences how much learners contribute
Pressure on language production	Talking to one or two learners is easier than presenting to the whole group and will encourage fluency over accuracy
Post task activities	Reading a transcript of their task can encourage accuracy; task repetitions can lead to more complex language

Source: Willis and Willis (2007: 154–74)

 Activity 11.4 Discussion What advice would you offer a colleague in the context described here:

I work with learners aged between ten and twelve for whom English is an additional language. They currently speak quite fluently. At the start of the next academic year, they will be going to secondary school where all the instruction will be in English and I would like to spend the twelve weeks of the summer term preparing them for this experience and help them to deal with the classes in science and mathematics. I have been allocated two hours a week of class time for this. How can I decide what should go into the programme and what would be the best format for the classes?

 11.6 Further reading

The most useful book on discourse analysis is Paltridge's (2012) *Discourse Analysis: An Introduction.* Both O'Keeffe et al.'s (2011) *An Introduction to Pragmatics* and Grundy's (2008) *Doing Pragmatics* are good on pragmatics. Several other approaches to patterns in grammar exist, for example, narrative structure (Labov 1999) and story grammars (Rumelhart 1975), but the core text on the linguistics of problem-solution is Hoey's (1983) *On the Surface of Discourse.* Martin and Rose (2008) and Nesi and Gardner are useful recent works in genre analysis.

Skehan's (1998) *A Cognitive Approach to Language Learning* and (2014) *Processing Perspectives on Task Performance* are good particularly on classroom tasks, and Dave and Jane Willis's (2007) *Doing Task Based Teaching* is good on designing pedagogic tasks.

Part IV

Language Skills

Chapter 12

Reading

12.1 Introduction

Being able to read in your mother tongue is necessary to be able to play a full part as a citizen in most parts of the world. Those who live in English-speaking environments or wish to study in Anglophone educational institutions likewise need to be able to read in English. Even in countries where English is not the main language, being able to read in English gives access to cultural and economic resources which are not so easily accessed through other languages. These incentives to learn to read in English are reinforced by examinations and educational systems more generally which treat reading as a central part of being able to use English, something which is perhaps reflected in the pedagogic advantages of a relatively permanent written text. All this means that most teachers of English are also teachers of reading and so are concerned with identifying ways they can help their learners read English better. This chapter is intended to offer such teachers some help by discussing the following three questions:

1 What is involved in reading?
2 How do people learn to read English?
3 How can teachers teach reading?

12.2 What is involved in reading?

Perhaps because so much of reading is unobservable, many of the people who write about reading have offered definitions of what the term means:

> Understanding a written text means extracting the required information from it as efficiently as possible. (Grellet 1981: 3)

> [Reading means] to work out the meaning of a written text with the purpose of being able to take some kind of action as a result. (Wallace 1992: 4)

> Reading is the ability to draw meaning from the printed page and interpret this information appropriately. (Grabe and Stoller 2013: 3)

These definitions underplay the wonder of reading.

> Readings appears to be at least as magic as pulling rabbits from hats, conjuring pigeons from coat sleeves, or producing dimes from behind someone's ear . . . readers are able to take arbitrarily

determined shapes presented against some appropriate background and turn them into meaning. (Hudson, 2007: 7)

The rest of this section looks at psychological, linguistic and social understandings of what is involved in reading.

12.2.1 Psychological aspects of reading

Reading draws on two sources of information – visual information from the written text, and non-visual information from what readers already know. The non-visual information is normally divided into what is described as bottom or lower level, linguistic information (discussed in the next section on linguistic aspects of reading) and higher or top level, non-linguistic information. When readers see a text, they retrieve the relevant linguistic knowledge and world knowledge from their long-term memory and bring this into their working memory (Baddeley et al. 2009) and the result is an interpretation of the text.

The lower-level information is processed very fast, at a rate of ten words per minute for fluent readers and the process is automatic, that is, it cannot be consciously controlled (Grabe and Stoller 2013: 15). Identifying word meaning is an important, if not the most important, product of the lower-level information reading process, and measures of the speed at which readers can identify words correlate very closely with their ability to read, but, to the extent that the use of lower- and higher-level information can be distinguished, lower-level information results in semantic propositions related to phrases or clauses rather than individual words.

The higher-level information includes background information about the world. This information is often described as being organized into cognitive structures known as schemas or schemata. Grabe (2009: 79) describes them as 'variable and messy networks of knowledge that are called up, or activated by the active information in working memory', and some writers now avoid the term schema. However, reading cannot happen unless readers make extensive use of their knowledge of the world. If, for example, a text starts with the mention of a judge, readers may activate the network related to judges and court cases within their long-term memory and so will assume that lawyers, a defendant and possibly a jury will be involved. Readers will use their schemata to resolve ambiguities in the text so they will know that 'sentence' is more likely to refer to the punishment the defendants receives rather than a unit of written language and, as readers move through the text, the network of activated items will be refined (Nassaji 2007). The lexical items related to the judge will be primed and, if a word such as 'sentence' appears in the text, readers will be able to retrieve it faster than if the judge had not been mentioned.

The content of information networks will not be the same for all readers. Lawyers educated in England or Wales might distinguish between different levels of courts – for example, a magistrate's court without a jury, a crown court with a jury – and kinds of law, a civil case with a plaintiff and a criminal case with a prosecutor, where non-lawyers would not make such distinctions until they had read further into the text. Similarly, readers from different cultures bring different kinds of background knowledge to a text, and this may result in different understandings of what the text means.

Table 12.1 Grabe's behaviour of strategic readers

1. Predict what the text will be about
2. Monitor for comprehension
3. Relate text information to prior knowledge
4. Form questions and find answers in the text
5. Pay attention to text structure
6. Initiate comprehension support processes when comprehension is unclear
7. Form a summary of the information in the text
8. Reflect on the information in the text after reading

Source: Grabe (2009: 241)

The use of higher-level information is less automatic and more under the control of readers than the use of lower-level information. Readers monitor their own reading processes, evaluate how well the reading process is going and make plans to deal with any problems that arise. For some readers, these processes are conscious. Earlier in this section you might have consciously noticed 'schemata'; if you had not come across the term before, you may have decided that it was an irregular plural of schema or that it was not necessary for you to understand what you were reading and so could be ignored. However, it is possible that the decision not to worry about the word was not made consciously. Where this is a conscious process, it is usually described as a strategy and, where it is not conscious, it is a sub-skill or habit (Grabe 2009: 221). This means that the same behaviour may be a strategy or a skill, depending on whether it is conscious or not. It is possible to find many different lists of both skills and strategies (see Table 12.1). However Hudson notes that 'while the detailed lists of skills may be helpful in curriculum development and textbook design, the actual operationalization of simple unitary skills is problematic' (2007: 103). This does not mean that skills and strategies are not an important part of reading but that readers use skills and strategies in response to problems created by the texts they are reading and what the readers are doing with the texts. Activity 12.1 relates to the strategies one learner used in reading a text.

 Activity 12.1 Strategies

Here is a text and following it is a think-aloud protocol from a student who read the text.

Vitamins

Food contains only minute quantities of the substances called vitamins, but they are vital for good health. For example, if you eat a diet of meat, bread, sugar, and fat, you may become ill with a disease called scurvy. This is caused by a deficiency in vitamin C, which is found in fruit and vegetables.

About fifty different vitamins have been identified, and a deficiency in many of these can lead to illness. Vitamin A is most important for good eyesight, but is also important for general good health. Liver contains a considerable amount of vitamin A, but vitamin A is also found in fish, meat, milk, butter, some fruits and vegetables.

Vitamin B in fact consists of twelve different chemicals, which are found in eggs, cheese, butter, wholemeal flour and vegetables. If a person has an inadequate amount of vitamin B in his diet, this may affect his whole body, particularly the skin, the nervous system, and the heart. Deficiency in vitamin B results in a disease called beriberi.

Vitamin C prevents scurvy and helps to heal injuries. Some doctors believe that large quantities of vitamin C help people to avoid colds. Fruits and uncooked vegetables are rich in vitamin C, but when they are cooked, or left for a long time, they lose most of their vitamins.

Vitamin D is essential for the growth of bones and teeth and is found in fish, liver, oil and milk. Vitamin D is the only vitamin which the body can make for itself, but it can only do this if there is sufficient sunlight. A lack of both sunlight and vitamin D can result in a disease called rickets, which causes bones to soften and to be deformed.

Vitamins are only needed in very small quantities. A quantity sufficient for a whole life would weigh only a quarter of a kilogram. Vitamins can be manufactured and are sold as additions to our food, but a well-balanced diet will provide an adequate amount of vitamins.

Here is an excerpt from a transcript of what the student said while she was reading the text. This kind of transcript is called a protocol because it describes what the student does while she reads. What strategies or skills did the student use? Can you relate these to the strategies identified in Table 12.1?

I am going to read the passage … to get the main idea. I read just the first sentences of every paragraph. Vitamin A. Vitamin B. I am still reading the third paragraph. I read the passage and … I am in the 4th paragraph. OK. I finished this passage and I am going back to read it again sentence by sentence. Do I know what the text is about? Yes, it's about vitamins, types of vitamins. A, B, C, D. And what foods contain them.

I will read the sentence in the 1st paragraph. The 1st sentence … yes, . . . there is one word in the first sentence I couldn't have the meaning. What's that word? It's minute. Minute, second, hour, does not make sense. No. Minute. Minute. Minute. Oh /maɪnjuːt/. Yes, may be. I . . . I know this. Yes, it's minute. The last paragraph. Oh … Oh … Very small quantities. OK. I read the sentence and I get the meaning. All other words are known for me. And I am going to the second sentence.

While the lower-level information process results in semantic propositions, as readers move through a text, these proposition are combined using higher-order skills to form a coherent model of the text meaning that relates to the readers' purpose for reading the text (Kintsch and Rawson 2005).

The psychological view of reading provides insights into reading. However, this approach does not take into account differences in the ways that different readers approach different texts, or even the same text, so it needs to be supplemented with insights about texts which the linguistic approach provides and insights about readers and their roles in society that the social view offers.

12.2.2 Linguistic views of reading

This section explores in more detail the lower-level information that is part of the psychological views of reading. However, it extends the notion of linguistic information beyond orthography, phonology, lexis, grammar, phonology to include discourse.

When reading, less familiar words may be processed letter by letter, and sometimes using information about their phonology. For example, readers who first encounter a word such as 'gryphon', will use

Activity 12.2 **Linguistic knowledge in reading**

When we read, we bring a lot of different kinds of knowledge to what we see on the page or the screen. This activity is intended to make you think about these kinds of knowledge. What makes these language samples easy/difficult to read?

1. gnidneherpmoc dna gnidoced htob sevlovni gnidaeR
2. lexicalaccessorwordrecognitionsyntacticparsingandsemantic propositio nformationaretypicallyseenaslower levelprocessesthatoccurrelativelyaut omaticallyforthe fluent reader
3. 他送我一本书。
4. ρεαδινγ καν βε διφφικυλτ
5. Ανάγνωση μπορεί να είναι δύσκολη
6. Tā sòng wǒ yī běn shū
7. Be high level comprehend process that close represent what we typical consider read comprehend
8. Hij gaf me een boek
9. *'Twas brillig, and the slithy toves* did gyre and gimble in the wabe.
10. A book give he i

their knowledge of the fact that in English, unlike some other languages, writing move from left to write and spaces indicate the beginning and end of words, and of the Roman alphabet, to reconstruct the word 'gryphon' (see Chapter 2), possibly making the identification of the word based on the unusual combination of 'gry-'. They will then retrieve the typical pronunciation of the letters, taking into account the digraph 'ph' that 'y' represents a vowel, to produce something like /ɡrɪfən/ (see Chapter 8) and compare the resultant acoustic image with the words in their mental store or lexicon. If the reader knows that a gryphon is a mythical creature resembling a lion with the head and wings of an eagle, that understanding will cue expectations related to the topic and genre of the text. If readers do not know the word, they will either ignore it or work out its meaning somehow. In contrast a word like 'cat' will probably be processed as a semantic unit, without drawing on orthographic information, though, even with words like this, phonological information is probably retrieved (Walter 2008).

With lower level information, the focus has been on identifying word meanings but as items seven and ten in Activity 12.1 may suggest, without syntax and morphology, reading is not possible though, as Grabe notes, 'the role of grammar in reading comprehension is not a common topic in books on reading' (2009: 199). If you do not know any English grammar, it is not possible to read any but the shortest English text but beyond that it is difficult to estimate how important grammar is. However, just as with spoken language, some grammatical patterns are characteristic of particular genres of written language. For example, readers of academic text need to be able to process nominalizations as in the grammatical subject of the sentence:

Students' monitoring of their comprehension is often identified as a major reading strategy that improves main-idea comprehension. (Grabe and Stoller 2013: 143)

Here the writers could have used 'students monitor whether they have understood what they have read'. This kind of compression in written language means that the information which might have been spread over three sentences is expressed in one sentence and readers need to process the semantic proposition expressed by the nominalization before moving on to the next part of the sentence.

If reading is conceptualized as a communicative task, the central question is why somebody is reading this text and the main linguist framework for identifying communicative tasks is genre theory, discussed in Chapter 8. The key element of genres are their communicative purposes. When we read a text, what counts as success will depend on the genre of the text is being read. For example, someone reading a dictionary will generally be regarded as successful if they find the information they need about a particular word. Someone reading a novel may expect to end up with a broader awareness of human nature. Someone reading a twitter feed may be deciding what tweets they want to forward to their own followers or which tweets need a response. Hyon's programme in Table 12.2 indicates how genre can be used to structure a reading programme. Several commentators have produced lists of reading purposes, independent of the texts (e.g. the seven purposes in Grabe and Stoller 2013: 6), which may be useful in course design.

12.2.3 Social views of reading

Reading is a social process. As in listening and speaking, somebody is producing language to express a message and someone is reconstructing that message from marks on paper or on screen. To read is to be involved in a slow, often very slow, interaction with the author or authors of a text that parallels what happens in listening. In the same way that we are limited in the people to whom we can speak, the kinds of text to which people have access and the purposes for which they can use those texts will vary depending on their place in society. For example, in many countries the process of becoming a lawyer, involves learning to read legal texts and this is not easy. First-year law undergraduates in England read law reports very differently from third year students (Badger 2003) and this is not simply a question of learning new language but of understanding the role of law reports in the legal system. For those who have not completed this training, these texts will be very hard to access.

More generally, an important part of most educational systems is learning what kinds of text written by what authors need to be read and in what ways they should be read. The social view of reading focusses not just on the reader and the text but the social and communicative context in which it take place, what Heath describes as the literacy event (1982). For example, where learners are reading an academic paper, the literacy event would include the ways in which they have access to that paper, online or in print, on their smart phone or on a desk top computer, the context in which they read the paper and the associated acts, such as writing an essay and receiving feedback on that essay. Being able to decode the text and relate the propositional meaning to the relevant background information is an important part of this but reading is more than this and so the aims of the reading class need to be more than decoding and comprehending.

12.3 How do people learn to read English?

All the models of learning discussed in Chapter 3 see some form of practice as a necessary part of learning to read. Within information processing models, practice should be preceded by some kind of

Table 12.2 A genre programme of EAP reading (Hyon 2001)

	Hard news	Feature article	Textbook	Research article
Content	Recent events of some importance or interest	Various factors involved in a large current issue	Concepts in a particular field	A new scientific investigation carried out by the author(s)

Structure	Inverted pyramid structure (information presented in descending order of importance)	1. Anecdotal lead
		2. Connection of anecdote to larger issue
		3. Discussion of various factors involved in the issue
			Cyclical patterns for presenting concepts	1. Introduction
				  a. Establishing research area importance
				  b. Indicating a gap
				  c. Filling the gap
				2. Method
				3. Results
				4. Discussion

Language style	'Objective': writer attributes opinions to other sources using quotations and citations; balanced with dramatic and emotional language	Subjective: writer may express opinion to appeal to readers' emotions and to offer an interpretation of the issue	Sure and authoritative: characterized by lack of hedging and lack of reference to evidence or controversy	Cautious: characterized by hedging and reference to experimental evidence
Purpose	To report newsworthy events in the most efficient and objective way	To draw readers into the whole article; to entertain readers and offer an interpretation of the issue	To present the 'facts' of a particular filed in a patterned manner	To present an interpretation of a timely investigation

input. This has often meant that learners need to have relevant linguistic information, usually particular vocabulary, or background information related to the topic of the text. More recently, the input has been widened to include 'strategic and metacognitive instruction' (Hudson 2007: 292) about the strategies such as those listed above.

In the monitor model, the necessary element is that learners should be able to understand more or less what they are reading. This has parallels with sociocultural views of learning where providing the appropriate support and then withdrawing it is how learning is seen to happen. Deciding what support is appropriate requires an understanding of the resources that learners bring to the classroom.

Learners who are already able to read in the first language bring the important knowledge that written symbols carry meaning, but this will vary depending on the writing system used in their first language. Some of these differences and the impact these differences have on learners of English are described in Chapter 8. However, one of the insights of the social view of learning is that learners who can read in their first language do not simply bring knowledge of the orthography of that language but also their experience of literacy practices in that language. The fact that young learners have been read to by their parents in their first language or in English is something that can be built on in the English reading class and indeed being read to may be the first stage in learning to read. Learners may bring other experiences to the language classroom. Gregory (2008: 20) describes working with a four-year-old boy called Tony who was learning to read his first language, Chinese, and English at the same time. In the Chinese class, Tony copied out the text before reading it and wanted to do the same in English. His English teacher had seen copying out words as part of the process of learning to write rather than learning to read but was able to adapt her teaching style to take advantage of Tony's copying skills. Understanding the resources that learners bring to the class and managing these resources is an important part of effective teaching.

12.4 How can teachers teach reading?

The previous sections have described the reading process and how learners develop the reading abilities as ways of helping teachers identify the aim of their reading lesson. Within a task-based approach, the aim is likely to be a task which involves reading but is not limited to reading, such as the description of reading an academic paper discussed in the social view of reading. Preparing learners for this reading task would be very demanding and it would need to be broken down into more specific aims, that is, identifying the genres that learners will need to read or the purposes that they need to achieve. In weak communicative approaches, the aim of the reading lesson is often to understand a particular text, which may be chosen because it is in the course book or is selected by the teacher. If it is the latter, Grabe and Stoller (2013: 132) suggest involving learners in the choice selection where possible but, even if this is not possible, using texts with are interesting, attractive and accessible. This may lead to the selection of authentically produced texts but Grabe and Stoller's point about accessibility is more important than their source. If learners cannot make sense of a text, it will not be authentic for them.

12.4.1 The sequence of the reading lesson

Once teachers have identified their reading text, they need to structure the overall lesson. Reading classes or those parts of the class devoted to reading typically consist of three stages:

1 *Pre-reading*, which focuses on providing learners with the appropriate linguistic (often lexical) and world knowledge needed to understand text,

2 *While-reading*, where the learners read the text and demonstrate their understanding of the text, often by answering comprehension questions and

3 *Post-reading*, where learners respond to the text by, for example, discussing the topic of the text or using the information from the text in a piece of writing.

12.4.2 Activities in the reading lesson

The world knowledge that learners need to make sense of a text will depend on what the learners know and the particular text. One aspect of background knowledge that needs to be covered to ensure that readers engage in as authentic way as possible with the text is the reason why the learners are reading the text. This will enable the learners to understand the role their reading is playing in an act of communication and to identify what kind of information they will be looking for when they read the text. Common pre-reading activities include a discussion about the topic or the use of visuals. Many of the tasks described in Table 15.2 in Chapter 15 can be adapted for this purpose.

The choice of words to pre-teach reflects a dilemma in the typical reading class between whether the aim is to help learners read the current text or to read future texts. Teachers may ask learners to identify the words they need to understand or they can use their own intuitions to identify what the key vocabulary items are for the text. Teachers should draw on frequency data to identify what vocabulary learners need for future texts, perhaps supplemented by words that the learners identify. Particularly for future-oriented items, learners need to be able to recognize them very quickly and techniques such as the use of flashcards or apps such as *Memrise* can be useful. Table 12.3 is part of a word recognition exercise which is designed to help with increasing the number of words learners recognize at sight. Learners identify which of the phrases on the right matches the phrase in the left column as fast as possible. Grabe and Stoller suggest using this kind of activity with twenty to twenty five words or phrases on a regular basis to build up learners' sight vocabulary. Research carried out by Walter (2008) suggest that the speed at which readers can form an acoustic image of words is an important part of reading fluency and reinforces the need to include the pronunciation of words in reading lessons. Chapter 10 provides more examples of techniques for introducing and practicing new vocabulary.

The pre-reading stage can also be used to develop learners' reading strategies. This can be in the form of a discussion with the learners about how they will approach the text or the teacher may want to introduce a new strategy. As discussed earlier, strategies are normally a response to a problem with a text and so pre-planning what strategies to teach can be difficult. However, one widely used generic strategy for reading academic texts is survey, question, read, recall (or recite) and review (SQ3R).

Table 12.3 Word recognition exercise (based on Grabe and Stoller 2013: 135)

Key phrase	Distractors			
1. By the way	By the time	By the way	On the way	By the end
2. Word list	Wired list	Word list	Wild fist	Weird list
3. Determine	Determine	Decline	Decease	Deceive

Table 12.4 A generic strategy: SQ3R (adapted from Fairbairn and Winch 2011: 36 et seq)

Survey	Survey the text to get an overall grasp of what it is about, and decided whether it is worth reading in more detail
Question	Next, think carefully about what you hope to get from this text. What do you want to know and were in the text might you find it?
Read	Squeeze as much useful information as you can out of the text. This will probably include skimming, scanning and detailed reading
Recall	Now try to recall what you have learned, reciting or listing it to yourself, whether by remember inside you head, saying it out loud or writing notes on a fresh piece of paper or computer file
Review	Finally, review what you have done and what you should do next. Is there, for example, any further reading you should do?

Teachers can present this to their learners but it is probably most effective to illustrate how it might be used with a think aloud protocol, where the teacher reads a text aloud and adds comments on the application of the particular stages of the strategy at appropriate points.

Ness and Kenny (2016) illustrate modelling a strategy with a lower level class using a think-aloud protocol. See Table 12.5. They suggest that before the class, teachers need to identify where they are going to pause, what strategy they are going to exemplify and consider what they will actually say.

12.4.3 While-reading activities

During the while-reading stage, the standard procedure is for learners to read silently and on their own. Some teachers ask their learners to read aloud. This is a useful technique for beginner learners as it can

Table 12.5 Using a think-aloud protocol to model a strategy (Ness and Kenny 2016: 457)

Text	Possible script	Strategy
'How clever you are', it said to the spider	'I'm not familiar with the word *clever*, so I'm going to use context clues to try to figure out what it means. The spider can jump from plant to plant, and it leaves string to make a web. That's tricky to do, and something that can do that must be skilled and smart. I'm guessing that *clever* means smart or bright.'	Using context clues for unknown vocabulary

help teachers identify and monitor problems that learners have. However, reading aloud slows down the reading process and so can make comprehension difficult because learners forget earlier parts of the text before they have understood the later section. Once teachers are confident that learners are reading reasonably well, they should encourage them to read silently. Where readers need to be helped to read more quickly, some teachers find it useful for their learners to follow the text as the teacher reads it aloud or as a recording of the passage is played back.

A related activity is shadow-reading (De Guerrero and Commander 2013). The learners are paired, with one member of the pair reading the text orally in chunks which allow both members of the pair to identify the propositional meaning, and the other repeating the text, first aloud, secondly in a low voice and then silently. See Table 12.6, which illustrates how the technique operates and also that the word 'sibling', which the teacher assumed was not known to either of the pair did not seem to cause any difficulty in understanding the text.

During the while-reading activity, learners need to demonstrate their understanding of the text. This is often done by answering questions on the text. It is important that these questions address what a reader outside the language classroom might be expected to understand. For example, if teachers want their learners to demonstrate a general understanding of the text, a useful question is to give the text a title and asking learners to identify the referents for pronoun is an easy way of checking that the learners are bringing together information from more than one sentence. An alternative to asking questions is for the learner to transfer the information into another format, such as labelling a diagram. This activity can be facilitated using technology such as using software to produce mind maps of texts (Liu et al. 2010). See Figure 12.1. Where a class is reading more than one different text or reading separate parts of one text, teachers can ask learners who have read different texts to form groups and discuss the texts together. This can be more structured, in jigsaw reading activities, where some learners have the questions and others have the textor where the questions need learners to combine information from more than one text.

12.4.4 Web Quests

Where learners have access to the internet, teachers can create reading activities that require learners to visit a range of website and collection information to carry out a particular task. This kind of activity

Table 12.6 Shadow reading (De Guerrero and Commander 2013: 443)

R	that they have another sibling
SH	They … oh, jeez … can you repeat please?
R	that they have another sibling
SH	that they have another sibling (out loud)
	that they have another sibling (low voice)
	----------------------------------- (silent shadowing)
R	His name is David …
SH	oh, my God, this is the brother of the Bob and Eddy.
R	Yeah … it's the brother.
SH	OK, OK.

R = reader; SH = shadower.

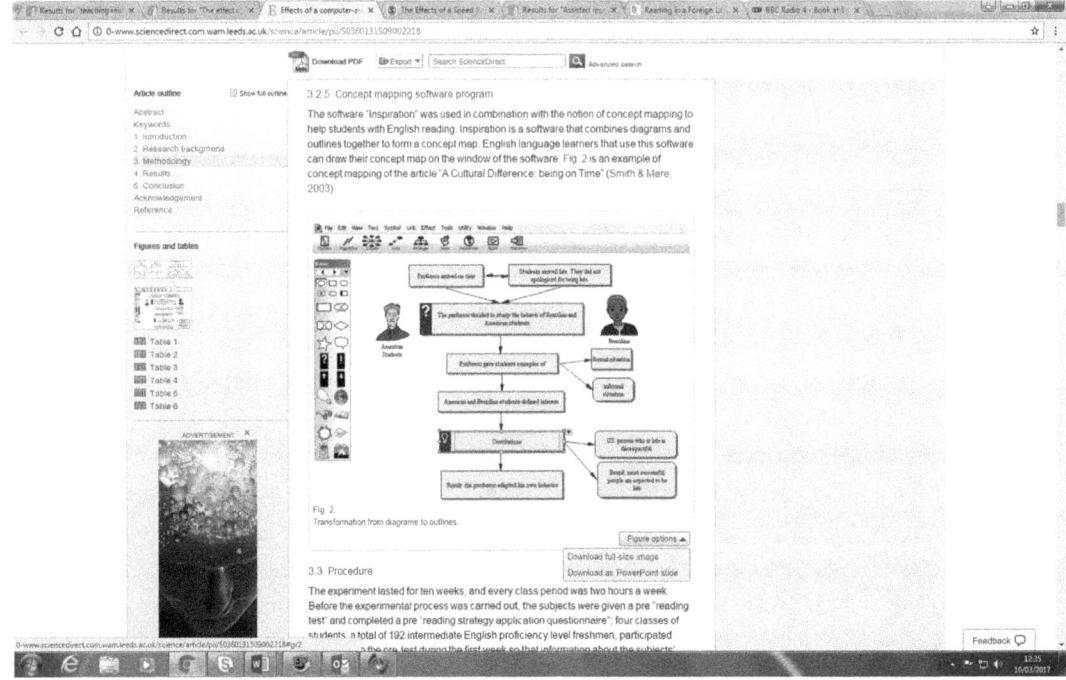

Figure 12.1 Mind maps as information transfer (Liu et al. 2010)

is known as a web quest. Dodge (2007), one the originators of the idea of web quests, says that 'a webquest is an inquiry-oriented lesson format in which most or all the information that learners work with comes from the web'.

The web quest designer identifies a topic or issue that is of interest to the learners and then selects web sites which will help the learners to carry out a task related to the topic or issue. For example, teachers might design a web quest on the cost of flying from where the learners are to, say, London and the relevant web sites would be those of airlines or travel companies. In its simplest form, the learners are given

- a description of the issue/problem they need to address and
- a list of web sites.

The learners then address the issue, question or problem using the websites. In more sophisticated versions, the web quest designer will use special software to design a web page which contains all the information and ensures that the learners do not get lost as they roam the web.

Here is an example of the teaching context that led one teacher to design a web quest.

The six learners with whom I used the web quest formed an elementary level group who had been learning English for approximately four to six months. The group consisted of five Arabic speakers and one Portuguese speaker. They had recently been following a course book unit about food and restaurants, had practiced vocabulary about describing restaurants and used basic dialogues about how to order food in a restaurant. During the lessons, I noticed that learners were less than motivated and reluctant to communicate with one another. At one point during the unit, I asked the learners whether they had had much experience with eating in local restaurants. The response was a resounding 'no'. Their reasons for this included that food was 'bad' in Britain or that restaurants in the local area were too expensive. There was some comment that they were reluctant to use English in restaurants or would find it difficult to read the menus, perhaps because the language contained in the average menu from a restaurant is usually above elementary level English. It was at this point that I realized that the learners didn't feel that they would actually use most of the language being presented during the lessons and this, in turn had resulted in low enthusiasm for the lesson.

The Town X web quest in Figure 12.2 was the teacher's response to this situation and she was aiming to do three things: improve learner motivation in the classroom, practice restaurant-related language, and encourage her students to go to a restaurant in the town where they lived.

The Town X restaurant web quest
Your friend is coming to visit you in Town X. You'd like to take your friend for a meal at a restaurant. She then listed four websites for restaurants in Town X and asked her learners to complete this chart:

Name of restaurant	Address	Phone number	Kind of food	Price

2. Now discuss the following questions.
    a. Which restaurant would you like to take your friend to? _____
    b. Why? _____

Figure 12.2 The Town X website

12.4.5 Post-reading activities

For some reading lessons, the demonstration of comprehension is not easy to distinguish from the post-reading activity but in principle, the post-reading activity should mirror what would happen when the text is read outside the language classroom.

Where the lesson has a strategic or metacognitive aim, learners can usefully reflect on how well they can demonstrate their understanding of the text with a view to identifying knowledge, skills or strategies which they or other learners in their class might seek to improve. For example, one learner had to decide if the statement 'Roy only copied paintings by two famous artists' was true, after reading the following extract:

This, of course, gives rise to much shaking of heads among art experts. After all, the whole point of art is to be creative and original. Even so, Roy was proud of his ability to reproduce Picassos, Van Goghs and so on, so accurately they seemed like the real thing.

The learner justified her decision that the statement was false by saying:

OK, in the text it says, 'Even so, Roy was proud of his ability to reproduce Picassos, Van Goghs and so on.' So that's false, because 'so on' means something more and that means that he did not only copy paintings by two famous artists. (Kremmel et al. 2015: 12)

This would have demonstrated to the teacher that the learner had understood the phrase 'so on' and might also have served as input for other learners.

The approach to organizing readings lessons described above can be described as intensive reading and the main focus is on understanding a particular text, though the approach may develop particular reading skills/strategies or linguistic knowledge that can be used on other text. This kind of lesson is useful and common. Two other kind of activities are useful in developing reading abilities but receive less attention than they should: reading fluency development and extensive reading.

12.4.6 Reading fluency

Reading fluency activities are intended to increase the speed at which people read and, while not explicitly linked to the notion of deliberate practice discussed in Chapter 3, are consistent with that idea. Teachers have used speed reading techniques to do this. For example, Yen (2012) used twenty texts written at the 1,000-word level (Nation 2017). Each of the passages was 550 words long and was accompanied by ten comprehension questions. The learners who read the texts increased their speed from about 120 words per minute to about 165 words per minute and increased their reading speed after the course.

Taguchi et al. (2012) used a repeat reading approach with the same overall aim. This study looked at one learner. The texts were taken from two novels. The learner chose how much she read in each session but averaged about eight hundred words. For each session, she

1 read a passage silently timing herself,

2 read the same passage three more times while listening to the audio recording,

3 read the same passage two more times silently while timing each reading with a stopwatch,

4 wrote thoughts and comments about the repeat reading session in a diary.

Over six sessions, she increased from about 130 words per minute to just under 190.

12.4.7 Extensive reading

Extensive reading means that learners read books, often graded readers, that they find easy to understand and enjoy reading. The idea that extensive reading leads to improvements in reading is intuitively plausible and it has been described as the 'magic carpet' to language development in general and reading abilities in particular but 'the "magic carpet" remains firmly nailed to the floor' (Macalister 2014: 389), despite the evidence suggesting its benefits (e.g. Nakanishi 2015). The limited use of extensive reading is because its results are largely to do with reading efficiency and a more positive attitude to English and reading. These are not aspects that are highly valued by all examination systems and so extensive reading is seen as an unnecessary luxury. Extensive reading is also relatively expensive. It requires a library of readers and logistical support in terms of a place to keep the books, a mechanism for learners to borrow and return them and support for the learners as they read. When I worked in Malaysia, I was fortunate enough to have a principal who was sufficiently in favour of English language education to agree to the purchase of relevant readers but, perhaps more importantly, the school had a room where the books could be kept.

Where teachers can set up extensive reading schemes, the following are useful guidelines (Day and Bamford 2002: 137–9):

1 The reading material is easy.

2 A variety of reading material on a wide range of topics must be available.

3 Learners choose what they want to read.

4 Learners read as much as possible.

5 The purpose of reading is usually related to pleasure, information and general understanding.

6 Reading is its own reward.

7 Reading speed is usually faster rather than slower.

8 Reading is individual and silent.

9 Teachers orient and guide their students.

10 The teacher is a role model of a reader.

The Extensive Reading Foundation (2011) runs a website on extensive reading and a downloadable guide.

12.5 Summary

This chapter examined the process of reading from a psychological, linguistic and social perspective and briefly examined how people learn to read to inform the teaching of reading in the final section. This section provides information about structuring reading classes as well as suggestions related to reading fluency and extensive reading activities.

 Activity 12.3 Discussion

What would you suggest that the teacher in this context does to help the student improve their reading?

I teach adults in a college in California in a low intermediate (B1+) class. The students are mainly migrants who have moved to California to find work. Although they enrol on a twelve-week course, their attendance is poor because job interviews, migration formalities and family responsibilities take precedence over English language courses. However, they are very motivated, particularly wanting to learn spoken English and the written language associated with dealing with bureaucracies and potential employers. If they attended all their classes I would see them for seven and a half hours a week and they would also have classes with a colleague for the same amount of time.

I have agreed with my colleague that my focus should be on reading, particularly job advertisements and application forms. However, I cannot be sure who will come to my classes from day to day and I need to find a way to organize my teaching and the work they do outside the class so that the classes are useful both to learners who comes to every class and those who are not so regular.

12.6 Further reading

My favourite book on reading is Hudson's (2007) *Teaching Second Language Reading* but Grabe's (2009) *Reading in a Second Language: Moving from Theory to Practice* and Grabe and Stoller's (2013) *Teaching and Researching Reading* are good, and the latter has a chapter on research-informed reading teaching.

Gregory's (2008) *Learning to Read in a New Language: Making Sense of Words and Worlds* is very good on social aspects of learning to read, particularly with younger learners, and Snowling and Hulme's (2005) *The Science of Reading: A Handbook* provides an authoritative account of reading in a first or second language, particularly from a psychological point of view.

Chapter 13

Writing

13.1 Introduction

Being able to write is a key to educational success and is also the main way in which people can access cultural and economic resources. Being able to write in English unlocks many educational and economic resources particularly in Anglophonic countries but also in many countries across the world, and this gives it a similar status to being able to read in English. However, one important difference is that writing is a productive skill, and this means it is easier to understand how people write than how they read, and people often have stronger memories of the process of learning to write in their first language than they do of learning to read. Perhaps for this reason debates about the nature of writing and of how people learn to write have been more heated than those related to reading. This chapter argues that these different views of writing and learning to write are best seen as different perspectives rather than competing views. The effective teaching of writing involves a reconciliation between the different views. The chapter aims to support that reconciliation by addressing three questions:

1 What is involved in writing?

2 How people learn to write English?

3 How can we teach writing?

 Activity 13.1 Thinking about the writing class

Think of a lesson where you aim to improve a group of learners' writing abilities in English and try to address the following questions:

1 For what reasons do the learners need to be able to write in English? For some learners, this may just relate to an examination, but many learners also need to be able to write for other reasons.

2 What are the aims of the writing class? How closely is this related to your answer to question 1?

3 What kinds of activities happen in the writing class? Do writers spend most of their time writing, or are they working on other aspects of language such as grammar?

4 What kinds of things does the teacher do? Does the teacher spend their time talking about writing, giving learners feedback on their writing?

5 How well can the learners write in languages other than English? How might this knowledge help them when they write in English?

6 How good are the learners at the skills such as planning involved in writing?

7 How well does the writing element in the programme help the learners achieve the aims identified in question 1?

13.2 What is involved in writing?

Theories of writing provide teachers with a way of describing what it is that they want to achieve in their writing lessons.

13.2.1 Theories of writing

The term writing has been understood in a range of ways (Hyland 2009, 2003b; Ivanič 2004). These are often described as approaches. In most areas of English language teaching, an approach is a way of teaching. However 'approaches' to writing provide limited guidance on how writing should be taught rather than what writing is and so I am using the term theory here instead.

The different ways of understanding writing can be described in two dimensions. The first is whether the word 'writing' is treated dynamically as a verb (as in I am writing) or synoptically as a noun (writing is difficult), and the second dimension relates to whether the focus is on the individual creativity of the solitary writer in the garret or the more social view of writing as communication. The two dimensions give four theories, though the boundaries between them are often fuzzy. The theories are described below.

The different theoretical positions are often described in agonistic terms as being opposites (Badger 2006; Hyland 2003a; Kammler 1995; Tannen 2002) or as a progressivist narrative reflecting our growing understanding of writing with the most recent model seen as being the best (Ivanič 2004). However, the approaches are complementary rather than competing. It is better to see the theories as capturing different aspects of writing with decisions between the models as reflecting what is appropriate for particular contexts. These ways of thinking about writing or theories of writing provide a diagnostic tool for the writing teacher. When working with a group of learners, teachers need to think about what they need to learn and the theories of writing can help them achieve this. If they lack knowledge of the appropriate vocabulary, then the product view of writing is most appropriate and if they are not good at planning their work, then a process view is better. See Table 13.1.

13.2.2 Product theories

Product views see writing as mainly to do with knowledge of grammar, vocabulary, spelling, punctuation and cohesive devices. This often leads to pieces of writing whose main aim is to allow learners to show off particular grammatical constructions. Indeed Racelis and Matsuda use the term grammar-writing to describe this view of writing and offer the following illustration of what a grammar writing class might aim at:

Table 13.1 Perspective on teaching writing

	Synoptic	Dynamic
Individual	**Product** e.g. spelling, punctuation, grammar, vocabulary	**Process** e.g. generating ideas, planning, editing
Social	**Genre** e.g. purpose, audience, topic, text structure	**Literacy** e.g. investigating what people do with writing

> Focusing mostly on experiential writing, my grammar-writing prompts looked like this: *What has been the happiest moment in your life? What happened? Describe and explain.* This writing prompt appeared on the top of a page, followed by blank lines. It was presented with little additional instruction or discussion. Students were expected to provide a rich description using the present perfect, past perfect, and simple past tenses. (Racelis and Matsuda 2013: 383)

This view of writing sees the writing lesson as an extension of what happens in grammar (Chapter 9) and vocabulary (Chapter 10) lessons, and most teachers will have a richer conceptualization of writing, but sometimes the reason learners have difficulty writing is because of their lack of knowledge about grammar and vocabulary and, in these circumstances, grammar and vocabulary can be appropriate aims for a writing lesson.

13.2.3 Process theories

Process views of writing emerged from mother tongue teaching, where knowledge of grammar and vocabulary could be assumed, and so process theories focus on the skills people use in writing, which makes this a dynamic view of writing. They were originally used in second language teaching contexts with more advanced learners, but this view of writing does have insights into how even beginners can be helped to improve their writing.

In a very influential article, Flower and Hayes (1981) argued that 'the process of writing is best understood as a set of distinctive thinking processes which writers orchestrate or organize during the act of composing' (p. 366). The Flower and Hayes model was a description of L1 writing, but it has been successfully adapted to make sense of the L2 writing process (Leki et al. 2008; Silva 1993). Table 13.2 summarizes five models of the writing process: Flower and Hayes (1981); an early book for L2 teachers on the process approach to teaching writing (White and Arndt 1991); and three research-based models (De Larios 2008; Sasaki 2000; Wang and Wen 2002). While there are similarities in all the models, the terminology used to describe the writing process varies, and this can be problematic. Table 13.2 attempts to indicate what terms are equivalent in different process theories.

One particular issue is the term 'translation' which Flower and Hayes, rather confusingly for teachers of second languages, used to describe putting thoughts into words. However, translating between languages does figure in second language writing, and the impact of translation on writing quality seems to be mixed. Gosden (1996) found that translation is used more by less skilled L2 writers, and

Table 13.2 Process models of writing

Flower and Hayes (1981: 370)	Wang and Wen (2002: 232)	White and Arndt (1991: 11 et seq.)	Sasaki (2000: 290)	Roca De Larios et al. (2008: 36–7)
The rhetorical problem	Task examining	Generating ideas	Generating ideas	Reading the prompt
				Task conceptualization
Generating	Idea generating			Planning
Planning / Organizing / Goal setting	Idea organizing	Focusing ideas / Structuring ideas	Planning / Retrieving	
Translation	Text generating / Re-viewing	Drafting	Verbalizing	Formulation
Reviewing / Evaluating	activities	Evaluating	Evaluating	
Revising	Process controlling	Re-viewing	Re-reading	
Monitor			Translating, other	Meta-comments

Figure 13.1 White and Arndt's model of the writing process

Woodall (2002) found that intermediate students used the L1 between two and three times as much as advanced learners depending on the writing task. However, Kobayashi and Rinnert (1992) found that L2 writers using translation produced better writing than those who wrote directly in English. Similarly, in Sasaki's (2000) study, both skilled and less skilled L2 writers benefitted from translation in writing, but skilled writers improved their English expression with the help of L1 while less skilled writers translated ideas word-by-word from L1 into L2.

Table 13.2 misrepresents the idea of writing as a linear process. In fact, the writing process is recursive. The Flower and Hayes model recognizes the recursive nature of writing through the concept of the monitor, that is, the ways in which writers decide when to move onto a new stage. This recursion is also a feature of L2 writing (Raimes 1983; Silva 1993; Zamel and Spack 1998), and White and Arndt present their model diagrammatically as a cycle. See Figure 13.1. Second language writers move back and forth between the processes of planning, drafting and revision, and between the written and the emerging text to carry out the problem-solving task that composing entails (Manchón et al. 2007). De Larios et al. (1999) describe this as 'backtracking', which they gloss as L2 writers' actions 'to take stock of the ideas and constraints of the text produced so far in order to bring them to bear on current needs' (p. 14).

For example, where learners need to write a letter of complaint, the focus would be on the process that might lead to the letter. The aims of the lesson might include what people complain about, producing a first draft or proof-reading a letter.

A criticism of process views is that they see sees all kinds of writing as broadly the same so planning and revising would be seen as a part of many different kinds of writing, though this may not be true of text messages and many emails. Process theories also underplay the role of specialist knowledge about kinds of writing. Secondary school learners will need to learn about the conventions of writing in a range of disciplines, for example, writing a description of an experiment. This would go beyond what a process view can contribute and is where genre theory can provide some insight.

13.2.4 Genre theories

Genre models developed in two main contexts. The first was mother tongue English language classes where learners were writing what should have been, for example, science reports as the stories they were familiar with from their English classes. The second context was where speakers of languages other than English were preparing to study in Anglophonic universities and did not understand the conventions of academic writing.

Genre models differ from process approaches in that their focus is on language knowledge and they differ from product approaches in that the areas of knowledge they see as most important are about texts and their relationship with the social environment. The idea of genre is examined in more detail in Chapter 11 but, in short, a genre is a group of texts which share the same social purpose and so have similarities in terms of who reads and writes them, what they are about or their topic and how they are structured. As not all learners will need to produce all kinds of written genres, this has implications for syllabus design.

A typical genre lesson or series of lessons would have an aim like writing a letter of complaint about, say, a delayed bus or producing an academic essay and the focus would be on how such pieces of writing are structured and the ways in which the grammar and vocabulary are used to achieve the overall aim.

The weakness of genre views of writing is that they underplay the role of the writer and this means that they sometimes present genres as more fixed than they really are and ignores the potential for creativity. The view that genres are relatively fixed can have social implications. Where, for example, language learners have to use particular genres to apply for jobs, sometimes the problem is not simply that the learners do not understand the genre but that the genre is structured in a way that favours particular groups in society so that aims should be not to prepare learners to use the genre but to change the genre (Cooke and Simpson 2008).

13.2.5 Literacy theories

Literacy theories in English language teaching came out of lessons with people who had moved to English speaking contexts and were often socially disadvantaged such as ELL clauses in North American and ESOL and EAL classes in the UK. Writing here is just one aspect of language use and the speaking, listening and reading that go on around writing as well the multimodal resources such as the use of images, are as important to the production of writing as making marks on paper or typing on a keyboard. A literacy practice will often include writing but will rarely consist only of writing.

Literacy theories see writing as a social practice within a historical context. Ivanič says:

> All our writing is influenced by our life histories. Each word we write represents an encounter, possibly a struggle, between our multiple past experience and the demands of a new context. Writing is not some neutral activity which we just learn like a physical skill, but it implicates every fibre of the writer's multifaceted being. (1998: 181)

This view of writers means that the aim of the writing lesson is not just to develop the learners' writing abilities but also to empower learners.

Not only do writers have personal histories but also what we write is historical. The kinds of things that we write are changing (e.g. text messages, Facebook entries, online job applications) and the development of new and different kinds of writing have implications that go beyond what happens in the classroom so learners need to develop an awareness of why particular discourses and genres are the way they are.

Literacy approaches differ from process approaches because they see writing as essentially social and from genre approaches in that they see writers as having more agency but also recognizing that many texts are often not produced by individual authors. A typical literacy writing class would aim to help learners to produce letters of complaint about, say a delayed bus, but would also look at the way producing this involves spoken and written language and to look more generally at the social role of public transport.

 Activity 13.2 How do we learn to write?

Look at the following kinds of writing or aspects of writing and consider how you learnt them. Were you given instruction? Did you observe other people producing similar texts or was something else involved?

1. Forming letters/ characters	2. Revising
3. Shopping lists	4. E-mails
5. Formal letters	6. Academic assignments

13.3 Learning to write

Product and genre approaches to writing align mainly with psychologically oriented theories of learning (Chapter 3) with learners developing declarative knowledge from the teacher and their own analytical processes and proceduralizing this through practice.

Process and literacy approaches are less clear about how they see learning happens but both assume that much information will be picked up implicitly through engaging in writing and watching others carrying out the same activities. So Ivanič says that within literacy approaches, people 'learn implicitly by participating in socially situated literacy events which fulfil social goals which are relevant and meaningful to them' (2004: 235). This is consistent with implicit learning followed by practice within psychologically oriented theories of learning but is probably most clearly seen as focussing on learners developing by work within their zone of proximal development supported by scaffolding from the teacher and other learners within a sociocultural paradigm.

13.4 Approaches to teaching writing

This section covers the four approaches to teaching writing mentioned above and has a final section on feedback.

13.4.1 Product

In this approach, learning to write has four stages which closely parallel PPP (presentation, practice and production) – familiarization, controlled writing, guided writing and free writing. The familiarization stage aims to make learners aware of certain features of the target writing. In the controlled and guided writing sections, the learners practise the skills with increasing freedom until they are ready for the free writing section, where learners may use writing within a communicative task.

A product lesson for a letter of complaint

1 Familiarization – learners look at examples of complaint letters, possibly written for this purpose and identify grammatical patterns and appropriate lexis.

2 Controlled writing – learners produce some simple sentences about their complaints from a substitution table.

3 Guided writing – learners produce a piece of writing based on a complaint suggested by the teacher or course book writer.

4 Free writing – learners write a letter of complaint.

13.4.2 Process

Process writing classes involve learners engaging in the writing process. This is learning by doing rather than learning by instruction so the stages would depend on the teacher's view of the stages of the writing process. See Figure 13.1. A lesson or series of lessons might have four stages: prewriting, composing/drafting, revising and editing (Tribble, 1996: 39).

A process lesson for a letter of complaint

1 Pre-writing or generating ideas

   a Individually, learners think about a situation in which they have complained about faulty good or bad service (or have felt like complaining) and tell a partner.

2 Planning

   a Focussing ideas – in groups, learners put the ideas from 'generating ideas' into a mind map.

   b Organizing ideas – in groups, learners organize the mind map into a plan.

3 Drafting

   a First draft – in groups, the learners produce a draft letter of complaint . . . They are told not to worry about formal features of the letter, such as grammar and spelling at this stage.

   b Second draft/revising – the groups of learners exchange drafts and write comments on the content of each other's drafts. Sometimes, the teacher will also look at drafts at this stage. The learners then produce a second draft of their letters of complaint.

   c Final draft/proof-reading – in groups the learners proof-read their own draft and produce a third draft of the letters of complaint.

Figure 13.2 A multimodal brainstorm (Amicucci and Lassiter 2014: 589)

Activities common in a process approach writing class

Brainstorming

Process approaches see writing as an action of creativity and this has led to a focus on helping learners develop ideas that they wish to communicate in writing and a common way of doing this is through brainstorming. Rao (2007) suggested a three-stage approach. First the learners spent five minutes individually thinking about the title of their piece of writing, in this case the merits and demerits of keeping pets. They then formed pairs or larger groups and combined their ideas. They were told not to be judgmental at this stage but to find some way of organizing the two sets of ideas. This could be done on paper if the learners wished. The final stage was to present their ideas to the class and one group would act as scribes to produce a class brainstorm on the board. This is a very structured approach to brainstorming but Rao was using this as way of introducing the notion of brainstorming to his learners and it had a positive effect on the quality of their writing. Brainstorming can be done with a combination of words and pictures and this can be useful for younger learner. See Figure 13.2 for a brainstorm on 'place'.

Writing conferences

A conference in the writing class is a meeting between the teacher and one or more learners. Maliborska and You (2016) investigated writing conferences in a course for speakers of other languages who were studying in the United States. Once the teacher had given the essay title, learners produced a first draft and had a group or individual conference about that draft, produced a second daft and then had an individual conference about the second draft. They found that learners preferred individual to group conferences and wanted the conference to last more than typical in this context, fifteen minutes. They also found that the attention switched from ideas and organization in the first conference to grammar and vocabulary in the second conference, something that mirrors the division between evaluating and revising in Flower and Hayes's characterization of the writing process. As with Rao's work on brainstorming, they did find that conferencing is not natural to learners and that they may need to be taught how to make best use of conferences by strategies such as preparing questions for the teacher before the conference.

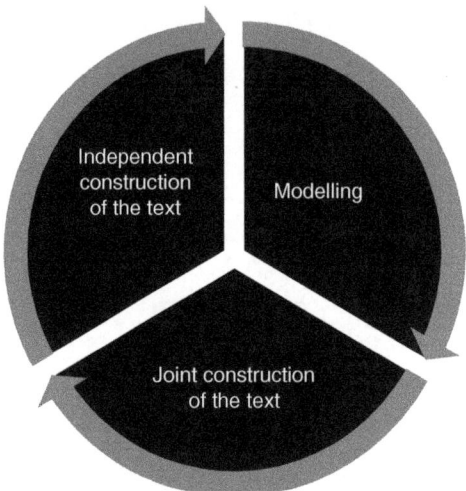

Figure 13.3 The wheel model of genre literacies pedagogy
(Cope and Kalantzis 1993)

13.4.3 Genre

Genre approach writing lessons can be taught in a range of ways but the wheel model in Figure 13.3 has received a lot of attention. This essentially has three stages modelling the target genre, where learners are exposed to examples of the genre they have to produce; the construction of a text by learners and teacher; and, finally, the independent construction of texts by learners. The cycle can be repeated as and when needed. Dudley-Evans (1997: 154) also identifies three stages in genre approaches to writing. First, a model of a genre is introduced and analysed. Learners then carry out exercises which manipulate relevant language forms and, finally, produce a short text. This parallels product approaches very closely.

A genre approach writing lesson for a letter of complaint

1 Contextualization – the learners and teacher talk about when it would be appropriate to write a letter of complaint.

2 Language awareness – the learners look at two or three examples of letters of complaint. They will be guided to look for particular features of the letters, depending on what aspects the teachers think they need help in, for example, the teacher may choose to focus on the layout or a particular aspect of grammar.

3 In groups, the learners write their own letter of complaint.

Activities common in genre approaches to teaching writing

Genre approaches are often text focussed and this is exemplified here with two activities for students. The first relates to the overall structure of academic articles and the second relates to the level of formality in academic writing and in particular the use of 'I'.

Text analysis: the structure of academic articles

Negretti et al. (2011) describe a course for native speakers of Swedish who were studying pedagogy at university. One of the tasks that the learners were asked to carry out was

> With your classmates, finish the analysis of the two ELT articles. Then, analyse and compare the two linguistics articles given to you. In particular, pay close attention to the following aspects: intended audience; structure of the article; introduction …; rhetorical aspects throughout the paper; and style (ex. tenses, verbs used, hedges etc.)

They found that this analysis of academic articles led to the learners developing declarative and procedural knowledge of the genre of academic articles but that this did not impact on the writing of all the learners in the study. It was not clear from the study if the genre knowledge would have become part of the writing of all the learners given time or if some other kind of learning would be needed first.

Levels of formality: using 'I'

This is an example from my own materials for people who want to study in English. Many learners have been told to avoid using 'I' in academic writing. However, in some fields the use of 'I' is acceptable (Hyland 2002), and this material is intended to help learners see what the practice is in TESOL and also develop their abilities to work out what happens in other academic disciplines. The aim here is not to identify rules but to help learners develop the skills so that they can identify patterns of use.

13.4.4 Literacy

Literacy approaches focus on trying to make what happens in the classroom as similar to what the learners will need to do outside the classroom. This is related to the concept of authenticity discussed in Chapter 4.

Read these text extracts and work out why the writer is using the pronoun 'I'
Extract A
In the preface of their work, Day and Bamford (1998) defined extensive reading as 'an approach to the teaching and learning of second language reading in which learners read large quantities of books and other materials that are well within their linguistic competence'. As I have personally developed my own reading competence by reading a large number of English novels, I have always been confident about the beneficial effects of extensive reading.
Extract B
Permission from the students willing to participate was also necessary and this leads to the second ethical aspect I considered: the people affected by the research. Before asking for my students' permission, I told them in Spanish what the Study was about, what it was for, what improvements it was expected to bring about and what the participants were expected to do.
Extract C
In the following section, I will discuss the necessity of equipping students – with regard to the above-mentioned context – with some strategies that would help them be less dependent on teachers and more aware of their learning process.

Figure 13.4 Using 'I' in academic writing

This means that teachers need to design activities in the lesson which relate to literacy based events outside the class room and are activities in which the learners would be likely to be involved. For example, Stewart (2010) chose the topic of migration for her class of learners who had come to live and work in the United States. Though the main target was to improve the learner's writing, they also read and analysed a wide selection of texts related to the topic. This was an important element as it validated the learners' own experience. For example, one participant said:

> I have the similar experience with the authors [of the texts we read] and I could imitate the wrighting [sic] style for my composition.

This also led to the students seeing their writing as more than a classroom exercise:

> I hope our writing can help Americans understand that like them, we are human beings and we are here to work hard and to do good things for their country.

A literacy or social practices writing lesson for a letter of complaint

1 Choosing the kind of writing

   a The lesson would start with a discussion of what the learners would want to complain about and what they want the letter of complaint to achieve. It is important that this comes from the learners rather than from the teacher and reflects the learners' own lives.

2 Identifying resources

   a In groups the learners then discuss what they already know about letters of complaint and what they need to know.

   b Learners now discuss how they will get the information that they need, often from the teacher but also from other sources.

   c The learners then do what they need to do to get the information they need. This might include reading timetables or photographs of the number of people on a bus.

3 Drafting the letter

   a The learners in groups or individually draft a letter

   b In groups or with the help of the teacher, the learners produce a final version of the letter, often from more than one person

4 Participating in communication

   a The learners send their letters of complaint to the relevant authorities.

Activities associated literacy approaches to teaching writing

Autobiographical writing

Autobiographical writing is important in literacy approaches as an acknowledgement of the learners' histories and the contribution of their histories to their language learning. Park (2013) describes how she used what she calls cultural and linguistic autobiographical writing with a group of adult language learners in the United States. She asked her learners to produce a portfolio of autobiographical writing about the themes of (1) family and early schooling, (2) initial experience in the United States, (3) experience of learning English in the United States and (4) reflection on the writing project. She found that there was a lot of variation in how learners responded to this but she found that it helped learners develop aspects of language more often associated with product and genre approaches:

> I had acquired a lot of useful techniques about writing. For example, I learned how to use subordinate clauses in paragraph, so that they wouldn't make your writing too monotonous. (Park 2013: 342)

It also helped establish their own identity:

> I think the more important thing is that I write the real me. It made me think a lot, I see many changes happened to me. (Park 2013: 343)

Finally, it served as a way of focussing their attention on what they wanted to achieve in the United States.

> I was able to organize my list to arrive to my final goal in the United States. So I know what is first and what I need to do to achieve those goals. (Park 2013: 342)

Using a class blog

Blogs are used in many writing classes but they are particularly relevant to literacy approaches because they provide opportunities for learners to communicate in an authentic way and also reflect the literacy recognition that texts may have multiple authors. Simpson (2013) describes the use of a blog as part of an intermediate class for people who had come to live in the UK. The opening post on the blog read:

> Hello everyone and welcome to our class blog. this is a place to practice your writing. we will use this throughout the year. first, click the comment icon. write the most important thing you learned last week. Say why this is important to you. second, look at this post. There are some mistakes. what are they? (p. 198)

For homework the teacher would set a question and the learners would produce a response to that question on the class blog. A typical interaction was:

> [Teacher] Last week you had only 7 spellings to learn. Do you get everything correct? If not, why not? Did you spend enough time studying? Or is there another reason?
>
> [Learner] Yes, my all spellings are correct. No, I don't think so enough time spend in study because I have too much housework and my son keep busy to me. (p. 189)

The teacher also used the blog during class time and the same learner who was involved in the interaction above wrote the following as part of a book review.

> [Learner]TYPE OF BOOK: Romance
>
> The setting of this book is in England and the Greek Island of Santorini (A Place in the Sun). This books main plot is How people fall in love, what is they expecting to there partner. Some men play with womens heart, they broken there heart and they can't bother. [Victoria and Ben]

[Teacher]Very interesting Shahedah. Remember to put a space after a comma and full stop:) Also, can you say something about your opinion of this book? Did you like the characters? Did you like the story?

[Learner] It's my common mistek, I'm always forgoten. Sorry. I like this book beacause it's gave me infomation about greek Island, riletionship, differant tipes people. I like victoria's and Kelly's characters. Intresting story. (Simpson 2013: 192)

The teacher found the blog was useful as a way of encouraging learners to write and the learner who produced the book report said she liked the blog because it was public, the teacher and the students could comment on her work and she could read other students' blog entries and use them as models for her own writing.

13.5 Feedback

As a teacher in Malaysia, I often spent my evenings with a stack of thirty or so exercise books gradually working my way through them with my red pen. I always felt torn between the desire to correct everything, which I thought of as providing maximum support to my learners, and trying not to discourage them. One of my learners complained that it looked as if someone had been bleeding over his homework and I could see that my good intentions were often discouraging my learners and had little impact on their writing. So this section discusses ways of providing feedback that I hope will have more impact than my Malaysian efforts did. There are two more important issues, what to give feedback on and how to give that feedback and two less important issues, when to give feedback and who should be giving the feedback.

 Activity 13.3 What do you give feedback on?

Imagine that you are a teacher of English working with learners aged between sixteen and eighteen. The learners have been asked to write a short piece of writing answering the question 'How to live a healthy life?' This is what one of your learners has produced. What feedback would you give to this learner? You can write on the text or in the margins and you can include some comments at the bottom of the piece of writing if you want.

Healthy is the most important thing in the lives. Without healthy, people cannot do anything els. Money can almost buy everything, but not healthy. If healthy is very important for us, why some people keep doing bad things to damage their health? We all know smoking, drinking, taking drugs and other things that will hurt our body, but some people still keep doing those every day. People need to realized how important to maintain their health, so they won't regret in the future. Daily exercise, good eating habit and rest can help us to maintain our healthy. Therefore, we need to remember that it's never too late to change! If you are doing something that is hurting your body, stop it before too late!

13.5.1 What to give feedback on

Feedback on learners' writing generally has one of four often overlapping aims: evaluation (does the writing reach the required standard); criticism (what is bad about the writing); suggestion (how can the writing be improved); and praise (what is good about the writing) (Hyland and Hyland 2001). The first aim is addressed in Chapter 6 but the others are covered here. Most research shows that teachers give much more negative than positive feedback. Lee (2009: 17) found over 90 per cent of feedback was about weaknesses in writing and, while Hyland and Hyland (2001) found more praise (44 per cent), quite of lot of the positive comments were followed by something negative.

> References very good. Two small problems. (1) Bibliography (at end of essay) – include initials of author. (2) Be careful about referencing inside the essay. Avoid 'said'. (Hyland and Hyland 2001: 192)

The focus on the negative is partly a reflection of the fact that improving learners' writing abilities necessarily implies identifying where there is room for improvement as well as what is being done well. However, it is important to remember that feedback is not just about the writing but also about learners' overall motivation. See Chapter 3. Some students will feel the need for positive comments, like my Malaysian student, but other students may feel like this:

> I think I've already got enough confidence so I don't need any more good comments. The problem, urn, I want development, so I want to know the weaknesses most. (Hyland 1998: 280)

Teachers have a range of options when they are providing feedback on mistakes in student writing:

1 Identify all mistakes

2 Identify no mistakes

3 Identify some mistakes

Some educational institutions have policies that say all errors should be identified (Lee 2009) and this is often a popular policy with parents but is difficult to apply in practice. Teachers would need to be very brave to go for option two but there is a line of research which suggests that improvements will happen without correction. See Chapter 9. Many teachers go for option three but then need to decide what criteria they adopt to make the selection.

 Activity 13.4 Selective feedback

Look back at the sample writing in Activity 13.3 and identify the principles you used in deciding what to provide feedback on. To what extent did you use one of the following principles? Do you use these principles in your current practice?

a Frequency – For example, the learner makes a lot of mistakes with 'healthy' (though the learners does get it right once).

b Errors and not mistakes – Some teachers distinguish between errors, when the learner does not know the rule, and mistakes, where the learner knows the rule but forgets it. In English, we use the base form of the verb after to, for example, to go, to look etc. In the sample, the learner gets this right in 'to damage' 'to remember' and 'to maintain' but gets it wrong in 'to realized'. Some teachers think mistakes should be corrected as this is part of the process of automatization. Errors are an indication that learners need to be helped to notice a rule that is new for them. They would require that learners learn something new and so would require a different response from the teacher.

c Communication – Some errors make it difficult to understand what the learner means. I do not think there are any examples of this in the sample but you may disagree. This criterion can lead to disagreement because different people will disagree what makes it hard to understand what the learner means.

d Importance – If a teacher is preparing learners for an examination or specific kind of writing, the teacher may feel that certain mistakes are more important. For example, I would see the use of exclamation marks in academic writing as likely to annoy a tutor and so would probably correct this. Again, there is an element of subjectivity in this.

e Teaching – Most teachers tend to focus on what they have just been working on. So if they have done a lot of work on organization, they are more likely to focus on problems with organization or praise examples of good organization.

13.5.2 How to give feedback?

The most important quality of feedback is that it is understood by the learners and it is very important that teachers check to make sure that comments which are clear to them are also clear to their learners. Here is an example of a misunderstood piece of feedback given to a student called Luo where the teacher wanted Luo to add a conjunction between 'lessons' and 'play games'.

> Excerpt from Luo's first draft: They forget their homework, their lessons, only play games in the internet!
>
> Teacher's comment: Use transitions to rewrite this sentence.
>
> Excerpt from Luo's revision: **But** they forget their homework, their lessons, only play games in the internet! (Changes are highlighted in bold print.) (Yang et al. 2006: 190)

Spoken feedback in writing conferences can often help ensure mutual understanding but is not a guarantee (Maliborska and You 2016: 11). Technologies now allow for relatively easy recordings of spoken feedback where it is not possible for teachers to meet their learners face to face. Teachers can also make use of a range of ways of providing written feedback electronically including blogs and wikis. In the university where I now work, students' assignments are submitted electronically and tutors provide feedback electronically. Many tutors find this more efficient than giving feedback on printed student scripts and this is becoming more common within the school system (Zheng et al. 2015).

Teachers also have to make decisions about how much information they give about particular errors. The first sentence of the learner text in Activity 13.2 reads:

> Healthy is the most important thing in the lives

Table 13.3 A coding system for providing feedback

Category of error	Code	Category of error	Code
Spelling error	sp	Preposition	prep
Word order error	wo	Wrong word	ww
Verb form error	V	Missing word	/
Tense error	T	Subject/verb concord	SV
Article error	Art	Sentence structure	SS

Here the teacher's feedback could go from a complete rewrite, 'Health is the most important thing in our lives', to a question mark indicating that something needs to be changed. The balance is difficult. Teachers try to ensure that learners understand what the problem is but also that the learners need to put in enough cognitive effort to make learning probable. If teachers provide too much help, learners can make a correction but no learning will happens. If teachers provide too little help, learners will not understand what is wrong and again no learning will happen.

One technique that is widespread is the use of a coding system (Lee 2009). See Table 13.3. Coding systems do save time and can encourage learners to think about their errors but, as with many of these techniques, it is important that learners are given training in any coding system and that the coding system is easily available to learners by, for example, a poster in the class.

13.5.3 When to give feedback?

In a product approach to writing, learners produce a piece of text, receive feedback on that and then move on to another writing task. Within a process approach, learners typically receive feedback when they have produced a first draft of their writing as well as on the completed texts. This means that learners can respond to the feedback they receive within a short time frame and this may be more effecting in helping them to proceduralize their knowledge about language than where they would have to wait for a new piece of writing where the feedback might not be relevant. The evidence for improvements between first and second drafts is strong (e.g. Yang et al. 2006). The evidence of improvement in later pieces of writing is less clear but positive (e.g. Hyland 1998).

13.5.4 Who should give feedback?

Traditionally feedback has been provided by the tutor but feedback can be provided by other learners in the class or by using digital resources. Peer feedback has been tried in many contexts but most often with adults and the results have largely been positive. When teachers use this out with their learners, learners need with training in how to give feedback and provide some kind of structure for their feedback. Research that I have been involved in (Yang et al. 2006) found that learners prefer feedback from their teacher to the peers and made more improvement as a result of teacher than peer feedback but the learners did benefit from peer feedback, particular where it related to the content of the writing rather than grammar and vocabulary. We also found that peer feedback encouraged learner autonomy.

Many learners have access to internet resources through laptops, tablets and smart phones and teachers can provide instruction in how to uses these resources effectively. Saadat et al. (2016) give the example of a learner who is not sure whether to write 'in accordance with' or 'in accordance by'. This can be checked by using online dictionaries (see Chapter 10) or concordances (see Chapter 9) or in the archives of online discussion groups.

13.6 Summary

This chapter looked at the teaching of writing in terms of three main questions:

1 What is involved in writing (to identify the aim of the writing lesson)?

2 How do we learn to write (to under what learners are doing when they learn to write)?

3 How should we teach people to write (to help teachers design writing lessons)?

The chapter examined each of these questions in terms of four theories or approaches to writing: product, process, genre and literacy. The approaches are not alternatives but, as a group, give us a reasonably complete way of thinking about teaching writing lessons. The sections on each approach identified differences in the aims, views of learning and organization of lessons. The section on teaching also had a subsection on feedback which looked at what teachers might provide feedback on and on the ranges of ways in which feedback can be given.

 Activity 13.4 Discussion

What would you suggest that the teacher in this context does to help the student improve their writing?

At my university, I teach the subject English Language. I teach first-year students doing their degrees in English language teaching, translation and research. In fact, in the writing class students analyse model academic paragraphs from the writing course books, considering the writer–reader relationship, the purpose for writing and the specific lexico-grammatical elements. The students write drafts at home and I give them written feedback on their drafts using the correction symbols, that is, I highlight students' mistakes without providing the right answer so that students use English dictionaries, the Internet and other learning resources to spot and self-correct the mistake

However, when checking students' second drafts, I have noticed that my students fail to correct some of the most serious lexico-grammatical mistakes. In fact, although spelling, verb tense and punctuation mistakes made in the first drafts are usually corrected in the second drafts, other mistakes are not corrected.

13.7 Further reading

The most useful guide for teachers is Harmer's (2004) *How to Teach Writing*. Ken Hyland is probably the leading researcher on second language writing, and his book *Teaching and Researching Writing* (2009) is a useful introduction to the literature on teaching writing. Literacy approaches are relatively new. Lillis's (1998) *Student Writing: Access Regulation Desire* looks at writing in higher education but mainly as first language writers, and Kern's (2000) *Literacy and Language Teaching* looks at the implication for ideas related to literacy on language teaching in general.

Chapter 14

Listening

14.1 Introduction

Listening can lay claim to being the skill to which least attention is paid. This is because, like reading, it is a receptive skill and, like speaking, is often not part of the assessment procedures by which learner development and teacher effectiveness are measured. However, listening is very important in the learning process and is central to all oral communication. Like reading, the receptive nature of listening means that it is not always obvious how listening happens or how people learn to listen and, again like reading, this has meant that listening lessons often consist mainly of practice rather than teaching. This chapter attempts to respond to these issues by addressing three questions:

1 What is involved in listening?
2 How do people learn to listen to English?
3 How can teachers teach listening?

14.2 What is involved in listening?

Listening, like reading, is a psychological, linguistic and social activity. This section mainly describes the linguistic contribution to the listening process, but two things need to be borne in mind while reading the section. First, the conventions of written text make it easier to describe the listening process as if it were a linear process drawing on different kinds of knowledge, the lower and higher levels of information discussed in Chapter 12, to make sense of the input. These kinds of information are not used in sequence. The listening process is a complex one and different kinds of information are used at all stages of the listening process. Second, for expert users of English, many of the processes described happen extremely fast and without any conscious effort or control, and so most expert users are not aware that these processes are happening.

> Beginning-level L2 listeners, however, have limited language knowledge; therefore, little of what they hear can be automatically processed. They need to consciously focus on details of what they hear, and given the limitations of working memory and the speed of speech, comprehension suffers. (Vandergrift 2004: 5–6)

Learners perceive speakers of English as speaking very fast because the learners' listening processes are struggling to keep up rather than because English speakers talk quickly. Teachers sometimes find it hard to understand the problems their learners are having listening because, as expert users, they are not aware of the processes that are causing problems to learners.

The processes of listening and reading have much in common, so Field's (2008b: 125) model of listening parallels the earlier discussion of reading.

> Decoding: translation of the speech signal into speech sounds, words and clauses, and finally into a literal meaning
>
> Meaning building: adding to the bare meaning provided by decoding and relating it to what has been said before.

What follows is based on Field's stages, but decoding is sub-divided into two parts: constructing phonemes and syllables; identifying words and clauses or parsing. However, as with reading there is a physiological stage or stages before you get to decoding or perception. The physiological stages cover how we get the sound waves that are produced by speakers, the substance of listening, into our heads. This stage normally only goes wrong if there is a physical problem with the signal or a physiological problem with some part of the ear. A listener may fail to understand something because the speaker's voice is too soft or because the listener's ear is too full of wax. If there are no physiological problems, we end up with what Field describes as the input or speech stream (Field 2008b: 126). The acoustic signal is not language and what happens at this stage would be the same if we were listening to the sound of a cat meowing or another person talking to us. As Field says of the input:

> What reaches our ears is not a string of words or phrases or even a sequence of phonemes. It is a group of acoustic features . . . We must not think of the words or phonemes of connected speech as transmitted from speaker to listener. It is the listener who has to turn the signal into units of language. (2008b: 127)

Once the acoustic signal has reached the section of the short-term memory called the phonological loop, it is then ready to be decoded.

14.2.1 Decoding

Constructing phonemes and syllables

The perception or decoding stage starts when listeners use their knowledge of the phonology of English, often described as bottom or lower-level knowledge, to interpret the substance, the phonetic data. This is not always a straightforward matching process because there is often more than one way of saying phonemes. The different ways of saying one phoneme are described as allophones. If you produce the letter 'p' in 'pit' with your hand in front of your mouth, you will find that you produce a puff of air while the 'p' in 'spit' does not produce a puff. However, listeners hear these physically distinct phenomena as the same sound in English. The sound [p] with or without aspiration can count as the phoneme /p/. There is more information about phonemes and allophones in Chapter 7 (Field 2008b).

English has about forty-five phonemes and a larger number of allophones, and this represents a considerable learning load for learners who speak other languages. The extent to which this is something that learners need to be taught or helped to learn will depend at least partly on the phonemes in other languages they speak. The number of vowels in English has been said to cause particular problems, and Jenkins (2002) has argued for a focus on consonants for speakers of ELF. See Chapter 7 for further discussion of this point.

Once listeners have constructed the phonemes, they group them into syllables, though in some cases they probably bypass phonemes and go straight to syllables. Syllable construction is not particularly easy in English. For example, Japanese has about seventy different syllables; Mandarin has about 1,600; and English is said to have up to 3,000 (MacWhinney 2008: 345). The process of putting phonemes into syllables or directly identifying syllables from the sound signal is at least as problematic as phoneme identification, and the level of difficulty will depend on who your learners are.

Words

Once listeners have constructed syllables, they need to convert these into words. The influence of written language has led to two misconceptions about spoken language which conceal the difficulty of identifying words. The first is that it is easy to identify words. Identifying words in written text is generally easy because of the blank spaces between words. We know that 'not happy' is two words because of the space between 'not' and 'happy' and 'unhappy' is one because there is no space between 'un-' and '-happy'. Many language users imagine that in spoken language there is a pause between words. However, spoken language does not work like this, and anyone who listens to a language they do not know will notice how difficult it is to decide when one word ends and another begins.

A second issue is that the regularity of written language, and particularly of print, encourages the view that the same word is normally said in the same way. Unfortunately, in spoken language, this is not true. Field gives the following different ways of saying 'actually', ordered from the most careful to the most casual pronunciation (2008b: 153):

/æktjʊəlɪ/

/ækʃʊəlɪ/

/æktʃʊlɪ/

/æktʃəlɪ/

/æktʃlɪ/

/ækʃlɪ/

/æʃlɪ/

The listener has to recognize all these different strings of phonemes as the same word.

Deciding where one word ends and another begins, what Rost (2011: 36) describes as segmentation, and whether two strings of phonemes are the realizations of the same word, what Rost describes as variation (p. 36), are key to listeners constructing words from what they hear.

Segmentation

The main cue for deciding where a word begins in English is stress. Like many, but not all, languages, English syllables are either stressed or unstressed. In a word like 'cooker', 'cook' is stressed and '-er' is unstressed. Unstressed syllables usually contain the vowels /ə/, /ʊ/ or /ɪ/. About 90 per cent of content or lexical words begin with a stressed syllable (Field 2008b: 178; Rost 2011: 36). Below is the first part of a nursery rhyme 'Mary had a little lamb', written without spaces to reflect the lack of gaps in spoken language but with the syllables marked for stress by capital letters:

MAryHADaLITTleLAMBItsFLEECEwasWHITEasSNOW

The stress here is a fairly reliable way of finding the start of the content words. However, nursery rhymes have survived because they are easy to understand and so it might be expected that they would have a regular link between syllables and words. But even here, there are some oddities. 'Had', which would normally be treated as a function rather than a content word, is stressed in "Mary had a little lamb". It is also clear that stress is less effective in helping listeners decide where the end of a content word appears. Is the word 'had' or 'hada'? Is it 'fleece' or 'fleecewas'?

If the same rule is applied to the first sentence of the previous paragraph, identifying the words gets a bit more complicated.

TheSTRESSisaFAIRlyreLIableWAYofFINDingtheSTARToftheCONtentWORDS.

The stress strategy would lead to listeners hearing the word 'liable' rather than 'reliable' and Listeners might hear 'stresses' rather than 'stress is'. Listeners must be using additional strategies. The most likely is a knowledge of function words such as 'a', 'its', 'was' and 'as' in 'Mary had a little lamb' and 'the', 'is', 'a' again, and 'of' in the other sentence. There are many fewer function words than lexical words and they are also much more common so it is reasonable to assume users of a language learn these words early on. Function words are not usually stressed so when users listen to English they can use these words to identify the boundaries of the lexical or content words. A combination of the assumption that content or lexical words start with a stressed syllable and knowledge of the function words of English would identify all the words in 'Mary had a little lamb'. The concepts of function and lexical/content words are looked at in more detail in Chapter 10 and stress is also covered in Chapter 7.

For the second sentence ('The stress here is a fairly reliable way . . .') language users would also need to rely on another strategy related to a knowledge of prefixes and suffixes, or, more technically, bound morphemes, such as '-ly', 're-' (to recognize 'reliable' rather than 'liable') and '-ing'. Again, these are a relatively small group of items and appear fairly frequently so it is plausible that language users learn to construct these morphemes fairly early on and, because, like function words, they are not usually stressed, they can then use this knowledge to identify word boundaries. Morphemes are discussed in Chapter 8 and affixes and prefixes in Chapter 7.

The negative side of the use of function words and bound morphemes in identifying word boundaries is that once they have been used to identify word boundaries many learners of English do not pay very much attention to them (Field 2008a) and this can mean that learners may have difficulty with the productive use of function words and bound morphemes. This can cause problems with the development of learners' grammar. See Chapter 8 for more about this.

The extent to which learners know about stress, functions words and suffixes/affixes in English will vary enormously. This is partly because of their knowledge about English but also the ways in which other language they use cue the identification of words. For example, Russian indicates the ends of some words by the use of an unvoiced consonant (Nathan 2008: 56) and French typically has the stress on the last syllable (p. 57) so the extent to which this is an issue in a particular class will depend on who the learners are and what they know.

Variation

The various possible pronunciations of 'actually' discussed above illustrates several of the problems in identifying a word. Often when learners are first exposed to a word they hear the full or citation form. For 'actually' this will be /æktjʊəlɪ/ if they are learning BBC English but, as the differences between this way of saying the word and the most causal /æʃɪ/ shows, citation forms are not always what listeners will hear. The two most important changes are elision, where a sound is left out (as in the omission of /ʊə/ in the most casual form of 'actually', and assimilation, where a sound changes because of the sounds around it, as in the change from /tj/ to / tʃ/. These features of continuous speech are discussed in Chapter 7.

Parsing

The parsing stage is where listeners identify clauses. Listeners need first to segment the words they have identified into clauses. I will illustrate this using an example of spoken language taken from the MICASE databases (Briggs et al. 2002). I have divided this into words because I am assuming that listeners will already have identified words but many listeners will not be completely sure of the words at this stage. The sentence below comes from the start of a lecture on psychology and the syllables in capitals are stressed.

We're basically DONE with HIStory, we're DONE with METHods and we're going ON to biopsyCHOLogy.

The process of parsing draws on a range of different kinds of knowledge, but two of the most important here are intonation and grammar.

Spoken English can normally be divided into tone units (discussed in Chapter 7). In the sample above we have three intonation units:

We're basically DONE with HIStory,

we're DONE with METHods

and we're going ON to biopsyCHOLogy.

Intonation units are usually also grammatical units and here all three intonation units are clauses. In addition, intonation units normally end with a rising or falling tone at the end of the sentence. Here 'history' and 'methods' would typically be said with a rising tone so listeners would expect there to be something more to come in the sentence. In contrast, 'biopsychology' would normally be said with a falling tone to indicate the end of the sentence (Brazil 1985; Dalton and Seidlhofer 1994).

At the same time, listeners will be using their grammatical information. When listeners hear 'we're', they can bring in their grammatical knowledge and, in particular, the fact that 'we're' can be followed by an optional adverb and then either an adjective, an -ing participle, for example, eating or an -en form or past participle, for example, eaten. This knowledge will activate the groups of words labelled as adverbs, adjectives and participles in the listeners' heads. This will make it easier for them to process the words 'basically', 'done' and 'going' when the speaker says them. They will also use grammatical information when they have heard to two instances of 'done' and the one instance of 'going'. All of these could be the end of the clause but they will also know that these words can be followed by prepositions. This will activate or prime prepositions and because they will know that prepositions are followed by nouns, nouns in their turn will be activated or primed. After the noun, they will know that this could be the end of the clause and the fact that this fits in with what their knowledge of intonation tells them may well be enough for them to decide that they have correctly parsed the sentence.

Problems identifying word and syllables

The process of decoding is complex and can go wrong. Two British comedians, known as the Two Ronnies, created a sketch in which a customer asked for a series of goods which were misunderstood by the shopkeeper. For example, the customer asked for 'Fork handles' and was given 'Four candles', where the /k/ could either be the end of the syllable beginning with /f/ or the start of a new syllable. Misunderstandings are also common in songs where the lack of context may mean listeners do not have enough information to rule out misinterpretation. A well-known example of this is from a Jimi Hendrix song in which he sang 'Excuse me while I kiss the sky', that has been widely heard as 'Excuse me while I kiss this guy'.

These are problems for all speakers of English but particularly where people speak two languages. For example, the phonetic substance, roughly transcribed as [ʒʌtʌdɒ], may be heard by an English speaker as 'Shut a door' or as a French speakers as 'Je t'adore' (I adore you). This is a slightly facetious example but it illustrates the need to remember that what a learner hears is not necessarily the same as what the teacher hears.

When I was learning Malay, one of the first sentences I was taught was 'Saya bekerga sebagai guru'. This means 'I work as a teacher' and 'sebagai' can be roughly translated as 'as'. This is not a content word and so was probably not said with as much force as 'bekerga' meaning 'work'. Perhaps because of this, I heard the first part of 'sebagai' as 'spag' and I used my knowledge of English/Italian to jump to the wrong conclusion. My teacher was rather surprised to hear me say 'Saya bejerga spaghetti guru'.

14.2.2 Meaning building and genre

The next section looks at how listeners progress from the words and sentences to the meaning of the message. What this means was explained by George Miller in this way:

> To understand what another person is saying, you must assume that it is true and try to imagine what it could be true of. (Rost 2011: 61)

Listeners draw on a range of different kinds of information when they build meaning. There have been various attempts to describe this. Here I use the linguistic framework of genre with the sub-categories of field, what the listening event is about, tenor, the people involved and mode, the organization.

Listeners will generally have some knowledge about the listening event that is the genre of what they are listening to. The students listening to the psychology lecture will have some knowledge of the genre of academic lectures. The concept of genre looks quite promising as a way of identifying different kinds of listening situations. Table 14.1 lists the genres identified by Field (2008b: 63) and this may be of some use as a kind checklist of different kinds of listening events.

Table 14.1 Listening genres

Face to face	Conversation
	Obtaining and giving information
	Negotiation
Distant but two-way	Phone conversation
	Taking a message
External to listener	Announcements
	Instructions
	Answer phone messages
Listening for pleasure	Drama excerpts
	Film clips
	Jokes
	Songs
Interviews	Discussions
	Sports commentaries
Instructional	English lessons
	Lectures
Persuasive	TV ads

Source: Adapted from Field (2008b: 63)

While this is a useful list for a listening course designer, we are not yet as a stage where a course designer can look at a list of all possible listening situations in the way that someone who is constructing a grammar syllabus can look at a book on grammar. Where you have a group of learners with specific needs, it may be possible to identify the set of listening genres that they will need to get engaged in but, for more general learners, deciding what should be taught is difficult.

14.2.3 Purpose

The most important feature of a genre is purpose. The purpose of students attending lectures is to understand the main ideas that the lecturer is expressing and to make notes that they can use later in their studies. The purposes will be different for other genres, for example, when listeners are in a conversation, they probably just want a general idea of what is being said but when someone is asking for the time at which a train leaves, they want the precise time.

The concept of purpose is also used to classify listening events outside the framework of genre theory. Wilson (2008) identifies four kinds of purpose. See Table 14.2.

This is a useful checklist but it is difficult to see how this could be the basis for a course or part of a course on listening.

14.2.4 Mode/organization

At the next level down, genre knowledge includes information about the organization of the genre. In an academic lecture, there will be some kind of an introduction and, as noted above, associated texts

Table 14.2 Purposes for listening

Listening for gist	The general idea of what is being said, e.g. watching a film
Listening for specific information	A specific piece of information, e.g. an answer phone message
Listening in detail	Listening for some specific information but we are not sure what, e.g. an academic lecture
Inferential listening	Finding out how the speaker feels, e.g. a conversation

Source: Adapted from Wilson (2008: 10)

such as handouts or PowerPoint slides accompanying the lecture. Listeners will know that the purpose of lectures is educational so they will aim to understand the main ideas that the lecturer is expressing.

14.2.5 Tenor/participants

One aspect of genre is the roles of those involved. Bell (1984: 160) identifies four possible roles of a listener:

Addressees – the person who is being spoken to and who has the same right to speak and the speakers. This would include the listener in a two-person conversation between friends.

Auditors – Listeners who are being spoken to but can only speak occasionally. The students in the psychology lecture would be addressees.

Over-hearers – Listeners whom the speaker knows are present but are not being spoken to. This would cover members of the public at a criminal trial who are listening to what the judge or a witness says.

Eavesdroppers – Listeners whom the speaker does not know are present but are not being spoken and have no right to speak. This would cover the situation of people listening to a conversation between people they do not know on a bus.

These roles indicate who can speak and when. A related distinction can be made between one way (e.g. listening to the radio) and the much more common two-way listening (e.g. talking to someone face to face). The rights associated with Bell's roles are norms but the differences in roles impact on the possible strategies that listeners can adopt if they fail to understand something or if they want further information. It would be unusual for someone eavesdropping on a conversation on a bus to intervene (though Lynch 2009: 59–60 provides an example of where someone eavesdropping on a telephone conversation feels able to take a more active role because the conversation has been so loud). Similarly, some people have been known to address questions to the television and machine/human interactions are blurring the one-way/two-way distinction.

14.2.6 Field/ Schemata

The field of the listening event means the topic. A useful way of describing this is as a schema, that is, a set of related knowledge about the world. This is a term borrowed from psychology and discussed and critiqued in Chapter 12. Lynch gives the following example of how a schema or group of schemata would be needed to make sense of the following, originally spoken, text.

When I first went into the System, I had to queue for ages. At first, the woman did not understand what I asked for, but eventually she found the bottles I wanted. Just as I was about to pay, the red light went on. It was a good thing that I had my passport with me. (2009: 56)

For many listeners, this would be quite hard to understand, not because of problems with phonology, vocabulary, or grammar but because they lack the information that 'System' is short for 'Systembolaget', a shop selling alcohol in Sweden. For someone who is familiar with Swedish culture, the use of the term 'system' will activate a series of ideas related to the purchase of alcohol so someone who is familiar with this network will find it easier to understand the mention of the passport because people buying alcohol in a 'System' are often required to provide proof of their age by showing a document such as a passport.

The essential idea here is that once the concept of say, psychology, is foregrounded in the listeners' head then a range of associated concepts and vocabulary will also be activated. So, when the lecturer mentioned 'History' and 'Methods', these words would have been relatively easy for anyone for whom this was part of an activated schema in which a psychology had branches such as the history of psychology or methods used to investigate psychology. The concept of schemata is also discussed in Chapter 12.

14.2.7 Using all sources of information

Listeners do not draw on one source of information and then another. Listening seems to be much messier then this. Where students are attending a lecture as part of a psychology course as in the example above, even before the lecturer speaks, the students have quite a lot of knowledge about what they are going to here. For example, they know that the lecture will be related to the topic of psychology and that it is part of a series of lectures in which, from the way that the lecturer talks about them in the extract, the history of psychology and the methods used to study psychology have already been discussed and, if they have studied the course outline, they will know that this lecture is about biopsychology. They may even have been given some reading to do before the lecture about biopsychology.

14.2.8 Top-down and bottom-up

The description of the listening process in the section of decoding and meaning building followed a sequence described as bottom-up. Knowledge about phonology is usually regarded as lower information and knowledge about genres is higher information. This does not imply that listeners draw on the different kinds of information in this order. Listeners make use of whatever information will help them make sense of the acoustic signal by using all kinds of knowledge. Without top-down information, listening would be very difficult and without bottom-up information it would be impossible. As Staehr says,

If listeners have not recognized a certain number of words in the input though bottom-level processing, they will not be able to draw on top-level cues, access the relevant contextual information, and construct an adequate meaning representation of the text. (2009: 581)

Activity 14.1 The listening process

1 Try listening to a short extract from a language you do not speak. If you have access to the internet, YouTube provides a lot of examples of this. Reflect on how you tried to make sense of what you heard.

2 If you know more than one language, consider how you learnt to listen in your second language. What difficulties did you have with listening? Are there any parallels between the problems you faced and the problems your learners have with listening to English?

3 Try reading these sentences with no pauses aloud to a friend and see what they write down.
   a Necks day
   b Wipe bird
   c Tem men
   d Bag cold
   e Streak credibility

In the psychology lecture, the higher-level information is not enough. The listeners need to be able to identify the phonemes, syllables and words that the lecturer is producing if they are going to achieve their purpose in attending the lecture. Listeners need to draw on all kinds of information.

Unfortunately, much discussion of the listening process talks of top-down and bottom-up approaches. A course which just taught learners bottom knowledge and how to use it would be extremely boring and not very effective. A course which focussed on the top end might be interesting but would not necessarily help learners to improve their listening. The real benefit of answering the question of how people listen and identifying the kinds of knowledge that are used in listening is as a diagnostic tool. Course designers and teachers need to decide what areas of knowledge are presenting problems to their learners and these areas should form the aim of the listening lesson.

Once the aims of the units of teaching have been identified, then teachers need to consider the topic of the next section, 'How do people learn to listen?'

14.3 How do people learn to listen?

This section draws on the theories of learning discussed in Chapter 3. The monitor model (Krashen 1989, 1981b) has made two key contributions to our ideas about how people learn to listen. The first is that affective factors are very important in learning to listen. Learners who fail to understand a word when they are reading can go back and read it again. This is generally not possible to do when they are listening so listeners often feel they have very little control over what they are listening. This lack of control can lead to high levels of stress. Teachers need to consider whether their learners are being made nervous by listening and, if necessary, consider ways in which they can reduce learners' stress level. A key element here is giving learners more control and there are some examples of ways of doing this in the teaching section of this chapter.

The second important contribution is that learners only learn from comprehensible input. Giving learners authentically produced texts they cannot understand will not lead to the development of their listening. Whether a text is comprehensible depends on an interaction between the text and the listeners so the most important aspect here is making sure that the texts are of an appropriate level for the specific learners. This is often difficult to do but the interaction hypothesis suggests one way of doing this.

The interaction hypothesis and notion of negotiation for meaning were first put forward by Long (1983, 1985) within an information processing model. When people are engaged in face to face interactions they often negotiate their way around possible incomprehension and this negotiation is a way of making it more likely that learners notice gaps in their language knowledge. This provides a rationale for the use of two-way interaction in the listening classroom but it is less easy to apply this notion to one-way listening. However, some attempts to do this will be discussed in the teaching section.

Information processing is probably the theory of learning that is most useful in understanding why listening lessons are carried out in the way that they are. It sees learning happening as the result of learners acquiring declarative knowledge about listening and then proceduralizing that knowledge. The teaching of cultural and lexical knowledge is often part of listening classes and this relates to cognitivism. However, while giving students access to this kind of information is part of language learning or developing students' declarative knowledge, it is less obvious that it is connected particularly with listening.

In recent years, critiques of listening classes have focussed on the lack of declarative knowledge about listening and have portrayed listening classes as being about practising listening rather than about learning to listen (Field 1998; White 2006). One important response to this is the idea that learners need to be taught is strategies for learning (Oxford 1990; O'Malley and Chamot 1990). Language use or communication strategies were discussed in Chapter 2 and learning strategies in general were discussed in Chapter 3. Strategies are often divided into three categories; cognitive, for example, learners infer the meaning of unknown words using context; socioaffective, for example, learners ask the teacher what a word means; and metacognitive, for example, learners checking whether their understanding of one part of the text is coherent with the rest of the text.

Goh (2002) takes a hierarchical view of the description of strategies so in the examples of inferring meaning from context, the overall strategy is cognitive, the sub-strategy is inferring and the tactic is using contextual clues. Another example would be if a learner decided to use a metacognitive strategy to listen to a television documentary. The learners would then select a sub-strategy, such as pre-listening and the tactic of previewing the content, by reading a description of the documentary in a TV listening magazine or webpage. People working in this area have devised lengthy and complex labelling systems for strategies. Table 14.3 exemplifies these systems by listing the sub-skills and strategies related to the metacognitive strategy.

There is some debate about how well this kind of a list reflects what learners actually do. Rees-Miller (1993) argued that the way strategies are used will vary widely between different learners, and Lynch describes the term socioaffective as 'ragbag' (2009: 81). While there is now some support for teaching strategies (e.g. Tudor 2001; Vandergrift and Tafaghodtari 2010; Vandergrift and Goh 2012), many learners will already use a range of strategies and teachers need to remember that the strategies they think are most useful will not necessarily be the most useful for their learners.

Less problematically, most if not all cognitivists, would agree that learners move from controlled use of skills to automatic or autonomous use of skills as a result of practice. People learn to listen, in other

Table 14.3 Metacognitive strategies for listening

	Sub-strategy	Tactics
Metacognitive	Pre-listening	Preview contents rehearse sounds, encourage oneself to relax
	Selective attention	Listen to words in groups, listen for gist
		Listen for content words, notice how information is structured
		Pay attention to repetitions, notice intonation
		Listen to specific parts of the input, pay attention to visuals
	Directed attention	Concentrate hard, continue to list in spite of difficulty
	Comprehension monitoring	Confirm that comprehension has taken place
		Identify words or ideas not understood
		Check current interpretation with content of the message
		Check current interpretation with prior knowledge
	Real-time assessment of input	Assess the importance of problematic parts that are heard
		Determine the potential value of subsequent parts of input
	Comprehension evaluation	Check interpretation against some external sources
		Check interpretation using prior knowledge
		Match interpretation with the context of the message

Source: Based on Goh (2002); Lynch (2009); Vandergrift et al. (2006)

words, by listening. This is more than an argument for lots of practice. The change from controlled to automatic frees up mental power. When listeners are controlling their actions, this needs quite of lot of cognitive effort but as the actions become more automatic, they need less and so they are able to do other things. Many learners will start noticing new things about the listening process and this will start a new learning event. The idea of deliberate practice (see Chapter 3) suggests that learners need to be motivated and focused when they do their practice if they are to benefit. This is often a problem with listening where it is harder for teacher to know exactly what the learners are doing.

 Activity 14.2 Learning and teaching listening

1   How similar is the listening that happens in English classrooms that you are familiar with to the kinds of listening that happens outside the classroom?

2   What aspect of your learners' listening would you like most to improve?

14.4 How can we teach people to learn to listen?

Styles in teaching listening have changed in the last fifty or sixty years. Goh (2008) sees the most recent development in teaching listening as a move to metacognitive instruction, largely related to the metacognitive strategies discussed in the previous section with a focus on completing tasks that reflect real-life communication (Vandergrift 2004). This parallels very closely the move to task based teaching with the problem-solving elements including, but not being limited to, metacognitive strategies. However, in many contexts the approach to teaching listening follow what is often called the comprehension approach and this is based on the idea that learners will get better at listening with lots of practice

14.4.1 The comprehension approach

In the comprehension approach, learners are typically exposed to recordings of texts which have been produced for non-language learning purposes or texts which have features of authentically produced texts. However, most language learners will not have the same decoding and meaning making knowledge that those for whom the text was intended would have and so the teacher will need to provide them with this knowledge before they engage with the text. Underwood et al. (1989: 25 et seq.) describes an early version of how a class might be structured in this approach using a three part model, a pre-listening stage 'where the context is established' (p. 28), a while listening stage which covers 'what students are asked to do during the time that they are listening to the text' (p. 45) and post-listening, which covers 'all the work related to a particular listening test … done after the listening is completed' (p. 74).

The comprehension approach is often more complicated than this. So teachers might start with some pre-teaching of vocabulary and possibly some background information related to the topic. Immediately after, or perhaps during a break in the listening, learners will be asked to answer general or gist comprehension questions. Typically, teachers will then play the recording again and ask the learners to do some more detailed comprehension questions. It is not completely clear why gist questions come before detailed question but there does seem to be an assumption that gist questions are easier. After the listening activities are complete, there is then some kind of extension activity on the same topic. This might involves the learners doing some writing or a speaking activity. Table 14.4 is White's description of the comprehension approach.

The comprehension approach offers teachers a useful template for listening classes and learners do benefit from this. Teachers who are new to teaching may find it a good way of organizing a listening class However, the comprehension approach is best seen as a starting point because it has two broad weaknesses: first, it misrepresents the nature of listening and, second, it gives very little attention to teaching. This means there are two complementary ways in which language teachers can improve on the comprehension approach. They can create lessons which are closer to listening outside the classroom, what I label the authentic listening approach, informed by broadly sociocultural views of learning, and they can create opportunities in their lessons for learning and teaching, the teaching listening approach, informed broadly by cognitive theories of learning. Many teachers do both.

14.4.2 Authentic listening

Goh sees the move to more authentic texts as one of the features of newer ways of teaching listening. However, the authenticity she is talking about is largely product authenticity, though the pre-teaching of vocabulary or content information can be seen as an attempt to help the learners engage authentically. Unfortunately, the fact that a text was not produced for language teaching purposes is no guarantee that learners will be able to process it in an authentic way. Product authenticity does not mean there will be process authenticity. Effective teaching requires a broader view of authenticity.

Table 14.4 The comprehension approach

1. Selection of listening materials	Either the teachers choose the materials which the students will listen to (a video or audio recording, usually in the form of CD or cassette), or it is a piece of listening in the course book.
2. Pre-listening	The teacher … does a warm-up on the topic of listening text along the lines of 'What do you know about.?' 'What do you think they are going to say . . .?' The teacher may pre-teach some difficult or key vocabulary items.
3. Gist questions	The teacher sets some gist questions for the students to answer after they have listened for the first time.
4. First listening	The teacher plays the audio or video tape for the first time so that students can work on the tasks after listening to it.
5. Checking answers to the gist questions	The teacher often does this by getting the students to check their answers in pairs, and then a whole class feedback.
6. Detailed questions	The teacher sets some tasks which require the students to listen for many information/details in the piece of listening.
7. Second listening	The teacher plays the audio or video tape again so that the students can complete the tasks. (Steps 6 and 7 may be repeated. The teacher probably will play the tape at least once for each task. The teacher and the students check the answers after each task.)
8. Extension activity (optional)	The teacher uses the topic or some of the language from the listening text as input for an 'extension' or 'transfer' activity in which students use other language skills. Perhaps the listening prompts a discussion, or a writing task, or leads on to some reading on the same topic.

Source: Adapted from White (2006: 116)

Outside the classroom, listeners listen to things which have some relevance to them. If teachers can choose what their learners listen to they should start by allowing their learners to choose their own teaching materials or selecting something that their learners would listen to outside the classroom. In some cases, the learners' needs and wants will be clear enough for teachers to identify enough listening texts for their learners. Those who teach learners whose needs are not so clear, such as young learners, may need to make informed guesses about what listening texts are relevant to their learners.

One aspect of this relevance is that listeners have reasons for listening. When teachers are designing exercises around a listening text, they need to start with the purpose that listeners would listen to the text. For example, if I listen to a weather forecast on the radio, I will normally only want to know what the weather is where I live, and so will focus only on that information. I may want to know if it will rain because, if it does, I will need to have my party indoors. If such a text were used in the classroom, it would be more authentic for learners to focus on one geographic location rather than trying to write down a general summary of the weather. Similarly, if I watch a documentary on television, my purpose is to have some general understanding of the topic rather than to become an expert. The measure of success in listeners is not whether the listeners have understood everything in the text, even if we could agree what that meant, but whether they have achieved their purpose. Understanding the text and achieving their purpose may be related but they are often different.

Second, the patterns of participation in listening classrooms are often very different from listening outside the classroom. Perhaps, the most obvious aspect of this is the use of recordings of texts which would normally be listened to with the speakers present. Listening to a recording of a conversation is very different from participating in a conversation and often more difficult. What teachers say to their students say may provide a more authentic listening experience for their learners than listening to a recording because of the possibility for participation. Even if the recording has other merits which mean it should be used, various techniques have been developed for increasing learners' participation.

Lynch suggests that one of the learners might be given control of the playback device and could stop the recording when somebody or an agreed number of learners raised their hands because something is hard to understand (Lynch 1996: 99). Then the learners decide what to do next. They may find from the discussion in the group that one member of the group has understood the recording and so they can go on. Alternatively, they may want to hear the problematic part of the recording again, look up something in a dictionary or ask the teacher. Another technique suggested by Lynch is indirect negotiation, where the recording includes a listener who has some problems in understanding the speaker or speakers so that learners can hear the negotiation for meaning at second hand. These techniques for helping the learners to listen in more authentic ways can be complemented with methods where the focus is on teaching listening.

The techniques we have discussed in the authentic listening section of this chapter have been about how what happens in the class can be made part of the process of leading learners to listen more effectively beyond the classroom. However, it is important to remember that many learners have opportunities to listen to English outside the classroom, whether in face-to-face interactions or through recordings of songs and films. Where learners have access to the internet, this can be a very rich source of listening activities and so teachers working in such contexts should provide the support and encouragement that their learners need to help them to make use of this resource. Particularly with older learners, it can be very useful to direct them to useful websites where they can listen to English language programmes that they select and that offers more control than would be possible in the classroom.

14.4.3 Beyond the comprehension approach

Teachers and commentators have come up with a range of ways of supplementing the comprehension approach so that there is more opportunity for learning and these are often structured around the notion of strategies.

The lists of metacognitive strategies such as that in Table 14.3 are not the basis for a listening syllabus. Learners need to learn to choose a strategy to address a problem that they are facing and this will depend on their own level of knowledge and skill as well as the task that they are hoping to accomplish. This means that the first stage of a strategic approach involves a diagnosis by the teacher of learners of what listening problems the learners face and how these problems can be best addressed. The second part then focuses on how learners can develop the skills and strategies that the diagnosis reveals. This is very similar to the sequence used in a task-based lesson.

Table 14.5 A metacognitive strategy for teaching listening

Question	Purpose	Examples of learner responses
1. What were you listening to?	Confirm comprehension	
2. What helped you to understand the text?	Elicit task knowledge (factors that influenced listening)	When the text repeats again, I can catch the point
3. What prevented you from getting the correct answers?	(Same as 2)	The reading is so fast that I choose the answers anyhow
4. What did you do to understand as much of the text as possible?	Elicit strategy knowledge (strategies for facilitating listening)	Look at question first to concentrate on the parts to pay special attention to

Source: Based on Goh and Taib (2006)

Diagnosing learners' problems with listening

A common way of diagnosing learners' problems is for the learners to carry out some task and either the teacher or the learners identify ways in which the learners could do better. Goh and Taib suggest a three-stage lesson for younger learners.

1 Listen

Learners listen to a conventional listening text

2 Answer and reflect

They answer the questions as normal and then answer the four questions in Table 14.5. This is meant to get individual learners to think about how they listen. This can be done individually or in groups.

3 Report and discuss

The learners report to the whole class on the factors that influenced listening and the strategies that they used to understanding the text

Sometimes the diagnosis stage will involve the teacher in carrying out an activity which is specifically designed to identify problems. One example of this approach to diagnosis is called the dictogloss. This is Wilson's 'dictogloss' version of the task (2003). The teacher chooses a short text at a level that can be largely understood but is presents some challenges for the learners.

1 *Listening* – in this phase learners do three things

  1.1 listen, without note-taking, to a short passage spoken at a natural speed.

  1.2 self-assess their listening comprehension.

  1.3 listen two more times taking notes.

2 *Reconstructing* – in this phases, learners form small groups and try to reconstruct the text.

3 *Discovering* – in this phase learners

3.1 compare their text with the original and attempt to classify the sources of mistakes.

3.2 assess the relative importance of their mistakes

3.3 listen again without reading the text and assess their performance.

The process of diagnosis will provide the teachers and, sometimes the learners, with information about where the listening process is not working as well as it should be and this diagnosis forms the basis of the next stage of the listening class.

Using the diagnosis

Using the diagnosis has been presented as if it were separate from the process of diagnosis. This can be true but it is also common for the process of diagnosis to reveal that some learners are using strategies that other learners are not. Often the most effective way for learners to develop a new strategy is from other learners.

Where no one in the groups of learners has can address a problem, the teacher needs to provide a framework for identifying the problems that arise. The list of strategies identified in Table 14.3 can be used for this purpose. Field (2008b: 298) offers an alternative approach which identifies four kinds of strategy:

1 Avoidance strategies mean the listeners decide that some information is not needed to achieve their purpose. For example, when you are listening to a recording of a flight announcement in an airport, deciding you will only listen to announcements related to your airline or your destination.

2 Achievement strategies mean that listeners use available information to make sense of what was said to achieve their purpose. If you are flying to Copenhagen on Eagle Airlines flight 724, but you only hear Cope and Eagle, you can probably guess that this announcement is about your flight.

3 Repair strategies involve seeking help from the speaker or other sources of information. If you are not sure which gate a flight announcement said you should go to, you can ask an official or check on an information screen.

4 Proactive strategies mean listeners decided to adopt a different approach in future so that the problem can be avoided. If listeners find numbers hard to decode, they may decide to repeat the number of their flight aloud, or ask someone else to do that before they listen to the flight announcements.

This kind of framework can form a useful basis for a discussion about what strategies learners should adopt and if there is sufficient common ground, this can be used as the basis for some whole class or group teaching. If a group feels that they are not sufficiently prepared, they can practice specific strategies such as rehearsing words that might be expected to come up in a recording.

The diagnosis process can also lead to teaching which is not related to strategies. For example, if a group of learners find it hard to distinguish between 'disguises' and 'the skies' (Field 2008b: 292) probably need help with their minimal pair perception of /ð/ as in 'the' and /d/ as in disguise. See the section on minimal pairs in Chapter 5.

14.5 Summary

This chapter presented a view of how listening happens as having two interacting stages, decoding and meaning building. Decoding depends on the quality of the acoustic signal and listeners' knowledge of the linguistic signal. English language learners may fail to recognize what is said in English for a range of reasons, varying from a lack of knowledge of English phonology to a lack of background information about what is being discussed.

The chapter drew on a range of theories of learning to make sense of how people learn to listen. The monitor model highlighted the importance of affect and comprehensible input in learning. Information processing theory emphasized the need for learners to expand their knowledge and skills and then practice these until they can be used automatically. Sociocultural approaches emphasized the importance of learners' interactions through listening in a supportive environment.

The final section examined some of the ways in which listening has been taught. One common pattern in the language classroom approach is the comprehension approach with a pre-listening stage, often focussing on vocabulary and reminding learners of relevant background knowledge, a while listening activity, focused on comprehension question and a follow-up activity related to a skill other than listening. The chapter also examined some ways in which the comprehension approach might be supplemented.

 ## 14.6 Further reading

My favourite book of listening is Field (2008b), but Lynch (2009) is also very good. Wilson's (2008) *How to Teach Listening* is a useful source of ideas for listening lessons. Rost's (2011) *Teaching and Researching Listening* is a good introduction to the research into second language listening.

 ## Activity 14.3 Discussion

What would suggest that the teacher in this context does to help the student improve?

Dmitry works for a UK-owned Investment Fund in, Eastern Europe He uses English on a daily basis in a variety of settings. He frequently travels on business trips to conduct negotiations with potential British or American investors and regularly takes part in business meetings with his native speaker business partners. Dmitry's general level of L2 proficiency is high. He speaks fluently and demonstrates a good command of grammatical and lexical knowledge, including specialized business vocabulary. However, his biggest challenge is related to listening skills, particular understanding native speakers' connected speech.

Dimitry studies English in one-to-one classes run in his company. He is supposed to have three one-hour lessons a week but because of travel he often misses at least one of these lesson. His teacher is an expert use of English who speaks the same mother tongue as Dmitry. She does not have a background in finance.

Lessons are normally based around the use of financial programmes recorded from the radio or TV. Typically, in the pre-listening stage, the teacher will have discussion with Dmitry about the topic and teach some key vocabulary. The while listening stage, involves Dmitry listening to the recording and orally summarizing the content of the recording. Sometimes, he needs to hear the recording twice. After the recording. Dmitry will construct a written summary of the recording with the help of the teacher.

Chapter 15

Speaking

15.1 Introduction

Speaking is central to how language is conceived. If someone says they can speak a language, this usually means they can do more than speak. In pedagogic terms, audiolingual approaches to teaching suggest that the starting point of learning a language is learning to speak, and my own experience of learning Malay is that this is a viable method of language learning and teaching. However, the fact that many people find speaking more stressful than using other skills and the problems the temporary nature of oral language present for language learning explain why speaking is the last skill to be covered in this book. As with other skills, the chapter addresses three questions:

1 What is involved in speaking?
2 How do people learn to speak English?
3 How can teachers teach speaking?

15.2 What is involved in speaking English?

When teachers are organizing a class focused on speaking, their aim should be a real-life communicative task with a spoken element. However, where teachers are not able to do this or where teachers need to help their learners to participate more effectively with such a task, an understanding of what is involved in speaking English will help teachers analyse their learners' performance and identify appropriate aims for pre-communicative teaching, and this section is intended to help teachers do this. Speaking draws simultaneously on psychological, linguistic knowledge and social skills, and these are addressed below.

15.2.1 The psychology of speaking

Producing spoken language involves three stages – conceptualization (what the speaker wants to mean), formulation (expressing that meaning in vocabulary and grammar) and articulation (producing the appropriate sounds). However, speakers are also listening to themselves so self-monitoring is a fourth element in speaking. A version of this model based on De Bot (1992: 3), Kormos (2006) and Goh and Burns (2012: 36) appears in Figure 15.1.

For example, if a speaker wanted to explain that tomorrow is Black Friday, a day on which many shops have special offers and many people go shopping, the conceptualization would be the

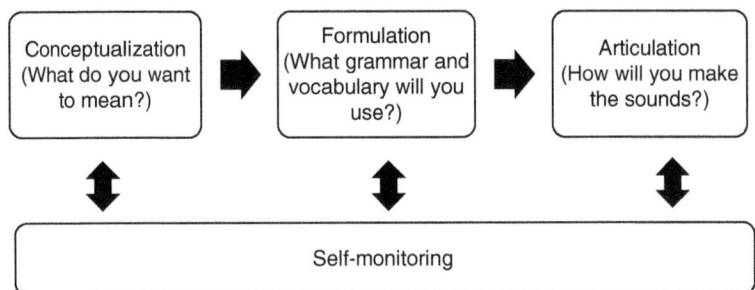

Figure 15.1 A model of speech production (based on De Bot 1992: 3)

connection between the knowledge the speaker has about 'tomorrow' and the knowledge of 'Black Friday'. Whether this information is known or not known to other people in the conversation will help the speaker decide what to include, for example, whether the speaker can use the term 'Black Friday' or if it will need to be explained. The conceptualization is not in a particular language but would be marked in some way as needing to be expressed in a particular language. This information is then passed onto the formulator where the idea is put into English.

Often the starting point of this process is retrieving from long-term memory the verb, in this case 'be', and the grammatical patterns that this implies, for example, subject/predicator/subject complement/ optional adverbials. The speaker here would be making choices between 'Tomorrow is Black Friday', 'Black Friday is tomorrow', and 'It is Black Friday tomorrow', depending on what the speaker's monitoring of what other people were saying was appropriate. Bilingual speakers may have problems at this stage if their English and L1 lexicon are not completely distinct because information about the equivalent of 'be' in L1 may be used to construct the utterance in English. Once the utterance has been constructed, the speakers would then identify the phonemes needed to express the utterance. This is then passed onto the articulator where the tongue, lips and vocal cords produce the actual sentence. All of this needs to happen extremely quickly. Where the speech processing system works well, it leads to fluent speech, that is, 'the rapid, smooth, accurate, lucid, and efficient translation of thought or communicative intention into language under the temporal constraints of on-line processing' (Lennon 2000: 26)

15.2.2 The linguistics of spoken English

To produce the sentence 'Tomorrow is Black Friday' requires a knowledge of the discourse, grammar, vocabulary, phonology and phonetics of English as well as sufficient background knowledge. For most purposes, the linguistic knowledge needed for speaking is the same as it would be for writing, but speakers typically have less preparation time than writers and also have an audience in front of them. Both factors impact on spoken English.

The lack of time for planning means that 'speakers do not usually speak in sentences' (Luoma 2004: 12), and the research literature avoids the term sentences for spoken language, preferring the term utterances. The Luoma quote includes the word 'usually' because speakers who have plenty of time to plan often do produce sentences, and the amount of time allowed for production is the key element here. The following complex sentence was spoken but has many of the features of written language:

> Burgess was a writer with his earliest roots and inspirations deep in popular culture, a lonely child who read out silent movie speech cards to illiterate neighbour kids in the cinema, a warily intelligent adult who addressed popular forms as an observer, a creator and one of the UK's earliest authors to embrace the possibilities of television. (Kennedy 2017)

Similarly, the following extract was part of an online written interaction but has many of the features of spoken language (Carter and Mccarthy 2015: 12):

A: gotta go
B: ttyl [talk to you later]
A: ok
B: which means tomorrow right?
A: I'd forgot that
B: cos we're seeing David.
A: Must go. Alright.

This reinforces the point made in Chapter 11 that teachers need to know the genres with which their learners need to engage. For example, in spoken academic discourse, Basturkmen (2001: 7–8) identifies a three-stage structure to questions comprising (a) introducing the topic, for example, 'You mentioned the possibility of a merger', (b) the question, for example, 'but did you consider the possibility of an alliance with other organizations' and (c) justifying the question, for example, 'I notice one of two of the large supermarkets like Safeways have now got dry cleaning franchises in them so that services are like where people are rather than attracting people to them.' Where teachers can identify specific spoken genres, this kind of information will benefit their teaching.

However, generally speech is unplanned, produced very rapidly and so typically less grammatically complex than written language with more coordination than subordination. The lack of planning also has an influence on the vocabulary used at the formulation stage. So speakers adopt communicative strategies such as using vague words like 'thingy' instead of someone's name or 'stuff' for a more specific noun. They also produce 'fillers' such as 'er' and 'um' but also 'like', 'you know', 'what I am trying to say is', which may serve, at least in part, to give speakers time to plan what they will say next.

The lack of time also leads to grammatical patterns that are not common in written language: 'Black Friday, it's tomorrow'. This construction, sometimes called a header (Carter and Mccarthy 2006: 10), is probably produced because the idea was passed on to the formulator faster than normal and so the idea had not been completely conceptualized. A similar explanation accounts for the complementary tail structure: 'It's tomorrow, Black Friday.' The speed of processing also leads to the violation of some grammatical features (Cullen and Kuo 2007), for example, the use of a singular verb where a plural would be expected, for example, 'There's lots of things left to do'. See also Table 15.1.

The fact that the audience is present for much speech also has an impact on the grammar and vocabulary that is used. Some aspects of this were discussed in Chapter 11, particularly the section on politeness, and below in the section on social aspects of speaking, but this is also reflected in other

Table 15.1 An example of a spoken interaction between a tutor and a student (adapted from MICASE; Simpson et al. 1999)

---

1. S1 Okay what are you working on today?
2. S2: Um, I'm in uh English um one-twenty-five, [S1: Okay] and I have um essay that I wrote and maybe you could, maybe, look at it, maybe revise it.
3. S1: Okay what was the assignment?
4. S2: Um, this one is autobiography.
5. S1: Right.
6. S2: And this one here is a synthesis essay which is based on a, essay that we read, about Columbus.
7. S1: Okay. [S2: So] Christopher Columbus?
8. S2: Mhm.
9. S1: And um these are both due for the end of this term? Is that it?
10. S2: Right right.

---

ways such as ellipsis in spoken English. Carter and McCarthy illustrate this with a conversation about wine (1995: 147):

(01) It's lovely
(02) Good winter wine that
(01) A terrific one
(02) Put hairs on your chest that one

The non-elliptical form of the final utterance would start with 'It will', but the speaker may have started by thinking that the subject could be reconstructed from the context by the audience and then added the tail 'that one' to prevent misunderstanding.

The differences between written and spoken forms of English are potentially problematic for learners of English who may have been exposed largely to the English typical of written genres. The research on spoken language has focused on native varieties, while research into spoken ELF is 'still in its infancy' (Seidlhofer 2004: 222), and it is not clear to what extent these features exist in ELF. However, Björkman (2008: 38–9) found some features of spoken English described above (e.g. fronting 'This report, we'll do it later' and non-marking of plurals '300 degree') occurred in the ELF used a Swedish university and, interestingly, found no evidence that these features impeded communication. This suggests that at least some of the features of spoken English are a result of processing problems rather than differences in the grammatical or lexical system underlying spoken English, but learners will need to be made aware that the oral English that is the target in the speaking class is not identical with the aim of the writing class.

15.2.3 Social aspects of speaking

Many forms of speaking such as conversations involve two or more speakers and this means that the parties to the interaction need to avoid two people speaking at once. Some of the features of spoken interaction are illustrated in Table 15.1. First, the two participants manage to avoid overlaps, except in two places, right at the start where S1 says 'Okay' even though S2 is still speaking, perhaps because S2 had produced a grammatically coherent clause and, later in utterance 7. As the transcript shows, the speakers change at grammatically boundaries and this will probably be reinforced by intonational factors not recorded in the transcript. Both speakers use back channel signals to indicate that they have heard what has been said but do not wish to speak, for example, 'right' in utterance 5 and 'Mhm' in utterance 8. The interaction includes the use of interactional communication strategies (Goh and Burns 2012: 66) in the clarification request in utterance 3 and the confirmation request in utterance 9, where S1 asks 'Is that it?' to make sure that the two assignments are due at the end of the term.

This section introduced what is involved in speaking as a way of suggesting what might be the aims of speaking classes or parts of classes focusing on speaking. Activity 15.1 is intended to make you reflect on the features of spoken English. We now turn to how learners might develop their speaking abilities.

 Activity 15.1 Planning to speak

In order to engage in a spoken communicative event, planning is needed and the model of speech production can be used to think about this. For example, if you wanted to buy some fruit you would need to conceptualize your intentions in terms of what fruit you wanted and how much of the fruit you wanted. The conceptualization might also include how much you would be willing to pay. At the formulation stage, you would need to work out what grammar and vocabulary you would need as well as have some idea about the discourse structure of the interaction with the shopkeeper. At the articulation stage you would need to be able to produce the appropriate sounds and intonation. You would also need to know what gestures are appropriate to indicate fruit. You will need to have some fillers or useful fixed phrases that you can include in case your mind suddenly goes blank.

Can you do a similar analysis for one of the following?
Asking for direction to a bank
Buying a bus ticket
Ordering a meal in a restaurant
Making an appointment with a doctor

15.3 Learning to speak English

All the theories of learning discussed in Chapter 3 can be applied to learning to speak. The Monitor Model and connectionism would suggest that learning will happen when learners are exposed to understandable samples of language without the need for anything else. However, the dominant theory is that of information processing, where there is a distinction between a phase of learning to speak and a phase of speaking. Vygotskyan theories also make the movement from learning to speak and speaking as a development from scaffolded or other directed speaking to autonomous speaking.

The information processing theory means that learners need to have the appropriate knowledge of discourse, grammar, lexis and pronunciation as declarative and then proceduralized this knowledge.

The development of procedural knowledge means that they will need to practice the psychological processes of speaking, discussed above if they are to become effective speakers of English.

The development of declarative and procedural information is dependent on what learners bring to the classroom. This will partly relate to knowledge of the spoken language in their first language and issues such as those addressed in Chapter 11. Learners may bring different ideas of how the spoken and written languages are connected. Arabic speakers may expect a clearer division between everyday English and its written forms (Said 2002). Everyone who can speak a language will be able to use the processes outlines in Figure 15.1, though they may not be conscious of this, but the speed at which they are able to process language will vary depending on their expertise in English.

Teachers need to consider the level of speaking ability of their learners when they consider what learning activities are appropriate. For example, the qualities of the speech that learners produce can provide some indication of the state of their declarative and procedural knowledge. Where learners are not able to correct themselves, the issue is likely to be declarative knowledge and they need language input. If they are pausing for extended periods of time but producing accurate and appropriate language, this indicates that they have not progressed far enough with the automatization of procedural knowledge and need more practice.

Speaking is not simply a cognitive challenge. The monitor model suggests that learners may not choose to speak in English for a considerable time, possibly a year, after they have started being exposed to English and implies that making learners speak has a negative impact on their learning. Speaking in a second language classroom presents a particular risk of a loss of face (see also the discussion of politeness in Chapter 11) as the learners' speech may be being evaluated by their teachers and fellow students. Peng (2014: 3) noticed that some students in speaking classes 'preferred to stealthily read a brick-thick vocabulary book hidden under the textbook of handouts in from of them' to answering the teacher's questions and many teachers will have had similar experiences.

One way of understanding the reluctance to speak is the concept of 'willingness to communicate'. Learners who are not willing to communicate are unlikely to make progress in speaking. The concept was borrowed from studies of mother tongue speakers. The original idea was that stress associated with speaking depends on, first, the size of audience, with public groups as the most stressful and talking to a single person the least, and, second, their relationship with the speakers, with strangers as most stressful and friends as least stressful (Macintyre 2007). Both factors would be arguments for allowing learners to speak in pairs or small groups before they speak to the whole class.

The notion of willingness to speak has been developed within second language learning to cover individual and situational factors. So Peng identifies three kinds of personal factors: cognitive (e.g. how well learners know the topic), linguistic (how highly learners rate their ability to speak English) and affective (level of anxiety). Situational factors are also important. Teacher attitudes to correctness are key. So one student said of a teacher:

C is a very kind person. When I speak in his class I feel comfortable and not stressed. I think what makes him different from other professors is that he is not much concerned about your pronunciation. (Zarrinabadi 2014: 293)

But less obvious teaching procedures such as the amount of time teachers allow for responses to their questions are important as this allows learners more planning time. One learner became less willing to communicate after this event:

> I paused for some seconds. Suddenly the teacher asked another one to continue. He thought I don't want to go on while I was thinking. (Zarrinabadi 2014: 293)

Often the attitudes of classmates and learners' self-rated language ability combine.

> I was kind of afraid of losing face when speaking English in front of the class. [...] Because I often make mistakes in prepositions and grammar in my expressions, in high school my classmates often laughed at me. I am kind of scared. (Peng 2014: 104)

Sometimes the culture of the classroom can reduce willingness to communicate. Another learner was unwilling to speak because

> I was concerned that others would think I like to show off or that I am I'm always pre-empting others. (Peng 2014: 132)

This last quote is important because the culture of the classroom will vary dramatically from one context to another but also because class culture can be changed. Creating a supportive classroom culture and making use of activities which encourage willingness to communicate is an important part of enabling learners to improve their speaking.

15.4 Teaching speaking

Once teachers have decided their aim and considered how learners will achieve this aim, they need to identify an overall framework for the class and decide what activities would be appropriate.

15.4.1 Sequences in the speaking class

Teachers of speaking broadly have a choice between presentation, practice, production (PPP) (Figure 4.2) and a problem-solving sequence (Figure 4.3). However, variations on both two sequences exist for the teaching for speaking. Thornbury (2005) has recast PPP as awareness, appropriation and autonomy (AAA; see Chapter 4) to reinforce the centrality of what the learners learn, rather than what the teacher teaches, and but has kept the division between awareness (presentation) and appropriation (production) to reflect the distinction between declarative and procedural knowledge in an information processing theory of learning.

Goh and Burns (2012: 153) have produced an extended version of the problem-solving sequence to include metacognitive or reflection activities. Figure 15.2 illustrates what Goh and Burns describe as the holistic model. The most distinctive elements of this model are stages one and six. In stage one, learners should think about how they are learning to speak. At the start of a course, this might relate to the whole speaking programme. Learners might think about how to increase their willingness to communicate in class or identify what features of their spoken English they want to improve. More specifically, it might relate to how they will use the next task to develop their speaking by, for example, planning what they are going to say and anticipating what their interlocutor will say. The point of this stage is to help learners to think about their learning or, in other words, develop their metacognitive awareness.

Stage six is also an addition to the problem-solving approach, and complements stage one with the learners reflecting back on what they have learned from the earlier stages of the cycle. Goh and Burns see metacognition as a central part of learning but do not argue that it should be included in all speaking lessons.

Despite the clear differences in the overall sequence and what is or is not included, one of the complications in deciding which sequence is appropriate for a particular context is that the different sequences offers more or less detailed analysis of different parts of the lesson. For example, where language input is addressed in the 'language practice' stage by Willis and Willis (2007) and by Goh and Burns (2012) in the stage labelled 'focus on language discourse/skills/strategies', Thornbury (2005) distinguishes between awareness, how learners increase their declarative knowledge and appropriation, where learners develop their procedural abilities. Again, Goh and Burns's 'conduct speaking task' seems to map on to both Willis and Willis's 'task planning' and 'task reporting'. However, the mark of a good lesson is not whether it follows a particular sequence but how much the learners benefit from the lesson so teachers should be guided by what is appropriate for their group of learners rather than consistency with what they have read. For example, a problem-based approach, whether is it task-based teaching or a holistic approach, is generally to be preferred over the sequence of PPP or AAA, but this would not stop teachers drawing on the division between awareness and autonomy in how their lessons were planned.

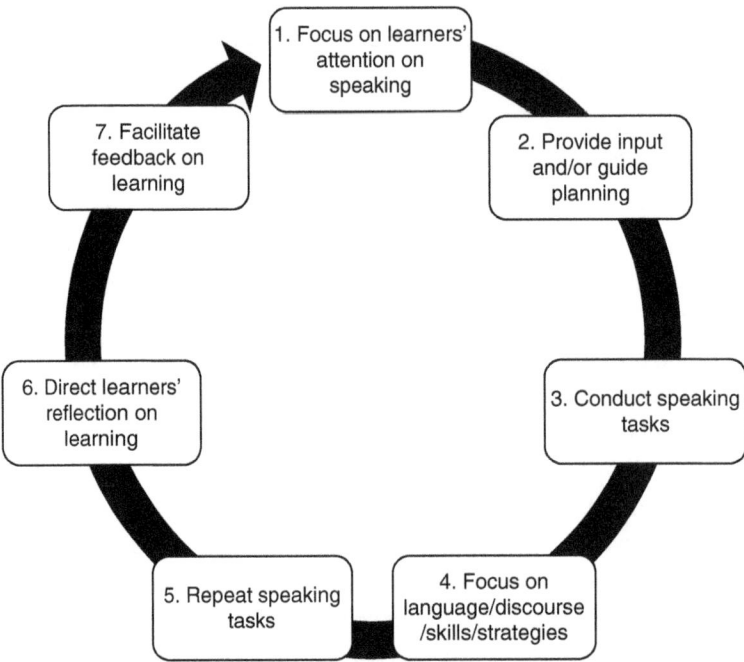

Figure 15.2 The teaching speaking cycle (Goh and Burns 2012: 153)

15.4.2 Activities in the speaking class

This section draws on the sequences outlined above to consider how teachers can design activities under the headings of:

a the speaking task,

b language focus (awareness),

c language focus (appropriation) and

d reflection.

The speaking task

The central element in a speaking class or group of classes is when the learners engage in a communicative task that is as similar as possible to spoken communication outside the language classroom, such as the service encounters discussed in Chapter 11. The choice of task may depend on the needs of the learners or on a specification from the syllabus or the teaching materials. Once the task has been identified, teachers will need to consider how best to set up the task in the class. However, teachers also need to consider what the learners also already know (Swan 1985b: 86). See Chapter 4. Where learners do not have the necessary language knowledge and skills to engage meaningfully with the task, the teachers will need to provide some form of language support before learners do the task. This might be providing relevant vocabulary but could be much more extensive. For example, if the target task was to engage in a discussion about appropriate levels of punishment for different crimes, it might be appropriate for the learners to carry out a pre-communicative task of listing crimes in the order or seriousness (e.g. stealing a book compared with exceeding the speed limit in a car). Activity 15.2 asks you to compare two different ways of helping learners to ask someone to repeat what they have said.

 Activity 15.2 Providing input: asking someone to repeat what they said

What would you see as the advantages and disadvantages of exercise one and two below as ways of helping learners to ask someone to repeat what they have said? Would it be useful to combine the two exercises?

1 Look at the following extracts from conversations and see how one speaker indicates that they did not understand what was said by the other speaker.

   a I went to a new restaurant near Headrow on Friday?

     Sorry. Where did you say?
     Near Headrow. Near the Light.
     OK. OK. The Light.

   b Have you read that stuff on the psychological processing of written text yet?

     Sorry I didn't quite catch that. Could you say it again?
     The stuff on psychological processing, have you read it yet?
     Oh no. Not yet.

2 In English, when you find it hard to understand what someone has said, you can ask them to repeat what they have said. Here are some useful words and phrases for this: Sorry, Come again, I didn't quite hear what you said, Could you repeat what you just said?

In this session, practice your interview protocol on others in the class. Make a recording of your interviews. One of you asks the question items. The other observes and makes notes about any difficulties. You may need to elaborate on the actual question items you have prepared. If your respondent does not understand the question, rephrase it and think how you can clarify it for the final version. The aim is to practice your protocol and get feedback from others in the class about how easy or difficult it is to understand the interview items. Help your peers by giving them good feedback and by explaining how you understood the question items. When you have finished, listen again to your recording. How did you ask the questions and how could you improve on them? Revise any questions you need to.

Figure 15.3 Improving an interview protocol (Basturkmen 2002: 29)

Equally learners can be helped to prepare for a task by giving them time and guidance about how they might plan for what they are going to say. The planning time will enable learners to draw more fully on what they know and encourage the learners willingness to communicate. A similar idea is built into the Willis and Willis suggestion that learners first carry out the task in groups before presenting the task to the whole class. A more extended version of this kind of task repetition to help learners develop the skills necessary to carry out research interviews is described in Figure 15.3.

Other activities which might be used to help learners prepare for a task are described under language input. The distinction between what activities should be part of the preparation and what activities should be part of the potential language focus after the learners have carried out the task depends on teachers' judgment about how well the learners will carry out the task, with the aim that learners will be able to carry out the task more or less successfully.

Identifying the focus of the language input

Some approaches to language teaching allow teachers to identify the focus on the language input in advance and this allows time for preparation. Goh and Burns (2012: 226–7) suggest where a task-based teaching approach is used with large classes, teachers may have to pre-select language input, though this would also allow for the input to be included in the preparation for the main task. Within most task-based teaching approaches, the language input section will depend on how the learners have performed the task and teachers need to be expert at analysing the language that learners use when carrying out the task to identify what aspects they need help with. Activity 15.3 provides an example of some learner language that you might analyse to decide on the follow up language input. Most teachers will not have the resources to produce these transcripts or the time between lessons to produce this kind of analysis and many teacher rely on more informal monitoring of learner language.

Activity 15.3 Analysing learner language in a task-based teaching approach

Two learners are having a conversation about what television programmes they like to watch. This is a long turn from one of the learners about an episode of a programme from the United States called *Friends*. What language input does the learner need to better tell a story? This may relate to vocabulary, grammar or discourse or the extent of proceduralization.

They see is a cheesecake in front of a neighbour door, and the cheesecake is there like for a whole day and nobody catches, and Rachel and Chandler decide to get it. And they open the box and . . . see a really beautiful cheesecake, and they decided to try it. And when they tried it they get a love for a the cheesecake because it was so tasty and … they start to eat eating it, eating it like crazy people, and in the end of the cheesecake they realized that there was no more cheesecake for the person that ordered. So . . . they gone to start to pick an another cheesecake to put in the door of thenother [*sic*] neighbour, and they eat it again and they couldn't stop to eat it. And . . . then, Chandler said it's really better than Monica's cheesecake, and they can't stop to eat and it falls on the floor and they just grasp some folks[forks] and keep on to eat it. So it's really nice and I remember it because we have a a a Brazilian friend that make the cheesecake we already tried it . . . .

In some contexts, learners can analyse their own language production. In a class of pre-university learners (5.5 IELTS), Lynch (2001, 2007) made audio recordings of pairs of learners carrying out a role play in which they asked a tutor for an extension for their assignment. Each pair chose a section of about two minutes to transcribe. They reformulated the transcription as they thought fit. The transcription and reformulation took place out of class. The teacher also reformulated the transcript and discussed the differences between the learners' and teacher's reformulation were discussed with the pair of learners. The learners found this activity motivating and noticed many of grammatical oddities. Although the study suggests that this kind of activity is more appropriate for higher level language learners used to analytical learning, this is an effective way of identifying an appropriate aim for the language focus.

Language input (awareness)

Once the language focus is clear, teachers will need to decide if learners lack knowledge (i.e. related to declarative knowledge and learner awareness) or have the knowledge and are not using it effectively (i.e. related to the automatization of procedural knowledge and appropriation).

Learners can be helped to become aware of particular aspects of language by exposure to language samples. These may be provided by the teacher demonstrating the target language use. For example, if learners are learning to tell stories in English, as in Activity 15.3, the teacher might tell a story and ask learners to focus on, for example, the start and end of the story, an aspect of grammar or pronunciation. This might also be provided by more expert learners in the class. The same function might be achieved by using an audio or video recording, which learners themselves might be able to find on line. Many awareness activities are based on transcripts of spoken English because the relative permanence of the written form allows more time for noticing activities.

For example, where the learners' performance sounds more like written than spoken language, teachers may decide that learners need to be more aware of the features of spoken English. It would be possible to do this by taking features of spoken English, such as the use of heads, discussed above, and teaching this as a grammatical item. An alternative approach would be to expose the learners to an extract of authentically produced spoken language of their target variety. Such transcripts may be included in the course book or available through on line corpora such as MICASE (Simpson et al. 1999). Timmis (2005) suggests a four-stage approach to using such transcripts:

1 Cultural access – relating the context of the transcript to the learners' culture

2 Global understanding – ensuring that the learners have a general understanding of the text so that they appreciate the links between linguistic patterns and overall meaning

3 Noticing tasks – designed to help learners see the differences between their expectations of spoken English (Activity 1 in Figure 15.4) and spoken varieties of other languages they may speak (Activity 2).

4 Language discussion tasks – aimed to investigate the learners understanding of the relations between levels of formality, personal relationship and the language used.

Noticing activity 1
Look at the Chris/Trudy/Enid dialogue below and put brackets around any words you think might not be necessary in informal spoken English,
For example,
How are you?
I am fine thanks and how are you?
I am fine too. It's very cold isn't it?
How are you?
[I am] fine thanks and [how are] you?
[I am] fine [too]. [It's] very cold isn't it?

Chris: Oh, hello Enid. It's nice to meet you.
Trudy: Hello, how's the family?
Enid: They're very well. How are your family?
Trudy: They are smashing.
Chris: It's a beautiful day, isn't it?
Enid: Yes, it is.
Chris: Is your business booming?
Enid: Well, it's not too bad you know.

Now listen/watch and check which words are missed out on the video dialogue.
Noticing activity 2
1. Look at the dialogue [see dialogue in sample noticing task 1] and translate it into your language.
2. Now translate it back into English without looking at the original.
3. Now look at the original and find any differences between your dialogue and the original.

Figure 15.4 Working with the grammar of spoken English: noticing tasks (Timmis 2005: 125)

The learners are not required to produce the features of spoken English represented in the transcript, but whether it would be appropriate for learners to do this might be a part of the language discussion task and the language input might impact an appropriation activity.

The square brackets are intended to indicate possible responses to noticing activity 1 and would not be in the transcript given to the learners.

Language input (appropriation)

Within an information processing view of learning, appropriation activities relate to the automatization of procedural knowledge and so follow on from language awareness activities. However, within sociocultural models of learning, appropriation happens as a result of providing learners with the support they need to carry out an activity and then gradually reducing the support so that learners can carry out the activity independently. This idea means awareness activities would not be seen as essential and learning might happen during the different stages of an appropriation activity.

When designing or selecting appropriation activities, teacher need to consider what their purpose is. This section focused on three categories of activities: drills, communicative activities and repetition. A key part of the speaking process is retrieving elements of the language from memory, so memorization techniques and in particular drills can be an important part of appropriation.

Drills, a technique most associated with the audiolingual approach, can be used to help learners with their fluency and accuracy. Drills are not widely discussed in current research literature. Indeed Wong and Patten (2003) wrote an article entitled 'drills are out' and excessive use of drills can be 'awfully boring' (Saito 2008: 58). However, many learners, albeit from particular cultural backgrounds, report that memorization is an important element in language learning. Saito (2008) found his Japanese learners rated drills positively. Here is a comment from a Chinese learner:

> One day, I approached the most fluent speaker who always showed impatience in talking with me because of my hesitating English. I offered to discuss with him about such topics as intellectual copyright and laid-off workers. He was shocked by my incessant speaking with sensible arguments while he was at a loss to find appropriate English words to express himself . . . But he never knew that I had just memorised some episodes from China Daily and poured them out to him. (Yu 2014: 665)

Again a Chinese winner of a nationwide speaking competition reported:

> All of us agreed that the greatest benefit from our middle school study was that we had memorized some material. As a result, we can speak and write a little more accurately [than students from other middle schools], we have a little better feel for the language, we are a little more like native speakers, and there are collocations we can use but others cannot. We learned our English through recitation. (Ding 2007: 276)

Ding (2007: 278) argues that memorization allows learners to acquire a knowledge of 'the formulaicity of language, a feature linguists may overlook', something which has been put forward as an explanation for the production of fluent speech (Pawley and Syder 1983). However, some learners also find memorization helps with developing knowledge of grammar

> One thing that I felt especially beneficial from learning texts by heart is that I could choose the right answer in the multiple choice section without second thought. (Yu 2014: 663)

Thornbury (2005: 64) suggests that drilling may be a useful noticing technique 'since it draws attention to materials that learners might not otherwise have registered'. However the most obvious role for drills is in proceduralizing existing knowledge, and in particular the process of articulation and, where the learners make grammatical or lexical choices, formulation. Some drills can involve conceptualization but this is relatively unusual, though, memorized phrases or chunks can act as 'islands of reliability' (Thornbury 2005: 64), which enable learners to produce something which is grammatically accurate and, because, they allow more time for conceptualizing or formulating what comes next, improve fluency.

Drills can vary both in terms of classroom organization and in terms of the linguistic demands on learners. The simplest form of a drill is where the teacher says an utterance or plays a recording of the utterance and the whole class repeats this. It is difficult for teachers to hear what individual learners are saying but choral repetition reduces the potential for loss of face.

The teacher then nominates particular learners to repeat the utterance. It is fairly easy to use the same process for a recorded dialogue and even solitary teachers can model a dialogue, by, for example, holding out the left or right hand to indicate who is speaking. A dialogue of two utterances, such as a question and an answer, means that the individual stage can be followed by pair work or by dividing the class into two.

Drills can also be organized as whole class interactions. If the language input was focused on 'would like to' plus a verb, learners could be asked to identify a musical instrument they would like to play, a country they would like to visit and a singing group they would like to meet, from a limited selection listed on the whiteboard. The learners circulate around the class trying to find someone who has made the same choices by asking the questions 'What instrument would you like to play' 'What country would you like to visit?' 'What group would you like to meet?'

The linguistic demands on the learners can also vary. Drills are typically based on repeating spoken language and this restricts the length of the utterance. It is possible to extend this by introducing the utterance in chunks:

Where

Where can you get

Where can you get the best

Where can you get the best fish and chips?

Another approach to this is to write the whole dialogue on the board and gradually rub it off as the learners are able to repeat it. A related version of this activity is where each learner in a group is given a written version of one of the utterances in a dialogue, which they memorize, returning the printed version to the teacher when they are confident of it. The group then has to reconstruct the original dialogue. Written cues are important but the advantage of a purely auditory cue for a drill is that learners are not distracted by features of the written language such as spelling.

Drills can also be graded in terms of how much choice the learners need to make. Simple repetition is the easiest. Learners may go on to substitute a word or a phrase. So if learners are able to say 'Where can you get the best fish and chips?' the teacher might use the cue 'pasta' and the learners would be expected to say 'where can you get the best pasta?' These kinds of drills aim to improve articulation.

	Gilbert	Becky

1. Look at the dialogue and read out loud.
2. See the first line in the dialogue, then look up and say it out loud. Continue line by line.
3. See the first line, then look up, look at your partner, and talk with emotion. Continue line by line.
4. Now don't look at the dialogue. Look at your partner, and talk with emotion (It doesn't have to be exactly the same as the dialogue). Keep practising until you feel comfortable.
5. Talk with emotion, looking at your partner and using gestures.
6. Change roles, and repeat rounds 1 to 5.

Figure 15.5 A goal-driven pair drill (Saito 2008: 60)

Figure 15.6 A simple image for describe and draw

However, it is possible to include some grammatical or lexical choices. So a follow up from the utterance 'They are from France. They're French' might be followed by the cue 'Korea' with the expected response of 'They are from Korea. They are Korean.' This includes an element of formulation. This can be taken a stage further with an element of personalization, for example, 'What is your favourite food?' 'X' followed by 'Where can you get the best X?' 'In Y'.

Figure 15.5 describes the procedure for what Saito calls a goal-driven pair drill. This can be for a live or recorded dialogue with a transcript. Before doing the drill the learners would complete a comprehension activity based on the dialogue and Saito suggests that the learners either perform the dialogue for the class or make a recording as a final part of the drill.

Whatever role drills play in a class, appropriation activities will include more communicative activities such as information gap activities, where two partners have different information. One version of this is 'describe and draw', where one member of pair has a drawing which they describe to their partner who tries to draw the image without looking at the original. A simple version of this is illustrated in Figure 15.6. It is also possible to create similar activities where the two partners have similar but slightly different pictures or the same pictures in a different sequence and have to identify differences between them without looking at each other's pictures. Many learners enjoy these activities but the artificiality of the information gap can reduce motivation.

As useful resource for devising discussion based appropriation activities is the list of tasks identified by Willis and Willis (2007) in Figure 15.1.

Table 15.2 Task as appropriation activities

Task type	Example of a cat-related task
Listing	Make a list of why people like/don't like cats
Sorting	Classify things that cats like doing into nice things and no such nice things
Matching	Match photos of cats with descriptions of them
Comparing	Cats or dogs: which make the best pets
Problem-solving	Ways to stop your neighbour's cat from coming into your garden

Source: Based on Goh and Taib (2006)

Repetition is an important part of appropriation. It is one of the rationales for the use of drills and many of the more communicative activities discussed in the section require that learners repeat language. Here we are concerned with repetition of a task. Task repetition is built into task-based teaching approached as much of the research in this area has explored the impact of repeating task under different conditions. Table 11.12 in Chapter 11 looks at some task conditions that teachers can change when they ask learners to repeat a task again.

One variation that applies to spoken tasks is the use of a different modality. So learners may be asked to produce a written version of a spoken task. Research also indicates that participating in text based computer-mediated chat helps learners develop oral skills (Razagifard 2013), possibly because more planning time is allowed and the risk of loss of face is reduced. This can also allow learners to practice some aspects of their spoken English outside the classroom.

A more direct form of repetition was used by Lynch and Maclean (2000: 236–9) when they were preparing a group of learners for a medical conference. The group was divided into pairs and each pair read a different academic article and produced a poster based on their article. One person in each pair stood by their poster and the other people in the class moved around the class and spent three minutes asking about the posters. The extracts below come from the first and fourth visit to the poster.

> Q-TWIST is a new method of calculation. And we calculated the ... quality adjusted ... outcome ... It is a method to find out how, how much of the time the patients live without tumour and without toxicity ... how much of this is really good for them ... So it was a calculation on a ... meta-analysis of breast cancer studies ... all applying the same. (Lynch and Maclean 2000: 236)

> And we take this time ... and some others (yeah) to do the Q-TWIST calculation ... (yeah) and what we get is the result that ... the time without symptoms is not different for patients ... who (yes) received tamoxifen (yeah) or tamoxifen plus chemotherapy. (yes) So in regards to this aspect (yes) there is no difference between the two groups. (Lynch and Maclean 2000: 239).

The language development is less to do with being able to use appropriate vocabulary and grammar than in producing a more coherent explanation of what the academic paper meant but the repetitions do seem to have led to language improvement.

Reflection

Reflection is an important part of the learning process. Zhang and Head (2010) made use of reflection when working on a three year programme with a group of university learners who during the first year were reluctant speakers. At the start of second year course, they asked their learners to discuss the following questions in groups

1 Why did they want to speak good English?

2 How could they could learn to speak good English?

3 What classroom activities could help them improve their speaking skills?

The responses to these questions were was used to design classroom activities within the framework of topics determined by the course book. The learners also completed a self-evaluation form at the start of the second year and again at the end of the course. The first three questions of this form were:

1 I give myself the following grades for progress on this course. (Score 1–10)

Speaking: _____ / Listening: _____ / Using learning strategies as much as possible: _____

2 I speak English in class: as much as possible/a lot/often/a little

3 I speak my own language in class: only when necessary/often/a lot/too much

The figures on question two changed from 49 per cent (a little) at the start of the second year to 53 per cent (as much as possible) by end. The respective figures for question three were 37 per cent (often) and 44 per cent (only when necessary). This approach is most obviously relevant to older learner but Goh and Taib (2006) have used a similar approach for listening with young learners. See Chapter 11.

15.5 Summary

This chapter explored psychological, linguistic and social perspectives on speaking. It has used information processing theory, supplemented with Vygostkyan ideas, to explore how people learn to speak English and the kinds of knowledge and skills that speakers of other language bring to the learning process. The final section has looked at sequences in the speaking class, primarily the AAA model and the problem-solving model before looking at using speaking tasks in the classroom and how different kinds of language input activities, either related to awareness or appropriation, and reflection can contribute to the speaking lesson.

 Activity 15.4 Discussion

What advice would you offer to a colleague working in the context described below?
I teach the top form in a boys high school in an urban setting in Southeast Asia. Most of my learners will be going on to study business and business related subject at university after school. There are about twenty-five students in each class and I see them for six one hour lessons a week. Most of them have access to the internet outside school and play games such as Minecraft and Clash Royale with English speakers players from around the world. Their spoken English is fluent but their language is often very informal and

grammatically inaccurate and this may be problematic for the more formal genres they will need at university and I think for their future careers. The university entrance exam does not include any speaking and so this receives little attention in the course book. However, I would now like to spend one hour a week helping them learn to make formal presentations as I know this will be part of their assessment at university. How can I best use this time?

 ## 15.6 Further reading

The two most useful books on speaking are Goh and Burns's (2012) *Teaching Speaking: A Holistic Approach* and the more classroom-oriented Thornbury's (2005) *How to Teach Speaking*. Goh and Burns provide a clear description of the psychological processes involved in speaking, and Kormos's (2006) *Speech Production and Second Language Acquisition* provides more detail. The best source on the grammar of spoken English is Carter and McCarthy's (2006) *The Cambridge Grammar of English*. The concept of willingness to communicate is largely addressed in articles, but Peng's (2014) *Willingness to Communicate in the Chinese EFL University Classroom* is clearly written and shows how the concept helps make sense of a particular context. Thornbury's explanation of AAA is easy to follow and he provides numerous examples of relevant activities. Willis's (2007) *Doing Task-Based Teaching* remains the best description of a problem-solving sequence and again provides lots of examples of activities related to different stages of the lesson. Goh and Burns are good on reflection but this is still an area of language teaching that is developing.

Part V

Conclusion

Chapter 16

Professional Development

16.1 Introduction

This aim of this book was to help English language teachers to support their learners to become better users of English. This concluding chapter takes a step back from language learners to focus on how teachers can improve. Helping teachers to improve is often going to also help learners but may be more directly linked to the quality of life of teachers (Hanks 2017: 117). When I realized I did not have to spend my evening marking every mistake in my learners' homework, the main impact was that I had more free time rather than any direct benefit to my learners.

This chapter addresses the issue of professional development by, first, considering the knowledge and skills that might be developed, the processes by which teachers might develop, analogues of the theories of language learning discussed in the rest of this book, and some techniques for professional development. This can be expressed through three questions:

1 What skills and knowledge might be the focus of teacher development?

2 How can these skills and knowledge be developed?

3 How can teachers develop their skills and knowledge?

16.2 What skills and knowledge might be the focus of teacher development?

Shulman (1987: 6) identified six aspects of teacher knowledge or understanding. See Table 16.1. A slightly simpler framework is offered under the head of personal practical knowledge (Golombek 1998). This divides teacher knowledge into four categories:

1 knowledge of self,

2 knowledge of subject matter,

3 knowledge of instruction and

4 knowledge of contexts.

The two categories are more similar than they appear as a knowledge of contexts will include knowledge of learners and of educational end. Schulman sees these forms of knowledge as coming from research into English and research in English language teaching, educational documents and practices, and the 'wisdom of practice' (Shulman 1987: 11), that is, teachers' experience of learning and teaching.

Table 16.1 Schulman's areas of teacher understanding

1. General pedagogical knowledge	What are the general principles and strategies of classroom management and organization?
2. Curriculum knowledge	What I aspects of English need to be taught?
	What resources do I have to teach these things
3. Pedagogical content knowledge	How do I teach English?
4. Learners	Who are my learners? What they want to achieve?
5. Educational contexts	How do the learners in my class interact?
	How my educational institution operates?
	How my educational institution fits into larger structures
6. Educational ends	Why English is important in the education system?
	What are the purposes for learning English?

However, the personal practical knowledge framework (sometimes known as PPK) focuses particularly on the wisdom of practice both as a source of information in its own right but also as a way of framing other sources of knowledge. Teachers may have developed their initial understanding of teaching English from teacher training programmes, but these understandings have been framed and structured by the teacher's individual experiences. As the term 'practical' suggests, this approach also tries to bridge the gap between knowledge and skills because personal practical knowledge is 'oriented to practice' (Golombek 1998: 452) and perhaps is best seen as what Schön (1983: 3) describes as 'knowledge-in-action'.

These characterizations of teacher knowledge and skills can be seen as a kind of syllabus for teacher development, and a formal programme of teacher development might use one of these frameworks to structure the programme content. However, teacher development is not something that just happens on teacher education programmes. The starting point for most teacher development is where teachers identify a problem they would like to solve (Farrell 2007: 3) or a puzzle they would like to understand better (Hanks 2017: 20). As with information processing models of learning, the starting point is noticing a gap between what you know and what you would like to know, or what you do and what you would like to do.

16.3 How can these skills and knowledge be developed?

Most teachers develop their knowledge and skills through a process of reflection. One well-established model of reflection is outlined in Figure 16.1. The first two stages of the reflective cycle – concrete experience, that is, teachers doing something, and observation and reflection, that is, teachers thinking about how what they have done does not meet their expectations – are what leads to teachers noticing the gap, described above.

All teachers are involved in concrete experience whenever they engage in teaching activities, in or out of the class, and the stage of observation and reflection may not seem very challenging. But for most teachers, teaching their classes is so complicated that many aspects have become routine. These are activities that teachers do almost automatically. I did not realize that marking every mistake on my learners' homework was not leading to a clear benefit for several months, and it did not occur to

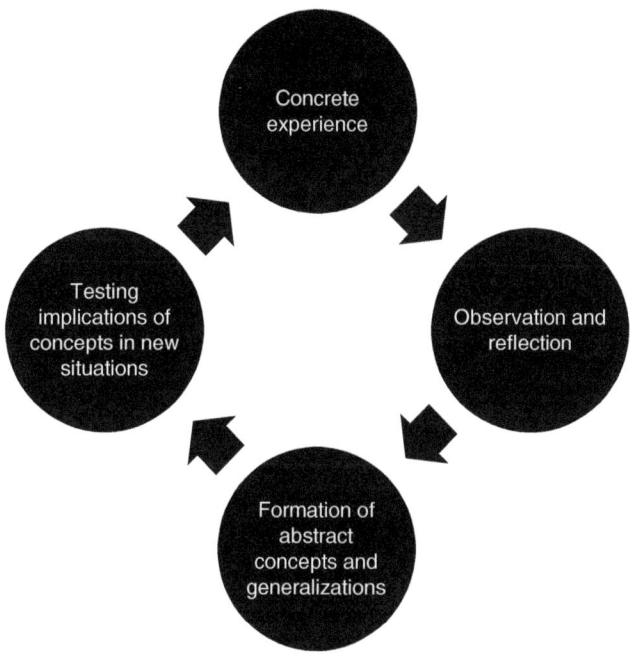

Figure 16.1 The experiential learning model (Kolb 2015: 53)

me that there might be some other way of doing this. It was not until the event I noted above, when a learner said I had been bleeding over his work, that I was able to pull back from my routine and consider what alternatives I had. Reflecting on what you had done is not something which happens all the time, and some ideas about how to encourage reflection are examined in Section 16.4.

The next stage in the reflective cycle is the formation of abstract concepts and generalizations, that is, the development of a personal theory about what has happened. For me, this was a move from thinking about marking as something that was an intrinsic part of a teacher's role, to the idea that marking might be demotivating my learners. At the time when this happened to me, I had limited access to published research, and I initially thought back to my own teacher education when it was suggested that using a green pen might make correction less threatening to learners.

This took me to the fourth part of the reflection cycle – testing implications of the concepts in new situations. For two weeks, I switched to a green pen but kept on trying to mark all the mistakes. At the end of two weeks, the monitor in one class approached me at the end of the class and told me that the class had bought me a present and gave me a red pen. At this point, I realized that my initial theory had been wrong and I was back at stage 3 of the reflection cycle. My theory that the red pen was demotivating was wrong, rather my marking was giving my learners more information than they could process. I then consulted a colleague and he suggested correcting only the grammar points that had been most recently taught. When I tried this approach out, a second attempt at stage 4, it went well.

My experience marking with a red pen led to a relatively clear outcome, but sometimes the cycle results in a more general development. A teacher in Canada (Shi 2002: 141–2) was working with a learner from India who found it difficult to distinguish /s/ and /ʃ/. To help the learners, she suggested that he adopt the English name 'Sam' as a way of building in more practice of the problematic /s/ sound and, incidentally, addressing the fact that his Indian name was difficult for the teacher and his fellow learners to pronounce. That evening she reflected on this decision and in particular the fact that mispronunciations of her own Chinese name had made her unhappy. This made her decide to reverse her original advice to the learner. The next day she asked the Indian learner to teach the class how to say his name properly and this went well. This had a beneficial impact on the class and the learners did learn to distinguish /s/ and /ʃ/. For the teacher the event was not about pronunciation but the links between language and identity. This ties in with the exploratory practice view of professional development (Allwright and Bailey 1991; Hanks 2017) where the focus is on understanding more than problem-solving, though, of course, understanding is likely to lead to changes in practice.

16.4 How can teachers develop their skills and knowledge?

The two instances of teacher development arose, in my case, from a comment from a learner, and in Shi's case from her own experience. Your learners can trigger some reflection on your part, but this is unlikely to happen on a predictable basis, so many teachers try to build in interactions with the colleagues. This can be done on a formal basis where teachers observe each other's classes and offer comments. Some institutions make this a part of normal procedures. Mutual observations are more likely to lead to reflection than one person observing another because unilateral observation can become more like an inspection. The aim is for the observer to be a critical friend (Farrell 2007: 148), and most teachers respond better to advice from a friend than someone who has power over them, where the observed teacher may feel defensive. In some institutions, expert teachers sometimes do classes which are observed by several colleagues, and this can be effective where teachers can make the links between the expert classes and their own. Where teachers are working together with similar classes, discussions in the staff room and opportunities to exchange materials or ideas about how to use materials are good ways of encouraging reflection and professional development.

Where teachers can reflect on their own lessons without an intervention from a colleague, this will expand the potential for teacher development. Critical incidents such as the name change discussed above do not happen on a regular basis. One way of generating reflection is for teachers to write notes on their lesson plans or keep a teaching journal in which they reflect on what went well and what went less well. Many teachers will not be able to do this for all their lessons, but if you have the time to do this once a week, it can lead to significant teacher development.

Another way of encouraging reflection and developing your PPK is reading other people's writing. When I worked in Malaysia, the organization for which I worked produced a newsletter which contained articles written by other English teachers about ideas for teaching. This often made me think about how my own practice related to what other teachers did and tempted me to try out new approaches. Reading what other people did also led me to writing descriptions of what I did, and I found the process of writing about my lessons encouraged me to reflect on what I had done and why. At the time, I was studying for an MA and so also had access to some research literature. This required more work from me before I could understand how it related to my own teaching, but as I became more familiar with the genre of the research article and research monograph, I found it easier to decide where they contained ideas that would help my teaching. For example, I read about cohesion (Halliday and Hasan 1976) and found it interesting, but am still not completely sure how it might inform my teaching while the concept of genre (Swales 1990), which I at first found hard to understand, now seems to me to be central to the teaching of academic literacy. One of my aims in writing this book is to encourage teachers to think about how they can use their own experience.

16.5 Summary

This chapter briefly examined professional development, looking, first, at what might be the focus of teacher development; second, at how reflection might lead to professional development; and third, at some ways in which teacher development can happen.

 Activity 16.2 Discussion

This chapter has not included any activities as I feel that professional development should be based on your own experience of the language learning classroom, but here is a framework which should enable you to think about your previous professional development and structure what happens in the future.

1. Identify an aspect of teaching knowledge and skills that has happened outside formal teacher education.
2. What was the trigger for this? What made you notice the gap in your professional knowledge or practice?
3. What resources did you draw on to address the gap? This might include fellow teachers, research or your own reflection.
4. What impact did the resources have on your understanding or practice in the classroom?
5. How might you develop your ability to notice gaps in your professional knowledge or practice?

 16.6 Further reading

Farrell's (2007) *Reflective Language Teaching* is a good introduction to reflection and professional development, and Johnson and Golombek's (2004) *Teachers' Narrative Inquiry as Professional Development* includes many insightful stories from the classroom. If you are interested in exploratory practice, Hanks's (2017) *Exploratory Practice in Language Teaching: Puzzling about Principles and Practices* is a good introduction.

References

Aitchison, J. 2003. *Words in the mind: An introduction to the mental lexicon*. Oxford: Blackwell.

Alderson, J. C. and Wall, D. 1993. Does washback exist? *Applied Linguistics* 14(2), 115–29.

Alexander, L. G. 1993. *Practice and progress: An integrated course for pre-intermediate students*. Harlow: Longman.

Allan, R. 2009. Can a graded reader corpus provide 'authentic' input? *ELT Journal* 63(1), 23–32.

Allwright, D. 2005. From teaching points to learning opportunities and beyond. *TESOL Quarterly* 39(1), 9–31.

Allwright, D. and Bailey, K. 1991. *Focus on the language classroom: An introduction to classroom research for language teachers*. Cambridge: Cambridge University Press.

Alrabai, F. 2015. The influence of teachers' anxiety-reducing strategies on learners' foreign language anxiety. *Innovation in Language Learning and Teaching* 9(2), 163–90.

Amicucci, A. N. and Lassiter, T. 2014. Multimodal concept drawings: Engaging EAL learners in brainstorming about course terms. *TESOL Journal* 5(3), 523–31.

Anderson, J. 2015. Affordance, learning opportunities, and the lesson plan pro forma. *ELT Journal* 69(3), 228–38.

Anderson, J. R. 2010. *Cognitive psychology and its implications*. 7th ed. New York: Worth.

Arneil, S., Holmes, M., and Street, H. 2017. *Hot potatoes*. Accessed 1 January 2017 from https://hotpot.uvic.ca/.

Austin, J. L. 1962. *How to do things with words*. Oxford: Clarendon Press.

Bachman, L. F. 1990. *Fundamental considerations in language testing*. Oxford: Oxford University Press.

Bachman, L. F. and Palmer, A. 1996. *Language testing in practice*. Oxford: Oxford University Press.

Bachman, L. F. and Palmer, A. S. 2010. *Language assessment in practice: Developing language assessments and justifying their use in the real world*. Oxford: Oxford University Press.

Backhaus, P. 2009. Politeness in institutional elderly care in Japan: A cross-cultural comparison. *Journal of Politeness Research – Language Behaviour Culture* 5(1), 53–71.

Baddeley, A. D., Eysenck, M. W. and Anderson, M. 2009. *Memory*. Hove/New York: Psychology Press.

Badger, R. G. 2003. Legal and general: Towards a genre analysis of newspaper law reports. *English for Specific Purposes* 22(3), 249–63.

Badger, R. G. 2006. Investigating agonism in linguistics. *Journal of Pragmatics* 38(9), 1442–56.

Badger, R. G. and MacDonald, M. 2010. Making it real: Authenticity, process and pedagogy. *Applied Linguistics* 31(4), 578–82.

Baecher, L., Farnsworth, T. and Ediger, A. 2014. The challenges of planning language objectives in content-based ESL instruction. *Language Teaching Research* 18(1), 118–36.

Basturkmen, H. 2001. Descriptions of spoken language for higher level learners: The example of questioning. *ELT Journal* 55, 1–10.

Basturkmen, H. 2002. Learner observation of, and reflection on, spoken discourse: An approach for teaching academic speaking. *TESOL Journal* 11(2), 26–30.

Bauer, L. and Nation, P. 1993. Word families. *International Journal of Lexicography* 6(4), 253–79.

Beaken, M. 2009. Teaching discourse intonation with narrative. *ELT Journal* 63(4), 342–52.

Bell, A. 1984. Language style as audience design. *Language in Society* 13(2), 145–204.

Berkel, A. V. 2005. The role of the phonological strategy in learning to spell in English as a second language. In: Cook, V. and Bassetti, B., eds. *Second language writing systems*. Clevedon: Multilingual Matters, pp. 97–121.

Beuckens, T. 2016. *English Language Listening Library Online*. Accessed 11 November 2017 from www.elllo.org/.

Biber, D., Johansson, S., Leech, G., Conrad, S. and Finegan, E. 1999. *Longman grammar of spoken and written English*. Harlow: Pearson Education.

Björkman, B. 2008. 'So where we are?' Spoken lingua franca English at a technical university in Sweden. *English Today* 24(2), 35–41.

Björkman, B. 2011. The pragmatics of English as a lingua franca in the international university: Introduction. *Journal of Pragmatics* 43(4), 923–5.

Black, P. and Wiliam, D. 1998. *Inside the black box: Raising standards through classroom assessment*. London: King's College London.

Blake, A. 2016. *The first Trump-Clinton presidential debate transcript, annotated*. Accessed 30 September 2016 from www.washingtonpost.com/news/the-fix/wp/2016/09/26/the-first-trump-clinton-presidential-debate-transcript-annotated/.

Block, D. 2003. Review of Michel Thomas's language course. *Language Learning Journal* 27(1), 74–8.

Bloor, T. and Bloor, A. M. 2004. *The functional analysis of English: a Hallidayan approach*. 2nd ed. London: Arnold.

Borg, S. 1999. Studying teacher cognition in second language grammar teaching. *System* 27(1), 19–31.

Borg, S. 2007. Research engagement in English language teaching. *Teaching and Teacher Education* 23(5), 731.

Bot, K. D. and Lowie, W. 2005. *Second language acquisition*. London: Routledge.

Bourdieu, P., Thompson, J. B., Raymond, G. and Adamson, M. 1991. *Language and symbolic power*. Cambridge: Polity.

Bourke, J. M. 2006. Designing a topic-based syllabus for young learners. *ELT Journal* 60(3), 279–86.

Brazil, D. 1985. *The communicative value of intonation in English*. Birmingham: English Language Research, University of Birmingham.

Brazil, D. 1997. *The communicative value of intonation in English*. Rev. ed. Cambridge: Cambridge University Press.

Breen, M. 1985. Authenticity in the language classroom. *Applied Linguistics* 6(1), 60–70.

Breen, M. 1987a. Contemporary paradigms in syllabus design 1. *Language Teaching* 20(2), 81–92.

Breen, M. 1987b. Contemporary paradigms in syllabus design 2. *Language Teaching* 20(3), 157–74.

Brett, D. 2004. Computer generated feedback on vowel production by learners of English as a second language. *ReCALL* 16(1), 103–13.

Brezina, V. and Gablasova, D. 2015. Is there a core general vocabulary? Introducing the new general service list. *Applied Linguistics* 36(1), 1–22.

Briggs, S., Simpson, R., Ovens, J. and Swales, J. 2002. *Michigan Corpus of Academic Spoken English*. Accessed 17 December 2004 from www. lsa.umich.edu/eli/micase/index.htm

Brooks, G. 2015. *Dictionary of the British English spelling system*. Cambridge: Open Book Publishers.

Brown, G. D. A. and Ellis, N. C. 1994. *Handbook of spelling: Theory, process and intervention*. Chichester: John Wiley.

Brown, G. D. A. and Loosemore, R. P. W. 1994. Computational approaches to normal and impaired spelling. In: Brown, G. D. A. and Ellis, N. C., eds. *Handbook of spelling: Theory, process and intervention*. Chichester: John Wiley, pp. 320–35.

Brown, P. and Levinson, S. C. 1987. *Politeness: Some universals in language usage*. Cambridge: Cambridge University Press.

Brumfit, C. 1991. Problems in defining instructional methodologies. In: De Bot, K., Ginsberg, R. B. and Kramsch, C. J., eds. *Foreign language research in cross-cultural perspective*. Amsterdam: Benjamins, pp. 133–44.

Brumfit, C. 1997. How applied linguistics is the same as any other science. *International Journal of Applied Linguistics* 7(1), 86–94.

Butler, Y. G. 2015. Parental factors in children's motivation for learning English: A case in China. *Research Papers in Education* 30(2), 164–91.

Butt, D., Fahey, R., Spinks, S. and Yallop, C. 1995. *Using functional grammar: An explorer's guide*. Sydney: National Centre of English Language Teaching and Research.

Butt, G. 2008. *Lesson planning*. London: Continuum.

Byrne, D. 1986. *Teaching oral English*. Harlow: Longman.

Cambridge English First. 2016. *Handbook for teachers from 2016*. Cambridge: Cambridge English Language Assessment.

Canagarajah, S. 2016. TESOL as a professional community: A half-century of pedagogy, research, and theory. *TESOL Quarterly* 50(1), 7–41.

Canale, M. and Swain, M. 1980. Theoretical bases of communicative approaches to second language teaching and testing. *Applied Linguistics* 1(1), 1–47.

Carroll, L. and Blum, A. A. 2008. *Alice in wonderland*. Oadby: Thorpe & Porter.

Carter, R. and McCarthy, M. 1995. Grammar and the spoken language. *Applied Linguistics* 16(2), 141–58.

Carter, R. and McCarthy, M. 2006. *The Cambridge grammar of English: A comprehensive guide*. Cambridge: Cambridge University Press.

Carter, R. and McCarthy, M. 2015. Spoken grammar: Where are we and where are we going? *Applied Linguistics* 38(1), 1–20.

Cauldwell, R. 1996. Stress-timing: Observations, beliefs, and evidence. *Eger Journal of English Studies* 1, 33–48.

Celce-Murcia, M., Brinton, D. M. and Goodwin, J. M. 2010. *Teaching pronunciation: A course book and reference guide*. Cambridge: Cambridge University Press.

Cervatiuc, A. 2009. Identity, good language learning, and adult immigrants in Canada. *Journal of Language, Identity & Education* 8(4), 254–71.

Chapelle, C. A. and Voss, E. 2016. 20 years of technology and language assessment in language learning & technology. *Language Learning and Technology* 20(2), 116–28.

Chase, W. G. 1973. *Visual information processing: Proceedings of the Eighth Annual Carnegie Symposium on Cognition*, Carnegie-Mellon University, Pittsburgh, Pennsyvania, May 19, 1972. New York/London: Academic Press.

Chomsky, N. 1969. *Aspects of the theory of syntax*. Michigan: MIT Press.

Chomsky, N., Mukherjee, N., Patnaik, B. N. and Agnihotri, R. K. 2000. *The architecture of language*. Oxford: Oxford University Press.

Clark, M. M. 2016. Learning to be literate: Insights from research for policy and practice. *Improving Schools* 19(2), 129–40.

Cogo, A. and Dewey, M. 2006. Efficiency in ELF communication: From pragmatic motives to lexico-grammatical innovation. *Nordic Journal of English Studies* 5(2), 59–93.

Cohen, A. D. and Macaro, E. 2007. *Language learner strategies: Thirty years of research and practice*. Oxford: Oxford University Press.

Coles, M. and Lord, B. 1976. *Access to English: Getting on*. Oxford: Oxford University Press.

Connor, U. 2002. New directions in contrastive rhetoric. *TESOL Quarterly* 36(4), 493–510.

Connor, U., Nagelhout, E. and Rozycki, W. V. 2008. *Contrastive rhetoric: Reaching to intercultural rhetoric*. Amsterdam/Philadelphia: John Benjamins Pub.

Conor, U. 1996. *Contrastive rhetoric: Cross-cultural aspects of second-language writing*. Cambridge: Cambridge University Press.

Cooke, M. 2006. 'When I wake up I dream of electricity': The lives, aspirations and 'needs' of adult ESOL learners. *Linguistics and Education* 17(1), 56–73.

Cooke, M. and Simpson, J. 2008. *ESOL: A critical guide*. Oxford: Oxford University Press.

Cooper, W. A., Lam, D. C. L., O'Toole, S. A. and Minna, J. D. 2013. Molecular biology of lung cancer. *Journal of Thoracic Disease* 5, S479–90.

Cope, B. and Kalantzis, M. 1993. *The powers of literacy: a genre approach to teaching writing*. London: Falmer.

Council of Europe. 2001. *Common European Framework of Reference for Languages: learning, teaching and assessment*. Cambridge: Cambridge University Press.

Coxhead, A. 2000. A new academic word list. *TESOL Quarterly* 34(2), 213–38.

Coyle, D., Hood, P. and Marsh, D. 2010. *CLIL: Content and language integrated learning*. Cambridge/ New York: Cambridge University Press.

Coyle, Y. and Gracia, R. G. 2014. Using songs to enhance L2 vocabulary acquisition in preschool children. *ELT Journal* 68(3), 276–85.

Crossman, E. R. F. W. 1959. A theory of the acquisition of speed-skill. *Ergonomics* 2(2), 153–66.

Crystal, D. 2010. *The Cambridge encyclopedia of language*. Cambridge: Cambridge University Press.

Cullen, R. and Kuo, I. C. 2007. Spoken grammar and ELT course materials: A missing link? *TESOL Quarterly* 41(2), 361–86.

Dalton, C. and Seidlhofer, B. 1994. *Pronunciation*. Oxford: Oxford University Press.

Dalton-Puffer, C. 2007. *Discourse in content and language integrated learning (CLIL) classrooms*. Amsterdam/ Philadelphia: John Benjamins Pub.

Darvin, R. and Norton, B. 2015. Identity and a model of investment in applied linguistics. *Annual Review of Applied Linguistics* 35, 36–56.

Day, R. and Bamford, J. 2002. Top ten principles for teaching extensive reading. *Reading in a Foreign Language* 14(2), 136–41.

de Bot, K. 1992. A bilingual production model: Levelt's 'speaking' model adapted. *Applied Linguistics* 13(1), 1–24.

de Guerrero, M. C. M. and Commander, M. 2013. Shadow-reading: Affordances for imitation in the language classroom. *Language Teaching Research* 17(4), 433–53.

De Larios, J. R., Murphy, L. and Manchón, R. M. 1999. The use of restructuring strategies in EFL writing: A study of Spanish learners of English as a foreign language. *Journal of Second Language Writing* 8(1), 13–44.

De Larios, J. R., Manchón, R., Murphy, L. and Marín, J. 2008. The foreign language writer's strategic behaviour in the allocation of time to writing processes. *Journal of Second Language Writing* 17(1), 30–47.

Deci, E. L. and Ryan, R. M. 1985. *Intrinsic motivation and self-determination in human behavior*. New York/ London: Plenum.

DeKeyser, R. 2006. Skill acquisition theory. In: VanPatten, B. and Williams, J., eds. *Theories in second language acquisition: An introduction*. Mahwah, NJ: Lawrence Erlbaum, pp. 97–113.

DeKeyser, R. M. 1995. Learning second language grammar rules. *Studies in Second Language Acquisition* 17(3), 379–410.

Denhovska, N., Serratrice, L. and Payne, J. 2016. Acquisition of second language grammar under incidental learning conditions: The role of frequency and working memory: Frequency and implicit learning of L2 grammar. *Language Learning* 66(1), 159–90.

Ding, Y. 2007. Text memorization and imitation: The practices of successful Chinese learners of English. *System* 35(2), 271.

Dodge, B. 2007. *The WebQuest page*. Accessed 8 February 2017 from http://webquest.org/index.php

Dörnyei, Z. 2005. *Psychology of the language learner individual differences in second language acquisition*. Mahwah/ London: Lawrence Erlbaum.

Dörnyei, Z. 2009. The L2 motivational self system. In: Dornyei, Z. and Ushioda, E., eds. *Motivation, language identity and the L2 self*. Bristol: Multilingual Matters, pp. 9–42.

Dörnyei, Z. and Csizer, K. 1998. Ten commandments for motivating language learners: Results of an empirical study. *Language Teaching Research* 2(3), 203–29.

Dörnyei, Z. and Ushioda, U. 2011. *Teaching and researching motivation*. 2nd ed. Harlow: Pearson Education.

Downing, A. and Locke, P. 2005. *English Grammar: A University Course*. London: Routledge.

Ducate, L. and Lomicka, L. 2009. Podcasting: An effective tool for honing language students' pronunciation? *Language Learning and Technology* 13(3), 66–86.

Dudley-Evans, T. 1997. Genre: How far can we go, should we go? *World Englishes* 16(3), 351–8.

Educational Testing Services. 2012. *The official guide to the TOEFL Test*. 4th ed. New York: McGrawHill.

Ellis, N. C. 2006a. The associative-cognitive CREED. In: VanPatten, B. and Williams, J., eds. *Theories in second language acquisition: An introduction*. Mahwah, NJ: Lawrence Erlbaum, pp. 137–54.

Ellis, N. C. and Schmidt, R. 1997. Morphology and longer distance dependencies. *Studies in Second Language Acquisition* 19(2), 145–71.

Ellis, R. 2006b. Current issues in the teaching of grammar: An SLA perspective. *TESOL Quarterly* 40(1), 83–107.

Ellis, R. 2015. *Understanding second language acquisition*. Oxford: Oxford University Press.

Ericsson, K. A. 2013. Training history, deliberate practice and elite sports performance: An analysis in response to Tucker and Collins review-what makes champions? *British Journal of Sports Medicine* 47(9), 533–5.

Ericsson, K. A., Krampe, R. T. and Tesch-Romer, C. 1993. The role of deliberate practice in the acquisition of expert performance. *Psychological Review* 100(3), 363–406.

Extensive Reading Foundation. 2011. *Guide to extensive reading*. Accessed 14 March 2017. from www.erfoundation. org/ERF_Guide.pdf

Fairbairn, G. and Winch, C. 2011. *Reading, writing and reasoning: A guide for students*. Maidenhead: Open University Press.

Faircloth, B. S. and Miller, S. D. 2011. Enabling enriched, empowered education: Insights from Jere Brophy's legacy. *Theory into Practice* 50(4), 262–8.

Farrell, T. S. C. 2007. *Reflective language teaching: From research to practice*. New York: Continuum.

Field, J. 1998. Skills and strategies: Towards a new methodology for listening. *ELT Journal* 52(2), 110–18.

Field, J. 2005. Intelligibility and the listener: The role of lexical stress. *TESOL Quarterly* 39(3), 399–424.

Field, J. 2008a. Bricks or mortar: Which parts of the input does a second language listener rely on? *TESOL Quarterly* 42(3), 411–32.

Field, J. 2008b. *Listening in the language classroom*. Cambridge: Cambridge University Press.

Flege, J. E. 1987. A critical period for learning to pronounce foreign languages? *Applied Linguistics* 8(2), 162–77.

Flower, L. and Hayes, J. R. 1981. A cognitive process theory of writing. *College Composition and Communication* 32(4), 365–87.

Foster, P. and Ohta, A. S. 2005. Negotiation for meaning and peer assistance in second language classrooms. *Applied Linguistics* 26, 402.

Foster, P. and Skehan, P. 1999. The influence of source of planning and focus of planning on task-based performance. *Language Teaching Research* 3(3), 215–47.

Fulcher, G. 2010. *Practical language testing*. London: Hodder Education.

Gao, Y., Zhao, Y., Cheng, Y. and Zhou, Y. 2007. Relationship between English learning motivation types and self-identity changes among Chinese students. *TESOL Quarterly* 41(1), 133–55.

Gardner, R. C. 1985. *Social psychology and second language learning: The role of attitudes and motivation*. New York: Basic Books.

Gardner, R. C. and Lambert, W. E. 1959. Motivational variables in second-language acquisition. *Canadian Journal of Psychology* 13(4), 266–72.

Gardner, R. C. and Lambert, W. E. 1972. *Attitudes and motivation in second-language learning*. Rowley, MA: Newbury House.

Gardner, S. and Nesi, H. 2013. A classification of genre families in university student writing. *Applied Linguistics* 34(1), 25–52.

Gass, S. M. 1998. *Second language learning data analysis*. 2nd ed. Mahwah/London: Erlbaum,.

Gerlach, D. 2016. Reading and spelling difficulties in the ELT classroom. *ELT Journal*, 1–10.

Gilmore, A. 2004. A comparison of textbook and authentic interactions. *ELT Journal* 58(4), 363–74.

Gilmore, A. 2007. Authentic materials and authenticity in foreign language learning. *Language Teaching* 40(2), 97–118.

Gilmore, A. 2015. Research into practice: The influence of discourse studies on language descriptions and task design in published ELT materials. *Language Teaching* 48(4), 506–30.

Gnutzman, C. 2000. Lingua franca. In: Byram, M., ed. *Routledge encyclopedia of language teaching and learning*. London: Routledge, pp. 356–9.

Goh, C. 2008. Metacognitive instruction for second language listening development. *RELC Journal* 39(2), 188–213.

Goh, C. and Taib, Y. 2006. Metacognitive instruction in listening for young learners. *ELT Journal* 60(3), 222–32.

Goh, C. C. M. and Burns, A. 2012. *Teaching speaking: A holistic approach*. Cambridge: Cambridge University Press.

Goh, G. and Christine. 2002. Exploring listening comprehension tactics and their interaction patterns. *System* 30(2), 185–206.

Golombek, P. R. 1998. A study of language teachers' personal practical knowledge. *TESOL Quarterly* 32(3), 447–64.

Golombek, P. R. and Johnson, K. E. 2004. Narrative inquiry as a mediational space: Examining emotional and cognitive dissonance in second-language teachers' development. *Teachers and Teaching* 10(3), 307–27.

Gosden, H. 1996. Verbal reports of Japanese novices' research writing practices in English. *Journal of Second Language Writing* 5(2), 109–28.

Grabe, W. 2009. *Reading in a second language: Moving from theory to practice*. Cambridge: Cambridge University Press.

Grabe, W. and Stoller, F. L. 2013. *Teaching and researching reading*. Abingdon: Routledge.

Graddol, D. 1994. What is a text? In: Graddol, D. and Boyd-Barrett, O., eds. *Media texts: Authors and readers*. Clevedon: Open University and Multilingual Matters, pp. 40–50.

Graddol, D. 2006. *English next: Why global English may mean the end of 'English as a foreign language'*. London: British Council.

Granger, C. and Hicks, T. 1978. *Contact English 2*. London: Heinemann.

Graves, K. 2000. *Designing language courses: A guide for teachers*. London: Heinle & Heinle.

Green, A. 2014. *Exploring language assessment and testing: Language in action*. London: Routledge.

Gregory, E. 2008. *Learning to read in a new language: Making sense of words and worlds*. Thousand Oaks/London: Sage.

Grellet, F. 1981. *Developing reading skills: A practical guide to reading comprehension exercises*. Cambridge: Cambridge University Press.

Grundy, P. 2008. *Doing pragmatics*. 3rd ed. London: Hodder Education.

Gu, Y. 1990. Politeness phenomena in modern Chinese. *Journal of Pragmatics* 14(2), 237–57.

Guiora, A., Beit-Hallami, B., Brannon, R. C. L., Dull, C. and Scovel, T. 1972. The effects of experimentally induced changes in ego states on pronunciation ability in a second language: An exploratory study. *Comprehensive Psychiatry* 13(5), 421–8.

Haladyna, T. M., Nolen, S. B. and Haas, N. S. 1991. Raising standardized achievement test scores and the origins of test score pollution. *Educational Researcher* 20(5), 2–7.

Halliday, M. A. K. 1961. Categories of the theory of grammar. *Word* 17, 242–92.

Halliday, M. A. K. 1978. *Language as a social semiotic*. London: Edward Arnold.

Halliday, M. A. K. and Hasan, R. 1976. *Cohesion in English*. London: Longman.

Halliday, M. A. K. and Matthiessen, C. M. I. M. 2004. *An introduction to functional grammar*. 3rd ed. London: Arnold.

Halliday, M. A. K. and Matthiessen, C. M. I. M. 2014. *Halliday's introduction to functional grammar*. 4th ed. London: Routledge.

Han, Z. 2000. Persistence of the implicit influence of L1: The case of the pseudopassive. *Applied Linguistics* 21(1), 78.

Hanks, J. 2017. *Exploratory practice in language teaching: Puzzling about principles and practices*. London: Palgrave Macmillan.

Harmer, J. 2015. *The practice of English language teaching*. 5th ed. Harlow: Longman.

Harris, R. 1996. *Signs, language and communication*. London: Routledge.

Harwood, N. 2010. *English language teaching materials: Theory and practice*. Cambridge: Cambridge University Press.

Heath, S. B. 1982. Protean shapes in literacy events: Ever-shifting oral and literate traditions. In: Tannen, D., ed. *Spoken and written language: Exploring orality and literacy*. Norwood, NJ: Ablex, pp. 348–71.

Heaton, J. B. 1988. *Writing English language tests*. London: Longman.

Hedge, T. 2000. *Teaching and learning in the language classroom*. Oxford: Oxford University Press.

Henderlong, J. and Lepper, M. R. 2002. The effects of praise on children's intrinsic motivation: A review and synthesis. *Psychological Bulletin* 128(5), 774–95.

Henderson, A., Frost, D., Tergujeff, E., Kautzsch, A., Murphy, D., Kirkova-Naskova, A., . . . Humanistiska, F. 2012. The English pronunciation teaching in Europe survey: Selected results. *Research in Language* 10(1), 5–27.

Heritage, J. and Maynard, D. W. 2005. *Communication in medical care: Interaction between primary care physicians and patients*. Cambridge: Cambridge University Press.

Heuven, W. J. B. 2005. Bilingual interactive activation models of word recognition in a second language. In: Cook, V. and Bassetti, B., eds. *Second language writing systems*. Clevedon: Multilingual Matters, pp. 260–88.

Hewish, A., Bell, S. J., Pilkington, J. D. H., Scott, P. F. and Collins, R. A. 1968. Observation of a rapidly pulsating radio source. *Nature* 217, 709–13.

Hill, K. and McNamara, T. 2015. Validity inferences under high-stakes conditions: A response from language testing. *Measurement: Interdisciplinary Research & Perspectives* 13(1), 39–43.

Hockett, C. F. 1960. The origin of speech. *Scientific American* 203, 88–101.

Hoey, M. 1983. *On the surface of discourse*. London: George Allen & Unwin.

Holliday, A., Hyde, M. and Kullman, J. 2004. *Intercultural communication: An advanced resource book*. London: Routledge.

Holtgraves, T. 2002. *Language as social action: Social psychology and language use*. Mahwah, NJ: Erlbaum.

Howarth, P. 1998. Phraseology and second language proficiency. *Applied Linguistics* 19(1), 24–44.

Huang, S. C. 2016. Language learning strategies in context. *Language Learning Journal*, 1–13.

Hudson, T. 2007. *Teaching second language reading*. Oxford: Oxford University Press.

Hyland, F. 1998. The impact of teacher written feedback on individual writers. *Journal of Second Language Writing* 7(3), 255–86.

Hyland, F. and Hyland, K. 2001. Sugaring the pill – Praise and criticism in written feedback. *Journal of Second Language Writing* 10(3), 185–212.

Hyland, K. 2002. Authority and invisibility: Authorial identity in academic writing. *Journal of Pragmatics* 34, 1091–112.

Hyland, K. 2003a. Genre-based pedagogies: A social response to process. *Journal of Second Language Writing* 12(1), 17–29.

Hyland, K. 2003b. *Second language Writing*. Cambridge: Cambridge University Press.

Hyland, K. 2009. *Teaching and researching writing*. 2nd ed. Harlow: Longman.

Hymes, D., H. 1979. On communicative competence. In: Brumfit, C.J. and Johnson, K. eds. *The communicative approach to language teaching*. Oxford: OUP, pp. 5–27.

Hyon, S. 2001. Long-term effects of genre-based instruction: A follow-up study of an EAP reading course. *English for Specific Purposes* 20 (suppl 1), 417–38.

Ivanič, R. 1998. *Writing and identity: The discoursal construction of identity in academic writing*. Philadelphia, PA: John Benjamins.

Ivanič, R. 2004. Discourses of writing and learning to write. *Language and Education* 18(3), 220–45.

Jenkins, J. 2000. *The phonology of English as an international language: New models, new norms, new goals*. Oxford: Oxford University Press.

Jenkins, J. 2002. A sociolinguistically based, empirically researched pronunciation syllabus for English as an international language. *Applied Linguistics* 23(1), 83–103.

Jenkins, J. 2007. *English as a lingua franca: Attitude and identity*. Oxford: Oxford University Press.

Johnson, K. 1996. *Language teaching and skill learning*. Oxford: Blackwell.

Johnson, K. 2005. *Expertise in second language learning and teaching*. Basingstoke: Palgrave Macmillan.

Johnson, K. E. 2002. Language as a skill. *ELT Journal* 56(2), 190–91.

Jones, C. and Waller, D. 2015. *Corpus linguistics for grammar: A guide for research*. Oxford: Routledge.

Kachru, B. 1983. Models for non-native Englishes. In: Smith, L., ed. *Readings in English as an international language*. Oxford: Pergamon, pp. 69–87.

Kammler, B. 1995. The grammar wars. *English in Australia* 114, 3–15.

Kaplan, R. B. 1966. Cultural thought patterns in inter-cultural education. *Language Learning* 16(1–2), 1–20.

Kennedy, A. L. 2017. Burgess at 100. *Burgess and the morality of contemporary culture*. [Podcast]. Accessed 28 February 2017 from www.bbc.co.uk/programmes/b08g4flp

Kenworthy, J. 1987. *Teaching English pronunciation*. Harlow: Longman.

Kintsch, W. and Rawson, K. A. 2005. Comprehension. In: Snowling, M. J. and Hulme, C., eds. *The science of reading: A handbook*. Oxford: Blackwell, pp. 210–26.

Klapper, J. 2003. Taking communication to task? A critical review of recent trends in language teaching. *Language Learning Journal* 27, 33–42.

Kobayashi, H. and Rinnert, C. 1992. Effects of first language on second language writing: Translation versus direct composition. *Language Learning* 42(2), 183–209.

Kolb, D. A. 2015. *Experiential learning: Experience as the source of learning and development*. Upper Saddle River, NJ: Pearson Education.

Kong, S. 2015. Designing content-language integrated learning materials for late immersion students. *TESOL Journal* 6(2), 302–31.

Kormos, J. 2006. *Speech production and second language acquisition*. Mahwah, NJ: Lawrence Erlbaum.

Krashen, S. 1981. *Second language acquisition and second language learning*. Oxford: Pergamon.

Krashen, S. 1987. *Principles and practice in second language acquisition*. New York: Prentice Hall.

Krashen, S. 1989. *Language acquisition and language education: Extensions and applications*. New York: Prentice Hall.

Krashen, S. D. 1985. *The input hypothesis: Issues and implications*. London: Longman.

Kremmel, B., Brunfaut, T. and Alderson, J. C. 2015. Exploring the role of phraseological knowledge in foreign language reading. *Applied Linguistics*. pamv070.

Kumaravadivelu, B. 2003a. *Beyond methods: Macrostrategies for language teaching*. London: Yale University Press.

Kumaravadivelu, B. 2003b. A postmethod perspective on English language teaching. *World Englishes* 22(4), 539–50.

Labov, W. 1999. The transformation of experience in narrative. In: Jaworski, A. and Coupland, N., eds. *The discourse reader*. London: Routledge, pp. 221–35.

Lado, R. 1961. *Language testing: The construction and use of foreign language tests, a teacher's book*. London: Longmans.

Lamb, M. 2004. Integrative motivation in a globalizing world. *System* 32(1), 3–19.

Lantolf, J. P. 2007. Sociocultural theory and second language learning. In: VanPatten, B. and Williams, J., eds. *Theories in second language acquisition: An introduction*. pp. 201–24.

Larsen-Freeman, D. 1991. Research on language teaching methodologies: A review of the past and an agenda for the future. In: De Bot, K., Ginsberg, R. B. and Kramsch, C. J., eds. *Foreign language research in cross-cultural perspective*. Amsterdam: Benjamins, pp. 119–32.

Larsen-Freeman, D. 2003. *Teaching language from grammar to grammaring*. Boston, MA: Thomson Heinle.

Larsen-Freeman, D. and Anderson, M. 2011. *Techniques and principles in language teaching*. 3rd ed. Oxford: Oxford University Press.

Latham-Koenig, C. and Oxenden, C. 2013. *English file: Beginner student's book*. Oxford: Oxford University Press.

Latham-Koenig, C., Oxenden, C. and Seligson, P. 2013. *English file: Elementary*. Oxford: Oxford University Press.

Laufer, B. and Hulstijn, J. 2001. Incidental vocabulary acquisition in a second language: The construct of task-induced involvement. *Applied Linguistics* 22(1), 1–26.

Laufer, B. and Shmueli, K. 1997. Memorizing new words: Does teaching have Anything to do with it? *RELC Journal* 28(1), 89–108.

Laufer, B. and Waldman, T. 2011. Verb noun collocations in second language writing: A corpus analysis of learners' English. *Language Learning* 61(2), 647–72.

Lazaraton, A. 2010. From cloze to consequences and beyond: An interview with Elana Shohamy. *Language Assessment Quarterly* 7(3), 255–79.

Lee, I. 2009. Ten mismatches between teachers' beliefs and written feedback practice. *ELT Journal* 63(1), 13–22.

Leech, G. 2007. Politeness: Is there an east-west divide? *Journal of Politeness Research-Language Behaviour Culture* 3(2), 167–206.

Leeds City Council. 2017. *Wedding ceremony options*. Accessed 8 February 2017 from www.leeds.gov.uk/

Leki, I., Silva, T. and Cumming, A. 2008. *A synthesis of research on second language writing in English, 1985–2005*. London: Routledge.

Lennon, P. 2000. The lexical element in spoken second language fluency. In: Riggenbach, H., ed. *Perspectives on fluency*. Ann Arbor: University of Michigan Press, pp. 25–42.

Levelt, W. J. M. 1989. *Speaking: From intention to articulation*. Cambridge/London: MIT Press.

Lewis, M. 2000. *Teaching collocation: Further developments in the lexical approach*. Hove: Language Teaching Publications.

Lewis, M. and McCook, F. 2002. Cultures of teaching: Voices from Vietnam. *ELT Journal* 56(2), 146–53.

Lewis, M. Paul 2009. *Ethnologue: Languages of the world*. Available from www.ethnologue.com/.

Lightbown, P. and Spada, N. M. 2013. *How languages are learned*. Oxford: Oxford University Press.

Lightbown, P. M. and Spada, N. 2006. *How languages are learned*. 3rd ed. Oxford: Oxford University Press.

Lin, M. H. and Lee, J.-Y. 2015. Data-driven learning: Changing the teaching of grammar in EFL classes. *ELT Journal*, 264–74.

Liu, C. C., Wu, L. Y., Chen, Z. M., Tsai, C. C. and Lin, H. M. 2014. The effect of story grammars on creative self-efficacy and digital storytelling: Story grammars and digital storytelling. *Journal of Computer Assisted Learning* 30(5), 450–64.

Liu, P.-L., Chen, C.-J. and Chang, Y.-J. 2010. Effects of a computer-assisted concept mapping learning strategy on EFL college students' English reading comprehension. *Computers and Education* 54(2), 436–45.

Long, M. 1983. Native speaker/non-native speaker conversation and the negotiation of comprehensible input. *Applied Linguistics* 4, 126–41.

Long, M. H. 1985. Input and second language acquisition theory. In: Gass, S. and Madden, C., eds. *Input in second language acquisition*. London: Newbury House, pp. 377–93.

Long, M. H. 1991. A design feature in language teaching methodology. In: De Bot, K., Lowie, W. and Verspoor, M. H., eds. *Foreign language research in cross-cultural perspective*. Amsterdam: Benjamins, pp. 39–52.

Long, M. H. 2005. *Second language needs analysis*. Cambridge: Cambridge University Press.

Long, M. H. 2016. In defense of tasks and TBLT: Nonissues and real issues. *Annual Review of Applied Linguistics* 36, 5–33.

Long, M. H. and Norris, J. M. 2000. Task-based teaching and assessment. In: Byram, M., ed. *Routledge encyclopedia of language teaching and learning*. London: Routledge, pp. 597–602.

Luoma, S. 2004. *Assessing speaking*. Cambridge: Cambridge University Press.

Lynch, T. 1996. *Communication in the classroom*. Oxford: Oxford University Press.

Lynch, T. 2001. Seeing what they meant: Transcribing as a route to noticing. *ELT Journal* 55, 124–32.

Lynch, T. 2007. Learning from the transcripts of an oral communication task. *ELT Journal* 61(4), 311–20.

Lynch, T. 2009. *Teaching second language listening*. Oxford: Oxford University Press.

Lynch, T. and Maclean, J. 2000. Exploring the benefits of task repetition and recycling for classroom language learning. *Language Teaching Research* 4, 221–50.

Macalister, J. 2014. Teaching reading: Research into practice. *Language Teaching* 47(3), 387–97.

Macaro, E. 2006. Strategies for language learning and for language use: Revising the theoretical framework. *Modern Language Journal* 90, 320–37.

MacDonald, M., Badger, R. and White, G. 2000. The real thing? Authenticity and academic listening. *English for Specific Purposes* 19(3), 251–67.

Macintyre, P. D. 2007. Willingness to communicate in the second language: Understanding the decision to speak as a volitional process. *Modern Language Journal* 91(4), 564–76.

Mackey, A., Gass, S. and McDonough, K. 2000. How do learners perceive interactional feedback? *Studies in Second Language Acquisition* 22(4), 471–97.

MacWhinney, B. 2008. The competition model. In: Robinson, P. and Ellis, N. C., eds. *Handbook of cognitive linguistics and second language acquisition*. New York/London: Routledge, pp. 314–72.

Maliborska, V. and You, Y. 2016. Writing conferences in a second language writing classroom: Instructor and student perspectives. *TESOL Journal* 7(4), 874–97.

Manchón, R. M. and de Larios, J. R. 2007. On the temporal nature of planning in L1 and L2 composing. *Language Learning* 57(4), 549–93.

Martin, J. R. and Rose, D. 2008. *Genre relations: Mapping culture*. London: Equinox.

Matsuda, A. Y. A. and Friedrich, P. 2011. English as an international language: A curriculum blueprint. *World Englishes* 30(3), 332–44.

Matsumoto, Y. 2011. Successful ELF communications and implications for ELT: Sequential analysis of ELF pronunciation negotiation strategies. *Modern Language Journal* 95(1), 97–114.

Mayer, S. R. T. 1874. Leigh Hunt and Charles Ollier. *St. James's Magazine*, 406.

McCarthy, M. and Carter, R. A. 1994. *Language as discourse: Perspectives for language teaching*. London: Longman.

McCarthy, M., O'Dell, F. and Shaw, E. 1997. *Vocabulary in use upper intermediate reference and practice for students of North American English*. Cambridge: Cambridge University Press.

McCarthy, M., O'Keeffe, A. and Walsh, S. 2010. *Vocabulary matrix: Understanding, learning, teaching*. Andover: Cengage Learning.

McCrostie, J. 2007. Examining learner vocabulary notebooks. *ELT Journal* 61(3), 246–55.

McNamara, T. 2000. *Language testing*. Oxford: Oxford University Press.

McNamara, T. 2007. Language assessment in foreign language education: The struggle over constructs. *Modern Language Journal* 91(2), 280–82.

McNamara, T. F. and Roever, C. 2006. *Language testing: The social dimension*. Malden/Oxford: Blackwell.

Meddings, L. and Thornbury, S. 2009. *Teaching unplugged: Dogme in English language teaching*. Peaslake: Delta.

Mehisto, P., Marsh, D. and Frigols, M. J. 2008. *Uncovering CLIL: Content and language integrated learning in bilingual and multilingual education*. Oxford: Macmillan Education.

Méndez García, M. d. C. and Pavón Vázquez, V. 2012. Investigating the coexistence of the mother tongue and the foreign language through teacher collaboration in CLIL contexts: Perceptions and practice of the teachers involved in the plurilingual programme in Andalusia. *International Journal of Bilingual Education and Bilingualism* 15(5), 573–92.

Messick, S. 1989. Validity. In: Linn, R. L., ed. *Educational measurement*. 3rd ed. Phoenix, AZ: Oryx Press, pp. 13–103.

Messick, S. 1996. Validity and washback in language testing. *Language Testing* 13(3), 241–56.

The Michigan Corpus of Academic Spoken English. 1999. *The Michigan Corpus of Academic Spoken English*. Accessed 25 May 2017 from www.hti.umich.edu/m/micase/

Milton, J. and Meara, P. 1995. How periods abroad affect vocabulary growth in a foreign language. *ITL Review of Applied Linguistics* 107/8, 17–34.

Mitchell, R. and Myles, F. 2004. *Second language learning theories*. 2nd ed. London: Arnold.

Moor, P., Crace, A., Cunningham, S., Comyns-Carr, J., Albert, D. and Cheetham, C. 2013. *Cutting edge. Elementary*. Harlow: Pearson.

Moyer, A. 2013. *Foreign accent: The phenomenon of non-native speech*. Cambridge: Cambridge University Press.

Moyer, A. 2015. Autonomy in second language phonology: Choice vs. limits. *Language Teaching*, 1–17.

Murphy, D. 2011. An investigation of English pronunciation teaching in Ireland. *English Today* 27(4), 10–18.

Murphy, L. and Roca de Larios, J. 2010. Searching for words: One strategic use of the mother tongue by advanced Spanish EFL writers. *Journal of Second Language Writing* 19(2), 61–81.

Murray, N. 2012. English as a lingua franca and the development of pragmatic competence. *ELT Journal* 66(3), 318–26.

Naiman, N. 1996. *The good language learner*. Clevedon: Multilingual Matters.

Nakanishi, T. 2015. A meta-analysis of extensive reading research. *TESOL Quarterly* 49(1), 6–37.

Nam, K. M. 2017. How young children make sense of two different writing systems: Korean written in the Hangul alphabet, and English written in the Roman alphabet. *Journal of Early Childhood Literacy*. p146879841668538.

Nassaji, H. 2007. Schema theory and knowledge-based processes in second language reading comprehension: A need for alternative perspectives. *Language Learning* 57(s1), 79–113.

Nathan, G. S. 2008. *Phonology: A cognitive grammar introduction*. Amsterdam: John Benjamins.

Nation, I. S. P. 2001. *Learning vocabulary in another language*. Cambridge: Cambridge University Press.

Nation, I. S. P. 2013. *Learning vocabulary in another language*. 2nd ed. Cambridge: Cambridge University Press.

Nation, P. 2017. *Professor Paul Nation*. Accessed 15 March 2017 from www.victoria.ac.nz/lals/about/staff/paul-nation

Nation, P. and Waring, R. 1997. Vocabulary size, text coverage and word list. In: Schmitt, N. and McCarthy, M., eds. *Vocabulary description, acquisition and pedagogy*. Cambridge: Cambridge University Press, pp. 6–19.

Negretti, R., Kuteeva, M., Engelska, I., Stockholms, U. and Humanistiska, F. 2011. Fostering metacognitive genre awareness in L2 academic reading and writing: A case study of pre-service English teachers. *Journal of Second Language Writing* 20(2), 95–110.

Nesi, H. 2007. *The British Academic Spoken English Corpus*. Accessed 22 June 2017 from www.coventry.ac.uk/researchnet/d/503

Nesi, H. and Gardner, S. 2012. *Genres across the disciplines: Student writing in higher education*. Cambridge: Cambridge University Press.

Ness, M. and Kenny, M. 2016. Improving the quality of think-alouds. *Reading Teacher* 69(4), 453–60.

Nesselhauf, N. 2003. The use of collocations by advanced learners of English and some implications for teaching. *Applied Linguistics* 24(2), 223–42.

Nesselhauf, N. 2004. *Collocations in a learner corpus*. Amsterdam: J. Benjamins.

Nikula, T. 2015. Hands-on tasks in CLIL science classrooms as sites for subject-specific language use and learning. *System* 54, 14–27.

Nishida, R. and Yashima, T. 2010. Classroom interactions of teachers and elementary school pupils as observed during a musical project in a Japanese elementary school. *System* 38(3), 480–90.

Norris, J. M. and Ortega, L. 2000. Effectiveness of L2 instruction: A research synthesis and quantitative meta-analysis. *Language Learning* 50(3), 417–28.

Norton, B. and Kramsch, C. 2013. *Identity and language learning: Extending the conversation*. Bristol: Multilingual Matters.

Nunan, D. 2004. *Task-based language teaching*. Cambridge/New York: Cambridge University Press.

O'Keeffe, A., Clancy, B. and Adolphs, S. 2011. *Introducing pragmatics in use*. London: Routledge.

O'Malley, J. M. and Chamot, A. 1990. *Learning strategies in second language acquisition*. Cambridge: Cambridge University Press.

O'Neal, G. 2015. Segmental repair and interactional intelligibility: The relationship between consonant deletion, consonant insertion, and pronunciation intelligibility in English as a Lingua Franca in Japan. *Journal of Pragmatics* 85, 122–34.

O'Regan, J. P. 2014. English as a lingua franca: An immanent critique. *Applied Linguistics* 35(5), 533–52.

Oller, J. W. 1973. Cloze tests of second language proficiency and what they measure. *Language Learning* 23(1), 105–18.

Oxenden, C. and Latham-Koenig, C. 2009. *New English file: Beginner student's book*. Oxford: Oxford University Press.

Oxford, R. L. 1990. *Language learning strategies what every teacher should know*. Boston: Heinle.

Oxford, R. L. 2010. *Teaching and researching language learning strategies*. Harlow: Longman.

Oxford, R. L., Griffiths, C., Longhini, A., Cohen, A. D., Macaro, E. and Harris, V. 2014. Experts' personal metaphors and similes about language learning strategies. *System* 43, 11–29.

Paltridge, B. 2012. *Discourse analysis: An introduction*. London: Bloomsbury.

Park, G. 2013. 'Writing is a way of knowing': Writing and identity. *ELT Journal* 67(3), 336–45.

Parrott, M. 2010. *Grammar for English language teachers*. Cambridge: Cambridge University Press.

Pawley, A. and Syder, F. H. 1983. Two puzzles for linguistics: Nativelike selection and nativelike fluency. In: Richards, J. and Schmidt, R. W., eds. *Language and communication*. London: Longman, pp. 191–228.

Payack, P. J. J. 2014. *Number of words in the English language: 1,025,109.8*. Accessed 15 January 2017 from www.languagemonitor.com/number-of-words/number-of-words-in-the-english-language-1008879/

Peirce, B. N. 1995. Social identity, investment, and language learning. *TESOL Quarterly* 29(1), 9–31.

Peng, J.-E. 2014. *Willingness to communicate in the Chinese EFL university classroom: An ecological perspective*. Bristol: Multilingual Matters.

Pennington, M., C. 1996. *Phonology in English language teaching*. Harlow: Longman.

Pennington, M. C. 2013. *Phonology in English language teaching: An international approach*. New York/London: Routledge.

Perez-Vidal, C. and Roquet, H. 2015. The linguistic impact of a CLIL science programme: An analysis measuring relative gains. *System* 54, 80–90.

Peters, M. L. 1985. *Spelling: caught or taught? A new look*. London: Routledge/Kegan Paul.

Pienemann, M. 2006. Processability theory. In: VanPatten, B. and Williams, J., eds. *Theories in second language acquisition: An introduction* London: Routledge, pp. 137–54.

Pimsleur, P. 1980. *How to learn a foreign language*. Boston: Heinle and Heinle.

Pimsleur, P., Reed, D. and Stansfield, C. 2004. *Pimsleur language aptitude batters: Manual*. Bethsda, MD: Second Language Testing Inc.

Poehner, M. E. and Lantolf, J. P. 2005. Dynamic assessment in the language classroom. *Language Teaching Research* 9(3), 233–65.

Poehner, M. E., Zhang, J. and Lu, X. 2015. Computerized dynamic assessment (C-DA): Diagnosing L2 development according to learner responsiveness to mediation. *Language Testing* 32(3), 337–57.

Potts, D. and Park, P. 2007. Partnering with students in curriculum change: Students researching students' needs. In: Rice, A. ed. *Revitalizing an established program for adult learners*. Alexandria, VA: TESOL, pp. 181–201.

Prichard, C. 2013. Using social networking sites as a platform for second language instruction. *TESOL Journal* 4(4), 752–8.

Prodromou, L. 2008. *English as a lingua franca: A corpus-based analysis*. London: Continuum.

Qin, Y., Carter, C. S., Silk, E. M., Stenger, V. A., Fissell, K., Goode, A. and Anderson, J. R. 2004. The change of the brain activation patterns as children learn algebra equation solving. *Proceedings of the National Academy of Sciences of the USA* 101(15), 5686–91.

Racelis, J. V. and Matsuda, P. K. 2013. Integrating process and genre into the second language writing classroom: Research into practice. *Language Teaching* 46(3), 382–93.

Raimes, A. 1983. *Techniques in teaching writing*. Oxford: Oxford University Press.

Rao, Z. 2007. Training in brainstorming and developing writing skills. *ELT Journal* 61(2), 100–106.

Razagifard, P. 2013. The impact of text-based CMC on improving L2 oral fluency. *Journal of Computer Assisted Learning* 29(3), 270–79.

Rea-Dickins, P. 2006. Currents and eddies in the discourse of assessment: A learning-focused interpretation. *International Journal of Applied Linguistics* 16(2), 163–88.

Rees-Miller, J. 1993. A critical Appraisal of learner training: Theoretical bases and teaching implications. *TESOL Quarterly* 27(4), 679–89.

Richards, J. C. and Rodgers, T. S. 2014. *Approaches and methods in language teaching*. Cambridge: Cambridge University Press.

Rifkin, B. 2003. Guidelines for foreign language lesson planning. *Foreign Language Annals* 36(2), 167–79.

Roach, P. 1982. On the distinction between 'stress-timed' and 'syllable-imted' languages. In: Crystal, D., ed. *Linguistic controversies essays in linguistic theory and practice in honour of F.R. Palmer*. London: Edward Arnold, pp. 773–89.

Roach, P. 2004. British English: Received pronunciation. *Journal of the International Phonetic Association* 34(2), 239–45.

Roach, P. 2010. *English phonetics and phonology: A practical course*. 4th ed. Cambridge: Cambridge University Press.

Roberts, C. and Cooke, M. 2009. Authenticity in the adult ESOL classroom and beyond. *TESOL Quarterly* 43(4), 620–42.

Robinson, J. D. 2005. Soliciting patients' present concerns. In: Heritage, J. and Maynard, D. W., eds. *Communication in medical care: Interaction between primary care physicians and patients*. Cambridge: Cambridge University Press, pp. 22–47.

Robinson, P. 2001. Task complexity, task difficulty, and task production: Exploring interactions in a componential framework. *Applied Linguistics* 22(1), 27–57.

Robinson, P. 2003. Attention and memory. In: Doughty, C. and Long, M. H., eds. *The handbook of second language acquisition*. Malden/Oxford: Blackwell, pp. 631–78.

Rogers, V. E., Meara, P., Aspinall, R., Fallon, L., Goss, T., Keey, E. and Thomas, R. 2016. Testing aptitude: Investigating Meara's (2005) LLAMA tests. *EUROSLA Yearbook* 16, 179–210.

Rost, M. 2011. *Teaching and researching listening*. 2nd ed. Harlow: Longman.

Rumelhart, D. 1975. Notes on a schema for stories. In: Collins, D. G. B. A., ed. *Representation and understanding: Studies in cognitive science*. New York: Academic Press.

Rundell, M. 2002. *MacMillan English dictionary for advanced learners*. Oxford: MacMillan.

Ryan, R. M. and Deci, E. L. 2000. Self-determination theory and the facilitation of intrinsic motivation, social development, and wellbeing. *American Psychologist* 55, 68–78.

Saadat, M., Mehrpour, S. and Khajavi, Y. 2016. Internet-mediated corrective feedback for digital natives. *TESOL Journal* 7(1), 233–45.

Said, E. W. 2002. Living in Arabic (the distinction between classical written and demotic spoken Arabic). *Raritan-A Quarterly Review* 21(4), 220–36.

Saigh, K. and Schmitt, N. 2012. Difficulties with vocabulary word form: The case of Arabic ESL learners. *System* 40(1), 24–36.

Saito, H. 2008. A framework for goal-driven pair drills. *ELT Journal* 62(1), 56–65.

Saito, K. and Lyster, R. 2012. Effects of form-focused instruction and corrective feedback on L2 pronunciation development of /r{turned}/ by Japanese learners of English. *Language Learning* 62(2), 595–633.

Sampson, G. 2015. *Writing systems*. Sheffield: Equinox.

Sasaki, M. 2000. Toward an empirical model of EFL writing processes: An exploratory study. *Journal of Second Language Writing* 9(3), 259–91.

Saville-Troike, M. 2006. *Introducing second language acquisition*. Cambridge: Cambridge University Press.

Schmidt, R. W. 1990. The role of consciousness in second language learning. *Applied Linguistics* 11(2), 129–58.

Schmitt, N. 2000. *Vocabulary in language teaching*. Cambridge: Cambridge University Press.

Schmitt, N. and Schmitt, D. 1995. Vocabulary notebooks: Theoretical underpinnings and practical suggestions. *ELT Journal* 49(2), 133–43.

Schön, D. A. 1983. *The reflective practitioner: How professionals think in action*. New York: Basic Books.

Schultz, F., Utz, S. and Göritz, A. 2011. Is the medium the message? Perceptions of and reactions to crisis communication via Twitter, blogs and traditional media. *Public Relations Review* 37(1), 20–27.

Schwarz, C., Davidson, G., Seaton, A. and Tebbit, V. 1988. *Chambers English dictionary*. Edinburgh: Chambers.

Scrivener, J. 2010. *Teaching English grammar: What to teach and how to teach it*. Oxford: Macmillan Education.

Scrivener, J. 2011. *Learning teaching: The essential guide to English language teaching*. Oxford: Macmillan Education.

Searle, J. R. 1976. A classification of illocutionary acts. *Language in Society* 5(1), 1–23.

Seidlhofer, B. 2004. Research perspectives on teaching English as a lingua franca. *Annual Review of Applied Linguistics* 24, 209–39.

Seidlhofer, B. 2005. English as a lingua franca. *ELT Journal* 59(4), 339–41.

Seidlhofer, B. and Widdowson, H. G. 2009. *Accommodation and the idiom principle in English as a lingua franca*. Basingstoke: Palgrave Macmillan.

Shi, L. 2002. *A tale of names*. Cambridge: Cambridge University Press.

Shulman, L. S. 1987. Knowledge and teaching: Foundations of the new reform. *Harvard Educational Review* 57(1), 1–22.

Silva, T. 1993. Toward an understanding of the distinct nature of L2 writing: The ESL research and its implications. *TESOL Quarterly* 27(4), 657–77.

Simpson, J. 2013. Identity alignment on an ESOL class blog. *International Journal of Applied Linguistics* 23(2), 183–201.

Sinclair, J. 1987. *Collins Cobuild english language dictionary*. London: HarperCollins.

Sinclair, J. M. 1991. *Corpus, concordance, collocation*. Oxford: Oxford University Press.

Singleton, D. 2005. The critical period hypothesis: A coat of many colours. *International Review of Applied Linguistics in Language Teaching* 43(4), 269.

Skehan, P. 1996. A framework for the implementation of task-based instruction. *Applied Linguistics* 17(1), 38–62.

Skehan, P. 1998. *A cognitive approach to language learning*. Oxford: Oxford University Press.

Skehan, P. 2003. Task-based instruction. *Language Teaching* 36(1), 1–14.

Skehan, P. 2014. *Processing perspectives on task performance*. Amsterdam: John Benjamins.

Skehan, P. and Foster, P. 1999. The influence of task structure and processing conditions on narrative retellings. *Language Learning* 49, 93–120.

Skinner, B. F. 1974. *About behaviourism*. London: Penguin.

Smith, F. 1994. *Understanding reading*. Hillsdale, NJ: Erlbaum.

Soars, J. and Soars, L. 2000. *Elementary student's book: New Headway english course*. Oxford: Oxford University Press.

Sonbul, S. and Schmitt, N. 2010. Direct teaching of vocabulary after reading: Is it worth the effort? *ELT Journal* 64(3), 253–60.

Stæhr, L. S. 2009. Vocabulary knowledge and advanced listening comprehension in English as a foreign language. *Studies in Second Language Acquisition* 31, 577–607.

Stewart, M. A. 2010. Writing with power, sharing their immigrant stories: Adult ESOL students find their voices through writing. *TESOL Journal* 1(2), 269–83.

Stirling, J. 2005. Review: Teaching English spelling: A practical guide. *ELT Journal* 59(3), 263–8.

Stirling, J. 2011. *Teaching spelling to English language learners*. Raleigh, USA: Lulu.

Swaffar, J. K., Arens, K. and Morgan, M. 1982. Teacher classroom practices: Redefining method as task hierarchy. *Modern Language Journal* 66(1), 24–33.

Swales, J. M. 1990. *Genre analysis: English in academic and research settings*. Cambridge: Cambridge University Press.

Swan, M. 1985a. A critical look at the communicative approach (1). *ELT Journal* 39(1), 2–12.

Swan, M. 1985b. A critical look at the communicative approach (2). *English Language Teaching Journal* 39(2), 76–87.

Swan, M. 1994. Design criteria for pedagogic language rules. In: Bygate, M., Tonkyn, A. and Williams, E., eds. *Grammar and the language teacher*. London: Prentice Hall, pp. 45–55.

Swan, M. and Smith, B. 1987. *Learner English: A teacher's guide to interference and other* Taguchi, E., Gorsuch, G., Takayasu-Maass, M. and Snipp, K. 2012. Assisted repeated reading with an advanced-level Japanese EFL reader: A longitudinal diary study. *Reading in a Foreign Language* 24(1), 30–55.

Takanashi, Y. 2004. TEFL and communication styles in Japanese culture. *Language Culture and Curriculum* 17(1), 1–14.

Tannen, D. 2002. Agonism in academic discourse. *Journal of Pragmatics* 34, 1651–69.

Terry, M. and Wilson, J. 2004. *Focus on academic skills for IELTS*. Harlow: Longman.

Thompson, S. E. 2003. Text-structuring metadiscourse, intonation and the signalling of organisation in academic lectures. *Journal of English for Academic Purposes* 2(1), 5–20.

Thomson, R. I. and Derwing, T. M. 2015. The effectiveness of L2 pronunciation instruction: A narrative review. *Applied Linguistics* 36(3), 326–44.

Thornbury, S. 1999. *How to teach grammar*. Harlow: Longman.

Thornbury, S. 2002. *How to teach vocabulary*. Harlow: Longman.

Thornbury, S. 2005. *How to teach speaking*. Harlow: Longman.

Timmis, I. 2005. Towards a framework for teaching spoken grammar. *ELT Journal* 59(2), 117–25.

Tomlinson, B. 2008. *English language learning materials: A critical review*. London: Continuum.

Tomlinson, B. 2012. Materials development for language learning and teaching. *Language Teaching* 45(2), 143–79.

Tomlinson, B. 2013. *Developing materials for language teaching*. London: Bloomsbury.

Tomlinson, B. 2016. Special issue: Innovation in materials development. *Innovation in Language Learning and Teaching* 10(2), 73–153.

Torbe, M. 1978. *Teaching spelling*. London: Ward Lock.

Tribble, C. 1996. *Writing*. Oxford: Oxford University Press.

Trofimovich, P. 2016. Interactive alignment: A teaching-friendly view of second language pronunciation learning. *Language Teaching* 49(3), 411–22.

Trubetzkoy, N. S. 1969. *Principles of phonology*. Berkeley: University of California.

Trudgill, P. and Hannah, J. 2002. *International English: A guide to varieties of Standard English*. London: Arnold.

Tudor, I. 2001. *The dynamics of the language classroom*. Cambridge: Cambridge University Press.

Tutuola, A. 1961. *The palm-wine drinkard and his dead palm-wine tapster in the Deads' Town*. London: Faber and Faber.

Underhill, A. 2005. *Sound foundations: Learning and teaching pronunciation*. Oxford: Heinemann.

Underhill, A. and Casey, M. 2011. *Sounds(3)*. [Mobile App.] [20 Nov 2017].

Underwood, M., Kenworthy, J., and Rost, M. 1989. *Teaching listening*. London: Longman.

Ur, P. 2012. *A course in English language teaching*. 2nd ed. Cambridge: Cambridge University Press.

Ur, P. and Wright, A. 1992. *Five-minute activities: A resource book of short activities*. Cambridge: Cambridge University Press.

Ushioda, E. 2011. Language learning motivation, self and identity: Current theoretical perspectives. *Computer Assisted Language Learning* 24(3), 199–210.

Uysal, H. H. 2010. A critical review of the IELTS writing test. *ELT Journal* 64(3), 314–20.

van Lier, L. 2000. From input to affordance: Social-interactive learning from an ecological perspective. In: Lantolf, J. P., ed. *Sociocultural theory and second language learning*. Oxford: Oxford University Press, pp. 245–59.

Vandergrift, L. 2004. Listening to learn or learning to listen? *Annual Review of Applied Linguistics* 24(1), 3–25.

Vandergrift, L. and Goh, C. C. M. 2012. *Teaching and learning second language listening: Metacognition in action*. London: Routledge.

Vandergrift, L. and Tafaghodtari, M. H. 2010. Teaching L2 learners how to listen does make a difference: An empirical study. *Language Learning* 60(2), 470–97.

Vandergrift, L. et al. 2006. The metacognitive awareness listening questionnaire: Development and validation. *Language Learning* 56(3), 431–62.

VanPatten, B. 2002. Processing instruction: An update. *Language Learning* 52(4), 755–803.

VanPatten, B. and Williams, J. 2007. *Theories in second language acquisition: An introduction.* Mahwah, NJ: Lawrence Erlbaum.

Ventola, E. 1984. Orientation to social semiotics in foreign-language teaching. *Applied Linguistics* 5(3), 275–86.

Vygotsky, L. S. 1966. *Development of the higher mental functions. Psychological research in the USSR.* Moscow: Progress.

Vygotsky, L. S. 1978. *Mind in society: The development of higher psychological processes.* London: Harvard University Press.

Wall, D. and Alderson, J. C. 1995. Examining washback: The Sri Lankan impact study. In: Cumming, A. and Berwick, R., eds. *Validation in language testing.* Clevedon: Multilingual Matters, pp. 194–236.

Wallace, C. 1992. *Reading.* Oxford: Oxford University Press.

Walter, C. 2008. Phonology in second language reading: Not an optional extra. *TESOL Quarterly* 42(3), 455–74.

Wang, M., Koda, K. and Perfetti, C. A. 2003. Alphabetic and nonalphabetic L1 effects in English word identification: A comparison of Korean and Chinese English L2 learners. *Cognition* 87(2), 129–49.

Wang, W. and Wen, Q. 2002. L1 use in the L2 composing process: An exploratory study of 16 Chinese EFL writers. *Journal of Second Language Writing* 11(3), 225–46.

Wang, X. and Munro, M. J. 2004. Computer-based training for learning English vowel contrasts. *System* 32(4), 539–52.

Wang, Y. H. and Young, S. S. C. 2015. Effectiveness of feedback for enhancing English pronunciation in an ASR-based CALL system. *Journal of Computer Assisted Learning* 31(6), 493–504.

Webb, S. A. and Nation, I. S. P. 2017. *How vocabulary is learned.* Oxford: Oxford University Press.

West, M. 1953. *A general service list of English words, with semantic frequencies and a supplementary word-list for the writing of popular science and technology.* Rev. and enl. ed. London: Longmans.

Whipple, J., Cullen, C., Gardiner, K. and Savage, T. 2015. Syllable circles for pronunciation learning and teaching. *ELT Journal* 69(2), 151–64.

White, G. 2006. Teaching listening: A time for a change in methodology. In: Uso Juan, E. and Martinez Flor, A., eds. *Current trends in the development and teaching of the four language skills.* Berlin: M. de Gruyter, pp. 111–38.

White, R. and Arndt, V. 1991. *Process writing.* Harlow: Longman.

Widdowson, H. G. 2000. English. In: Byram, M., ed. *Routledge encyclopedia of language teaching and learning.* London: Routledge, pp. 193–6.

Wilkins, D. A. 1976. *Notional syllabuses: A taxonomy and its relevance to foreign language curriculum development.* London: Oxford University Press.

Willis, D. 1990. *The lexical syllabus: A new approach to language teaching.* London: Collins ELT.

Willis, D. 2015. *Winning the grammar wars: What grammar really is and how we use it.* Kendal: Willis-ELT.

Willis, D. and Willis, J. 2007. *Doing task-based teaching.* Oxford: Oxford University Press.

Willis, J. 1996. *A framework for task-based learning.* Harlow: Longman.

Wilson, M. 2003. Discovery listening – Improving perceptual processing. *ELT Journal* 57(4), 335–43.

Wilson, J. J. 2008. *How to teach listening.* Harlow: Longman.

Wong, W. and Patten, B. 2003. The evidence is IN: Drills are OUT. *Foreign Language Annals* 36(3), 403–23.

Woodall, B. R. 2002. Language-switching: Using the first language while writing in a second language. *Journal of Second Language Writing* 11(1), 7–28.

Woodford, K. and Jackson, G. 2003. *Cambridge advanced learner's dictionary*. Cambridge: Cambridge University Press.

Woodrow, L. 2006. English in academic setting: a postgraduate course for students from non-English speaking backgrounds. In: Snow, M.A. and Kamhi-Stein, L. eds. *Developing a new course for adult learners*. Alexandria, VA: TESOL, pp. 197–218.

Woods, D. 1996. *Teacher cognition in language teaching: Beliefs, decision-making and classroom practice*. Cambridge: Cambridge University Press.

Woodward, T. 2001. *Planning lessons and courses: Designing sequences of work for the language classroom*. Cambridge: Cambridge University Press.

Wright, T. 2005. *Classroom management in language education*. Basingstoke: Palgrave Macmillan.

Xie, X. 2013. Vocabulary explanation in English-major university classrooms in China. *ELT Journal* 67(4), 435–45.

Yang, M., Badger, R. G. and Yu, Z. 2006. A comparative study of peer and teacher feedback in a Chinese EFL writing class. *Journal of Second Language Writing* 15(3), 179.

Yen, T. T. N. 2012. The effects of a speed reading course and speed transfer to other types of texts. *RELC Journal* 43(1), 23–37.

Yu, X. 2014. The use of textual memorisation in foreign language learning: Hearing the Chinese learner and teacher voice. *TESOL Journal* 5(4), 654–77.

Zahedi, K. and Shamsaee, S. 2012. Viability of construct validity of the speaking modules of international language examinations (IELTS vs. TOEFL iBT): Evidence from Iranian test-takers. *Educational Assessment, Evaluation and Accountability* 24(3), 263–77.

Zamel, V. and Spack, R. 1998. *Negotiating academic literacies: Teaching and learning across languages and cultures*. Mahwah, NJ: Lawrence Erlbaum.

Zarrinabadi, N. 2014. Communicating in a second language: Investigating the effect of teacher on learners' willingness to communicate. *System* 42, 288–95.

Zhang, X. and Head, K. 2010. Dealing with learner reticence in the speaking class. *ELT Journal* 64(1), 1–9.

Zhao, J., Quiroz, B., Dixon, L. Q. and Joshi, R. M. 2016. Comparing bilingual to monolingual learners on English spelling: A meta-analytic review. *Dyslexia* 22(3), 193–213.

Zheng, B. et al. 2015. Middle school students' writing and feedback in a cloud-based classroom environment. *Technology, Knowledge and Learning* 20(2), 201–29.

Index